POLITICAL CULTURES IN THE ANDES, 1750–1950

A BOOK IN THE SERIES
LATIN AMERICA OTHERWISE:
LANGUAGES, EMPIRES, NATIONS

Series editors:
Walter D. Mignolo
Irene Silverblatt
Sonia Saldívar-Hull

POLITICAL CULTURES IN THE ANDES 1750–1950

EDITED BY Nils Jacobsen

AND Cristóbal Aljovín de Losada

DUKE UNIVERSITY PRESS

DURHAM AND LONDON

2005

Printed in the United States of America on acid-free paper ∞
Designed by Sam Potts Inc.
Typeset in Stempel Garamond by Keystone Typesetting, Inc.
Library of Congress Cataloging-in-Publication Data appear on the last printed page of this book.

Publication of this work has been supported by a grant from the Research Board of the University of Illinois at Urbana-Champaign.

CONTENTS

ABOUT THE SERIES

Latin America Otherwise: Languages, Empires, Nations is a critical series. It aims to explore the emergence and consequences of concepts used to define "Latin America" while at the same time exploring the broad interplay of political, economic, and cultural practices that have shaped Latin American worlds. Latin America, at the crossroads of competing imperial designs and local responses, has been construed as a geocultural and geopolitical entity since the nineteenth century. This series provides a starting point to redefine Latin America as a configuration of political, linguistic, cultural, and economic intersections that demands a continuous reappraisal of the role of the Americas in history, and of the ongoing process of globalization and the relocation of people and cultures that have characterized Latin America's experience. *Latin America Otherwise: Languages, Empires, Nations* is a forum that confronts established geocultural constructions, that rethinks area studies and disciplinary boundaries, that assesses convictions of the academy and of public policy, and that, correspondingly, demands that the practices through which we produce knowledge and understanding about and from Latin America be subject to rigorous and critical scrutiny.

This collection of essays examines the cultural politics of nation-building in the Andes. Comparisons extend across countries—Bolivia, Peru, Ecuador, and Colombia—and across time, from the half century before independence through the middle of the twentieth century. Its focus is on the cultural tensions generated by the extraordinary transformations involved in state-making: in other words, it looks at struggles between and across ethnic groups, genders, and the Andes' few elite and many subaltern peoples.

We have no comparative studies of this kind which make clear both the significance of the cultural dimensions of power and the varied courses that cultrual politics can take. The volume as a whole is a strong argument that Andean politics cannot be understood without a careful analysis of its cultural forms, of the ideological and social complexities through which state power is represented, expressed, built, rejected, challenged, and reworked. It is a strong argument that contemporary questions regarding the direction and the hope of Andean politics must be grounded in its turbulent cultural past.

ACKNOWLEDGMENTS

This book had its origin in an international conference held at the University of Illinois at Urbana-Champaign in March 2000. Only the chapter by Derek Williams was commissioned subsequent to the conference. We wish to thank the following conference participants for their ideas, critical comments, and contributions to the discussion, all of which have significantly influenced this volume: Enrique Ayala Mora, Rossana Barragan, Kim Clark, Tom Cummins, Carlos Espinosa, Thomas Fischer, Carlos Forment, Zephyr Frank, Michel Gobat, Tulio Halperin, Sudir Hazareesingh, Peter Klaren, Thomas Krüggeler, Carlos Mamani, Nelson Manrique, Ulrich Mücke, Scarlett O'Phelan Godoy, Andrew Orta, Vincent Peloso, Cynthia Radding, Frank Safford, Mary Kay Vaughan, Mary Weismantel, and Norman Whitten. A companion volume, including several papers from the March 2000 conference that do not appear here, will be published in Spanish by Universidad Nacional Mayor de San Marcos in Lima in 2005.

In preparing both the conference and this volume we received generous help from the following persons: Anita Bravo, Peggy Cook, Clare Crowston, Nicanor Dominguez, Teresa Jacobsen, Sam Martland, Robert Sanchez, Nan Volinsky, Michelle Wibbelsman, Ariel Yablon, and Kathy Young. At Duke University Press we received wonderful help to make this book as good as it could be from Miriam Angress, Kate Lothman, and above all Valerie Milholland. It has been an honor for us to work with Valerie, who over the past fifteen years has done so much for the publication of excellent and innovative work on Latin American history.

We are grateful for generous funding for the conference from the following sources: the National Endowment for the Humanities (Grant for Collaborative Research), the Center for Latin American Studies at the University of Chicago (then directed by Tom Cummins), the Center for Latin American and Caribbean Studies at the University of Illinois (under its director, Joseph Love, and interim director, Cynthia Radding), International Programs and Studies at the University of Illinois (under Associate Provost Earl Kellogg), and the Department of History at the University of Illinois (Peter Fritzsche, chair).

Above all we thank the contributors for their patience with and dedication to this project. We sincerely hope that the long wait in seeing their work on this volume completed and published will have been worth it.

Nils Jacobsen and Cristóbal Aljovín de Losada
Champaign-Urbana and Lima, April 2004

THE LONG AND THE SHORT OF IT

A PRAGMATIC PERSPECTIVE ON POLITICAL CULTURES, ESPECIALLY FOR THE MODERN HISTORY OF THE ANDES

Nils Jacobsen and Cristóbal Aljovín de Losada

It is hardly surprising that the study of political cultures has gained in popularity over the past decade. A confluence of major political events and reorientations of intellectual currents has once again focused attention on the production of consent and dissent in all types of political regimes, while questioning mechanistic linkages between economies and polities. The fall of the Soviet Union, the wave of democratization (however shallow), the resurgence of ethnic nationalism and communalism, and, among intellectual currents, the fall from grace of Marxism, "the linguistic turn," and the broad-based critique of Eurocentrism signaled some of the most salient trends of the late twentieth century on a global scale. In the case of Latin America, the winding down of the region's "thirty years war" (Jorge Castañeda) between military-authoritarian regimes and guerrilla movements, along with the upsurge in "new social movements" of women, shantytown dwellers, and indigenous and black groups, put issues of democracy, inclusion in the political arena, and the role of civil society at center stage.

Political culture assumes that culture provides meaning to human actions. We understand culture as a malleable ensemble of symbols, values, and norms that constitute the signification linking individuals to social, ethnic, religious, political, and regional communities. A pragmatic political culture perspective does not a priori exclude other approaches to the understanding of historical and contemporary polities, such as political economy and institutional analysis.

Still, behavior of individuals and groups cannot be derived in a linear fashion from interests or institutional constraints. As the case studies in this book will show, human actions are always involved in a complex language of symbols and values that make them intelligible to self and others. In focusing on the meaning with which public symbols, rituals, discourses, sequences of actions, and institutions are imbued by individuals and groups, the political culture perspective illuminates the production of consent and dissent to regimes, parties, movements, or political leaders. It yields insights into the mechanics by which polities sustain themselves or are challenged or toppled.

Relations of power undergird any political process. They necessarily draw on subjective, cultural, *and* interest and institutional dimensions.[1] In the modern era, publicly wielded power, as well as the key dimensions of a polity—citizenship, laws, institutions—is related to the state. Thus the nature of the state, the nature of civil society, and the nature of their contested relationship are crucial subjects for the political-culture perspective. The way a state operates and is institutionalized sets the framework of politics and shapes political practices and identities.

The kind of perspective on political culture advocated here is helpful for bringing into a common frame of discussion various conceptual approaches to nation-state formation and the construction of power in Latin America, approaches which often fail to communicate with each other. To simplify, we can identify two broad clusters of approaches: the "Gramscians," foregrounding the issues of hegemony, subalternity, and postcolonialism; and on the other hand, the "Tocquevillians," focusing on civil society, the public sphere, the ideological and institutional nature of political regimes, and citizenship.[2] While scholars working in the Tocquevillian perspective have tended to focus on urban topics, those working in the Gramscian perspective have focused on indigenous and black populations and how their values, practices, and institutional traditions related to and interacted with those of elites. While the Tocquevillians tend to highlight the emancipatory aspects of political modernity, the Gramscians tend to highlight the manner in which subaltern groups suffered exclusion and repression through elite groups, especially during the period of nation-state formation. The concept of political culture can serve as neutral ground for practitioners of both approach clusters as it privileges issues important for each. This book brings together contributions from scholars on either side of this conceptual divide, and includes scholars trying to bridge that divide.

This book pursues three goals: First, to provide historical depth for current debates about transitions to and ongoing redefinitions of democracy in Latin America. Issues of democracy, authoritarianism, citizens' rights, and the exclusion or inclusion of people based on notions of "race," ethnicity, gender, and class have been at the forefront of political debates and social movements in the region since the waning days of the colonial regime some two hundred years ago. These struggles have profoundly imprinted the values and practices of diverse groups and have influenced many institutions at issue in today's debates.

Our second goal is to advance an understanding of the formation of modern Andean political cultures through state-of-the-art case studies covering the two formative centuries of nation-state formation in the region. We reject the notion of one specifically Andean political culture. Our case studies from four Andean nations—Colombia, Ecuador, Peru, and Bolivia—demonstrate how even a focus on the same issue—for example, the deployment of race for the definition of citizenship—can have distinct meanings, depending on specific constellations of power and ethnic identity. The volume clarifies which issues have been prevalent in the construction of Andean nation-states.

Finally, we endeavor to exemplify the rich potential of a pragmatic political culture perspective for deciphering the processes involved in the formation, reconstruction, or dissolution of historical polities. The carefully crafted case studies, a comparativist conceptual essay, and the broad reflections in this introduction will help clarify the concept of political culture.

This volume cannot cover all major themes and issues of Andean political cultures between 1750 and 1950. Themes that do not receive the attention they deserve include electoral campaigns, working-class movements, popular religiosity, and the meaning of laws. Even so, the volume's broad chronological, spatial, and thematic coverage gives greater precision to the specificities of Andean political cultures within the comparative frame of Latin America. In this introduction we trace the history of the notion of political culture, discuss specific problems for the modern political culture perspective, and outline major issues of Andean political cultures on which scholars have focused to date.

THE HISTORY OF THE NOTION OF POLITICAL CULTURE

The modern scholarly use of the term "political culture" first appears in an article published by Gabriel Almond in 1956.[3] However, its subject matter has been debated at least since Plato and Aristotle sought to relate certain virtues or values to regime types. Among modern social scientists, Max Weber unquestionably has been most influential in preparing the later formal concept of political culture. He inserted culture (substantively) and meaning (methodologically) into the analysis of societies and greatly influenced the North American social scientists who pioneered the approach. Although for Weber most actions were prompted by material or ideal interests identifiable in terms of groups (class, religion, region, caste, ideology, etc.), he conceived them as molded and processed by customs, traditions, and values through which each individual derived meaning (*Sinn*). As Raymond Aron put it, for Weber "the contradiction between explanation by interests and the explanation by ideas is meaningless."[4] In Weber's scheme of classifying action from a subjective perspective, goal-oriented rational pursuit of group interests was only one in a wide range of potential individual motives for action that also included hatred or friendship and custom or ritual.[5] Moreover, Weber retained Hegel's distinction between civil society and the state. He emphasized that "the belief in a legitimate order differs in kind from the 'coalescence of material and ideal interests' in society."[6] A state with claims of legitimacy on its subjects or citizens is not just "the executive committee of the bourgeoisie" or of any other dominant group. Its stable functioning needs explanation regarding its relation to society that goes beyond ascertaining interests.

The conjuncture that gave rise to the concept of political culture occurred from World War II to 1960. The Nazi dictatorship and its modern politics of irrationality and genocide discredited both liberal and Marxist notions about the inevitability of achieving bourgeois-democratic or socialist societies in the "most advanced" nation-states. The breakup of the colonial empires and the foundation of new nations across Africa and Asia urgently raised the issue of whether democratic governance depended on more than economic development.[7] One school of thought, at the intersection of psychology, anthropology, and political science, "sought to explain recruitment to political roles, aggression and warfare, authoritarianism, ethnocentrism, fascism and the like in terms of the socialization of children—infant nursing and toilet-training patterns, parental disciplinary patterns and family structure."[8] Another literature—with a troubling heritage of geographic and racial determinism—attempted to establish distinct "national characters" through statistical definitions of "modal characters" showing a nation's predominant value and behavior patterns based on methods of child rearing, family structures, and religious beliefs.[9]

The initial political culture approach arose in close proximity to those literatures, yet "in reaction against . . . [their] psychological and anthropological reductionism."[10] One seminal study launched the first wave of political culture studies: *The Civic Culture: Political Attitudes and Democracy in Five Nations,* by Gabriel Almond and Sidney Verba (1963).[11] Worried about the threat of totalitarianism and the stability of the officially democratic political systems of West Germany, Italy, Japan, and the new nations of Africa and Asia, Almond and Verba sought to explore the characteristics of the political culture best suited to strengthening democratic regimes. The authors reacted also against the institutional and constitutional orientation then dominating the field of comparative politics. If democratic political systems were to take root in continental Europe, Africa, and Asia, more than a transfer of institutions was needed, because "a democratic form of participatory political system requires as well a political culture consistent with it."[12]

The authors defined political culture as "specifically political orientations—attitudes towards the political system and its various parts, and attitudes toward the role of the self in the system."[13] They developed behaviorist methods to test the relation between political attitudes and the political system as a whole. Based on Talcott Parsons's classification of action (cognitive, affective, evaluative) and Almond's own systems-theoretical approach, the authors designed a matrix scoring the attitudes of individuals to a variety of structural elements of political systems. Depending on how the interviewed citizens responded to elaborate questionnaires, a political culture could be classified as

> *parochial* (political orientations not separated from religious and social orientations, little expectation of change initiated from political system; example: Ottoman Empire)

subject (frequent orientation toward differentiated political system and its "output aspects," but hardly any orientation to "input aspects," i.e., bottom-up demands on political system, and to self's active participation; example: imperial Germany)
participant (orientation toward input and output aspect of political system, and to activist role of self in the polity).[14]

These were ideal types; contemporary political cultures usually would be mixtures of these types. Older—parochial or subject—orientations often were not fully relinquished as citizens adopted additional orientations. In fact, the authors saw the currently most adequate political culture for sustaining a democratic political system, the *civic culture* of the United States and the United Kingdom, as a "mixed culture, combining parochial, subject and participant orientations." This specific mix of orientations helped balance activity and passivity toward the political system allowing citizens to participate, but also to withdraw into quiet lives in the community. Yet, in other mixes, the ghosts of the past could produce regressive effects.[15]

While Almond and Verba accepted diversity within political cultures through specific "subcultures" and "role cultures," these were subsumed within the aggregate political culture, without providing a force for change.[16] On the critical issue as to whether this approach to political culture could *explain* why certain political systems were democratic and others not, all the authors would claim that it "demonstrating the probability of some connection between attitudinal patterns and systemic qualities."[17] While their behavioral approach called for radical empirical verifiability or falsifiability, their systems-theoretical approach required correlations—or, in Weberian terminology, elective affinities—rather than logically and chronologically sequential cause-effect relations.

During the 1960s and early 1970s, this approach to political culture spawned numerous case studies and further theoretical elaborations among political scientists.[18] But it soon ran into heavy opposition, and, by the 1980s, had gone out of fashion among political scientists.[19] Almond himself blamed this development on "reductionisms of the left and the right," to wit, various types of Marxist analyses and rational choice theory. For these approaches, the study of attitudes and values could contribute little to explaining political structures and processes.[20] Certainly the loss of a broader optimistic consensus around modernization theory undermined the appeal of the political culture approach during the 1970s. Yet, whatever the merits of Almond and Verba's model, it had serious flaws, partly rooted in the 1960s grand theory approach to political science, which entailed

an evolutionist, ahistorical tendency in the analysis of modernization
a static model of cultural traits
a behaviorist bent and reliance on quantitative data for determining subjective, cultural phenomena
a bias toward one particular model of Western political culture
an indeterminacy of cause and effect between political culture and political system[21]

Although Almond and Verba, along with many of the comparative politics and societies theorists of the 1950s and 1960s, came out of the Weberian tradition, they bent that tradition in a certain direction. They weakened Weber's own intricate linkage between "explaining" (analysis) and "understanding" (interpretation), between historical contingency and social science modeling, between cultural and socioeconomic causation. By trying to turn the study of the subjective in politics into a "hard," empirical science, this approach to politics called forth reactions espousing entirely different methods and epistemologies.

Since the 1980s, political culture has become a prominent field of inquiry in history and anthropology. These disciplines were in the grip of powerful new or rejuvenated theories and epistemologies, which gave a different orientation to historical and anthropological studies of political culture. We shall name five of these new approaches:

the "linguistic turn"[22]
redefinitions of culture from a social science category to a humanities category, and, in a second step, from an essentially unified, substantive entity to a more fragmented and processual concept[23]
the critique of "Eurocentrism," associated, on the one hand, with studies of subalternity and postcolonialism,

and, on the other, with a critique of the notions of progress and social evolution

the turn toward hegemony and power relations as central to understanding both state–civil society relations and relations between various social, ethnic, and gender groups

the rediscovery of the "public," and of civil society as central variables for modern polities[24]

These theoretical turns increased the interest of historians and anthropologists in the notion of political culture. In their writings the concept differs considerably from the model developed by political scientists during the 1950s and 1960s. In U.S. history, the breakthrough for political culture came with the discovery of "republicanism": values and cultural orientations stressing public virtues over inherited privilege that originated in the Renaissance underpinned the norms of Jeffersonian revolutionaries and Jacksonian working-class democrats.[25] One political scientist noted admiringly that American historians of political culture escaped "the necessity of choosing between interests and culture as explanations, instead using political culture to transcend that dichotomy."[26] For example, Gordon Wood's 1992 magisterial work, *The Radicalism of the American Revolution,* analyzed the shifting political culture of the thirteen colonies during the eighteenth century by demonstrating how various classes of people construed the meaning of their political rights, their social condition, and the legitimate exercise of power. Interconnection between social, political, and cultural dimensions also underlies Lynn Hunt's approach to the French Revolution. "The values, expectations and implicit rules that expressed and shaped collective intentions and actions," she wrote in 1986, "are what I call the political culture of the Revolution; that political culture provided the logic of revolutionary political action."[27]

Other proponents of a political culture approach to the French Revolution have committed to a full-blown cultural/semiotic methodology. Keith Baker has penned the most frequently cited definition of the concept:

> [Political culture] sees politics as about making claims; as the activity through which individuals and groups in any society articulate, negotiate, implement, and enforce the competing claims. . . . It comprises the definitions of the relative subject

> positions from which individuals and groups may (or may not) legitimately make claims one upon another, and therefore of the identity and boundaries of the community to which they belong. It constitutes the meanings of the terms in which these claims are framed, the nature of the contexts to which they pertain, and the authority of principles according to which they are made binding. It shapes the constitutions and powers of the agencies and procedures by which contentions are resolved. . . . Thus political authority is, in this view, essentially a matter of linguistic authority.[28]

Baker's linguistic approach limits human agency, but does not deny it. "Human agents find their being within language; they are, to that extent, constrained by it. Yet they are constantly working with it and on it, playing at its margins, exploiting its possibilities, and extending the play of its potential meanings, as they pursue their purposes and projects."[29] This heterogeneity of languages, localized in different political traditions or regional histories, is part of the study of political culture.[30] The reading of a symbol or a discourse can be subversive or favor the status quo, depending on who receives it and what s/he does with it. Many social movements build a contestatory discourse out of the official one. For instance, the republican discourse of citizenship, reason, and law has had two different sides, one subversive and the other conservative.

Still, this semiotic approach to political culture, staying for "explanations" of change purely within systems of linguistic or other types of symbols, opens itself up to the charge of "cultural determinism."[31] As Emilia Viotti da Costa has recently lamented, "the result of the shift from one theoretical position [scientistic Marxism] to another was an inversion: we simply moved from one reductionism to another, from economic to cultural or linguistic reductionism. To one type of reification we have opposed another. Both are equally unsatisfactory."[32] A pragmatic perspective on political culture seeks to avoid this reductionism.

POLITICAL CULTURES IN THE ANDES: ISSUES AND DEBATES

Andean scholars took up cultural approaches to the study of politics once again after the early 1980s. Influenced by French debates about *mentalité*,

Peruvian historians Alberto Flores Galindo and Manuel Burga developed the notion of an "Andean utopia." They understood this as a unique blend of Andean and European social and political projects, emerging out of the overlay of the Andean notion of repeated *pachacutis* (cataclysms of cosmic proportions) and Judaeo-Christian linear eschatology. From the early seventeenth century to the present, repeated eruptions of Andean utopian projects used the Inca past as a model for an ideal future polity, adapted to ongoing economic, political, and cultural change.[33] Even before Flores Galindo and Burga had published on Andean utopia, a heated debate about indigenous peasants' engagement with the Peruvian nation in the context of the devastating War of the Pacific and its aftermath had opened up a culturalist perspective on republican politics.[34]

The concern with the Incas for modern-day political struggles is primarily a Peruvian perspective, much less important in Ecuador and Bolivia, and virtually absent in Colombia. In Bolivia a cultural perspective first arose around bold new interpretations of indigenous movements fighting for economic and political rights since the late-colonial period. Silvia Rivera Cusicanqui criticized conventional Marxist and modernization theory analyses of "peasant revolts" as sudden "expressive" outbursts lacking realistic "instrumental" strategies for achieving their far-fetched goals. Rivera showed how the altiplano's Aymara "peasants" and their leaders had repeatedly organized their struggles around real and invented traditions of their communities and macroethnic groups. Rather than weakness, it showed their strength that they had taken on the white and *misti* (mestizo) authorities and ruling groups in their cantons, provinces, and the entire republic, *on their [the Andeans'] own terms,* that is, stepping outside the frame of reference prescribed by the colonial and republican regimes.[35] More broadly, the Taller de Historia Oral Andina (THOA) by the late 1980s began to uncover and reconstruct the vision of Bolivia's highland indigenous groups of their own history under colonialism and republicanism. Simultaneously, THOA sought to strengthen that autonomous consciousness and organizing capacity among the Aymara and Quechua communities.[36] Not for the first time, grassroots organizing among Andeans and elite intellectual debates were closer to each other in Bolivia than in Peru.

In Ecuador as well, scholars first introduced cultural perspectives into the study of politics in the context of the struggle of the indigenous peoples from the Oriente and the highlands for autonomy and land rights within a multicultural nation, a struggle that became surprisingly intense in July of 1990.[37] Deeply influenced by French poststructuralist social and cultural theory, Andrés Guerrero published a series of important studies deconstructing semiotic systems of representing "the Indian" in Ecuadorian administrative practice and elite discourse. Administrative institutions and practices of the early postcolonial republic disempowered the ethnic authorities and their political space. During the late nineteenth century, liberalism imposed its political imaginary onto indigenous leaders and their projects, turning their discourse into "ventriloquist speech." The elites' discourse showed telling continuities in their construction of poor helpless "Indians" in need of salvation by paternalistic hacendados and the civilizing mission of the nation-state.[38]

Colombian scholars took up the political culture perspective between the mid-1980s and early 1990s focusing on the issue of political violence and the relation of civil society to the state. At the time, political elites and the Colombian public increasingly felt that the institutions of the republic were failing and "the only solution was to refound the state."[39] The resurgence of a multifaceted *violencia* and the ineffectiveness and corruption of the judicial and executive branches of government persuaded politicians to enter into a process of deliberating a new constitution, which was promulgated in 1991. Scholars began to ask new questions about the connections of violence to a broad array of regional and national political institutions, practices, and attitudes. They sought to understand the perceived weakness of Colombian civil society that had failed to translate the long tradition of multiparty elections and strong regional power sharing into effective democracy and rule of law. The new constitution did take up the human rights of the republic's indigenous groups and large Afro-Colombian constituency. Yet Colombian scholars were more hesitant than those of Ecuador, Peru, and Bolivia to incorporate the issues of the racial order and remnants of the colonial caste system into their discussions of the nation's political culture.[40] These issues would be introduced more forcefully by foreign scholars.[41]

Intense communications among scholars from the Andean region, Europe, and North America, as well as the politics of scholarly training between the North Atlantic and Latin American regions, have led to a broadening range of issues studied from a political culture perspective. As a result, our understanding of Andean politics during the past 250 years now looks considerably different from the notions developed by several generations of historians and social scientists until the 1980s. Liberal, nationalist, and Marxist approaches to politics in the Andes had defined normative trajectories of state power, nation building, the development of the rule of law, and the interplay between political institutions and civil society, derived from a limited set of idealized North Atlantic models. They had portrayed the failures in the trajectories of the Andean republics—the violence, political corruption, weak and routinely subverted institutions, the horrific levels of poverty wracking the region until today, the gendered nature of power structures, the racialist and social exclusiveness—as deficits and breakdowns from those prescribed models.

The political culture perspective has helped to historicize those models and associated discourses, practices, and power constellations, and opens the view to the plasticity of each historical moment. We are beginning to perceive different futures and trajectories from the past embraced by various actors during critical conjunctures and over the long stretches of quiet life, work, and struggle in communities, confraternities, mines, sugar *ingenios*, factories, tenements, *chicherias* (Andean pubs), barracks, mutual aid societies, fire brigades, schools, and all the other spaces of political socialization. The political culture perspective has been instrumental in getting beyond an image of modern Andean political history as the boringly repetitive struggle of various elite and military sectors battling it out for control of the state. In that worn-out vision, Andean farmers, other popular groups, and women only appeared as victims, clients, or bystanders. The focus on attitudes and values of different social, ethnic, and gender groups, on rituals and practices in the political arena and the public sphere, emphasizes their agency. The best work in the political culture perspective on the Andes highlights the interaction of attitudes, norms, and practices regarding the political sphere with changing institutions, structures, and interests.

The literature to date has focused on a limited number of topics and periods of Andean political cultures. Not surprisingly, the indigenous experience under imperial Spanish and republican national rule has been a focal point of scholarship. The roots of this literature lie in the Andean anthropology and ethnohistory boom associated with John Murra, Tom Zuidema, María Rostworowski, Franklin Pease, and their students. From different theoretical vantage points they sought to decipher the functioning and inner logic of "Andean" society and culture.[42] Between the late 1970s and late 1980s, a related scholarship on "Indian resistance" grew out of a contestatory socioeconomic ethnohistory on Andean peoples. Karen Spalding was one of the first to apply Murra's analytical tools—reciprocity, redistribution, and vertical intraethnic exchange—to the analysis of postconquest Andean communities, their continuities, and ruptures in terms of society and economy, but also of authority structures and religion.[43] Tristan Platt inserted even the most "traditional" Andean communities into the field of politics and nation-state formation by emphasizing the effect of different state policies on Chayanta's communities—from the colonial "compact" to the disentailment of communal property and free trade in grains after 1874–78.[44]

During the 1980s the literature on indigenous resistance and rebellion gradually shifted emphasis from stressing economic and social issues to emphasizing the cultural logic behind the mobilization of Andean communities.[45] Steve Stern's 1987 edited volume, significantly titled *Resistance, Rebellion and Consciousness in the Andean Peasant World, Eighteenth to Twentieth Centuries,* contained diverse perspectives on peasant agency, ranging from political economy and social network analysis to full-blown semiotic and culturalist interpretations such as those by Jan Szeminski and Frank Salomon. In the introduction Stern himself set the tone by merging political economy with the logic of historically specific Andean notions of legitimate rule in eighteenth-century peasant mobilizations.[46]

Since the late 1980s, the culturalist turn has taken this scholarship considerably further by giving weight to indigenous political projects and agency. Anthropologists have most boldly asserted different, partly autonomous trajectories for Andean peoples' postconquest and postcolonial political imaginaries. Joanne Rappaport has shown how the Paez of Colombia's Cauca region constructed their own postconquest identity through oral and written memory, seemingly merging the two, and through these processes repeatedly put forth autonomous political projects.[47] In his ambitious ethnography and history of the Bolivian altiplano's K'ulta "people," Thomas Abercrombie uses the notion of "social memory" to suggest how the community has constantly regenerated its own cultural, social, and political identity, sharply delimited from misti and *cholo* outsiders through cultural practices and asymmetrical power constellations. At the same time, the K'ultas have engaged the Hispanic-dominated power structure and culture of the colonial regime and the Bolivian nation. This involved the K'ulta in a Bolivian national "interculture," participating willy-nilly in asymmetrical power relations and symbolic and material exchanges.[48] Both Rappaport and Abercrombie fully incorporate the dynamic changes of values and practices underlying native peoples' political cultures. Yet, more than most historians, they insist on an essential wholesomeness (not to say separateness) of native polities within Hispanized colonial and national states.

Much work about native peoples within Andean political cultures focuses on negotiation, compacts, issues of inclusion and exclusion, on the one hand, and representations of race and racial orders on the other. A number of scholars—often associated with the Yale school of Latin American history—take a Gramscian approach to subaltern studies, highlighting the vital political role Andean peoples have played in both sustaining and subverting colonial and national orders.[49] They stress increasing internal differentiation among indigenous groups (often explained as class formation), alliances of native elites with Hispanic power contenders, and the vital role of "organic intellectuals" for "counterhegemonic projects" of Andeans. Most importantly, they have highlighted the diminished political autonomy of Andean indigenous peoples as nation-states consolidated in the second half of the nineteenth century. Florencia Mallon has suggested that in the crises of postcolonial nation-state formation in Peru, certain groups of Andeans elaborated a national project of their own. Obliged to forge alliances with mobilized peasants, Hispanic elite sectors made concessions to subaltern national imaginaries. But in the crises' aftermath, Peruvian elites repressed their erstwhile allies. Mallon and others writing in this vein portray a stark choice of trajectories for Latin American postcolonial regimes: "hegemonic rule" based on inclusion and partial acceptance of subaltern groups' demands, or repression to prop up exclusivist, neocolonial regimes.[50]

Authors differ widely on what precisely makes a regime hegemonic.[51] Alternative elite policies toward indigenous peoples are equally problematic: the liberal dismantling of ethnic political authorities and institutions, on the one hand, and, on the other, the nationalist *indigenista* policies, reemerging since the 1890s, which inscribed racialized images of "Indians" in protective legislation, including the recognition of communal landholding. Moreover, the engagement of republican politics by Andean communities did not erupt suddenly in the crises of nation-state formation. Recent scholarship shows it to be an ongoing process bringing both losses—e.g., divisive politics within the communities and between them—and gains. New forms of association first promoted by liberals and later by anarchists, socialists, communists, populists, and Catholic Action groups in some regions strengthened communal identities and native social movements.[52]

The place of native peoples in Andean postcolonial polities also depended on how they weathered the Bourbon civilizing project and what role they assumed during the insurgencies fought for independence from Spain. Apart from demographic tendencies and economic pressures, this varied considerably between Andean territories according to the strength of communal institutions and their centrality for the colonial state and elites: generally greater in the south (from central Peru through the Bolivian altiplano) than in the north. Indigenous political projects and multicultural alliances with significant native participation and leadership were increasingly repressed. Yet in many places native authorities and commoners developed a new culture of politics, imbuing updated notions of ancient rights with ritual practices and meaning influenced by the Enlightenment.[53]

People of African descent also played a strong role in Andean political cultures, especially before the 1850s. Enslavement had largely deprived them of the corporate privileges and organization that made native Andeans such formidable factors in the statecraft of colonial and republican Andean political elites.[54] But in urban and rural areas of Colombia's Atlantic coast and Cauca Valley, Esmeraldas, Ecuador, and along Peru's entire coast they deployed autonomous organizing activities—in guilds, religious brotherhoods, and *cabildos,* autonomous hamlets, maroon societies, and bandit groups—that made them forces to be reckoned with. Recent scholarship has shown how they engaged exclusive politics and laws through contesting Hispanic honor codes, assuming important roles in the late-colonial and independence-era militias, forging alliances with elite political factions, fighting in urban electoral campaigns, and taking emancipation from slavery into their own hands.[55]

After 1850, liberal elite race politics posed a difficult political juncture for people of African descent. Racial imaginaries of the national elites of Colombia on the one hand, and Ecuador, Peru, and Bolivia on the other, took different courses after emancipation. In Colombia the liberals embraced the notion of creating an ever whiter Hispanic-Andean mestizo nation through "breeding out" the native populations in the central highlands. The large Afro-Colombian populations were seen as dangerous outsiders, to be marginalized and repressed, or their existence to be denied, wherever possible.[56] In the other Andean republics elites more thoroughly expunged people of African descent from their imagined nation, while wavering on the "Indian problem" between liberal "civilizing" projects and neo-traditional protection policies. The literature on elite representations of race in the postcolonial Andes is contributing much to the understanding of shifting racial orders between the liberal era and the era of interventionist states, with their rhetoric of populist nationalism.[57]

Gender norms and their negotiation or subversion have played a vital role in the construction of power in the Andean area. In complex association with Catholic doctrine and popular religiosity, norms for proper behavior of men and women formed a metaphorical linkage between notions of individual honor and morality and the construction of legitimate power. During the late-colonial period and the early decades after independence, public roles for respectable women were largely circumscribed to the sphere of church activities. Yet the late-colonial insurrections, the revolutions for independence, and the civil wars of the postindependence decades saw women assuming critical, quasi-public roles in local and national contests over power. Contemporary respectable opinion lionized pure virtuous women martyrs for independence. But it treated political activity, such as that of Micaela Bastidas and Bartolina Sisa during the Great Rebellion (1780–82), and "La Mariscala" (the strong-willed wife of Peruvian President Agustin Gamarra), with derision or moral condemnation. Only later popular, nationalist, and feminist currents of opinion underscored their importance. As Sarah Chambers has shown, while women were excluded from formal political participation, their role as behind-the-scene advisors, as friends giving advice from a womanly perspective, could be accepted and effective.[58] Against narrowly drawn elite norms, women's protagonism for the defense of community and family against abusive authorities, hacendados, or traders and the injustice of slavery had a long tradition among people of color in the Andes.[59]

The nineteenth-century "domestication" of women, along with patriarchal republicanism, has also been discussed in the literature on the Andes. Yet the transition was not as drastic as in some of the North Atlantic nations for which these models were developed. Andean liberalisms invested polarized gender roles with new urgency for the formation of the nation and for achieving modernity. While removing some of the legal and educational impediments to women's civic participation, elite opinion assigned women special functions around the moral progress of the nation.[60] The literature suggests that by 1920, strategic sectors of popular women—as market vendors and *chicheras*—confronted political authorities and male power structures by appealing to their importance for the nation, social justice, and notions of occupational "respect" that contravened elite racialized honor codes.[61]

The complex relationship between republicanism, constitutional rule, and personalist, authoritarian regimes is crucial for political culture research in the Andes. For a long time, citizens in the Andean republics did not *automatically* view military or civilian caudillos as antidemocratic. While formalistic Andean constitutional studies have a long tradition, to date few scholars have approached the republics' legal and constitutional trajectories from a social and cultural perspective. For the colonial period, John Leddy Phelan's studies of bureaucracy, law, patrimonial rule, and society in seventeenth-century Quito and of the linkage between social movement and defense of "constitutional" rights in Nueva Granada's Comunero rebellion of 1780 were pioneering.[62] For the republican period, Fernando Trazegnies' notion of "traditional modernization" highlights the repeated Andean practice of bringing legal codes up to the most "modern" standard (often defined by foreign elites) as a way to buttress entrenched power constellations and socioethnic orders.[63]

François-Xavier Guerra's *Modernidad e independencias* shifted emphasis in Latin American political history by combining constitutional issues, political philosophy, and ideology with the study of sociability and the public sphere. Guerra helps us understand the new polities in relation to the liberal ideology expressed through the constitution and political practice.[64] Recent studies have shown for Peru and Bolivia that the justification of most nineteenth-century revolutions was the defense of the constitution. Caudillos routinely claimed that they wanted to found a stable, truly republican system and accused their predecessors of despotism and fraudulent elections.[65] Other studies provide insight into the social and cultural construction of caudillo regimes: the centrality of coalition building, gaining control of local spaces through hierarchies of subaltern authorities, and expressing the expectations and understandings of popular groups.[66]

Since the 1990s, electoral studies have become important for understanding nineteenth-century Latin American politics. Previously, scholars had seen most pre-1930 elections as rigged elite affairs with miniscule popular participation, devoid of any consequence. Much of that criticism is justified. Nevertheless, elections created a public space and forced caudillos and oligarchic parties to launch political campaigns and organizations.[67] By the 1870s, Peruvian politicians put much effort into electoral campaigns and many mestizos, people of African descent, and native Andeans participated even if they could not vote.[68] Elections were the only way to acquire legal and legitimate power in the postcolonial Andean republics.

A field of increasing importance for Andean political cultures concerns the public sphere and civil society. Both in the Tocquevillian and various Marxist traditions, "modern" means of communication and associational activity are considered vital for democracy or hegemonic regimes. Because of difficult transportation, low literacy rates, and the habitual claim of the Catholic Church to fill the needs for nongovernmental public communication, public sphere and civil society—in this modern sense—long remained thin in the Andean republics. They lagged behind other Latin American societies even during the liberal era after 1850, when hundreds of new civic organizations were founded in Peru alone, from fire brigades to mutual aid associations, philharmonic societies, and electoral clubs.[69] But more informal, popular arenas for the formation of public opinions continued to flourish, from peasant community assemblies and chicherías to religious and civic fairs and festivities.[70] These spaces provided opportunities to discuss public issues and define common projects. Yet they largely limited access to elite-dominated spheres of power to clientelistic ties.

Decentered public spheres raise the issue of the regional or local origins of and contests over Andean nation-states. In Colombia, even by the mid-nineteenth century, regional elites found means to incorporate nonelite civil society, thus consolidating their power vis-à-vis the weak central government in Bogotá. In Ecuador the change from a tripartite regional elite struggle for power (Quito, Cuenca, Guayaquil) to a bipolar contest between Quito and Guayaquil during the massive political transformations from García Moreno's Catholic modernizing regime (1860–75) to Eloy Alfaro's Liberal Revolution of 1895 was accompanied by regionally distinct developments of communications and civil societies. The most dynamic and integrative developments occurred on the coast.[71] The multifarious Peruvian regional elites increasingly depended on linkages to the central state to control autonomous popular organizing and spheres of opinion. But just as the state began to gain strength—first briefly during the 1870s and then increasingly after 1895—it also began to adopt a more ambivalent attitude toward the pretensions of regional elites, increasingly viewed as "feudal" and antinational. Recent studies have highlighted the need to envision the formation of Andean nation-states from a less centralist perspective, paying closer attention to regional and local constructions of the nation and engagements with the state.[72]

Popular culture—its regional, social, and ethnic segmentation or hybridization—presents insights into the formation of national political imaginaries. When and how did various popular traditions—from music to food, sports, speech, and religious practices—broaden the political arena by subverting elite notions about proper public conduct? When did "polite society" embrace elements of Andean, African, or Chinese popular traditions? Did elites openly acknowledge the ethnic or lower-class origins of those practices, or did they try to neutralize their potentially déclassé and destabilizing connotations? Moreover, when and how did elites, the state, the Catholic Church, or commodity and cultural markets affect specific popular cultural traditions? We know much more about elite effects on popular culture than we do about the effects of popular culture on elite practices and identity. Varying regional and national power constellations and forms of conflict resolution have shaped the timing and modalities of incorporating popular traditions into elite practices. Not unlike the trajectories of race and nation, it is plausible that in the northern Andes (especially Colombia) elites embraced elements of popular culture—from *arepas* to the Cumbia—earlier (or at least more openly) than elites did in the southern Andes. After 1930, authoritarian nationalism and state interventionism combined to regulate and modernize ever more aspects of popular behavior and practices. This period marked a decisive wave in the "folklorization" of indigenous and African ceremonial and artistic traditions, as for example Cuzco's Incaic Inti Raymi festivities. Yet elite appropriation, reinterpretation, and cultural neutralization of popular culture was a drawn-out process, touching various traditions at different times. For example, the Señor de los Milagros—of syncretic pre-Hispanic and Afro-Peruvian origins—became Lima's most popular *and* elite-sponsored Catholic devotion no later than 1920. Yet even by the mid-1970s, after decades of massive migrations from the highlands, Andean music could only be heard on Lima's radio stations between 5 and 7 A.M., disappearing from the airwaves for the rest of the day when "respectable" society listened in. Political culture analysis for the Andes thus needs to carefully consider timing and modalities of popular culture shifts before connecting them to changes in the relative inclusiveness of power structures.

• • • • •

The chapters in this book tackle many of the issues we have presented here. They contribute to a newly emerging understanding of how, over the past

250 years, modern Andean political cultures were formed, challenged, and re-formed. In this introduction we have sought to outline the contours of a pragmatic perspective on political cultures.[73] Let us recall the shifts from the concept's origins as 1960s behaviorist political science theory within the modernization paradigm to the more interpretive, qualitative, and historicizing perspective now adopted by historians and anthropologists. This shift entails its own dangers. The pragmatic political culture perspective we advocate here has to navigate between "cultural reductionism" and "mechanistic voluntarism." Such a course portends the conceptual and methodological border crossings so central in Max Weber's work. It is evident today in the best political culture work on the Andes.

NOTES

1. For a processual approach to power, see Wolf, *Envisioning Power,* esp. chap. 1.
2. Of course, the theoretical lineages of approaches to the history of politics and power in Latin America are considerably more complex. Especially the impact (or lack thereof) of Foucauldian and postmodern ideas on practitioners in either of the two approach clusters creates a perpendicular fault line dividing scholars into those positing that history primarily concerns contested representations, and those believing that behind such representations there still exists a "reality" (even if objectively unknowable) that matters.
3. "Comparative Political Systems"; Formisano, "The Concept of Political Culture."
4. *Main Currents in Sociological Thought,* 2: 251, 264; see also Bendix, *Max Weber,* 46–47.
5. Aron, *Main Currents in Sociological Thought,* 2: 220–21.
6. Bendix, *Max Weber,* 494.
7. Almond, "The Study of Political Culture," 13.
8. Almond, "Foreword," ix; the seminal study in this school was Adorno et al., *The Authoritarian Personality;* for an update of this approach incorporating recent psychological research on emotional development, see Hopf and Hopf, *Familie, Persönlichkeit, Politik,* chap. 3.
9. Berg-Schlosser, *Politische Kultur,* 21–25; for a famous Latin American example, see Paz, *The Labyrinth of Solitude.*
10. Almond,"Foreword," x.

11. Almond and Verba, *The Civic Culture;* for a recent discussion of Almond's and Verba's concept concerning Colombia, see Jaimes Peñaloza, "Balance y reflexión."
12. Almond and Verba, *The Civic Culture,* 5.
13. Ibid., 13.
14. Ibid., 17–19.
15. Ibid., 29–31, 500–501.
16. Ibid., 32–33.
17. Ibid., 75.
18. See, e.g., Pye and Verba, eds., *Political Culture and Political Development;* Pye, *Politics, Personality, and Nation Building;* Eckstein, *Division and Cohesion in Democracy;* Berg-Schlosser, *Politische Kultur;* for early applications of political culture to Latin America, see Fitzgibbon and Fernandez, eds., *Latin America;* and contributions to Tomasek, ed., *Latin American Politics.*
19. By the 1990s, there were signs of a revival, but with little reference to the new political culture approach developed in history and anthropology; see, e.g. Eckstein, *Regarding Politics;* Thompson, Ellis, and Wildavsky, *Culture Theory.*
20. Almond, "Foreword," x–xi; for a more fine-grained classification of critics, see Almond, "The Study of Political Culture," 16–17.
21. Gendzel, "Political Culture," 229; among critical voices, see Pateman, "Political Culture"; Wiatr, "The Civic Culture"; Muller and Seligson, "Civic Culture and Democracy"; for discussion of Almond's and Verba's original cases in light of the criticism, see Almond and Verba, eds., *The Civic Culture Revisited.*
22. For its effects on history, see Appleby, Hunt, and Jacob, *Telling the Truth about History,* 207–17; Novick, *That Noble Dream,* chap. 15.
23. Geertz, *The Interpretation of Cultures,* esp. 3–30; on applications to political culture history, see Gendzel, "Political Culture," 233–35; for a critical account of recent notions of culture among American cultural anthropologists, see Kuper, *Culture,* esp. chaps. 3–7; on culture as praxis, see Ortner, "Theory in Anthropology."
24. Habermas, *Strukturwandel der Öffentlichkeit.*
25. Seminal works on republicanism include Baylin, *The Ideological Origins;* Pocock, *The Machiavellian Moment;* and Wood, *The Radicalism of the American Revolution.*
26. Welch, *The Concept of Political Culture,* 148–58.
27. Hunt, *Politics,* 10–11.
28. Baker, *Inventing the French Revolution,* 4–7.
29. Ibid., 6; see also Chartier, *Cultural Origins of the French Revolution;* Furet, *Interpreting the French Revolution.*
30. Baker, *Inventing the French Revolution,* 4–7.
31. Cf. Darnton's discussion of Baker and Chartier in "An Enlightened Revolution?"
32. Viotti da Costa, "New Publics, New Politics, New Histories," 20; for a critique of self-referential concepts of culture, see Kuper, *Culture,* passim; for a pragmatic anthropological approach to political culture bridging symbolic and social dimensions,

see Adler Lomnitz and Melnick, *Chile's Political Culture and Parties,* 1–16; see also Tejera Gaona, ed., *Antropología Política.*

33. Flores Galindo, *Buscando un inca;* Burga, *Nacimiento de una utopia.*

34. Bonilla, "The War of the Pacific;" Manrique, *Campesinado y nación;* Mallon, *The Defense of Community,* chap.3.

35. Rivera Cusicanqui, *'Oppressed But Not Defeated';* see also Albó, "From MNRistas to Kataristas;" Platt, *Estado boliviano.*

36. Mamani, *Taraqu;* Choque, *La sublevación.*

37. Ramón Valarezo, *Regreso de las runa;* Ibarra, *Indios y cholos.*

38. Guerrero, "La loi de la coutume," 331–54; Guerrero, *La semántica de la dominación;* Guerrero, "The Construction of a Ventriloquist's Image," 555–90.

39. Safford and Palacios, *Colombia,* 336.

40. Sánchez Gómez et al., *Violencia y democracia;* Sánchez Gómez, *Guerra y política;* Leal Buitrago and Zamosc, eds., *Al filo del caos;* for different perspectives on *violencia,* see Bergquist, Peñaranda, and Gonzalo Sánchez, eds., *Violence in Colombia.*

41. Rappaport, *The Politics of Memory;* Wade, *Blackness and Race Mixture;* Appelbaum, "Whitening the Region."

42. For an overview of those literatures, see Salomon, "Andean Ethnology in the 1970s," 75–128, Salomon, "The Historical Development," 79–98; Salomon, "Testimonies"; Poole, "Antropología e historia andinas," 209–45.

43. Spalding, "Kurakas and Commerce"; Spalding, *Huarochirí,* esp. chaps. 7 and 8.

44. Platt, *Estado boliviano y ayllu andino.*

45. O'Phelan Godoy, *Rebellions and Revolts;* a significant forerunner was Condarco Morales, *Zarate, el temible Willka.*

46. Stern, ed., *Resistance;* see also Szeminski, *La utopía;* the precursor for cultural interpretations of the Great Rebellion was Rowe, "El movimiento nacional inca."

47. Rappaport, *The Politics of Memory.*

48. Abercrombie, *Pathways of Memory,* esp. 109–25; Abercrombie, "To Be Indian to Be Bolivian," 95–130.

49. See Mallon, "The Promise and Dilemma of Subaltern Studies," 1491–515.

50. Mallon, *Peasant and Nation;* Mallon, "Indian Communities," 35–53; Thurner, *From Two Republics to One Divided;* on the western highlands of Guatemala (expressly referring to Andeanist historiographical models), see Grandin, *The Blood of Guatemala.*

51. For an insightful comparison of a broad gamut of different types of state formation in nineteenth century based on varying types of relations between the central state, the military, and popular groups during wars and civil wars, see López-Alves, *State Formation,* chap. 1, conclusion, and (on Colombia) chap. 3; for sarcastic anecdotes and linguistic erudition as tools of hegemony among nineteenth-century Colombian politicians (especially Conservatives), see Deas, *Del poder y la gramática,* esp. 45.

52. Diez Hurtado, *Comunes y haciendas,* chaps. 4 and 8; Clark, *The Redemptive Work,* chap. 6; Jacobsen, "Liberalism"; Jacobsen and Diez Hurtado, "Montoneras, la Comuna de Chalaco y la revolución de Piérola"; Gotkowitz, "Within the Boundaries of Equality."

53. Walker, *Smoldering Ashes,* chap. 3; O'Phelan Godoy, *Rebellions and Revolts,* chap. 5; O'Phelan Godoy, "L'utopie andine"; O'Phelan Godoy, "El mito de la independencia concedida"; Serulnikov, "Su verdad y su justicia," and essay in this volume; Thomson, "Colonial Crisis, Community, and Andean Self-Rule."

54. O'Phelan Godoy, "Discurso y etnicidad."

55. See articles by Garrido and Helg in this volume; Helg, "The Limits of Equality"; Hünefeldt, *Paying the Price for Freedom;* Aguirre, *Agentes de su propia libertad,* esp. chaps. 6 and 7; Blanchard, *Slavery and Abolition,* chap. 5.

56. Larson, "Andean Highland Peasants," 580–81; Safford, "Race, Integration and Progress"; Applebaum, "Whitening the Region."

57. See articles by Larson and Gotkowitz in this volume; Mendez, *Incas si, Indios no;* Poole, *Vision, Race and Modernity,* esp. chaps. 6 and 7; de la Cadena, *Indigenous Mestizos;* a cautionary note on elite essentialist racism in Mücke, *Das Indianerbild.*

58. Chambers, "Republican Friendship."

59. Silverblatt, *Sun, Moon and Witches,* chap. 10; Hünefeldt, *Paying the Price for Freedom,* 76–85.

60. Hünefeldt, *Liberalism in the Bedroom;* Denegri, *El abanico y la cigarrera;* Manarelli, *Limpias y modernas;* Barragan, *Indios, mujeres y ciudadanos,* 33–38.

61. Gotkowitz, "Within the Boundaries of Equality"; de la Cadena, *Indigenous Mestizos,* chap. 4.

62. Phelan, *The Kingdom of Quito;* Phelan, *The People and the King;* for recent interpretations of the Comuneros, see McFarlane, *Colombia before Independence,* 64–71.

63. Trazegnies, *La idea de derecho.*

64. Guerra, *Modernidad e independencias;* for the Andes, see Demelas-Bohy, *L'invention politique;* Garrido, *Reclamos y representaciones;* on nationalist and republican symbols in independent Nueva Granada, see König, *En el camino hacia la nación.*

65. Aljovín, *Caudillos y constituciones;* Irurozqui Victoriano, *"A bala, piedra y palo";* on violence as part of democratic politics in Colombia, see Pecaut, *L'ordre,* esp. 17.

66. Walker, *Smoldering Ashes;* de la Fuente, *Children of Facundo;* cf. striking similarities in the construction of a dictator in Kershaw, *Hitler.*

67. Among numerous studies on nineteenth-century elections and suffrage, see Barragán, *Indios, mujeres, y ciudadanos;* Irurozqui Victoriano, *'A bala, piedra y palo';* Peloso, "Liberals, Electoral Reform"; Chiaramonti, "Andes o nación"; Démelas-Bohy, "Modalidades y significación"; for Latin America in general, Sabato, "On Political Citizenship"; Sabato, *The Many and the Few;* Sabato, ed., *Ciudadanía política;* Posada Carbo, ed., *Elections before Democracy.*

68. McEvoy, “Estampillas y votos”; McEvoy, *La utopia republicana;* Mücke, *Der “Partido Civil” in Peru.*

69. Forment, “La sociedad civil y la invención de la democracia”; Forment, *Democracy in Latin America;* for the development of progressive Catholic associations and sociability in Antioquia, see Londoño-Vega, *Religion, Culture and Society in Colombia,* esp. 299–315.

70. On *chicherias*, see Rodriguez Ostria and Humberto Solares, *Sociedad oligárquica;* on women's networks of public opinion, see Chambers, *From Subjects to Citizens,* chap. 3 and 220–21; del Aguila, *Callejones y masones;* see also Jacobsen's chapter in this volume.

71. Ayala Mora, *Historia de la revolución liberal,* 69–71.

72. Nugent, *Modernity at the Edge of Empire,* 11–13, 315–23; Roldán, *Blood and Fire,* 298.

73. For a similar approach, see Formisano, “The Concept of Political Culture,” esp. 423–24.

IS POLITICAL CULTURE GOOD TO THINK?

Alan Knight

Discussing the utility of concepts is a tricky business, since (*pace* neoclassical economists) "utility" is a subjective thing, which will vary according to the interests and approaches of particular social scientists.[1] If someone believes that divine providence or the Hegelian world spirit offers the best explanations of history, empirical evidence is not likely to persuade him or her to the contrary. Furthermore, historians, more than most social scientists, can be cavalier with their concepts, failing either to scrutinize or clarify them adequately.

THE CONCEPT OF POLITICAL CULTURE

If we are to evaluate the utility of "political culture" in the Latin American context, however, we need some notion of what it means. Unfortunately, the recent explosion of cultural history, however rich in terms of its empirical foci and findings, has muddied more than clarified the conceptual waters.[2] The "new cultural history" has therefore failed to produce a clear consensus regarding "political culture." Its imperialistic urge to gather all human historical activity into its broad bosom may be correct, since all human activity is certainly cultural, in the sense of being mediated through words, ideas, symbols, discursive practices, etc.[3] Yet this is a form of self-defeating imperialism, which, by including everything, excludes nothing, and hence lacks any discrimination (and the one thing that useful concepts should do is discriminate).[4] If all human activity is cultural, the key qualifier is "political," hence political culture refers to all forms of political—as opposed to, say, economic or aesthetic—activity.

The political scientists who embrace the term do, at least, offer clearer definitions, which are worthy of attention. I stress this point since my critique of political culture has been seen as a kind of tilting at ancient windmills (e.g., Almond and Verba).[5] In fact, the windmills are by no means all ancient.[6] They are certainly not imaginary, and, whatever their faults, they at least present a clear and stable profile on the horizon, which is more than can be said of some of the will-o-the-wisp new cultural history, which often seems to make a virtue of obscurity and inconsistency. What is more, social scientists have methodological resources that historians—certainly historians of nineteenth-century Latin America—entirely lack: for example, survey data and participant-observation, which enable them to "operationalize" the concept in ways that historians cannot.[7]

Definitions of political culture vary, but one, which at least has the merit of capaciousness, brings together the "subjective propensities, actual behavior and the framework in which behavior takes place."[8] This does not seem to me radically different from—though it is perhaps a little more specific than—Keith Baker's definition, which historians regularly cite with apparent approval.[9] Political culture therefore embraces underlying attitudes (e.g., venality, parochialism, machismo), actual behavior (e.g., barrack revolts, rigged elections), and the (institutional?) framework within which behavior occurs (e.g., authoritarian or praetorian government).[10] However, it is the first that is usually associated with political culture—and not just in the key text of Almond and Verba.[11] This association seems semantically valid, to the extent that "culture" implies enduring beliefs and attitudes, whereas "actual behavior" could entail discrete events, amenable to quite different (noncultural) explanations, and "the framework" leads us to macroexplanations which, likewise, carry no necessarily "cultural" implications.

These different viewpoints may converge on the same historical phenomenon, but their approach is rather different. For example, if we state that, during the Porfiriato (1876–1911), Mexican elections were rigged, corrupt, and fairly meaningless, we could couch such a statement (a) in cultural/subjective propensity terms ("Mexicans were culturally attuned/accustomed/suited to such elections");[12] (b) in terms of actual behavior ("during elections, few voted, and those who did were dragooned"); or (c) in terms of the framework ("the Díaz government habitually rigged elections").

While these three perspectives are compatible, they approach the explanandum from different directions; indeed, we could say that the first might be favored by the cultural historian, the second by the political-narrative historian, the third by the political-institutional historian. Or, again, while a culturalist political scientist might endorse (a), a rational-choice theorist would prefer (b) and (c) over (a).

Though these three statements may be potentially compatible, their logical relationship is asymmetrical. While (a) would seem to require (b), since "subjective propensities" by definition must determine behavior, a propensity being "the quality of being inclined to something,"[13] (b) does not require (a), for behavior need not be seen as springing from prior propensities: a Mexican who fails to vote may do so because of illness, intimidation, bribery, a rational perception that voting is futile, or because he has something better to do on the day. None of these motives requires a subjective propensity. There is some psychological support for my argument. Stuart Sutherland discerns a "universal tendency to ascribe other people's behavior to their character traits or dispositions rather than to their situation"; hence the "error [of] attributing an action to a person's disposition rather than to the situation is extremely common."[14] So, we can—and usually should—analyze behavior without assuming subjective propensities. The reason is simple: we can observe behavior in abundance, but we usually guess at subjective propensities; indeed, we may, when we guess, simply invent them. After all, some subjective propensities are hard to get at, even in the contemporary world, where we have survey data and participant-observation to help. I do not mean transient and specific propensities—how a Mexican might vote in tomorrow's election, for example—but rather those kind of deep, enduring propensities that usually pass for political culture. Attempts to calibrate tolerance, trust, or democratic commitment are not entirely convincing. And if we are trying to plumb the subjective propensities of, say, insurgent peasants in nineteenth-century Latin America, the task is even more difficult, in many cases insuperable.[15] When the peasants of Comas resisted Chilean invaders during the War of the Pacific, did they do so in order to protect the Peruvian *patria,* or their own backyards? Was their resistance spurred by (proto-?) patriotism—a shared cultural trait—or by immediate self-preservation? The evidence does not, I think, permit a firm conclusion either way.[16]

So, even if such propensities exist (which they may not), they remain obscure. The best approach is to analyze actual behavior,which is what historians usually do: they record people working, trading, marrying, parenting, fighting, migrating, and so on. Behavior, including political behavior, may reveal distinct patterns: electoral participation or abstention, lobbying, litigation, land invasions, strikes, flight, riot and rebellion.[17] However, little is usually gained by attributing such behavior to underlying propensities; it is about as useful as Aristotle's explanation of gravity—things fall because it is in their nature to do so. In fact, the historical evidence for supposed underlying propensities is usually behavioral in the first place. We see a number of rebellions in Morelos or Juchitán and conclude that the Morelenses and Juchitecos are a rebellious lot (as Díaz himself observed, "those tramps of the south are tough").[18] But it would be a dangerously circular argument to invoke the rebellious disposition of the Morelenses as the cause of the Zapatista insurrection. Hence, statements about political culture are usually *descriptive at best:* to denote a particular political culture as, say, rebellious, deferential, democratic, corrupt, or violent is a shorthand way of saying that the group in question tends to *behave* in discernibly rebellious, deferential, democratic, corrupt, or violent ways.

Now this sort of shorthand may be harmless and may even, on occasions, be useful. So long as "political culture" is used *purely descriptively,* it may do no great harm. However, before we leap from bits of "behavior" to notions of a gestalt "culture," I think we should impose some basic criteria. Roughly, I assume that a pattern of recurrent actions denotes behavior; and a pattern of recurrent behavior (i.e., a great many cumulative actions), evident over time and, perhaps, space, may be *descriptively* referred to as culture.[19] A one-off revolt does not indicate a culture of rebellion. Still less—to return to modern survey data—does an intention to vote for a particular party denote a particular culture. (In passing, I would suggest that survey methods are best at establishing precisely such one-off, specific intentions and worst at revealing supposedly deep cultural traits. They can predict the result of an imminent election; they have yet to show that they can predict, say, a systemic democratic collapse). For "culture" to be employed, even in the purely descriptive sense I have outlined, as a shorthand for recurrent behavioral patterns, it must display both *durability* and *salience.*

By *durability* I simply mean that it must last: culture is not a fly-by-night, here-today-and-gone-tomorrow kind of phenomenon. It would be premature to talk of a "democratic political culture" in a country where, however fair and free the last election, and however large the turnout, the military had returned to barracks only weeks before. (Hence the current debates in Latin America have moved on from discussions of democratic "transition" to assessments of democratic "consolidation.") Party-political affiliations—the "liberal crescent" in nineteenth-century Mexico; Peru's *sólido norte Aprista*—imply a consistent allegiance over time, sometimes in the face of challenge and repression, not a transient (rational-choice?) calculation.[20] We could contrast these cases with, for example, contemporary Chihuahua or Baja California, swing states in the newly volatile universe of Mexican electoral politics, where party allegiances change from election to election, in response to particular events, economic vicissitudes, tactical voting, and the appeal of individual candidates. Conceivably, as I shall mention shortly, allegiances of unusual strength and durability might in some circumstances even qualify as genuinely explanatory as well as simply descriptive factors, but such explanatory claims must be proven, and, in fact, are often notoriously hard to prove.

If cultural characteristics must be durable, they must also be *salient.* They must attach to a broad cross-section of the group in question. If one swallow doesn't make a summer, one rebel doesn't make a rebellious political culture. While this may seem obvious, there are many intermediate cases where a broad "culture" is too readily imputed on the basis of a limited sample. Egregious examples would be the sweeping descriptions of Latin American (political) culture penned by Wiarda, Dealy, and others (descriptions that not only aggregate excessively but also boldly claim explanatory power).[21] Supposed national identities—especially, perhaps, those of large nations—are similarly vulnerable. Octavio Paz wrote a cultural portrait of the Mexicans that has received wide currency and even credence. However, not only is it based on poetic intuition rather than empirical evidence, it is also confined—so Paz tells us, although his qualification largely fell on deaf ears—to a "quite small" minority of Mexicans.[22]

Most national stereotypes, even if we generously or naively assume them to contain some elements of descriptive truth, are not really national: the *porteño* does not typify all Argentinians, while *tico* identity conveniently ignores Costa Rica's Atlantic Coast. Indeed, since the larger the unit, the harder, on balance, it becomes to detect any salient characteristics, it follows that regional identities—or political cultures—tend to be more meaningful than national ones. The image of the hardworking, entrepreneurial, Catholic Antioqueño, or his/her rough counterpart in Jalisco, Mexico (especially los Altos de Jalisco) at least contains sufficient descriptive power to merit consideration and provoke debate.[23] The contrasting political cultures of, say, Bogotá and Barranquilla, or Cuzco and Lima, are also worth taking seriously.[24] In fact, the most meaningful attributions of a distinct political culture may well be found at the local and municipal level: Red Líbano; radical Juchitan; pious San José de Gracia.[25] Of course, even these attributions are a little sweeping: not all Juchitecos are radical, not all Josefinos are *mochos* (pious political Catholics). But the salience of the attribute (and, I would repeat, its durability over time) tell in its favor. It follows, of course, that the greater the politicocultural variation at the lower level, the harder it becomes to accept the notion of a salient and meaningful political culture at the higher level. The politicocultural gulf between Lima, Cuzco, and Arequipa, or between Pasto, Bogotá, and Baranquilla, makes the notion of a distinct Peruvian or Colombian *national* political culture highly questionable, especially for the nineteenth century.

In the Mexican case a common pattern involves local dyadic rivalries between neighboring communities, who feud and fight, litigate and lobby, defining their very identity in terms of the old struggle (Juchitan vs. Tehuantepec; San José vs. Mazamitla; Amilpas vs. Soyaltepec).[26] While such disputes may involve broadly similar communities, whose quarrels concern local political preeminence or access to local resources, they can also serve to point up distinctive markers—ethnic, religious, and ideological—which set the rivals apart in terms of their (in part political) culture. Broader Latin American parallels spring to mind: León and Granada in Nicaragua; Acolla and Marco in the Yanamarca Valley of Peru.[27] Again, such dyadic rivalries make the notion of a coherent national—or even a coherent regional—identity/culture open to question.[28] Thus, while dyadic rivalry may be a (descriptively) significant part of Mexican political culture—i.e., it is a discernible pattern in Mexican political behavior and it may even help explain events —it militates against any notion of higher-level, especially national, politicocultural homogeneity.[29]

These examples concern geographical zones (regions, localities), but in a sense space serves to denote a range of nonspatial attributes, relating to race, class, ethnicity, and ideology. Mazamitla is Indian, San José Creole/mestizo; Tehuantepec is conservative, Juchitan radical (Juarista in the nineteenth century, Cardenista in the twentieth). But contrasting subnational political cultures need not be spatially defined. Nineteenth-century Latin America contained what might loosely be called sectoral cultures: for example, the artisans of Puebla, Bogotá, or Lima, who resisted free trade and foreign imports under the banner of protectionist caudillos and coalitions, who played a disproportionate role in urban politics, participated in elections, formed self-help groups, and rioted sometimes. Or the Catholic-clerical constituency which combined prelates, religious orders, and the devout laity, especially the *beatas* (pious ladies) of, for example, Guadalajara, Popayan, or Quito, who contested liberal reforms, and maintained a dense network of Catholic sociability exerting influence at the highest political levels.

Thus cultures—some, of course, more overtly political than others—come in myriad forms. Some are unique islands (there is only one San José de Gracia, just as there is only one Mexico, each uniquely defined by geographical space and historical experience). Some, however, are members of sprawling archipelagos—the artisan archipelago, the Catholic-clerical archipelago—linked by common ties of belief and interest. These ties may be latent or unconscious, or they may be manifest and conscious. Presumably one source of strength of the Catholic-clerical archipelago was that it was precociously aware of forming part of both a grand global network and an ancient historical tradition: those of the universal Church. These, as endless sermons, encyclicals, and pastoral letters reiterated, linked Rome to Mexico to San José de Gracia. Freemasonry in the nineteenth century and international socialism in the twentieth gave the anticlerical left something of the same sense of global belonging.

So far, I have stressed the purely *descriptive* character of political culture: it is, at best, a shorthand for a set of behaviors. But can political culture also serve as an explanatory concept? Are there times when, even bearing in mind the psychologist's caution against "dispositional" explanations, we can say with confidence: x happened because of y's political culture?[30] I think quite rarely. Usually, such an explanation is too tautological to be of use. If we attribute the failings of Porfirian elections to a deficient Mexican political culture, we are virtually saying: Mexicans behave like this because they behave like this (given that our evidence for a deficient political culture is primarily the way Mexicans have been seen to behave in previous elections).[31] So we are back with the Aristotelian "explanation" of gravity. Some potential explanatory power might be added if we advanced a kind of Pavlovian (strictly) behaviorist thesis: time, custom, and conditioning determine behavior; years of electoral corruption have inured Mexicans to electoral apathy and indifference; thus, even when given the opportunity of "a free vote and no boss rule," they fail to take it.[32] Political culture, in other words, is the product of prescription: "institutions heavily shape choices and behavior, and the 'habitual' practices of these choices and behaviors may eventually become embedded in intrinsic cultural values and norms."[33]

There are several problems with this argument, however. It is empirically questionable: Mexicans readily and enthusiastically rallied to Francisco Madero in 1910, when, after thirty-four years of electoral torpor, a genuine political opening beckoned. Recent research also stresses the rapidity with which the new electoral politics of the decade after 1810 was espoused in much of Latin America—and not just the major cities.[34] Centuries of colonial rule did not, it seems, prevent a swift espousal of representative forms of government, once the opportunity arose.[35] Events and interests trumped any residual cultural inertia. In both cases, however, the opening was brief—very brief in the case of Madero. Thus, we must conclude one of two things: either Mexico's democratic culture slumbered for a generation (or more) under Díaz, suddenly awoke in 1910–13, then went back to sleep for a further two generations. Or the dynamics of change were largely noncultural and had to do with events (the aging Díaz's mismanagement of the 1910 election) and interests (collective repudiation of the Porfiriato in 1910; collective repudiation of Madero leading to *cuartelazo*, in 1911–13).

By "interests"—which I am presenting as a counterpoint to culture—I refer to both economic advantage (individual or collective) and relationships of power (the two are clearly linked, but not identical). Both, I repeat, are culturally defined, since all human activities are culturally defined. But for the purpose of historical analysis and explanation, "interests" can—and should—be distinguished from "(political) culture." If Mexicans did not vote in Porfirian elections because they were *impelled* by (not simply characterized by) an undemocratic political culture, the explanation is cultural. If they did not vote because Mexico's rulers preferred to fix elections, in order to maintain their own political power and economic privileges, the explanation relates to interests.

Of course, the relation of interests to culture is complex. As James Scott has stressed, ostensibly cultural formulations (e.g., "naive monarchism") may be deceptive, since subalterns—e.g., Balzac's peasants—learn to speak the right "scripts," those which best serve their interests.[36] Such scripts should be read skeptically. Some bold "culturalists" have posited entire subaltern "(sub)cultures"—the "culture of poverty," the "Sambo" slave stereotype—which, on closer inspection, have been found seriously wanting.[37] Elites also deploy culture instrumentally. Latin American elites have regularly justified their political power and economic privilege on the basis of, for example, racial or religious legitimation. Objectively, of course, such justifications are worthless. Subjectively they are significant, at least to the extent that they were believed, especially by the elites themselves. (Again, we cannot know this for sure; but it seems likely that the self-regarding "public transcripts" of elites are more credible, at least to the elites, than the self-disparaging transcripts of subalterns are to subalterns. No one wants to consider himself a "Sambo"; many, given the chance, would like to be the "lords of humankind," by the grace of God or genetic inheritance.) This simple contrast illustrates a plausible and relevant rule of thumb: beliefs become credible to the extent that they reinforce interests. Yet when mutual reinforcement occurs—e.g., when elites cite scripture to justify elitism—it is difficult to disentangle the two. Cultural explanations are more cogent when they go against, rather than with, the grain of interest.

There may indeed be cases where affective cultural ties trump material (and other) interests.[38] A good case—unfortunately a twentieth-century case—is Costa Rican democracy, which seems to display a measure of consensus and durability greater than that in many Latin American democracies, notwithstanding its somewhat contingent genesis in the late 1940s.[39] Rhetoric and survey data both suggest a consistently high support for democracy in Costa Rica. Furthermore, Costa Ricans practice what they preach, and what they poll. Costa Rican democracy can fairly be said to be consolidated; it is "the only game in town."[40] In contrast, some Latin American democracies appear less consolidated and vulnerable to instrumental calculation: that is, democracy is fine so long as it serves immediate interests. But if it does not, it may succumb; other games are on offer, which may promise higher returns. Democracy, in this scenario, is not an affective value but an instrumental means—to secure stability, avoid bloodshed, and foster foreign trade, credit, investment, and approbation. If circumstances change, the logic of instrumentality may also change, mandating an alternative preference.

Another way of putting this would be to say that in Costa Rica democracy has achieved a "relative autonomy" of contingent (negative) circumstances. Come economic hell or political high water, democracy has a distinct staying power and is to a degree impervious to short-term instrumentalist calculations. Assuming this to be true, we can suggest that the affective appeal of democracy is a politicocultural factor of some explanatory power. It is durable (it has lasted over half a century), it is salient (it touches most Costa Ricans), and has a causal impact which cannot be reduced to prior interests. Costa Ricans do not espouse democracy simply because it will make them safer or richer or more powerful, but because they deem it to be a normatively superior system. Of course, differentiating norms from interests is, as I have said, a tricky business: sometimes apparently disinterested norms may reflect long-term interest.[41] And, in politics as in the market, short-term instrumentality can, in the long run, prove disastrous. My cautious conclusion—and chief concession to "culturalist" explanations—would be that some durable and salient allegiances cannot be reduced to interests and do suggest a genuine degree of cultural autonomy. "Political culture," in these cases, can help provide explanations. But the cases are few.

I have invoked the case of contemporary democracy because it is clearly political, has been much researched, and seems to fit the bill. Searching for comparable cases in the nineteenth century, unaided by survey data or participant-observation, is no easy matter. The alignments of royalists and patriots during the wars of independence (which I mention later) seem to respond primarily to political and economic interests, coupled with decisive, often external events. A couple of generations later, when patriots in Mexico and Peru resisted foreign invasion, it is hard to know whether disinterested patriotism (a cultural factor) or local self-interest prevailed. Did Peruvian peasants resist Chilean invaders because the latter were Chilean, or because they were rapacious? Or, to put it differently, since the easy answer might be "both," we should ask: how much causal "value-added" did the fact of their being Chilean generate? If the invaders had been Peruvian troops, or if the Chileans had behaved with punctilious rectitude toward civilians, would the response have been similar? Or consider the Brazilian antislavery and abolitionist movement which, like its British or U.S. counterparts, cannot be reduced to mere self-interest masquerading as philanthropy. Nevertheless, the defense of slavery correlated closely with slave ownership, indeed with slave ownership that remained profitable, but not so profitable that a switch to free wage labor was feasible.[42]

Finally, to take perhaps the best example nineteenth-century Latin America offers, consider Church-state conflict. Church and state, Catholics and anticlericals, fought to promote rival interests (economic resources, legal privileges, political power and patronage), but they also represented rival cultural conceptions, which enjoyed a certain autonomy and were not simply reflexes of those interests. Catholics really believed that they were party to a privileged and transcendental truth, which they were obliged to proselytize. Liberal and leftist anticlericals were no less sure that science, progress, and enlightenment were on their side, and promised a better society.[43] Instrumentality was often important. Thus, we find the Mexican clergy preaching against land reform and excommunicating *agraristas* in the 1920s, just as Brazilian priests had defended slavery sixty years before.[44] But Catholic allegiance was an autonomous, durable and, in some places, salient force, which affected politics and which cannot be reduced simply to prior interests. Patriotism and, a fortiori, religion would therefore seem to be two poles around which politicocultural battles often raged, somewhat autonomously of interests.

In some cases these rival cultural attachments were ancient and ingrained, the product of long-term acculturation. In Latin America, as in the France of André Siegfried, regions of Catholic/clerical political allegiance were often old and well defined.[45] They depended, for their reproduction, on a network of Catholic institutions, all answerable to the hierarchy and to Rome: churches, seminaries, convents, *cofradías,* and the array of lay associations called into existence by the encyclical *Rerum Novarum* of Pope Leo XIII.[46] Political Catholicism—perhaps the strongest manifestation of a distinct political culture in nineteenth-century Latin America—was not, therefore, the nimble, shifting, bottom-up phenomenon celebrated by many of the new cultural historians.[47] Rather, like the international communism of the 1930s and 1940s, it was dedicated, disciplined, hierarchical, and authoritarian. Furthermore, precisely in order to attain sufficient durability and salience, it relied on a barrage of institutions, without which it would not have existed. Analyses of political culture, especially if they wish to claim explanatory power, must squarely address these institutional prerequisites.[48]

On the other hand, some forms of cultural politics were more innovative and flexible. Indeed, they had to be, if Latin American political life was to receive occasional infusions of fresh blood—by which I mean not just people but also ideas and practices. The insurgent nationalism of Belgrano or Miranda or Fray Servando de Teresa y Mier did not derive from an ancient cultural legacy but instead involved novel formulations and, perhaps no less important, novel institutions (such as Masonic lodges).[49] Political culture was not all inert baggage but also involved prospective and even somewhat utopian visions of alternative futures. The independence period was, given its revolutionary climate, rich in such visions, some innovative and forward looking, some, such as Inca restorationism, backward looking, but radical nonetheless.[50] It is a defining characteristic of revolutions that such alternative visions flourish, that radical possibilities are scouted, and that autonomous politicocultural projects—those which go beyond the (still important) pursuit of quotidian material and political interests—acquire unusual force. Counterrevolutions—or, less dramatically, periods of postrevolutionary *tristesse*—involve not only physical repression but also cultural constriction: the visions fade and the hopes (or fears) subside. Wordsworth's "bliss was it in that dawn to be alive" (which greeted the French Revolution in 1789) gives way to the curmudgeonly conservatism of Burke, Pitt, and Coleridge. A similar process, perhaps, characterized early-nineteenth-century Latin America, as the initial liberal-democratic dreams soured and hardheaded, sometimes downright conservative, pragmatism prevailed, with respect to constitutions, elections, and fiscal policy.

Thus, political culture, on those occasions when it rises above mere description and offers causal explanations, does not necessarily imply prescription, tradition, or the status quo. It can also be allied to change and reform. Furthermore, new political cultures may arise quite suddenly; they do not necessarily mature for years like fine wines. This point, by the way, does not invalidate my argument for durability: a political culture can, obviously, be new, but—potentially—durable. Contemporary actors may not know this. Costa Ricans did not know they were witnessing the birth of an enduring democratic culture in the 1940s. (It is the same lack of hindsight that makes current debates about democratic "consolidation" inconclusive and somewhat scholastic.) Again, however, it is crucial for historians of political culture, especially if they wish to make causal claims, to address both the origins and the success of particular politicocultural innovations, of new historical "memes."[51] In other words—if we pursue the Darwinian metaphor—they must identify new politicocultural mutations as they arise and explain why, in certain times and places, some—probably only a few—survive and multiply in the battle for survival and reproduction, thus becoming both salient and durable. They do so, I would suggest, because they suit the circumstances, in which "culture" and interests achieve a mutually advantageous symbiosis; and because they acquire effective means of reproduction (e.g., schools, churches, parties, and a host of informal networks and institutions). Thus, liberal democracy frequently failed in nineteenth-century Latin America but proved a successful adaptation in late-twentieth-century Costa Rica. A fully Darwinian analysis of such contrasting outcomes would indeed offer a valid causal explanation of how political culture changes, and with what effect. In the two sections of this chapter which follow, I attempt a schematic approach to this problem, focusing on the period of independence and the late-nineteenth-century era of export-led growth.

POLITICAL CULTURE, POLITICAL ECONOMY, AND INDEPENDENCE (1780–1825)

If Argentina was "born liberal," the same was true, at least to some extent, for all the Americas.[52] As products of the "Atlantic Revolution," the republics of the Americas, north, central, and south, were all products of anticolonial movements which confronted monarchy and colonialism, and opted for independence and representative institutions. In the simplest terms, a system of hereditary monarchy gave way (with one major exception, Brazil) to a system of republican rule, based on notions of popular sovereignty. And even in Brazil, where the transition to independence was unusually smooth and managed (managed, in part, by the British), the result was a constitutional monarchy, vaguely Victorian in character, embodying representation and repudiating dynastic absolutism. Several caveats are, of course, in order. The new republics, if liberal, were not necessarily democratic. Large groups were disenfranchised (women, slaves, and Indians most obviously); constitutions were fragile and often honored in the breach; sporadic efforts were made to establish Spanish-American monarchies (the Mexicans tried twice, with Iturbide and Maximilian). And, in some cases, notably Paraguay, caudillos aspired to autocratic rule, dispensing with liberal-representative forms of government.

However, despite these many deviations, it is remarkable that the Spanish-American republics—and, indeed, the Brazilian (constitutional) monarchy—embodied principles of popular sovereignty and representation that remained staples of Latin American politics throughout and beyond the nineteenth century. Unlike Eurasia, Latin America avoided dynastic absolutism and other forms of royal, princely, ascriptive rule. Aristocracies were largely absent. Even authoritarian caudillos usually paid lip service to constitutional principle; they might ignore or amend constitutions, but they did not formally scrap them. Constitutions therefore remained, some of them quite durably, as "public transcripts" against which critics could judge and proclaim the failings of authoritarian administrations. Cycles of liberal (even democratic) opening and authoritarian closure, the subject of a great deal of recent political science discussion, are, it seems, as old as the republics themselves. A precocious democratization in the years between 1810 and 1830 was, in several cases, choked off by renewed conservative closure in the 1830s and 1840s. But a new generation of liberal reformers—Juárez, Sarmiento, Mosquera—returned to the fray around midcentury. And, even though the later nineteenth century, the era of export-led economic growth, saw a swing toward a positivistic (and racist) "liberalism" in, for example, Mexico, Guatemala, and Peru, this was offset by genuine liberalization and even democratization in the southern cone. There Chile, Uruguay, and Argentina formed part of Samuel Huntington's "first wave" of democratic advance across the globe.[53] I address this in my final section.

It is often taken for granted that the Latin American states assumed liberal, representative, and (outside Brazil) republican forms. But it is not entirely self-evident why this should be. The specificity of Brazil can be easily explained, at least in terms of the Anglo-Portuguese alliance and British mentoring of the fugitive Braganzas. But why did the Spanish-American flirtation with monarchy fail? After all, monarchy—constitutional and absolutist—remained the norm in most of Europe; even as the Ottoman and Habsburg empires shrank, and finally collapsed during World War I, they often spawned monarchical rather than republican successor states. It does not seem plausible to invoke the Monroe Doctrine which, for all its rhetorical ban on extensions of the European "system" into the Americas, lacked the military muscle to enforce its veto. If explanations of the republican-representative outcome are to be sought *within* Latin America, are they to be found lurking in some *cultural* corner of the continent? Did independence—triggered by the fortuitous Napoleonic invasion of Spain—make possible the efflorescence of a long-incubating liberal political culture in colonial Latin America, turning "hidden" into "public" transcript almost overnight? It would be somewhat surprising, given the chorus of historians and others who for years have descanted on Latin America's democratic deficit, illiberal "colonial legacy," lack of training in citizenship, and stultifying Hispanic-corporatist-authoritarian tradition.

More important—since much of that chorus may be little more than cacophony—the historical record itself does not reveal a pervasive, maturing liberalism, whether with respect to ideas or organizations, in colonial Latin America (compare British India, where forms of self-government were progressively, if grudgingly, introduced from the 1880s). Even if enlightened liberal ideas circulated, as of course they did, it does not seem that they detonated the independence movements, some of which were ambivalent about independence, *and* liberalism and the Enlightenment. It may be, in fact, that representative republican forms were finally adopted for lack of a better alternative. In a struggle against a colonial and (after 1814) absolutist metropolitan power, liberal republicanism was the most logical and appealing credo. Once Fernando VII—*el deseado* (the wished-for king)—had squandered his New World capital and, as a result, was no longer deseado, why should his rebellious New World subjects opt for another monarchy? The anticolonial struggle, unavoidable so long as Spain would not concede a measure of home rule, logically led to republican independence and representative government, premised on notions of popular sovereignty. Liberalism was the natural partner of patriotism, just as, in many twentieth-century anticolonial struggles, communism would become the natural partner of nationalism. This made possible the rapid adoption and even implementation of liberal representative systems throughout Latin America, an outcome that had less to do with deep cultural preconditions than with the pressing logic of the situation. Liberalism was an idea whose time had, rather unexpectedly, come. Or, we could say, it was a meme which suddenly acquired an unusual potency by virtue of the vagaries of historical natural selection.

A crucial additional factor—political economy—helps explain this precocious Latin American liberalism. It also helps explain the subsequent vicissitudes of liberalism through the nineteenth century, that is, its greater success in some places or periods than others, already mentioned in terms of cycles of opening and closure. I have, thus far, focused on political liberalism —the idea and practice of representative (usually republican) government, embodying a free (male) citizenry and constitutionally guaranteed rights. But political liberalism lived in uneasy symbiosis with economic liberalism;

and the former cannot be understood without taking the latter into account as well. In fact, the notion of an embryonic liberalism, growing in a colonial womb, is more plausible with regard to economic than to political liberalism. The Bourbon reforms did not promote self-government, representation, or civil rights; on the contrary, they tightened peninsular bureaucratic control, increased taxation without representation, cracked down on dissent, and established the first sizeable standing army in the American colonies. But they also took steps—sometimes ambivalent, shuffling steps—to promote *economic* liberalism: *comercio libre* (free trade), the abolition of monopoly *consulados,* and even a hesitant land reform, which would prefigure the liberal *desamortización* (disentailment) of the nineteenth century. In a sense, therefore, the Bourbons sought to accomplish a Barrington-Moore-style "revolution from above"—economic and administrative modernization, impelled by international competition, largely in the absence of serious sociopolitical reform.[54]

Like most such "revolutions from above," the contradictions of the project proved insurmountable. Yet it left a lasting legacy, in two distinct respects. First, the economic reforms fostered incipient export-led growth in several peripheral regions of the empire: the Río de la Plata, the Venezuelan lowlands, Cuba. The balance of power and prosperity began to shift, especially in southern South America. While this shift aggravated tensions in the old Andean heartland, it also generated frustrations of a different kind in the peripheries, where Creole elites sought genuine free trade with the rest of the world, especially Britain, and an end to taxation without representation. Hence, the second consequence: peripheral elites—especially Creole landlords with goods for export—began to see the attraction of combined economic and political liberalism. For the first would grant them access to world markets, while the second would give them greater control over their own destinies. Market freedom and political autonomy, which formed a neat philosophical couplet, thus exerted an unusual appeal. The lure of economic advantage conspired with the logic of political expedience, as already mentioned.

However, there was a price to pay for this option. Elites may favor market freedom and political autonomy for themselves, vis-à-vis an oppressive metropolis, but they have to consider the impact of these contagious principles on their own subalterns. Market freedom negates slavery and other forms of extra-economic coercion, while political autonomy, especially if couched in terms of liberal representation, implies civil rights and potentially democracy. Hence the classic dilemma of colonial elites: how far do they dare confront colonialism if, at the same time, they jeopardize their own socioeconomic privileges? At the risk of being overschematic (a recurrent risk in a chapter of this sweep), I can offer an answer, linking political economy and political culture, by resorting to a simple threefold typology. The peripheral Latin American societies which were beneficiaries of Bourbon rule at least with respect to foreign trade, fall into two rough categories: tropical lowlands, where the export sector consisted of plantations worked by black slaves; and temperate lowlands, dedicated to livestock farming, worked by cowboys, peons, and (rather fewer) slaves. The first included Cuba, coastal Peru, and Venezuela, the Colombian Chocó, and the Brazilian northeast. The second embraced the Río de la Plata and the Banda Oriental. Mexico had its own rough counterparts: Veracruz, Guerrero, and even Yucatán would fall in the first category, northern Mexico in the second. Both contrasted with the old colonial heartlands, where the sedentary Indian population remained large—indeed, had revived after the demographic nadir of the seventeenth century—and where mining and arable farming tended to hold sway.

The appeal of liberalism, both political and economic, affected these three regions differently. To put it crudely, contrasting political cultures were molded by contrasting political economies. (I admit to a frankly materialist formulation. In this instance at least, structures of production and class relations count for more than agency and identity.) In highland Indian Spanish America the colony survived longest, notably in Peru. The elite beneficiaries of colonial rule were concentrated in Peru and Mexico. Furthermore, fear of Indian and caste insurgency, never absent, had been exacerbated by the Túpac Amaru revolt of 1780 and subsequent rebellions in Andean Peru, and by the Hidalgo insurrection of 1810 in the Mexican Bajío. Creole demands for home rule or even outright independence were muffled by fears of class and caste war. Independence therefore came belatedly, either as a result of foreign invasion (Peru), or by virtue of a conservative Creole rebellion, directed against a now liberal metropolis, once the fear of popular insurrection had been quelled by royalist repression (Mexico). San Martín and Bolívar imposed independence on a somewhat reluctant Peru, while in Mexico Iturbide and the Trigarantine Army outflanked the weary forces of both *peninsular* royalism and popular patriotism. In the highland, Indian heartlands of the empire, therefore, liberalism remained a minority opinion (or, if you prefer, political culture). The promise of free trade alarmed merchant monopolists and could not attract hacendados who produced for limited domestic markets. The promise of representative government—free elections, civil rights, free expression—raised the specter of Indian and caste equality. If, as Iturbide's imperial debacle seemed to confirm, republican representative government could not be avoided, it at least had to be hedged about with guarantees: restricted suffrage, rigged elections, strong-arm caudillo rule.

In the economically buoyant peripheries, the attractions of free trade were powerful, and it is no surprise that the pacemakers of independence were to be found along the Atlantic littoral.[55] But when it came to political liberalism, a sharp—and logical—divergence appeared. Again, liberalism, with its promise of a homogenous citizenry and equality before the law, sat uneasily alongside coercive labor systems, which, reflecting ancient demographic patterns, were common along the Atlantic littoral. In particular, slavery, though usually associated with dynamic export-oriented economies, could hardly coexist with genuinely liberal government.[56] At the same time, the defense of slavery required a state apparatus capable of repression and undistracted by civil commotion. Slave owners might yearn for free-market opportunities, but they needed the backup of the colonial state and recoiled from revolution. As the dire lesson of Haiti suggested, "Cuba will be Spanish, or it will be African."[57] As a result, Cuba, the most dynamic slave society of the day, remained "always loyal" (to Spain). The Creole planters thus survived and, indeed, enjoyed the benefits of free trade under Spanish rule. But the intense conflicts over colonialism, home rule, and independence, which in mainland Latin America were resolved by the 1820s, continued to rack Cuba in the 1860s and 1890s, by which time the ending of slavery had removed the last best justification of colonial rule.

Of course, it is not historically impossible for a colony to achieve independence while clinging to coercive forms of labor. The United States managed to square the circle, spatially and ideologically cordoning off the slave/plantation sector. However, the outcome was tense and unstable, especially since the U.S. slave system was self-reproducing.[58] In South America, Brazil squared the circle, thanks to its unique, incremental, and generally peaceful transition to monarchical independence. Brazil also benefited from the built-in obsolescence of its slave system, once the external supply had been cut off in the 1850s. Abolition therefore came as a gradual but inevitable process. Like the United States, Brazil could live, at least for two generations, in a condition of structural political hypocrisy (again, perhaps, Victorian values helped?): representative institutions and parliamentary government coexisted with extensive chattel slavery, which in turn necessitated a strong central executive.[59] (Perhaps that helps explain why Portuguese America did not fragment into several individual republics as Spanish America did.) Abolitionists might denounce the palpable inconsistency of this outcome, but material interests would not be bound by ideological imperatives. Hence Brazil's political culture, like that of the United States, displayed a fundamentally schizoid nature.

At the time of independence, neither Cuba nor Brazil, with their close integration into world markets, could abandon slavery without facing serious economic repercussions. Cuba opted for continued colonial status, Brazil finessed the problem and achieved independence with slavery.[60] Venezuela and Argentina present contrasting cases. In the latter case, though slavery was common, it was less fundamental for the Argentine export economy, which relied on land-intensive livestock as well as entrepôt trade. Slave emancipation, logically implied by the promises of liberalism, was therefore accomplished early and easily, and Argentina established a more complete and unqualified liberal-republican politics, at least in its littoral/pastoral zone.[61] In Venezuela, however, the dilemma was more acute, since the country's cacao plantations relied on slave labor and, in some cases, the cacao planters struck the same Faustian bargain with the metropolis as their Cuban counterparts. But they were offset by other leaders—including planters like Bolívar himself—who either took their liberal principles more seriously (a culturalist explanation) or whose policies reflected the source of their support (for example, Páez's *llaneros*).[62] Slavery obstructed independence but could not block it entirely, as it had in Cuba. But neither could the Venezuelan planter elite finesse the problem, as in Brazil. Slavery ended amid bloody conflict; the plantations declined; but Venezuelan liberalism at least began life with a degree of ideological consistency. In highly schematic terms, then, we can posit a threefold typology of political behavior, and perhaps of incipient political culture, which derives in part from the imperatives of political economy: the Andean/Mesoamerican syndrome, where both political and economic liberalism were weak; and the Atlantic periphery syndrome, where economic liberalism (outwardly oriented, in respect of world trade) was strong, but political liberalism varied according to the nature of class relations, especially in the export sector, livestock production tending to be more favorable, plantation slavery intensely hostile. In crude terms, the prairies and pampas give us free labor and liberalism, while the plantation demands slavery.[63] Hence the continued colonialism of Cuba, the social upheaval of Venezuela, or the schizoid political culture of Brazil.

POLITICAL CULTURE, POLITICAL ECONOMY, AND POSITIVISM (1870–1920)

A striking feature of late-nineteenth-century Latin America is the ubiquity of liberals and liberalism, yet the bewildering variety of this phenomenon, which calls into doubt the very utility of the term. Of course, the fact that liberals termed themselves ("emically") "liberals" is of limited interest. Some of the most authoritarian parties in the world have flaunted a "Democratic" label. But there is a real ("etic") logic to the liberal label. Like the Bourbons, whose distant project they often emulated (*mutatis mutandis*), the liberals of the later nineteenth century were engaged in a sort of revolution-from-above, a point which Barrington Moore noted, *en passant,* in one of his rare references to the continent.[64] Like the Bourbons, the liberals were keen to promote trade, production, tax revenue, and territorial integration. But they did so not under colonial-monarchical auspices but rather with a view to emulating the progressive liberal states of Europe and North America. Unfortunately, the experience of the early nineteenth century made liberal elites leery of representative democracy, which too often seemed a solvent of order and progress. Cycles of liberal opening and conservative closure, punctuated by civil war and, occasionally, foreign invasion, had bred disillusionment, notably in Mexico, Central America, and the Andean Republics. Constitutional experiments had failed. The conclusion seemed to be that ruling elites should abandon, or at least postpone, the pursuit of "metaphysical" civil rights, in order to concentrate on the practicalities of economic development: exports, railways, ports, telegraphs, even industrial manufacturing. It is hardly surprising that positivism, offering a supposedly scientific rationale for this project, should captivate policymakers in Mexico, Peru, Brazil, and elsewhere. It also seems fair to refer to this as a shift in the prevailing political —or politicoeconomic—culture, comparable to the CEPALista turn of the 1940s and the neoliberal mass conversion of the 1980s.[65]

Positivism allowed for a strong, interventionist state, hence for a good deal of extraeconomic coercion. Slavery had all but vanished, but new forms of labor coercion flourished—Peruvian *enganche,* Mexican debt-peonage, the Guatemalan *mandamiento*—even while older forms (Bolivian *pongueaje,* Chilean *inquilinaje*) survived, or were actually enhanced, by economic growth. In the southern cone, by way of contrast, free-wage-labor systems prevailed and proved capable of attracting a stream of European migrants to the *fazendas* of São Paulo, and to the farms, *estancias,* and cities of Argentina. Reviewing this politicoeconomic panorama, it is again possible to sketch a tentative typology and relate it to the emergent political culture(s) of the period. Certain continuities appear. The old colonial heartlands—Mesoamerica and Andean America—now experienced unprecedented economic growth, with agricultural exports complementing minerals. Compared to mining, such exports required abundant land and labor, which in turn elicited either coercive labor systems or systematic dispossession of the landholding peasantry. The balance between these two alternatives—coercion or dispossession—tended to vary, depending on external demand, landlord muscle, demographic patterns, and the logic of the labor market. Three main patterns are evident; each carried a different potential for political conflict. Hence, we might say each significantly affected political culture, meaning by that the ways in which politics were conceived and conducted.

First, in central Mexico (classically, Morelos), El Salvador, and the Peruvian altiplano, landlords—both hacendados and prosperous kulaks—dispossessed peasant communities and converted peasants into wage laborers. This was a conflictual process, especially where the communities enjoyed old traditions of mobilization and protest (e.g., Morelos). In Mexico, the accumulation of conflict generated a social and agrarian revolution. In Peru and El Salvador, agrarian protest was contained and repressed.[66] Nevertheless, this clash between two competing sectors—landlord and peasant, hacienda and community—tended to create a climate (a political culture?) of class and ethnic hostility, clearly inimical to consensual or liberal-democratic politics. The extremes of repression and social revolution remained on the agenda.

Second, where commercial agriculture and peasant communities were spatially separated, landlords had to rely on forms of labor recruitment, often of a coercive kind. The mandamiento was designed to pry Indians from the Guatemala highlands and channel them to the new coffee fincas of the piedmont.[67] The Peruvian enganche brought labor from the sierra to the sugar plantations of the northern coast; while a similar system linked the coffee fincas of Soconusco to the Chiapas highlands.[68] In these cases the balance between coercion and incentives is hard to establish (coercion seems to have yielded to incentives over time, at least in Chiapas and Peru). Nevertheless, the system had a harsh, neocolonial quality and invited liberal critiques. It was scarcely conducive to political democratization. Coercion aside, such systems appear to have fortified an entrenched racism, especially in Guatemala where, Carol Smith suggests, the imperatives of the new coffee economy sharpened Indian/ladino divisions.[69] "Liberal" regimes thus implemented policies which were "liberal" only in respect to their external engagement with world markets. Internal economic relations increasingly became coercive and racist. Hence political systems tended to be authoritarian, exclusionary, positivistic, and, as a result, highly illiberal (e.g., under Díaz, Estrada Cabrera, Piérola). Not for the first time in history, a quickening of the market engendered not free labor and liberal democracy, but extraeconomic coercion and authoritarianism.[70] However, this syndrome does not appear to have generated such high levels of protest, compared to the dispossession of communities. Neither mandamiento nor enganche triggered large-scale popular insurrections. Chiapas was not a major center of revolution after 1910. The spatial segregation of haciendas and communities diffused conflict, and, it would seem, the expropriation of *land* provoked greater resistance than the appropriation of *labor.* The former threatened the very existence of often ancient communities, while the latter siphoned off population (yet also, sometimes, recycled resources back to the "donor" community).[71] The consequent popular protest, in fact, was likely to take the form of proletarian unionization on the recipient estates and plantations, as it did in Soconusco, Lambayeque, and Trujillo.

The third Andean/Mesoamerican syndrome concerned regions of weaker market activity, where landlords tended to rely on squeezing resources from a "traditional" "internal"—i.e., hacienda-resident—peasantry: peons, *colonos, pongos, inquilinos.* Demand for labor was limited and could be met locally; the demands of the market, similarly limited, made traditional (i.e., cashless) forms of remuneration attractive to landlords, while deterring landlords from expanding demesne (i.e., direct hacienda) production. Instead, landlords squeezed a surplus from resident peon/peasants; modernization stalled; and haciendas resembled a collage of peasant plots (e.g., Bolivian *sayañas*) or peasant flocks. Peasants often colluded with this outcome. While they resisted landlord demands for labor (especially for the hated *faenas,* or personal services), they also resisted expulsion and proletarianization. The modernization of Andean pastoral haciendas was obstructed as much by peasant resistance as by landlord backwardness.[72] Again, this syndrome, while it might produce minor skirmishes over sheep, llamas, faenas, and other labor obligations, did not generate extensive popular protest. In Bolivia, it seems, tensions in the hacienda sector only began to boil over in the wake of the Chaco War, as miners and MNRistas (members of the Movimiento Nacional Revolucionario) began to forge alliances with colonos in opposition to an antiquated, semifeudal landlord oligarchy. The agrarian component of the Bolivian revolution thus obeyed a somewhat different rationale compared to that of Mexico. In the former, haciendas faced a so-called internal siege, mounted by colonos and their allies; in the latter, external siege was waged by the free communities. The ensuing agrarian reforms removed the yoke of the hacienda from the bent backs of the *internal* peasantry in Bolivia, but broke up the hacienda and distributed it to the insurgent *external* peasantry in Mexico. Arguably, the first was a more typically "bourgeois" "antifeudal" reform, while the second represented a more radical challenge to bourgeois property rights.

Despite their differences, which in turn made forms of popular protest more or less likely, more or less radical, the fact remains that each of these patterns of agrarian change was premised on strong government, infused with positivistic and racist notions. Racism, of course, was not new. But the pseudoscientific racism of the later nineteenth century, which could easily cohabit with positivism, clearly fitted the ideological bill, given the prevailing socioeconomic trends. Elites espoused Darwin not because they had devoured *The Origin of Species* but because demotic "Darwinism" suited their preconceptions. As in the European colonial empires, where "lazy natives" were similarly being dispossessed and dragooned, Latin American elites readily advocated doctrines which rationalized forced labor, land expropriation, and increased military and police powers. Late-nineteenth-century Latin American liberalism thus had a quasi-colonial character, at least in Mesoamerica and Andean America. Needless to say, it frowned upon—or, at least, postponed *sine die*—any genuine democratization. The logic of positivism so required. In two major cases, Mexico and Bolivia, democratic breakthroughs occurred by virtue not of top-down liberal concessions but of bottom-up social demands, in 1910 and 1952 respectively.

If, in Mesoamerica and Andean America, the exigencies of export-led growth and agrarian commercialization made a genuine liberal politics unattainable, this was not true for much of the southern cone. There the same macroeconomic environment (growing world demand, faster and cheaper communications, and surplus European capital) had quite different political consequences. I argued above that the Atlantic littoral had proven unusually receptive to liberalism, both political and economic, around the time of independence. Late-nineteenth-century economic growth reinforced this association. In Argentina and Uruguay, above all, but also to a lesser extent in southern Brazil, growth demanded labor (land being abundant and export crops—wheat and coffee—being more labor-intensive than pastoral farming). Given the buoyancy of the market, landlords could afford to draw labor from Europe, in competition with the United States, Canada, and Australia. Immigrant labor implied better wages, an absence of coercion, and a more open, mobile society. It was not until slavery was abolished in São Paulo that the state became a magnet for European migrants. While migrants suffered discrimination, as they did in the United States, they did not encounter entrenched *estamental* barriers (based on corporate status) to their upward mobility. They were not, after all, "lazy natives" but industrious Europeans.

In the absence of labor coercion and caste barriers, the agrarian societies of the southern cone could practice a degree of genuine political liberalism. Political debate and a fairly free press flourished. Electoral competition became a staple of political life; and if, initially, votes were garnered by hard-nosed political bosses (Argentina's caudillos), the system allowed an expansion of the suffrage and political representation. Furthermore, the landed elite—in the Argentine littoral at least—did not oppose the extension of the suffrage proposed by President Saenz Peña. Rather, they welcomed it as a means of weakening the professional politicians, the caudillos and their cadres, who ran elections "relatively autonomously" of the landed "ruling class."[73] Thus, like Britain's Tories in 1867, Argentina's *estancieros* by 1912 were sufficiently confident of their socioeconomic station to risk the "leap in the dark" of mass suffrage. Nor were they too disappointed: the ascendant Radical Party (which, despite its petty-bourgeois image, included a good many estancieros) broadly respected landlord interests. Property, foreign trade, and social order remained Radical priorities: hence Irigoyen's conservative reaction to the postwar crisis of 1918–20. The repression inflicted on immigrants and leftists in Buenos Aires during the *semana trágica* and on the latifundia of Patagonia does not suggest a thoroughly liberal state or political culture. But, we should recall, it coincided with the Red Scare and Palmer raids in the United States, whose liberal-democratic credentials were pretty sound, if not impeccable.[74]

Thus, as Denoon has suggestively argued, the political and socioeconomic trajectory of the southern cone—Argentina, Uruguay, and Chile—roughly paralleled that of the British white dominions (Australia, New Zealand, South Africa).[75] "Settler" societies had to concede a measure of political freedom; or, to put it more bluntly, Europeans would not migrate en masse to societies where slavery, peonage, and other forms of extraeconomic coercion flourished. Liberalization—of the labor market and, by extension, of the polity—was the price paid for immigration, development, and profits. The elites of Mesoamerica and the Andes sometimes dreamed of becoming settler societies, but the politicoeconomic deck was stacked against them. Instead, they squeezed an indigenous peasantry, much as the British, French, Belgians, and Germans did in tropical Africa. Like the white dominions, the southern cone achieved a measure of liberal democratization, while Mesoamerica and Andean America took the path of authoritarianism, racism, and positivism. When the system failed—prematurely in Mexico, belatedly in Bolivia—the failure sometimes took the form of popular insurrection, in which the peasant mass, the infant labor movement, and a clutch of middle-class nationalist radicals came together in coalitions not unlike the national liberation movements of late-colonial Africa.

But there is, of course, an interesting twist to this story. Since our focus is the ("long") nineteenth century, it is probably wise to avoid further forays into the twentieth. However, it is worth noting that the liberal-progressive success stories I have been recounting—Argentina, Uruguay, perhaps southern Brazil—tend to lose the plot in the second half of the twentieth century. The reaction against liberal democracy and in favor of a new (bureaucratic? fascist?) authoritarianism occurred precisely in those prosperous southern cone countries where market economies, export growth, and liberal politics had been most evident. So the story is certainly not one of linear development. Nor is it a story of seamless political cultures maturing over generations. If, as has been argued, Argentina was afflicted by authoritarian and exclusionary "founding fictions," how do we explain the long period of immigration, assimilation, and democratization which accompanied the economic boom of c. 1880–1920? Conversely, if a culture of praetorianism and caudillismo had bitten deep into Mexico and Venezuela in the nineteenth century—and, indeed, still looked vigorous in the 1920s and 1930s—how do we explain the distinctive survival of civilian—and in Venezuela's case, democratic—politics after 1945? Finally, how do we explain the odd consolidation of liberal—and even "social"—democracy in Costa Rica, within a Central America more familiar with authoritarianism?

In these cases, the presumed path dependency imposed by political culture begins to look pretty indeterminate. Not only are sharp political discontinuities apparent; it is also hard to see how cultural explanations can begin to explain them. Even if we consider, as a good many comparativists have, the divergence between Argentina and Australia after c. 1930, it is not clear that the answer is to be found in Argentina's perverse political culture. Rather, particular *institutions,* which are in turn linked to specific interests, would seem to be relevant. These include the large estancias which had grown up from the late colony through the Rosas and Roca periods, encouraged rather than restrained by legislation; and the armed forces which, instead of fighting overseas wars, came to play an increasing role in domestic politics. Both "divergences" in turn, are related to Australia's membership in a global empire, a status which Argentina had abandoned in 1810. In this and other cases, I would suggest, the search for durable and salient politicocultural characteristics proves quite elusive. Even if such characteristics can be found, they tend to inhere in particular sectoral or spatial groups, and hence cannot be projected at the level of nations without grave risk of reification (which at times has an uncomfortably racist ring to it).

Trying to explain national trajectories in terms of contrasting political cultures is, therefore, largely chimerical. Even when patterns seem to emerge —more likely at the local and region level—they can often be traced back to prior politicoeconomic causes. In other words, political culture becomes the dependent variable. And, while political culture might then acquire some kind of inertial force (if only because of risk-aversion and the opportunity cost of learning new ways), it is striking how supposedly entrenched political cultures can change quite quickly in response to pressing circumstances. Hence the liberal-democratic opening of the 1820s and 1940s, and the liberal-democratic closures of the 1960s and 1970s. Hence, as we have seen, praetorian leopards (Mexico, Venezuela) can change their spots; and Uruguay, the "Switzerland of South America," can quite suddenly descend into military authoritarianism. While it may be possible to posit political culture as a genuinely autonomous factor in a few cases—such as Costa Rican democracy—it does not in general appear capable of explaining the various trajectories of the Latin American states in either the nineteenth or the twentieth centuries. Instead, we should look to interests, material and political, as mediated through the changing political economy of the region, and the vicissitudes of the international environment.

Thus, in response to the question originally posed—did nineteenth-century Latin America possess a common political culture?—I would answer in the negative. Any commonality shared by so diverse a collection of nations, regions, localities, sectors, ethnicities, classes, and ideological groupings is likely to be so low a common denominator that it denominates little and explains nothing. Indeed, this is probably even truer of the nineteenth than of the twentieth century. Of course, we could cite Catholicism or the Iberian heritage. But the first is too general (it fails to differentiate Latin America from much of Europe), while the second is too vague (it is a shorthand for a range of subcategories: Catholic, Spanish- and Portuguese-speaking, wheat-eating and wine-drinking). Both attributions, furthermore, gloss over wide variations and antagonisms. The more specifically political commonalities which seem to attach to nineteenth-century Latin America—republicanism, representative government, a loose liberal-conservative, jacobin-clerical political polarization—are similarly general and, for meaningful analysis, need to be disaggregated by time and place. Such disaggregation, which I have attempted in these pages, suggests considerable change over time and variation by place. Nations embody different regional political cultures within their (often sprawling) bulk. Regional political cultures likewise embody different local cultures. This does not imply an endless regress until we reach the quintessential carrier of a political culture—say, the ultimate ascetic, industrious, God-fearing, conservative Antioqueño. It means, rather, that, as for any historical or sociological inquiry, we have to strike a balance between intelligent generalization, without which history becomes one damn thing after another, and empirical accuracy, without which generalizations become dogmatic assertions. In seeking this balance, we need the right organizing concepts: those which usefully order the vast universe of empirical data and help us grope toward explanations of what happened and why.

I am not convinced that political culture is an organizing concept of great value.[76] It may (sometimes) offer a useful descriptive label—a way of summing up the political allegiances and practices of a given group, region, or locality. But for the label to fit, there should be evidence of both salience and durability—evidence which, in the absence of survey data or participant-observation, can only be inferred from actions or (dubious) transcripts. Even then, descriptive labeling begs the question of how such political cultures are engendered in the first place and reproduced over time. My brief analysis suggests that they tend to be dependent variables, the product of noncultural forces; and that they are both geographically and socially restricted. Hence, talk of national, let alone supranational, political cultures is misconceived. Furthermore, the leap from description ("political culture is thus") to explanation ("political culture is the *cause* of this or that") is long, risky, and rarely justified. There may be occasions when political culture can be shown to possess a genuine relative autonomy of interests, events, and institutions; when, therefore, it can figure as an explanatory factor; when, in other words, some explanatory "value-added" is achieved by introducing the concept. Religious—in this case, Catholic—political culture is probably the best example, which, in particular times and places, may exhibit salience, durability, and autonomy, while transcending political and material interests, and, of course, benefiting from a barrage of institutional supports. But this is a rare case, at least for nineteenth-century Latin America. And, of course, the political culture in question is far from being the bottom-up, voluntaristic, and democratic embodiment of subaltern resistance which, today, is often seen as the hallmark of cultural politics.

NOTES

1. At the conference that generated this book I was asked to reflect on the question "Did nineteenth-century Latin America have a common political culture?" I answered negatively, on the grounds (a) that "political culture" was a poor organizing concept, usually best left alone, and (b) that, insofar as it could be applied to Latin America, evidence of a common political culture was largely lacking. For the purposes of this book, the question has been rephrased to embrace "what 'political culture' might mean generally and specifically for Latin America and what it can do . . . to elucidate, analyze, and understand political regimes, political struggle, as

well as social movements [and] the role of civil society and [the] public sphere" (personal communication from Nils Jacobsen). I have rewritten (and cut) my original contribution in light of this change, although vestiges of the original question may still lurk in these pages. The paper originally contained a section (in between parts 2 and 3) that discussed the divergent development of Mexico and Peru in the "long" nineteenth century, thus bridging the gap between independence (part 2) and the period of export-led development (part 3).

2. Haber, "Anything Goes," offers a slashing critique.

3. Van Young, "The New Cultural History," 247; see the cast-iron definition of culture in Dennett, *Darwin's Dangerous Idea,* 338.

4. Knight, "Subalterns, Signifiers, and Statistics."

5. Almond and Verba, *The Civic Culture;* the criticism emerged during the conference and in subsequent comments on this chapter.

6. Indeed, Harry Eckstein, who traces "the political culture approach" to the "seminal works" of Almond and Verba, contends that it is experiencing "an early renaissance," and that it vies with rational-choice theory as "one of the two still viable general approaches to political theory and explanation proposed since the early fifties"; see his *Regarding Politics,* 266, 286; Inkeles, *National Character,* vii, proposes a culturalist explanation of politics at the national level, thus reviving the notion of "national character" ("which some people believe does not exist").

7. Cf. Seligson, "Toward a Model of Democratic Stability," 5–30.

8. Welch, *The Concept of Political Culture,* 6, citing Alfred Meyer.

9. Baker, "Introduction," xii.

10. I am defining institutions somewhat more narrowly than North (probably closer to North's "organizations"); see his "New Institutional Economics," 23.

11. The "touchstone of culturalist theory," states Eckstein, *Regarding Politics,* 267–68, is the "postulate of oriented action"; "orientations to action" are "general dispositions of actors to act in certain ways in certain situations"; Inkeles, *National Character,* xi, similarly stresses "attitudes, values and behavioral dispositions"; Lucien Pye prefers "attitudes, sentiments and cognitions," quoted in Diamond, "Introduction," 8, 12–13; the list of citations could be extended.

12. Obviously the choice of verb is significant, since it can suggest more or less deterministic "propensities."

13. In the Oxford English Dictionary definition.

14. Sutherland, *Irrationality,* 192–93.

15. Van Young, "To See Someone Not Seeing," 133–59.

16. Hence the interesting but inconclusive debate between Bonilla, "The Indian Peasantry," 219–31, and Mallon, "Nationalist and Anti-state Coalitions in the War of the Pacific," 232–79.

17. Historians have begun to take informal and covert forms of behavior much more seriously, partly influenced by Scott, *Weapons of the Weak.* Elsewhere, Scott argues

convincingly against inferring underlying subaltern attitudes or propensities from overt statements and behavior, for the good reason that the latter are designed to placate or deceive elites; see his *Domination and the Arts of Resistance.*
18. Womack Jr., *Zapata,* 20.
19. See Knight, "México bronco, México manso," 5–30.
20. Brading, *The Origins,* 96; Klaren, *Modernization, Dislocation, and Arpismo,* chaps. 7–8.
21. Dealy, "Prolegomena," 37–58; Howard Wiarda, "Toward a Framework," 206–36. For evidence of the continued appeal of such culturalist explanations, note Landes, *The Wealth and Poverty,* chap. 20.
22. Paz, *The Labyrinth,* 3.
23. Bushnell, *The Making of Modern Colombia,* 176–77; Gutiérrez Gutiérrez, *Los altos de Jalisco,* 31, 531.
24. Posada-Carbó, *The Colombian Caribbean,* esp. 229–51; Walker, *Smoldering Ashes,* 147–50. One reason for taking regional and local cultures seriously is that they may contain elements of self-fulfilling prophecy: that is, if a regional or local stereotype (presumably, a positive one) gains sufficient currency, people might try, consciously or not, to live up to it, particularly if they are spurred by vigorous, regional and local rivalries. Thus, Antioqueños *may* become more thrifty and hardworking in an effort to differentiate themselves from other Colombians. It strikes me as much less plausible to make a similar argument for the national level: for one thing, the kind of exchanges and encounters that might prompt such self-fulfilling stereotypes are far more common within nations than between them, especially for nineteenth-century Latin America. The story might be different for, say, Chinese treaty ports or the transnational communities of today.
25. Henderson, *When Colombia Bled,* chap. 6; Rubin, *Decentering the Regime;* González, *San José de Gracia.*
26. Rubin, *Decentering the Regime,* 30–36; González, *San José de Gracia,* 71, 111, 130; Dennis, *Conflictos,* 63ff.
27. Wortman, *Government and Society,* 235–36; Mallon, *The Defense of Community,* 106–7.
28. Some dyadic rivalries, it is true, may exist quite happily within a shared national culture (e.g., intercity rivalry among the Hanse towns of northern Germany: Nils Jacobsen, personal communication). Crucial considerations would be: (a) whether the rivalry reflects genuine differences in social or ethnic make-up, economic activity, or political interests and allegiances; (b) the strength of countervailing supralocal—especially national—institutions and interests; and (c) whether, as a result, rivalry is constrained within bounds (e.g., sporting contests) or breaks out in uncontrolled, violent, and nation-subverting conflict (as it often did in nineteenth-century Latin America).
29. Purnell, *Popular Movements,* illustrates the importance of local differences and rivalries within the Cristero heartland of Michoacan. Rivalries can sometimes help to

explain events, because they acquire a rationale and momentum of their own; they offer political and economic opportunities; they create vested interests (e.g., professional pistoleros); and they tend to be easier to maintain than to stop.

30. Sutherland, *Irrationality,* 191–98.

31. This is a common failing in contemporary Mexican political analysis, which identifies the country's deficient political culture as a cause of, say, electoral fraud, and advocates a renovation of that culture as a sine qua non of democratization. Yet institutional reform—the establishment of an effective Federal Electoral Institute, backed and funded by the government—has brought a rapid clean-up of electoral practices. The invocation of "culture"—as a kind of inertial drag—can thus serve as an excuse for inaction; see Diamond, "Introduction," 9–10.

32. The opportunity must be—and must be seen to be—genuinely free, with no fear of postelectoral reprisals. This is a demanding condition, of course.

33. Diamond, "Introduction," 7.

34. Posada-Carbó, ed., *Elections before Democracy.*

35. Regarding the vitality of colonial elections, I am not sure how far cabildo elections provided a true grounding in civic practices; my impression (based on Mexican sources) is that they were rather ritualistic and confined—in terms of both voting and office holding—to narrow elites; cf. Martin, *Governance,* 99–100; Whitecotton, *The Zapotecs,* 188–90; Haskett, *Indigenous Rulers,* chap. 2.

36. Scott, *Domination and the Arts of Resistance,* 96–103.

37. Lewis, *Five Families;* Elkins, *Slavery,* chap. 3.

38. See, e.g., Lauria-Santiago, *An Agrarian Republic,* 219, where, discussing the relationship between ethnicity and peasant production, the author notes that, around 1900, "Indian identity, while tied to communal landholding, transcended the nineteenth-century institution and in some respects *became independent of material forces*" (emphasis added).

39. Seligson, "Toward a Model of Democratic Stability"; Yashar, *Demanding Democracy,* traces the genesis.

40. Przeworski, *Democracy and the Market,* 26.

41. For example, what begins as an instrumental arrangement may harden into a more durable politicocultural trait (e.g., the Colombian National Front). It then becomes difficult to assess whether the trait is deeply rooted and hence relatively autonomous, or merely a self-interested continuation of the original pact (and hence vulnerable to reversal if the instrumental rationality fails).

42. Viotti da Costa, *The Brazilian Empire,* 147–48, 159–69.

43. See Knight, "Popular Culture," 393–444.

44. Gruening, *Mexico,* 216–19; Viotti da Costa, *The Brazilian Empire,* 138.

45. Siegfried, *Tableau politique.*

46. For a good case study, see Londoño, *Religion, Culture, and Society.*

47. Wolf, *Pathways to Power,* 410–11.

48. An ambitious, comparative analysis of political mobilization in nineteenth-century Latin America is currently being completed by Carlos Forment: see his "Sociedad Civil y la invención de la democracia en el Perú del tardío siglo XIX."
49. Guerra, "The Spanish-American Tradition," 7, discerns an "extremely rapid transition to modernity" of Spanish America at independence, with respect to both political ideals and forms of representation.
50. Flores Galindo, *Buscando un Inca;* Walker, *Smoldering Ashes,* chap. 4.
51. Blackmore, *The Meme Machine.*
52. Halperín Donghi, "Argentina," 99–116.
53. Huntington, *The Third Wave,* 16.
54. Moore, *Social Origins,* chaps. 5, 8; for another view of the Bourbon reforms as a broadly conceived, failing revolution from above, see Charles Walker's chapter in this volume.
55. Lockhart and Schwartz, *Early Latin America,* 419.
56. There were exceptions, e.g., Minas Gerais.
57. Martinez Alier, *Haciendas,* 95.
58. On the threat of the revolutionary war to U.S. slavery, see Kolchin, *American Slavery,* chap. 3.
59. Graham, *Patronage,* 44ff.
60. I realize that I am, for the sake of brevity, reifying entire countries. I mean certain key groups within countries, whose decisions counted.
61. Halperín Donghi, *Politics,* 58–59; Adelman, *Republic of Capital,* continues the analysis into the mid-nineteenth century.
62. Lynch, *The Spanish-American Revolutions,* 210–14.
63. Halperín Donghi, *Politics,* 59, describes how the Argentine littoral displayed "rapid politicization," an "openness toward innovation," and "an unexpectedly abstract conception of nature, structured according to economic criteria," all of which facilitated acceptance of new liberal-republican ideas and practices. These "cultural" features derived not from a generic "barbarism," but from the impact of European demand on a scantily populated region.
64. Moore, *Social Origins,* 428.
65. "CEPALista": policy prescriptions, including protection, state intervention, and ISI, associated with CEPAL (Comisión Economica para América Latina of the United Nations). *Mutatis mutandis,* the same sort of argument can be deployed for the 1940s and 1980s: *pace* Keynes, shifts in economic paradigm derived less from the cerebral reflections of policymakers than from pressing circumstances (depression, war, debt crisis) and powerful lobbies (unions, businessmen, bankers). Intellectual justification usually came after the event, reinforcing and legitimizing trends that were already underway. Prebisch, for example, did not invent ISI (import substitution industrialization); and the ISI which occurred by no means followed his precepts.

66. Womack, *Zapata,* chap. 2; Jacobsen, *Mirages of Transition,* chap. 6; Williams, *States and Social Evolution,* 69–78; though Lauria-Santiago, *An Agrarian Republic,* presents a more nuanced picture.

67. McCreery, *Rural Guatemala,* 167–68, 220–3.

68. Blanchard, "The Recruitment of Workers," 63–83; Benjamin, *A Rich Land,* 88–89.

69. Smith, "Origins of the National Question in Guatemala," 72–95.

70. Hence, New World slavery and the "second serfdom" of Eastern Europe.

71. An example of "raiding the cash economy," or, to use a quaint archaism, an "articulation of modes of production."

72. Martínez Alier, *Haciendas,* chap. 3.

73. Hora, *The Landowners of the Argentine Pampas,* chap. 3.

74. Credentials of this kind are always relative. Despite their sizeable "democratic deficits," both Argentina and the United states were, c. 1919, markedly democratic by global standards.

75. Denoon, *Settler Capitalism.*

76. For a healthy reaction against the present proliferation of "culture" as a conceptual blank check (on which see n. 7 above), note the trenchant critique of Kuper, *Culture,* esp. chap. 7.

HOW INTERESTS AND VALUES SELDOM COME ALONE, OR: THE UTILITY OF A PRAGMATIC PERSPECTIVE ON POLITICAL CULTURE

Nils Jacobsen and Cristóbal Aljovín de Losada

A sustainable political culture perspective has to address several challenges substantiated in Alan Knight's essay: (a) meaning and causality; (b) explanation of behavior or agency; (c) duration and changeability; and (d) scale of meaningful analysis (local, national, transnational).

Before addressing each of these challenges, we wish to define our understanding of such a pragmatic perspective, derived from both the historical overview of the concept and the best practices observable in recent scholarly work. By political culture we mean a perspective on processes of change and continuity in any human polity or its component parts which privileges symbols, discourses, rituals, customs, norms, values, and attitudes of individuals or groups for understanding the construction, consolidation, and dismantling of power constellations and institutions. The political culture perspective complements other approaches, such as political economy and institutional analysis.

MEANING AND CAUSALITY

Critics have claimed that the political culture perspective is not capable of explaining regime change. They argue that cultural variables rarely suffice as causes for major political processes. Knight largely concurs with this critique. He sees "affective" behavior in Latin American history limited to a few complexes: religion and politics; democracy in Costa Rica; and perhaps antislavery movements.

Although political culture's influence on the behavior of actors goes well beyond affects, it is true that contemporary political culture perspectives do not necessarily deal with cause and effect as fully and convincingly as, for example, political economy does.[1] A political culture analysis would have little to say about Bourbon fiscal reforms as causes for social unrest in the Andes during the eighteenth century.[2] Even so, by analyzing the discourses, rituals, and practices deployed by distinct actors in those conflicts, the political culture approach helps us understand the scope of choices available to contemporary actors, as well as the sociocultural contexts propelling social unrest.[3]

Natural scientists have long abandoned the illusion of certainty about ultimate causes, emphasizing instead quantum mechanics' statistical probability or chaos theory's orderly but seemingly random variability of outcomes. It thus seems a bit optimistic for historians to insist on being able to determine the causation of infinitely complex sequences of events and processes. Historians and social scientists of course cannot give up the quest for uncovering causalities. But cultural perspectives offer additional dimensions of understanding polities complementary to that quest: to wit, "the values, expectations and implicit rules that expressed and shaped collective intentions and actions" (Lynn Hunt), or the meaning actors attach to changes and continuities in policies, power constellations, and institutions. The cause-effect analysis honed by a "hard" social science approach presents the explanation scholars impose *retroactively* on change or continuity in the complex network of events, processes, and institutions of a given social unit of analysis. By contrast, the political culture perspective aims at understanding the *synchronic* subjective perception and meaning which different actors attach to the choices they make or which are imposed on them.[4] In that sense, political culture is vital to uncovering the range of historical futures and trajectories from the past that was imaginable by social groups and individuals in any specific context. Thus, to repeat, the pragmatic political culture perspective complements nonculturalist cause-effect analysis. It is also a safeguard against illusions of scientific precision in analyzing historical polities.

THE EXPLANATION OF BEHAVIOR, AGENCY, OR PRACTICE

Critics of the political culture perspective point out that behavior is often prompted not by attitudinal or cultural variables but by interests (material or ideal), the force of circumstance, and other noncultural dimensions. Alan Knight argues that the attitudes or propensities guiding specific behavior are often not knowable in the historical record. When scholars claim to know them, they often derive them by extrapolating from behavior itself, thus producing a dangerous circular argument. Moreover, even if we can reliably discern the attitude(s) underlying a behavior, this is of little heuristic value, merely describing the behavior itself in attitudinal terms.

We see little difference between the difficulties in ascertaining attitudes or interests as prompters of behavior. Individuals and groups commonly have more than one interest and do not automatically act on each interest politically. Thus deducing an interest from their sociopolitical, ideological, regional, ethnic, religious, or gender position does not suffice to claim interest-based behavior. The origins, motives, or subjective causes of behavior are always difficult to decipher, regardless of whether they are based on culture or interest. Yet if we take seriously that human agency is one central variable for understanding political processes, the attempt to decipher its subjective dimension must be made.

Historians and social scientists must approach this difficult task with an open mind, given the tremendous range of possible subjective causes. A priori assumptions of rational pursuit of interests, force of circumstance, or preponderant cultural causation will not do. Moreover, individuals always interpret their interests, the best behavioral response to a difficult situation, or the most appropriate behavior given accepted norms and discursive practices idiosyncratically. A carefully construed political culture perspective takes this subjective variability into consideration. Several contributions to this volume demonstrate how social or ethnic groups reinterpreted elite norms out of a mixture of self-interest and their own understanding of rights and obligations based on tradition or newly arising values, discourses, or ideologies. Colombia's "free persons of color," for example, in this way recast colonial notions of honor (see Margarita Garrido's chapter). Likewise, the late-colonial shift from traditional politics to revolutionary action in the communities of Norte de Potosí, analyzed by Sergio Serulnikov, built on subaltern reinterpretations of elite norms.

We have a hard time envisioning behavior of any type that is "explained" by specific interests or circumstances but does not occur in or show the patterning of a cultural matrix through which the actor gives it meaning and communicates it. Even behavior motivated by the rawest material interest in most cases will publicly be couched in and justified by the appeal to values considered legitimate in the broader social context (of course, in specific utilitarian political cultures raw self-interest may be lifted to the level of a core value). Without such legitimacy most actions would be routinely challenged by other members of society. In short, we doubt that it is sensible or even possible to neatly differentiate between behaviors/practices based on interests, force of circumstance, and more attitudinal/normative or symbolical factors. Which perspective(s) are foregrounded in the scholarly analysis and narration will depend on the subject studied, and on the cognitive goals of the project.

DURATION AND CHANGEABILITY OF A POLITICAL CULTURE

As Alan Knight correctly notes, if political culture is to have heuristic value, it must have a certain minimal duration. It would make little sense automatically to attribute any individual opinion expressed in an ad hoc fashion, any behavior or action, to an established culture of politics. The scholar would need to demonstrate that such individual acts form part of a pattern, an understanding among most members of the reference group about their cultural appropriateness or permissibility. Although political cultures are constantly undergoing change, they do not arise overnight (even in revolutions) and must have a minimum duration—usually measured in years or decades—in order to make them a meaningful category of analysis.[5]

In the older scholarship it was the other chronological extreme that made the political culture perspective unwieldy or even meaningless: the assumption of "cultural traits"—not changing over long periods of time (often centuries)—as a priori "causes" for political behavior or processes. In the case of Latin America, such long-term cultural explanations often revolved around the effects of Catholicism, authoritarianism, machismo, or, for indigenous groups, servility and rejection of innovation.[6] Clearly, the contemporary political culture perspective rejects those kinds of a priori assumptions, as they merely confirm stereotypes. The assumption of unchanging cultural traits eliminates the role of human agency and disregards the multiple social, economic, political, and cultural contextual events, processes, and institutions that intervene in the formulation of behavior and practices. Until the 1960s, the notion of rather stable cultural traits was linked to definitions of culture that considered specific rules for behavior, underlying institutions, and norms as innate or essential, inextricably tied to the very definition of ethnic, national, or religious groups.[7] The abandonment of such claims in contemporary political culture perspectives is closely linked to changed understandings of culture alluded to in our introduction.

A fruitful understanding of political culture, then, needs to navigate between the Scylla of the idealist, static "national character" tradition and the Charybdis of a mechanistic voluntarism conjured up by a definition of culture as nothing more than the never-stable, constantly changing outcome of conflicting human agency. To be sure, cultural identities and the political practices they entail are constantly updated. They shift in accordance with struggles over resources, new technologies, forms of communication, currents of ideas, and cultural practices. Yet the political culture approach allows us to see how, in this process of updating, groups recur to the memory and representation of older rights, identities, and foundation myths through rituals, discourses, visual and musical representations, and associational activities. In short, while political culture indeed is not unchanging, it builds on the reinterpretation of older values and practices. In the contemporary intellectual environment, the danger to a sensible political culture perspective is more likely to arise from mechanistic voluntarism than from static national character approaches.

Even if it is possible to identify periods of roughly comparable but by no means identical political cultures within Latin America, we envision a flexible time frame for each case. It will depend in part on the time-scale of the analysis, and may vary between local, regional, and national levels, and between specific dimensions of a political culture. For example, practices and values characterizing elite social clubs in major cities may not undergo significant change for many decades. Yet perhaps after as little as a decade, it may be useful to speak of an altered political culture of the same nation's congress—its rituals, practices of coalition building and patronage, and styles of oratory.

Political cultures of nation-states, their subdivisions, and dimensions may last from as little as a decade to hundreds of years. In any given political culture we would expect to find an amalgam of attitudes, rituals, discourses, norms, and practices some of which are just becoming "popularized," others which are "in their prime" (i.e., central for the practices and legitimacy of a regime), and others that are decaying, and losing their significance. The lifespan of specific elements of political cultures varies; sooner or later most become obsolete. Their symbolic or discursive power to mobilize consent or dissent melts away due to technological, socioeconomic, institutional, or cultural change. Even so, specific elements of an overall set of norms, rituals, and attitudes in a political culture may retain their potency for hundreds of years. Again, to avoid misunderstandings, it has to be proven—not assumed a priori—in each case that such ancient elements are still relevant; they never constitute the unchanging sum-total of a given political culture. Moreover, even if elements or fragments of ancient norms, rituals, or practices still play a political role, it does not mean that they are unchanged.[8] Appeals to a frequently changing concept of a just Incaic polity exemplify the contested "memory" or reconstruction of ancient traditions in modern Andean political rhetoric.

THE SCALE OF POLITICAL CULTURE ANALYSIS

Alan Knight doubts that in most cases political culture analysis can be meaningfully applied to large, complex polities such as nation-states. He suggests it should best be applied to towns, provinces, or circumscribed regions, and sectors of society. In these smaller spatial or social units within Latin America, specific political orientations, ideological preferences, and styles or traditions of politics have emerged since independence—Guy Thompson's "tincturing of the political landscape"—and at times even earlier. For nation-states as a whole, Knight finds little cultural or "affective" behavior relevant for deciphering the entire polity's trajectory.

Knight's skepticism reaffirms a fundamental point about Latin American nation-states: they were not born ready-made. One cannot reasonably claim that right after independence the notions, values, and practices of Aymara-speaking farmers in the province of Omasuyos (department of La Paz, Bolivia) and in the adjacent province of Huancané (department of Puno, Peru) were imbued with "Bolivianness" or "Peruvianness." Nor did they evidence specifically Bolivian or Peruvian national imaginaries or "projects." This is not to say that they did not begin to engage the politics of the separate republics suddenly claiming them as (second-class) citizens. Yet, for a long time, indigenous farmers on both sides of the altiplano's political divide continued to share practices and values through intense networks of communications, barter, travel, festive complexes, and, of course, their shared legacy of engaging the Incas and Spanish colonialism. Their political cultures for decades after independence remained more similar to each other than to those of farmers on Peru's north coast or Chiquitano villages in Bolivia's Oriente respectively.

The construction of national political cultures was a long, fitful process, at work—with different timing and rhythm—in villages, towns, and regions. The process began with the revolutionary struggles for independence and the new republics' establishment of national institutions, laws, emblems, and civic rituals. It touched every hamlet once a *teniente gobernador,* a tax collector, or gendarme appeared with the patent of his appointment, issued on the republic's own stamped paper and signed by a superior authority, demanding obedience in the name of the republic. National political cultures were formed through myriad friendly encounters, conflicts, communications, ceremonies, decrees, laws, and administrative routines, linking individuals or groups to the authority of the nation or its representation. As Benedict Anderson has shown, various types of public "circuits"—fiscal-administrative, judicial, military, and educational, for example—all could contribute to forging a "national imaginary," although in the postcolonial Andes their efficacy was hampered by institutional feebleness, partiality, and exclusivity. To grasp these drawn-out and multifaceted processes, we need a less rigid, elitist, and centrist understanding of the Latin American nation-states.[9]

Knight is correct in stressing the tremendous blockages and challenges for the formation of national political cultures in Latin America. There were attitudes, values, and practices showing indifference or hostility to specific national political projects and practices. Active or passive resistance arose from groups lending primacy to a religious, ideological, ethnic, social, or explicitly regionalist identity. The Catholic Church, with its universalist claims and hierarchy, is perhaps the most important institution for Latin America in this regard. Its impact on national political cultures varied from country to country and region to region, depending both on its institutional strength and the intensity of popular religiosity—relatively weak in most of Bolivia, strong in many parts of Colombia. Derek Williams's discussion about how Gabriel García Moreno discursively recruited women and native Andeans for forging an Ecuadorian "catholic people" exemplifies the instrumentalization of the church for building a national political culture.[10] These same kinds of policies, backed by regional or national church hierarchies, could easily turn divisive and delegitimize competing anticlerical national political projects. The universalist Catholic Church and the distinct regional, social, and ethnic forms of popular religiosity which it spawned has made what Hannah Arendt referred to as the sacralization of the secular nation-state an especially conflictive and ambivalent process for Latin American republics.

Other groups and institutions with a sense of their own civic-political identity had similarly ambivalent impacts on the formation of national political cultures. Indigenous communities and Andean ethnic groups for much of the nineteenth century wavered between an intense localism and projecting their own ideas about nation and republic into broader public spaces (for details, see our introduction and the case studies below). Masons, other freethinkers, doctrinaire liberals, and—in the twentieth century—anarchists, socialists, and communists understood themselves as part of an international brotherhood of values, which colored their construction of the nation-state, their approach to engaging its rules, legal frameworks, rituals, and claims on the citizens' allegiance. Nevertheless, their behaviors were shaped by the political culture of the specific place where they developed.

Still, all of these groups—including those embracing their particular *patria chica,* or the archipelagoes of urban artisans—sooner or later had to confront the challenges posed by nation-state formation. In fact, for many groups the very process of becoming aware of their local, regional, ethnic, or social identity was set in motion by interaction with authorities, brokers, or factions seeking to project or reconfigure more encompassing units of allegiance onto the local space. For some groups, especially Andean communities and macroethnic groups, this process was ongoing since the invasion of their realms by the Spaniards. But for all groups, including those closely identifying with the Catholic Church, these interactions took on entirely new qualities with the proclamations of independence.

Different social, ethnic, regional, and ideological groups struggled to impose their vision of (and interests in) the republic on the rest of the citizenry. A national political culture was gradually constructed and reconfigured in the processes and outcomes of those contests. From a political culture perspective, what is most revealing in these contests are the arguments adduced for and against specific projects, as well as the processes employed to mobilize support. They may demonstrate widely held notions about the relation between the state and the citizenry, or the mechanisms employed for putting together winning coalitions. In other words, what is most relevant for the configuration of a given society's political culture may not be the surface issues or political projects but the norms, ideologies, and rituals embedded within them or expressed through the routines of the political process itself.

Moreover, a sudden switch of "opinion" by a party, regional, ethnic, or ideological movement does not ipso facto invalidate political culture analysis. Political cultures, whether those prevailing in a locale, nation, party, social, ethnic, occupational, or corporate group, are frequently updated. Peripheral positions may be changed, redefined with the aim of strengthening those conceived of as fundamental. If what is changed lies at the core of a tradition, then indeed we have a new or different political culture.[11]

Many of the famous examples of local or regional Latin American political culture—pious San José de Gracia in Mexico, red Libano in Colombia, the solid Aprista north in Peru—cannot be explained exclusively from the local or regional perspective. This "tincturing" of the political map always comes about through the specifics of engagement between local power structures, interests, values, and practices with those at the provincial and national levels. We doubt if regional *identities*—movements exalting the cultural, ethnic, religious, or climatic distinctiveness of the patria chica—as opposed to regional socioeconomic and political *structures*—can develop before a region enters into intensive contact with the broader national (and international) world. Regionalists are forced to define their role(s) in that wider world: for example, close ties with merchant elites, with the state, or resisting imposition of mercantile practices, specific forms of taxation or political representation.[12] What is true for regionalists also holds for other groups projecting their identity onto the national political arena, whether they are devout Catholics, Andean communal farmers, Afro-Colombians struggling for autonomy or national representation, protectionist republican artisans, or middle-class urban communists. The formation and political mobilization of their civic identity, hence their political culture, is in part the outcome of interactions with other groups and authorities: agreements, conflicts, negotiations, and alliances concerning claims, rights, obligations, and representations within larger polities, the Spanish monarchy of patrimonial Habsburg origins, and increasingly bureaucratic-imperial Bourbon imprints during the late-colonial period, and the postcolonial Latin American republics.

• • • • •

In conclusion, we are arguing for a concept of political culture that privileges a dynamic and synchronic approach to understanding politics and relations of power. This perspective does not deny the force of interests, institutions, and contextual circumstances as *causes* for political change. But it goes beyond analysis of causes and effects by stressing the *meanings* which different social, ethnic, religious, sexual, ideological, and regional groups attach to political processes, structures, and institutions. Such a political culture perspective thus advances our understanding of the contested nature of politics and power relations in specific historical times and places. As the following case studies eloquently demonstrate for the Andes during the two critical centuries of nation-state formation, the pragmatic political culture perspective elucidates diverse historical futures. It thus offers an avenue for understanding how memories and imaginaries of just and legitimate political orders are updated and reconfigured in the day-to-day struggle over power.

NOTES

1. To be sure, Almond and Verba and their successors among today's political culture scholars in the field of political science insist on claiming the same power and precision for their findings as those of any other school in their discipline.
2. O'Phelan Godoy, *Rebellions and Revolts,* chap. 4.
3. For the late eighteenth century, see, e.g., Serulnikov's chapter in this volume;

O'Phelan Godoy, "L'utopie andine"; and Estenssoro Fuchs, "La plebe ilustrada"; for late-nineteenth- and early-twentieth-century southern Peru, see Calisto, "Peasant Resistance," chap. 6, and de la Cadena, *Indigenous Mestizos,* chap. 2; on Bolivia, see Larson, *Cochabamba, 1550–1900,* 378–90; Rivera Cusicanqui, *Oprimidos per no vencidos;* Condarco Morales, *Zárate, el temible Willka;* Mamani Condori, *Taraqu.*

4. Cf. the recent debate about Mexican cultural history in the *Hispanic American Historical Review* 92, no. 2 (1999), and Knight, "Subalterns, Signifiers, and Statistics."

5. Revolutions may launch new political cultures in a compressed span of time; yet if the catastrophes of the twentieth century have taught us anything, it is that considerable dimensions of the ancien regime political culture can and do survive quite vigorously.

6. On cultural legacies, see Adelman, "Introduction."

7. Ironically, some works founded in recent "identity politics" of subaltern ethnic, "racial," gender, or communal groups seem to be reviving the essentialism of older culture concepts.

8. Cf. Hazareesingh, *Political Traditions,* chap. 1; on changing radical republican popular traditions (derived from the French Revolution) in Colombia between 1810 and 1948, see Aguilera Peña and Vega Cantor, *Ideal democrático.*

9. Roldán, *Blood and Fire,* 296; Nugent, *Modernity at the Edge of Empire,* 11–13, 315–23.

10. On popular Catholicism and elite instrumentalization of a gendered Catholic morality in twentieth-century Colombia, see Ann Farnsworth Alvear, *Dulcinea in the Factory,* esp. chaps. 5 and 6; for nineteenth-century Ecuador, see also Demélas and Saint Geours, *Jerusalén y Babilonia.*

11. Cf. the compelling analysis of modern French "political traditions" in Hazareesingh, *Political Traditions.*

12. Van Young, "Doing Regional History"; Moerner, *Region and State;* Colmenares, "La nación y la historia regional"; Saignes, "Hacia la formación de sociedades nacionales"; Nugent, *Modernity at the Edge of Empire,* esp. 1–22.

PART ONE

STATE- AND NATION-BUILDING PROJECTS AND THEIR LIMITATIONS

The formation of states takes place through processes of building institutional capacity and autonomy that are "at least partially distinct from those that govern production and reproduction."[1] For political regimes to survive in the medium or long term, they must retain an aura of legitimacy among diverse constituencies of political actors strong enough to withstand severe shocks (e.g., economic crises, external wars, and civil conflicts). To get at the historically specific processes of state formation, these two sets of issues—state capacity and autonomy, and regime legitimacy—need to be approached from institutional, political economy, and political culture perspectives.

Political culture intervenes in many arenas that define a national project's meaning for and engagement of diverse social, ethnic, gender, regional, religious, and ideological groups. Nations necessarily construct an origin myth and make strong claims about the "fraternity" and equal rights of all those born and residing within their territory recognized as citizens. They thus provide discursive and practical tools for claiming such rights for those excluded. Republicanism and liberalism constituted further platforms for ideological negotiation and contestation over nation-state formation through the late eighteenth and nineteenth centuries, and other such platforms powerfully emerged in Latin America between the 1890s and 1930s (anarchism, socialism, communism, populism). Other ideological platforms, especially positivism and social Darwinism, primarily lent themselves to justifying less inclusive national projects.

Salient political culture issues that impacted nation-state formation in Latin America tended to link the issues of state capacity/autonomy and regime legitimacy. A few examples suffice to illustrate this point. The definition of citizenship mentioned above linked the legal scope of participation in the body politic with subjective experiences of inclusion/exclusion and the practices of mobilization in the public sphere around electoral campaigns and balloting. The state capacity and autonomy to preside over fair and free elections, the meaning of these elections to the voters, and the strategies deemed legitimate to achieve victory at the ballot box had a major impact on nation-state formation, regarding both its direction and its institutional solidity. The way states sought to implement reforms in the fields of public health, education, criminal justice, and urban planning had consequences both for state capacity and legitimacy. The more intrusive and coercive such reforms were, the greater was the likelihood that subalterns—the usual targets of such reforms—considered them illegitimate and worked to undermine them, resulting in protracted struggles or negotiations over state–civil society relations and the very meaning and legitimate function of the nation-state. Symbolic and ritual representations of the body politic—from independence day celebrations to national anthems, history and civics lessons, monuments, and the performing arts—also served important functions in building state capacity in the way they valorized or rebuffed popular groups as part of the body politic, mobilizing them for a national project, or, in the case of exclusion, delegitimizing the state for those excluded. The intricate linkages between institutional, political economy, and political culture aspects are especially clear in the struggles regarding military recruitment and taxation, perhaps the two most important arenas of constructing state capacity and regime legitimacy during the first century of nation-state formation in Latin America. The ethnic, social, and regional origin of conscripts and of taxpayers embodied both the interests of dominant social groups and state elites (regarding social control over and resource extraction from various subaltern groups) and the contentious normative ordering of the republic and how the rights of citizens were to be defined.

The four chapters in this section vividly exemplify some of these tensions and problems in Andean state- and nation-building projects between the late-colonial period and the mid-twentieth century. They all emphasize the fragility of attempts to foster state capacity/autonomy and regime legitimacy, and how these processes often resulted in outcomes quite different from those envisioned by elite colonial and postcolonial statemongers. Subtext in some, and central issue in others, the four chapters also discuss the entangled constellation of exclusion, paternalistic protection, and resistance between Hispanized elites and the large majorities of peoples of color, especially indigenous peoples, that has haunted Andean nation-building projects since their inception some two hundred years ago. Again and again the question arose on which terms and to which degree native Andeans, African Americans and other *casta* groups should be incorporated into the nation-state projects designed by various sectors of the Hispanized elites, or indeed whether such groups pursued visions of the nation-state entirely distinct and separate from those of Creoles. This multiple ambiguity in the processes of Andean nation-state formation—especially concerning the multiple Hispanic, native Andean, casta and African American political imaginaries and their negotiation or confrontation—appears in these chapters as a major factor shaping the quest for state capacity/autonomy and regime legitimacy. It played a major role in lending Andean nation-state building projects an especially instable, experimental character and limiting the spatial and social reach of state capacities and legitimacy.

Charles Walker's chapter shows that the Bourbon reform era constituted a formative experience for subsequent state-formation projects in the Andes. He highlights the sociocultural civilizing aspects of the reform project, especially in the cities. Madrid and the new cadre of "enlightened" bureaucrats in the Andes sought to change a whole gamut of popular cultural practices along with the physical appearance of the cities. They failed for a variety of reasons, among them resistance by those to be reformed. All that remained was a campaign to repress unruly plebeians, based on fears of the racialized other. But Walker sees the shadow of this failed state-building project looming large over subsequent Andean political cultures of the nineteenth century: it ushered in a stalemate between a "civilizing state" and various social and ethnic groups in the cities and rural spaces of the region that would complicate postcolonial nation-state formation.

Although not using the language of stalemate, Cristobal Aljovín's chapter on the political order that Andrés de Santa Cruz sought to create in Bolivia and Peru between 1835 and 1839 demonstrates the experimental and instable nature of Andean national projects in the postindependence era. Santa Cruz sought to stitch together a great variety of political traditions: liberal constitutionalism, Bonapartist and Bolivarian imperial ideas, and Spanish colonial and native Andean concepts of governance. While stressing personalism and the army as the key unifying forces of the Peru-Bolivian Confederation, standing above the fray of partisan interests, Santa Cruz did not understand these elements of rule as contradicting liberal constitutionalism, which his regime relied on for gaining legitimacy among the enfranchised (and largely white) notables. The Peru-Bolivian Confederation warrants further study as a major nineteenth-century attempt in the central Andes to use an eclectic amalgam of political practices and norms to overcome a narrow, Lima-based Creole republicanism.

Carlos Contreras's analysis of the fiscal decentralization campaign in Peru after the devastating War of the Pacific (1879–83) demonstrates the interplay between institutional conditions, state finances, and issues of political culture in limiting the room of maneuver for government reforms. The modernizing groups within Peru's political elite undertook a strenuous effort to make the collection of revenues throughout the republic both more efficient and less abusive. To that end they sought to increase state capacity in the provinces by establishing a new corps of tax commissioners independent from the abusive prefects, subprefects, and governors representing the executive power of the central government. The reform failed, and the new tax commissioners were cashiered within a few years of their appointment. They fell victim to the hostility of established provincial and local authorities, grossly insufficient funding, and the unwillingness of the taxpayers to accept them. It was their bad fortune that the key tax they were meant to collect, *contribución personal,* was extremely unpopular among the group supposed to pay it, largely consisting of Peru's indigenous peasantry. Contreras's lucid account of the rapid evolution of Peru's fiscal apparatus vividly demonstrates how the interplay of interest groups, power constellations, and norms and practices created outcomes entirely unforeseen by policy planners in the context of one of the most severe crises of the Peruvian state.

Laura Gotkowitz's essay on competing political visions about the place of Bolivia's majority Aymara and Quechua peoples in the nation during the critical decade before the 1952 revolution relativizes conventional notions that there existed a deep divide between *indigenista* and socially integrative populist projects. In twentieth-century Bolivian politics, there was no unilineal "transition from race to class." Leading members of the *Movimiento Nacional Revolucionario,* such as Hernan Siles Suazo, usually thought to be abandoning a racially/ethnically divisive notion of the nation through pursuing moderate social reforms, still could envision integrating the indigenous majority into the nation through "special legislation" creating an ethnically constituted system of local justice. Gotkowitz emphasizes how the Indigenous Congress of 1945 and the discourse of President Villarroel inadvertently empowered Bolivia's native Andeans. From longstanding moderate reformist demands (about land and *pongueaje,* the unpaid labor services) their new leaders—bridging the city and the countryside—forged a radical program focusing on "revolutionary law" that aimed at creating a completely different national Bolivian political economy and political culture. The essay powerfully demonstrates the ambiguity of political discourses and their multivocality during an era of crisis. Gotkowitz rightly views the vigor of these indigenous projects, disregarding state law, as a hallmark of twentieth-century Bolivian political culture (and perhaps having roots as far back as the second half of the eighteenth century, as Sinclair Thomson's recent study suggests). This has again become clear with the broad-based and diverse Bolivian indigenous rights movement of the past fifteen years.

NOTE

1. Charles Tilly, *Coercion, Capital, and European States, A.D. 990–1990* (Cambridge, Mass., 1990), as quoted by Fernando López-Alves, *State Formation,* 2.

CIVILIZE OR CONTROL?

THE LINGERING IMPACT OF THE BOURBON URBAN REFORMS

Charles F. Walker

Historians and other scholars largely agree that the roots of contemporary politics in Latin America can be found in the period bridging the eighteenth and nineteenth centuries. After independence, state makers created the institutions, structures, national boundaries, and other key characteristics that would mark the region until today. Many analysts believe that authoritarianism, instability, and exclusionary structures (as well as economic malaise) took hold in the postindependence period. Scholars are probing the development of the public sphere and rethinking institutions and processes such as elections with the hope of shedding light on contemporary political problems. Although analysts have long turned their attention to this period, only recently have the Andean countries been the subject of innovative monographs on broadly conceived "political history" that moves beyond the realm of presidents and generals. I use these studies to propose some ideas about change and continuity from 1750 to 1850.[1]

My essay focuses on the impact and legacy of the Bourbon reforms, particularly social reforms, in Lima. The Bourbons had an absolutist project that sought to reshape relations among different groups, especially vis-à-vis the state. Simply put, they strove to reorder society and change political culture. While they had halting success in implementing their reforms, their efforts influenced political practice for generations, shaping political responses and alignments even beyond independence. I examine how different groups responded to the Bourbons' absolutist efforts and the legacy of these responses. I contend that the reforms were ultimately reduced to kindred efforts to raise taxes and stop crime and insurgency. Their broader social and political components failed or stopped short due, among many factors, to wide opposition and to ambiguity among the Bourbon rulers and followers about the civilizing project. Nonetheless, opponents were unable to organize into a coherent movement, explaining the defeat of the Pan-Andean rebellions and the inconclusive social platforms of the wars of independence. This impasse between a frustrated, reform-minded, yet ultimately repressive state and active but inchoate opposition groups characterized Spanish America for decades after the defeat of the Spanish, and arguably into the twentieth century.

I concentrate on the social reforms of the Bourbon reforms—the efforts to civilize and control the population, particularly the urban lower classes. I examine why grandiose plans to "improve" Lima's infrastructure and illuminate the lower classes were abandoned, reviewing both the contradictions of the project itself as well as the broad opposition it met. Struggles over urban space shaped politics for decades, taking quite different forms and having different consequences than the more studied rural-based social movements. I review the political implications of the impasse between an authoritarian reformist state and a broad opposition that could not unify to present an alternative, a situation that endured well past independence. In doing so, I bring together recent innovative work on urban history that examines the public sphere, ritual, and gender and the politically driven history from below that dominated Andean studies for the past few decades and has produced groundbreaking work on peasants and politics. In essence, I want to link the analysis of elements of urban life, such as architecture and popular pastimes, with the examination of nation-state formation.

BOURBON REFORMS

Most definitions of the Bourbon reforms focus on the reorganization of the commercial, military, and administrative structures in the Americas during the eighteenth century. David Brading, John Lynch, and John Fisher among others provide astute analyses of the administrative changes. Immersed in frequent wars, the Spanish crown aimed to extract more resources from their American holdings. They succeeded.[2] The fascination with the Túpac Amaru and Túpac Katari uprisings has prompted an upsurge in studies on changes in the fiscal system, as historians have debated the relationship between taxes and rebellions. This interest has sparked less but nonetheless significant work on the military.[3] Research on the cultural project and social reforms of the Bourbons has been more sporadic, although interest has increased in recent years.[4]

The Bourbons had a cultural project that, I argue in this essay, lingers until today, manifesting itself in the difficult relations between the state and civil society, particularly the lower classes. The crown sought to centralize power in its American holdings and at the same time increase control over the unruly lower orders. The centralization campaign focused on streamlining the state and weakening its competitors. The diffusion and overlapping nature of the Habsburg "system" was transformed into a clearer hierarchy that, at least in theory, moved vertically up toward the viceroy and the crown itself. The colonial state sought to hem in local autonomy by clamping down on who could hold office in the city council, the high court, the militia, and in Indian communities, and by imposing discipline. Decrees from Madrid and Lima addressed virtually all aspects of social, cultural, and political life: rituals, dress codes, racial barriers, education, etc.[5] In terms of their competitors, the Bourbons sought to undermine the Church and dilute its considerable economic power. The expulsion of the Jesuits was an extreme act related to this order's independent ways, yet it epitomized such efforts to build an absolutist state. The colonial state also weakened, in typically halting fashion and with uneven success, corporate groups and the powerful upper classes of Lima and Mexico City, particularly Creoles.

The Bourbons' social project focused on controlling public space and homogenizing language and cultural practices. Brooke Larson summarizes their civilizing project in the following terms: "to turn unruly plebes and peasants into disciplined workers, soldiers, and taxpayers; to impose municipal control over public space, informal economies, and disorderly ceremonies; to rid the cities of superstition, crime, and vice; and to extend control over the forms of family organization, sexual practices, and moral and hygienic instruction."[6] These efforts form part of the European Enlightenment project. Other scholars have emphasized the drive to homogenize language and cultural practice. The Bourbons sought to hem in baroque rhetoric, make religious practice less profane, and unify literature, music, the fine arts, and other cultural expressions.[7]

The Bourbons attempted to reorganize and take control of city streets. They improved street signs and layout, created new agencies to oversee neighborhoods, regulated bullfights, cockfights, and public drinking, discouraged the discordant ways of popular religion, and invested, albeit frugally, in water canals and other infrastructure. Prior to midcentury, locations in cities such as Mexico City and Lima were designated on a block-by-block basis, and often in relation to a nearby landmark. Each block might have a name but also be referred to in terms of its proximity to a landmark, usually a church, or the residence of a distinguished citizen. For example, when Viceroy Manso y Velasco put key patriarchs in charge of supervising the rebuilding of Lima after the 1746 earthquake, he assigned Don Pedro Bravo the following area: "from his street until Juan Simón Street and in the block behind it from the Belén Church to the San Juan de Dios Church and all the way back to his house."[8] "His street," his house, and the San Juan de Dios and Belén churches constituted the key markers.[9] After midcentury, urban reformers standardized addresses, imposing single street names and coherent numerical systems and posting signs (tiles) with the information.[10]

In 1746, an earthquake and tsunami devastated the port of Callao and brought death and destruction to Lima as well. In its aftermath, Viceroy Manso y Velasco, titled the Count of Superunda (Over the Waves) for his rebuilding efforts, rationalized demarcation and sought to widen streets, eliminate second stories, and increase the circulation of air, goods, and people, all elements of the Enlightenment project of urban reform. In subsequent decades, Viceroys Amat, Guirior, Jáuregui, and de Croix named streets, divided the city into four quarters, each with ten districts, imposed new authorities, improved lighting and the water supply, and addressed sanitation problems. These changes followed the model of Madrid, where riots in 1766 had prompted a "program of discipline" that included the dividing of the city into tightly run quarters.[11] The reforms required the collection of information about the population, efforts that indicated not only the Enlightenment classification fixation but also just how much concerns about controlling the lower classes guided the Bourbon urban reforms. The 1785 "Division of Wards and Districts, and Orders Regarding the Establishment of District Mayors for the Capital of Lima," masterminded by Visitador

Jorge Escobedo, called for a census "because the governance [*buen govierno*] of this city requires the individual notice of its inhabitants and their occupations, as it is important to extirpate criminals and vagabonds." The document recommended including the categories of gender, occupation, and marital status, even for the city's many convents and monasteries, and prohibited anyone from moving without alerting the district mayor.[12] The information gleaned from the censuses aided efforts by Lima's rulers to change and regulate daily life.[13]

Escobedo's plan began by mentioning a number of ineffective decrees regarding public order dating from 1762 to 1770. Noting that "disorder is on the rise," it called for increased vigilance of the streets of Lima, roundups of beggars, vagrants, and the idle, heightened supervision of stores, cantinas, and flophouses, campaigns against gambling, and more street cleaning. It also ordered nightly patrols, instructing the district mayors to take two armed servants and to arrest any "person of color" out after 10 P.M. Those arrested were to be sentenced to eight days of public service, thirty if they were armed. This and other regulations of the 1780s indicate just how entwined urban reforms, race, and social fear were in late-eighteenth-century Lima.[14]

Equating population growth with progress, the Enlightenment project targeted poor sanitation and hygiene as obstacles to a healthy and thus growing population. This prompted the efforts to increase air circulation, to improve water supplies and lighting, and to clean streets. In a 1768 decree, Viceroy Don Manuel Amat, noting the difficulties in keeping Lima's streets clean, guaranteeing adequate water supplies, and improving trails and roads, named neighborhood mayors (*alcaldes comisarios de barrios*) to enforce sanitation rules. He called for lights that would last through the night and prohibited sheep and other livestock from entering the city as they not only dirtied the streets but also broke the ceramic covers of the water canals. Indicative of the difficulties in enforcing reforms, Amat made these authorities answer only to the Superior Government, thus allowing them to circumvent the multiple echelons of the justice system. The decree instructed authorities to have particular zeal about "Offenses against God, public sins, robberies, murders, and violence."[15]

These sanitation-public order concerns also motivated changes in how and where people were buried. Following similar reforms in Europe, late-colonial rulers created cemeteries outside the city walls to replace the custom of burials beneath churches, alleging that the dead poisoned the air. The cemeteries sparked heated debate and battles throughout the continent, prompting curious coalitions between Church members eager to protect their fundamental role in this ritual and lower orders such as Afro-Brazilians in Bahia who sought to maintain African traditions against the secularizing state and its enlightened allies.[16] Reforms also targeted the urban poor. In his request for the creation of a poorhouse in Lima in the late 1750s, Diego Ladrón de Guevara distinguished between *pobres,* deemed legitimate mendicants, and "phonies, idlers, and vagrants." Placing "legitimate beggars" in a poorhouse while incarcerating the "illegitimates" would beautify Lima's streets and allow the former to learn to work. As Silvia Arrom has shown for Mexico City, reformers sought to transform traditional notions of charity by institutionalizing efforts in state-run poorhouses, campaigns that continued into the republican era with mixed results.[17] In the latter decades of the eighteenth century, the Bourbons attempted to take control of streets, regulate civil society, inhibit "excessive" religious rituals and the Church's autonomy, and create a more disciplined population.[18]

From the perspective of the year 1800 (or 2000) these reforms by and large failed. Infrastructure and municipal organization improved—not too impressive an achievement in light of the Habsburgian abandonment of the cities—and grand neoclassical coliseums and plazas arose in the larger cities. But the lower classes remained unruly, the streets disorderly, and the workplace and domestic sphere distant from the colonial state's meddling. People of great cultural and racial diversity worked, performed, paraded, prayed, and enjoyed themselves in multiple ways in city streets, to the consternation of colonial authorities. Eighteenth-century authorities had created new institutions and legislation to facilitate urban administration. They had not fared so well in controlling the lower orders or extirpating baroque piety, let alone creating a new disciplined subject. In a 1780 plea to establish a police and judicial agency targeting property crimes in Lima just like Mexico's Tribunal de la Acordada, the author described the criminal inclinations and other defects of the lower classes: "That monstrous body of the plebe is the exterminator of wealth, of good costumes, and even of the lives of citizens. The majority are lazy bums." The author continued:

> The origin of the principal crimes of this country derives from the immense number of idlers and vagrants sheltered here. It is

> unlikely that any other city has such an abundance of noxious people. Just as it is easy to demonstrate that five-sixths of the population is made up of blacks, mulattos, and other *castas,* it can also be shown that three out of these very five, including Spaniards and white men, have no destination and live off fraud and crime. All of the censuses of Lima, ancient and modern, have recognized the excess number of plebes and the lack of Spaniards.[19]

The upper classes expressed their exasperation about out-of-control plebes in other periods of Peruvian history as well. Nonetheless, a review of texts from the last half-century of colonial rule indicates that representatives of the government and the upper classes increasingly felt that the Lima lower classes were growing in numbers and becoming more defiant. Documents supporting Escobedo's 1780s reforms described insolent vagrants wandering throughout the city in growing numbers, black bandits operating just outside the city limits, and various vices taking place in the city's center. One accusation brought together several anxieties of the era: excessive gambling, a growing vagrant population, and crimes by blacks. Vegetable and seed vendors from the Plaza de Armas complained about the "insults and robberies" that they suffered at the hands of the "vagrant and gambling" plebe. They claimed that house slaves sent to purchase something frequently gambled away the money and then robbed to recuperate it.[20] In the same period, authorities reported frequent attacks by black "evildoers" in the estates surrounding the city, who operated from the escaped slave haven outside Palpa.[21] Confidence in the civilizing project waned by the end of the century and it seems correct to conclude that programs to reorder society had been jettisoned and the desire to rectify the lower classes had narrowed into the obsession of merely controlling them. In the early 1800s, Lima authorities campaigned against taverns and public drinking and targeted vagrants, not to "improve" them but to incarcerate them or to put them to work. Even these more limited efforts—the attempts to clamp down on the daily activities, legal and illegal, of the lower orders—floundered.[22]

The impious and potentially subversive behavior of the lower classes motivated and shaped these reforms from the beginning. Social control formed a vertebral part of the European Enlightenment project but its importance was particularly prominent in Spanish America. Nonetheless, the efforts to enlighten, cleanse, and regulate were abandoned and the reforms reduced to their lowest common denominator: the control of the lower classes. In other words, the repressive elements came to dominate. Viqueira Albán highlights these contradictions and how they undermined efforts to improve life and to enact administrative change in Mexico City: "At the same time that the government tried to reform society and to bring the ideas of the Enlightenment to Mexico, it also tried to preserve the social peace by the perpetuation and even reinforcement of rigid legal divisions among the various social castes of New Spain."[23] The disdain for and fear of the lower classes, both urban and rural, weighed heavily on authorities and the upper classes in general in late-colonial Spanish America.

Reviewing the reasons for this failure of the civilizing project, or at least its devolution into mere social control campaigns, not only illuminates political and cultural struggles of the colonial period but also helps explain the contentious stalemate that characterized the postindependence period. Four related explanations emerge: financial concerns, uneasiness about race and society, the Bourbons' lack of commitment to their own "cultural program," and resistance from various quarters. As is well known, the key motivation behind the reforms was the need for money in order to keep Spain competitive with other European nations, particularly on the battlefield. It is reductionist but not incorrect to state that the Bourbons implemented the reforms in order to increase revenues, especially after the Seven Years War (1756–63). Effective urban reforms were costly, and the Bourbons proved by and large unwilling to invest. Of course, the structural obstacles were not only pecuniary. The Bourbons lacked effective administrators disposed to implementing the changes in the vast viceroyalties. Entrenched bureaucrats thwarted efforts that aimed to undermine their ties with local economic networks. They preferred the Habsburgian system based on the sale of positions and thus "collaboration" between authorities and merchants. Also, when doubts arose about the confusing decrees emanating from Spain, these administrators relied on precedent, weakening the reforms' impact.[24]

This reluctance to spend combined with deep-rooted concerns about race and social fragmentation to form a Habsburgian counter-reform reflex. Brooke Larson has correctly called race the Bourbons' "Achilles heel."[25] The Enlightenment civilizing project implied the acceptance, at least in abstract terms, of the possibility of a homogenous or united population. Even if they disparaged the lower orders for their backward customs, lack of virtue, or heathen ways, civilizing reformers of Europe and the Americas had to maintain some theoretical notion of an improved population, a belief that these groups could cast off their backward ways to become productive, disciplined subjects or even citizens. The Bourbons, however, premised their entire political project on reinforcing the colonial system, an assemblage of social hierarchies that positioned Indians as irremediable others. In the Andes, the fiscal reforms at the heart of the Bourbon project concentrated on increasing revenues from the Indian head tax. This required not only clamping down on corrupt or inefficient intermediaries but also confronting a growing population of mestizos and others who found themselves between the central categories of the caste system. The Bourbons dusted off and reinforced the founding dichotomy between Indians and Europeans, an undertaking that implied little confidence that Indians could be converted into productive subjects (non-Indians by the official definitions of the period). These anxieties greatly increased with the Andean rebellions of 1780–83.[26] In Lima, authorities consistently blamed the city's woes on the unruly nature of the black population, relinquishing any possibility of "civilizing" them. Although different interpretations of the multiethnic urban classes emerged in the eighteenth century, including the classificatory obsession of the casta or mestizaje paintings and the simpler yet highly racialized divide between "decent people" and the masses—these ideologies shared a common disdain for the lower classes.[27] The reinforcement of colonial social divisions shaped the Bourbons' project, attenuating the efforts to civilize the lower orders.

The Bourbons' reluctance to invest in the colonies and their reinforcement of racial codes that ultimately buttressed rather than reformed the colonial system are well-known explanations for the social and political weaknesses of these changes. Another related explanation—one that particularly helps explain the postindependence period—is that they simply were not that interested. The lofty goal of creating disciplined, productive, reverent subjects out of the unwashed urban masses ended up reduced to its minimum expression: stifling disorderly and potentially subversive activities. The dream of creating systematic, attractive, well-serviced cities collapsed into haphazard reform campaigns, improved yet unenforceable legislation, and the construction of neoclassical buildings.[28] With the confrontation between the utopian (or perhaps dystopian) view of the urban reformers and the messy streets and stubborn ways of the lower classes in Mexico City and Lima, the urban project was largely abandoned except for its repressive elements.

Discussion of "the Bourbon project" does not imply that it was cohesive or even coherent. In intellectual terms, no clear blueprint guided the reforms in the Americas—except for the search for increased revenues—and the measures incorporated a seemingly contradictory mix of neomercantilism and liberalism. In Spain itself, diverse and even contradictory intellectual currents supported the absolutist project. Scholars continue to debate the essence or even existence of the Enlightenment in Spain, and John Lynch deems its ideas "an influence but not a cause" of Spanish absolutism.[29] In social and political terms, differences between peninsulars and Creoles, hard-liners and reformers, and among the different echelons of the overseas administration need to be considered. José Gálvez was the key figure in the most intense period of reform in Spanish America, the 1770s to mid-1790s, implementing the intendancy system, reforming the military, increasing tax revenues, and diluting the administrative presence of Creoles. The opposition to his reforms from both sides of the Atlantic exemplifies the complexity of the Bourbon project and the obstacles it confronted. Creoles defended themselves from his efforts and accused him of nepotism and other charges. In Spain, rival groups criticized his reforms and his influence in the king's inner circle. The pace of reform slowed considerably in the 1790s.[30] In Spain, absolutism did not dislodge the aristocracy, and reforms in the Americas shared this cautious pattern. While the colonial state confronted and irritated the Church and the upper classes, it did not seek to displace them from the heights of power. Radical urban reforms required dismantling the elite's hold on power (symbolic, economic, and political), steps the Bourbons were not willing to take. Moreover, the absolutist kings, Carlos III and IV, faced broad opposition to their policies in Spain and frequent wars in Europe and beyond. Urban reforms in the Americas remained a low priority.

The colonial state had a sporadic presence in urban society, which helps explain the halting nature of these reforms. The state did not intercede in daily life, despite efforts to do so, but instead intervened in times of emergency and to control more obvious breaches of acceptable behavior. In colonial Lima, public and private space was organized in ways that contradicted official ideology, criminal laws, and moral teachings. The state and, arguably, the Church were not conceived of as a permanent presence regulating society but as forces that intervened episodically. Despite the efforts of the Bourbons to centralize political power, the colonial state did not have a great presence or influence except in times of crisis, when its moral and logistical authority rose. The 1746 earthquake, for example, allowed the viceregal state to show its prowess in emergency relief. It adeptly provided food and water supplies and imposed temporary order, in contrast to the feeble efforts of the cabildo. Yet it was much less effective in marshalling change in everyday life and creating the disciplined subject that the Enlightenment project sought. Scholars can find elaborate schemes and impassioned rhetoric about urban reforms in this period but need to review their implementation critically. Peter Campbell's admonition about European historians not adequately differentiating discourse and practice in the study of absolutism—"historians predisposed towards institutional history accepted legal and institutional statements such as royal edicts as proof of actual practice"—is particularly germane to Spanish America.[31]

The Spanish authorities' reluctance to spend and the contradictory nature of their absolutist project were not the only impediments, of course, to their social reforms. They also faced opposition from every front in the Americas. Some intellectuals bristled at Spanish control and the absolutist project (and European misinterpretations of the Americas) and developed alternative perspectives, ranging from (and combining) neoclassicism to protonationalism. It is difficult and perhaps even senseless to generalize about the political views and behavior of such a broad category as the "upper classes." Some opposed the centralization program of the Bourbons, others benefited, while almost all warily watched the increase in revolts, rebellions, and mass movements. Furthermore, leading and middling members of colonial society held governmental positions and thus the upper classes and the state were not discrete categories. Creoles struggled to maintain their positions. In terms of the social project of the Bourbons, the upper classes largely agreed with the efforts to clamp down on the lower orders yet chafed at the related efforts of the Bourbons to centralize power and to disrupt ties between authorities and local (American) economic interests. The crown sought to increase its control of colonial elites but knew that it could not displace them. In her study of illegitimacy, Ann Twinam shows that reformers ceded to the protests of the elite, ultimately placing them as "gatekeepers" of the social reforms.[32] The upper classes converged with the colonial state in their distaste, even repulsion, for the lower classes and "popular culture." The decrees and regulations of the era reflected the growing chasm between elite and popular culture in the eighteenth century, a chasm that would mark the postindependence period as well.[33]

The reforms also targeted the Church's autonomy and wealth. Not surprisingly, different groups and individuals, from archbishops to lay priests, objected. Reactions varied greatly. The Jesuits paid for their opposition (and their autonomy and wealth) by expulsion. In the 1750s, the Archbishop of Lima, Pedro Antonio de Barroeta, agreed with the campaign against the profanity of popular religion and the cacophony of popular culture. At the same time, however, he fought a behind-the-scenes battle against Viceroy Manso y Velasco over the question of who would lead the rebuilding of Lima after the earthquake and, in essence, over the comparative power of the Church and crown. In other words, the colonial state and Church authorities might agree on the need to discipline and "educate" the lower classes but battled over efforts by the Bourbons to centralize power. Indicative of the Church's complexity, priests and other members can be found on the side of the insurgents in the late-colonial rebellions as well as that of the defenders of the colonial regime. As was true throughout the colonial period and beyond, "the Church" comprised diverse doctrinal and institutional groups who expressed equally diverse political views. The Bourbons faced a variety of challenges to their absolutist project from religious sectors, ranging from quiet struggles over policy and etiquette to insurgent groups led by priests.[34]

These reactions, however, only make sense in the context of broad resistance by middle sectors and lower class groups throughout the Andes. The movements that culminated with the Túpac Katari and Túpac Amaru uprisings built on the manifold responses to the Bourbon reforms: intermediary groups squeezed by new tax codes, intellectuals incensed by Bourbon absolutism and influenced by events in Europe and the Caribbean, and lower-class groups fed up with the hyperexploitation of colonialism. These were not mere "reactions" to the reforms. As Sergio Serulnikov has shown, Indians and others incorporated Enlightenment notions of governance at the heart of the reforms into their own grievances.[35] These multiclass and multiracial movements gave pause to the upper classes, undermining their own opposition to the Bourbon project. At the same time, they fanned the flames of anti-Indian language and policies, deepening the more reactionary tendencies in the colonial state and its supporters. The large-scale rebellions in the late eighteenth century expressed the deep opposition to the colonial project as well as the powerful obstacles that awaited coalition-building leaders of the anti-Spanish forces.

Social movements, however, were not the only or the main response to the Bourbon reforms. In their sharp essays on late-colonial Mexico, both Cheryl Martin and Susan Deans-Smith stress negotiation and compromise.[36] Another crucial "weapon of the weak" against the civilizing project was simply to disregard it. In the eighteenth century and well beyond, the urban lower classes sang, celebrated, joked, urinated, etc. in outright disdain or indifference to the efforts of the state to discipline them. In the words of Sergio Rivera Ayala, "the merriment of the people defeated authoritarian speech."[37] Historians need to read the legislation regarding housing, neighborhoods, policing, etc. with great caution, asking whether these measures were enacted by the detached or ambivalent colonial state and whether the lower classes paid any attention. For example, a royal decree from August 3, 1745, lamented the "blasphemies, deaths, loss of honor and patrimony" caused by gambling and card games, especially by "vagrants and the depraved." It stipulated penalties for public gambling. Yet in 1786, Escobedo bitterly noted the failure of these efforts and the "pitiful extension" of dice and other prohibited games.[38] Travelers in Lima in the second half of the century almost unanimously describe the city's passion for gambling—Humboldt wrote that it "annihilated social life"—and nothing indicates a decline in this activity.[39] In the late eighteenth and early nineteenth centuries, Lima officials clamped down on vagrancy, drinking, and other forms of disreputable public behavior, but to little effect.[40] More needs to be known about plebeian culture and the "defense" of public space. Yet Foucault's commentary on Europe seems applicable: "the least-privileged strata of the population did not have, in principle, any privileges: but they benefited, within the margins of what was imposed on them by law and custom, from a space of tolerance, gained by force of obstinacy; and this space was for them so indispensable a condition of existence that they were often ready to rise up to defend it."[41]

Historians should be careful not to categorize every behavior that contradicted the state's social project as resistance. This categorization can convert mere disregard (based on custom, ignorance of the new codes, or the desire to do as one pleases) for the state-enacted social codes into a conscious effort that challenged the system. A member of the urban plebe ignoring laws about public conduct is not the same as a slave breaking production equipment or workers following orders but at the slowest possible pace.[42] Nonetheless, the colonial state attempted to take control of public space, yet failed. Part of the explanation for this failure lies in efforts by the lower classes to reject or simply disobey these campaigns. Despite draconian measures against them, the lower classes continued to cavort, dress, worship, and behave in ways that defied the civilizing process.[43]

BOURBON REFORMS BEYOND THE DEFEAT OF THE BOURBONS

The Bourbon social reforms were haphazardly put into practice and their effects were incomplete at best. They did not manage to foster a new disciplined subject nor did they create more manageable, rational cities. Key elements of the inconsistencies or contradictions in theory and practice of the colonial reforms continued well into the nineteenth century, beyond independence. Despite grandiloquent and even brilliant political tracts, different political reforms failed and the status quo by and large returned. In the Andes, this persistence of colonial patterns and even structures was most evident in the continued role of Indians as tax-paying, labor-performing subjects rather than citizens.[44] The pattern sketched here of waves of social reforms failing because of state inefficiency or ambivalence and societal opposition or indifference continued well into the twentieth century.[45]

The failure of the Bourbon reforms to reorder social and political relations in Lima according to the Enlightenment model does not mean that they were insignificant. The reforms altered administrative, economic, and military structures dramatically. Even if the Indian head tax symbolized the maintenance of colonial structures, social and political relations changed notably in the Andean countryside from 1750 to 1850.[46] And even if the urban reforms sputtered in the face of contradictory aims, haphazard implementation, and obstinate resistance, they changed urban society. Neoclassical buildings were constructed and infrastructure improved. Some of the changes, such as the institutionalization of charity, took place well into the postcolonial period and in incomplete fashion, but they altered state–civil society relations. Moreover, the reforms politicized a great deal of the population. The various responses to the reforms implied some type of questioning of Spanish rule, whether on traditional grounds (Habsburgian pact) or through some type of protonationalism, liberalism, and other enlightened currents. This is clearest in the highlands where the offensive against local autonomy and increase in taxes prompted changes in political culture and massive social movements. But the questioning of the urban reforms sketched here also prompted a variety of responses in Spanish American cities and could be at the root of broader political movements.

The urban reforms help explain why cities played a relatively minor role in the war of independence and in the early republic. The well-known explanation is that the Spanish concentrated their military forces as well as economic and political power in the cities. Conversely, the Andean interior bore the brunt of the rising tensions and contradictions of the Bourbon project: increased fiscal demands that fortified the Indian–non-Indian dichotomy and sparked broad opposition. These tensions burst into flame in the late eighteenth century with the Túpac Amaru uprising. Yet authorities and the upper classes feared riots and uprisings in Lima throughout the eighteenth century and the city was certainly not exempt from political conflagrations from 1750 to 1850. The fear of slaves and plebe insurrections prompted frequent calls for increased vigilance and harsh measures. In this sense, perhaps, the Bourbon reforms succeeded—they might not have illuminated or civilized the urban lower classes but they helped prevent lower-class political uprisings in Lima.[47]

A review of the urban reforms yields two other related explanations for the relative calm of the cities, besides these repressive measures. Controversies over public space and behavior—measures against vagrancy, drinking, gambling, inadequate dress, etc.—prompted short-term crises and conflicts that could lead to confrontations but usually were "resolved" without conflict. The state simply found it too difficult or too expensive to enforce its own regulations and thus withdrew. Even if the measures were put into effect, such as the crackdown on the poor that occurred in the late eighteenth century, they did not prompt broad, organized opposition. The lower classes confronted these urban reforms in a number of ways, including simply disregarding them. Unlike the Andean pattern of lawsuits, confrontations, and skirmishes in response to the increased economic demands and political intrusions of the colonial state, these urban responses did not tend to escalate into organized resistance. Cemetery reforms or antigambling raids might provoke riots, but not a revolution.

When opposition to the urban reforms organized and took to the courts and the streets, it often involved odd bedfellows. As noted, in his study of cemetery reforms in Bahia, João Reis found conservative religious groups allied with Afro-Brazilians in the defense of "tradition." The former defended Church prerogatives while blacks fought to maintain burial practices akin to African customs.[48] The Bourbon reformers targeted the excessive power of the Church and the upper classes and the disorderly ways of the lower classes. While the Lima upper classes distrusted the lower classes, many members shared their opposition to the Bourbon reforms. This could put them on the same side temporarily and informally in a battle against the colonial state and its elitist reformers. In the early republic, liberal reformers faced opposition from the recalcitrant Lima upper classes as well as the cantankerous lower orders. These groups converged only in their shared opposition to the civilizing project of the Bourbon reformers and their heirs. This did not turn into an effective political movement but did undermine the Bourbons and then the liberals. At a minimum, understanding this relationship overcomes the view of these arrangements as a reflection of ignorance by the lower classes. The urban poor had their reasons for opposing the civilizing campaign. While liberals had bastions of popular support in cities, conservatives counted on them as well. The roots of this relationship can be found in the colonial urban reforms.

The impact of the reforms transcended differences between urban and rural politics. The Bourbon reforms initiated a pattern of impasse or stalemate that reappeared repeatedly during the nineteenth century and beyond. Despite some inspired platforms and plans—the urban plans of Viceroy Manso y Velasco and his advisers, for example, were visionary—the state was unable to implement its project. As outlined here, it attempted to do so in despotic fashion, prompting discontent among its seeming allies. The colonial government faced internal divisions—disagreements about the reforms emerged at all echelons of the state—and many members expressed ambivalence about the acceptable and realistic extent of its reform plan. The upper classes, sectors of the Church, middle groups, and the lower classes resented different elements of the reforms, and challenged them in a variety of ways. While the reforms sparked broad, almost uniform opposition, the diverse groups had quite different motivations and ideological bases. Elite groups chafed at the centralization efforts while applauding the efforts at social control, Indians resented increased taxes, middle sectors felt marginalized, and the urban masses negotiated, disobeyed, and at times rioted. To back these and other attitudes, they invoked a variety of ideological platforms: protonationalism, Inca revivalism, Habsburgian traditionalism, elements of the Enlightenment, etc.

Throughout Spanish America, the broad opposition to Bourbon absolutism could not translate into functional, enduring multiclass and multiethnic alliances. The Bourbons faced opposition from almost infinite fronts, so broad, in fact, that "the opposition's" various components could not easily coalesce. This scenario of tense state–civil society relations that prevented the imposition of the state's broader platform but did not develop into an effective alternative would reappear, albeit with major differences, in the postcolonial period. After independence, state makers faced wide opposition and control of the state changed frequently. Liberal reformers, arguably the heirs of the Bourbons, also by and large failed to put into practice their views. The Bourbon stalemate, from this perspective, persisted well beyond independence from Spain. As the different essays in this volume demonstrate, causality is the sticking point where differences about the concept of political culture and its applicability emerge. I believe that the Bourbon reforms constituted a particularly clear or poignant manifestation of the pattern sketched here. While it would be an exaggeration to state that the Bourbon reforms caused this centuries-long stalemate, in the latter half of the eighteenth century deep state-society strains, severe class cleavages, and odd political alliances took form that had not emerged in the Habsburg era and would last well beyond the wars of independence.

The tense relations between the Church and the state highlight the ideological ambiguities and social thinness of early republican politics, particularly in regard to the liberals. They also highlight how these phenomena date from the failed Bourbon reforms. Liberal reformers initially attempted to clamp down on the Church, continuing in the Bourbon vein of asserting the state's right to dominate in spheres such as public welfare and identity rituals (birth, baptism, marriage, death) and in squeezing the Church's economic resources.[49] But the reformers rapidly pulled back, wary of such a battle in unstable times. If the liberals continued the Bourbons' efforts to weaken the Church, they also replicated their uneven success. Moreover, leading ideologues of different political camps harangued the profanity of popular religion and nervously questioned references to the Incas in song, dance, and festivities, echoing common eighteenth-century themes.[50] Elite writers shared a common derision for the superstitious, ignorant, and ultimately dangerous ways of the lower orders, including their processions and other religious celebrations.

This returns us to an enduring characteristic of the late-colonial era: the enormous divide between the upper and lower classes. On empirical grounds, it would seem logical that this divide narrowed in the early republic. In economic terms, turmoil and debt meant difficult times until the midcentury export-led development. While peasants weathered the storm, prominent members of the upper classes lost a great deal during the wars of independence and in the chaotic caudillo period.[51] Politically, the postindependence period saw the rise of many provincial mestizo leaders in the Andean republics and also allowed some mobility for other "middle sectors." Doubts about the postcolonial system ended up opening, at least temporarily, the constricted space in which intermediate groups operated. Nonetheless, the period from 1750 to 1850 witnessed the cementing of the divide between "*gente decente*" and the lower orders, as the upper classes eschewed any type of integrative notion of society. Elite ideologies reflected a fear of social disorder (despite the lack of revolts, urban and rural, in the early republic) and a visceral disdain for the dark-skinned lower classes. While the process of the construction of racialized social differences requires more study, hierarchies along class, race, gender, and geographic lines hardened in this period. This seems to be one particularly damning legacy of the late-colonial era.

◆ ◆ ◆ ◆ ◆

I have stressed the enduring echo of the failed Bourbon reforms, particularly its urban component: how an authoritarian state half-heartedly launched a reform project that ultimately was reduced to its repressive components. Even these efforts at social control only partially succeeded. The program met opposition from many sides, in fact from so many disparate groups with so many platforms and ideologies that an effective antistate coalition was difficult if not impossible. Urban policies followed this pattern of grandiose plans, little impact, and widespread disillusionment. Indeed, this characterized not only the urban reforms of the eighteenth century but subsequent campaigns as well.[52] In this regard, the political impasse prompted by the Bourbon reforms continues to mark Spanish America today.

It is difficult to chart changes in urban political culture, specifically that of the lower classes, over the course of the eighteenth and nineteenth centuries. Lima has not been the subject of the large number of culturally sensitive, politically focused studies that have characterized the best work on the highlands in recent decades. We have splendid studies of Lima's lower classes and the representation of race and class but few works that span decades and the colonial-republican divide.[53] This essay has underlined the gap between the goals and the results of the social reforms enacted in the second half of the eighteenth century. The analysis of struggles over popular culture and public space can explain with more precision why this occurred and suggest patterns and disruptions in the postcolonial period. The suggestion here that popular resistance to the civilizing project weighed heavily in this impasse needs to be substantiated. In this regard, the differences between the two schools outlined by the editors in the introduction—Gramscian and Tocquevillian—come to light.

The Gramscian approach has focused on the countryside and has moved beyond broad structural explanations to highlight local political practice and discourse. Studies such as these need to be conducted for Lima and other cities. The Tocquevillian school has provided important insights on political discourse and the public sphere. The work on public spaces—François Xavier Guerra and Annick Lempérière correctly point out the need for the plural—offers new perspectives on the relations between civil society and the state and thus the roots of contemporary politics.[54] My approach here seeks to make sure that the new political history and, in general, those invoking the concept of political culture, do not overlook the struggles over the control and nature of the national, regional, and local state or states. The examination of the struggles between a civilizing authoritarian state and stubborn popular culture offers an important opportunity to link these perspectives and gain important perspective on politics and culture in the Andes, past and present.

NOTES

1. For an incisive overview on scholars' treatment of "colonial legacies," see Adelman, "Introduction" in his *Colonial Legacies,* 1–13. For a thoughtful view on nineteenth-century politics, see Guerra and Lempérière, "Introducción," *Los espacios públicos en Iberoamérica,* 5–21; see also Sábato, ed., *Ciudadanía política y formación de las naciones.* I would like to thank Carlos Aguirre, Cristóbal Aljovín, Arnold Bauer, Mark Carey, Nils Jacobsen, and Andrés Reséndez for their suggestions for this essay.

2. Brading, "Bourbon Spain"; Lynch, *Spanish Colonial Administration;* Fisher, *Government and Society in Colonial Peru.*
3. O'Phelan Godoy, *Un siglo de rebeliones;* Stavig, *The World of Tupác Amaru;* Campbell, *The Military.*
4. Key works include Viqueira Albán, *Propriety and Permissiveness;* Beezley et al., *Rituals of Rule;* Estenssoro, *Música y sociedades.*
5. See Konetzke, *Colección de documentos.*
6. Larson, *Cochabamba, 1550–1900,* 355; see also Serulnikov, "Customs and Rules," and his chapter in this volume.
7. For efforts to replace the *policoralidad* or polysemic with the unison, see Estenssoro, "Modernismo, estética, música, y fiesta," 183–84.
8. Archivo General de Indias [hereinafter AGI], Audiencia de Lima, Legajo 511, 1748–1751.
9. Viqueira Albán, *Propriety,* 174–82. For street designations and urban reforms, see Moreno Cebrián, "Cuarteles, barrios y calles."
10. Viqueira Albán, *Propriety,* 174–82, and Ramón, "Urbe y orden," passim, discuss imposition of Cartesian notions of space.
11. Lynch, *Bourbon Spain,* 266.
12. Jorge Escobedo, "División de quarteles y barrios e instrucción para el establecimiento de alcaldes de barrio en la capital de Lima," 1785, Biblioteca Nacional del Perú [hereinafter BNP]. On Escobedo, see Fisher, *Government and Society,* 69–71, 241.
13. Key works on eighteenth-century Lima include Basadre, *La multitud;* Cosamalón A., *Indios detrás;* Flores Galindo, *Aristocracia;* Doering and Lohmann Villena, *Lima;* Moreno Cebrián, "Cuarteles"; Pérez Cantó, *Lima en el siglo xviii;* Ramón, "Urbe y orden," 295–324; Rizo-Patrón Boylan, *Linaje, dote.*
14. Escobedo, "Division," and Escobedo, "Nuevo Reglamento de Policía, Agregado a la Instrucción de Alcaldes de Barrio," 1786, BNP.
15. Manuel deAmat, "Habiendo sido uno de mis principales cuidados," 1768, John Carter Brown Library [hereinafter JCBL]; on these reforms, see Clement, "El nacimiento," 77–95.
16. Reis, "Death to the Cemetery," 97–113; Voekel, "Piety," 1–25; Casalino Sen, "Higiene pública," 325–44.
17. Arrom, *Containing the Poor,* passim; Ladrón de Guevara, "Exmo Sor. Don Diego Ladrón de Guevara, puesto a los pies de V.E. con el mas profundo rendimiento," Lima, 1757?, JCBL.
18. Creating disciplined workers also required meddling in the domestic sphere, as the Bourbons sought to remake gender relations; see Stern, *The Secret History of Gender,* esp. chap. 11; Twinam, *Public Lives;* Deans-Smith, "The Working Poor," 47–75; Rosas Lauro, "Educando al bello sexo," 369–413.
19. "Informe sobre el mal estado de policia, costumbres y administración de la ciudad de Lima y conveniencia de establecer en ella el Tribunal de la Acordada, a semejanza

del de México para mejorarlo," Lima, 1782?, 24–25, Biblioteca Nacional de Madrid [hereinafter BNM].

20. "Memorial de los abastecedores de semillas y verduras de la plaza mayor de Lima al Superintendente General, sobre los insultos y robos que padecían por la plebe desocupada y jugadora," Lima, 1785?, BNM.

21. "Informe al Virrey sobre los excesos cometidos por los negros armados y refugiados en los montes de Palpa," Lima, 10 November, 1786, BNM; on maroon activities in the 1780s see also Espinosa Descalzo, *Cartografía de Lima.*

22. For the antidrinking campaign, see Cosamalón A., *Indios detrás,* 205–20.

23. Viqueira Albán, *Propriety,* 9; for Lima, see Estenssoro, "Los colores."

24. Twinam, *Public Lives,* 291; Coatsworth, "The Limits of Colonial Absolutism," passim.

25. Larson, *Cochabamba,* 374; for a critical perspective on the Bourbons' absolutist project, see Fontana, *La crisis.*

26. Walker, *Smoldering Ashes,* chaps. 2–3.

27. Flores Galindo, *Aristocracia,* 95–99; Estenssoro, "Los colores."

28. These urban dreams can be found in the memoirs of the viceroys.

29. Lynch, *Bourbon Spain,* 254.

30. Brading, *The First America,* 473–91, 502–13.

31. Campbell, *Power,* 14. For breach between policy and practice regarding race, see, e.g., Cope, *The Limits of Racial Domination,* and Seed, "Social Dimensions of Race," 569–606.

32. Twinam, *Public Lives,* 313.

33. Key works include Aguirre, *Agentes;* Flores Galindo, *Buscando un inca;* Basadre, *La multitud;* Chambers, *From Subjects to Citizens;* Méndez, "Incas sí"; Abercrombie, "Q'aqchas and *la plebe*"; Thurner, *From Two Republics.*

34. On Barroeta and Manso y Velasco, see AGI, Audiencia de Lima, Leg. 511; Vargas Ugarte, *Historia del Perú, virreinato,* 3: 281–90; Estenssoro, "Modernismo," 182–84.

35. Serulnikov, chapter in this volume, and "Customs and Rules," 268.

36. Deans-Smith, "The Working Poor," Martin, "Public Celebrations," 95–114.

37. Rivera Ayala, "Lewd Songs," 36.

38. "Informe sobre el mal estado," f. 224.

39. Real Cédula, Aug. 3, 1745, Archivo del Cabildo Metropolitano, Lima, Serie B, Cédulas Reales y otros papeles, 2. Humboldt, *Cartas americanas,* 106–7 (letter of Jan. 18, 1803).

40. Cosamalón A., *Indios detrás,* 205–20.

41. Foucault, *Discipline and Punish,* 82.

42. Scott, *Weapons of the Weak;* see also Ortner, "Resistance," 173–93, and Voekel, "Peeing on the Palace," 183–208.

43. For a rich comparative case, see Martin, "Public Celebrations" and *Governance and Society.*

44. This is a central point of Méndez, "Incas sí," Thurner, *From Two Republics,* and Walker, *Smoldering Ashes.*
45. For superb examinations of continuities and change, see Van Young, "Conclusion: Was There an Age," and "Conclusion: The State as Vampire."
46. Serulnikov, "Customs and Rules," and Thomson, " 'We Alone Will Rule.' "
47. There are many other reasons, of course, to explain the absence of large-scale uprisings. Lower-class atomization and the existence of alternative forms of accommodation and resistance come to mind. Flores Galindo, *Aristocracia,* esp. 230–36; Aguirre, *Agentes,* passim; and the incisive essay by Halperín Donghi, "The Cities of Spanish America," 63–75, esp. 65–66.
48. Reis, "Death to the Cemetery," Voekel, "Piety and Public Space."
49. For an innovative analysis, see Burns, *Colonial Habits,* chap. 7; also Armas Asín, *Liberales,* passim.
50. Méndez, "Incas sí"; Cahill, "Popular Religion," 67–110; Walker, *Smoldering Ashes,* chap. 6.
51. See Halperín Donghi, *The Aftermath,* passim.
52. On limited success in confronting the crime wave of the 1990s, see Guillermoprieto, *The Heart that Bleeds.*
53. Aguirre, *Agentes;* Cosamalón A., *Indios detrás;* Flores Galdindo, *Aristocracia;* Estenssoro, "Los colores"; Wuffarden, "Los lienzos."
54. Guerra and Lempérière, "Introducción."

A BREAK WITH THE PAST?

SANTA CRUZ AND THE CONSTITUTION

Cristóbal Aljovín de Losada

The Peru-Bolivian Confederation (1836–1839) exemplifies the rich range of possibilities for nation-state building in Latin America in the early nineteenth century. For the new states created after the collapse of the Spanish empire, the first decades of their republican history were a political laboratory. It was a time of experimentation, when Latin American political cultures crystallized and gave rise to a most complex and contradictory relation between notions of legality and legitimate behavior of political actors. The Confederation did not escape this. It was an attempt not merely to redraw the political map of South America, thus transforming social and political identities, but also to construct a new type of political order.[1] The latter would be a blend of liberal, military, and Andean institutions, on the one hand, and on the other the typical political behavior of the caudillo, based in this case on the figure of Andrés Santa Cruz as protector and founder of the Confederation.

Santa Cruz portrayed himself as a legislator and described the Confederation as a new kind of state organization that would create a culture of peace.[2] He simultaneously envisioned himself as both a Simón Bolívar and a Napoleon Bonaparte. Like the French emperor, he and a group of lawyers prepared (or commissioned) legal codes (*códigos civiles, penales y de procedimientos*). These codes were to establish "modern institutions" corresponding to a civilized country, and to leave behind forever the old and outdated colonial codes. Reflecting the cult of Santa Cruz's personality, the codes bore his name.[3] Santa Cruz also participated eagerly in the preparation of both the constitutional arguments that justified the 1835–36 intervention of the Bolivian army in Peru and the constitutions that would frame the Confederation and its constituent states. This is not to suggest that all this was the work of one man, as many pamphlets published for or against Santa Cruz suggested. Rather, he and his advisers developed ideas, prepared laws, and made political decisions that reflected the range of political notions currently debated in Bolivia and Peru. This essay focuses not so much on establishing the *lineage* of the ideas of the Confederation as on highlighting the *construction* of its political ideas and agendas. Political ideas, much like religious, moral, and other ideas, are socially constructed. And the elite, especially a small inner group, usually has a major role in their creation and in making them important. Yet there is a relationship between constitutional building and political culture, shaped by different sectors of society.

POLITICAL IMAGINATION

In the political imagination of Santa Cruz and his group we find the whole range of constitutional ideas available at the time, and the way they shaped political legitimization in the early nineteenth century. According to François Guerra, the liberal constitutional theory dominated the political discourse. This theory gave rise to a clash between the mandates of the liberal constitution, based on equality (a society of citizens) and political representation, and a traditional society, based on a hierarchical order with ascribed identities. According to Guerra, the liberal paradigm began to predominate as the way to obtain political legitimacy (far more in America than in Spain) as early as the debates that took place prior to the Cortes of Cádiz (1808–10). This was a revolution in the way society (based on citizens) and authority (legitimized through elections) were conceived.[4]

Guerra is in general right about this. However, there are cases that do not fit neatly into his model, or are not as radical as he tries to depict them. Santa

Cruz, for instance, was not as radical as he believes, while Bolívar was so in some respects but not in others. Both can be thought of in chiaroscuro images. Bolívar developed a political outlook where military leaders led and instilled civic virtues in society. In the case of Santa Cruz—who greatly admired Bolívar and was one of his most loyal officers—there is a much greater distance between his view and modern constitutional ideas. Even so, Santa Cruz followed the appraisal Bolívar made of military leadership. He had an extremely corporatist view of society, which he inherited from the Andean tradition. And like Bolívar, Santa Cruz tried to evade or reduce the relevance of elections. Both feared popular anarchy.

Santa Cruz's constitutional understanding was due, in part, to his close connection with the southern *serrano* tradition of politics, authority, and power. It was an aristocratic and elitist understanding of politics, to which his family background contributed. Santa Cruz came from a family that belonged to the Andean elite of La Paz (Bolivia). His father, Don Joseph de Santa Cruz Villavicencio, was a Creole from Huamanga who belonged to the military order of Santiago, which means that he was a nobleman. His mother, Doña Juana Bacilia Calahumana, was daughter to the *maestre de campo* Matías Calahumana y Yanaiqui and María Justa Salazar Manzaneda. From his mother Santa Cruz inherited the *cacicazgo* of the town of Huarina, close to Lake Titicaca, in the province of Omasuyos. His mother's family was wealthy: her dowry was 65,442 pesos. Santa Cruz was proud of his lineage and saw himself as a descendent of the Inca dynasty. His political imagination was shaped by his Indian and Creole aristocratic background. Although his mother was a mestiza, Santa Cruz's certificate of baptism classified him as a white man (*español*).[5]

Santa Cruz was born in La Paz and spent a great part of his life in the highlands. He built his political power there, and was elected president of Bolivia in 1828 before assuming the mantle of Protector of the Confederation. It thus comes as no surprise that his constitutional ideas were connected to the highlands and not to Lima. In this he was quite different from Agustín Gamarra and his followers, who imagined Peru from a "Limeño" perspective. Although Gamarra was also a serrano with close connections to Cuzco, as Charles Walker has recently noted, his national vision was constructed from Lima.[6] Lima and its hinterlands were, however, quite different from the southern sierra. The population was overwhelmingly formed by whites, mestizos, *castas,* and free and slave African Americans. The Indians formed a small minority. Meanwhile, the sugar plantation dominated the rural landscape on the central Peruvian coast. This social and economic milieu was quite different from that of the southern Andes, where Indians, both in communities and haciendas, were the majority.

Santa Cruz's political imagination was also related to his experience in the army. His earliest experience, like that of many of his contemporaries, was in the Spanish army. He became a patriot only later during his military career with San Martín. Then he campaigned with Bolívar and afterward with the Peruvian and Bolivian national armies. During the wars of independence, both the Spanish and the patriotic armies construed a discourse wherein they were the solution against anarchy. They played a key role in politics because they pretended to represent the national interest, while civilians were pursuing their own, particular interests.[7] The military had begun occupying key state positions since the Bourbon reforms in the late eighteenth century, when the crown discarded Habsburg *pactista* philosophy and redefined the role of the Church.

POLITICAL AUTONOMY

Compared with other leaders of his time—in Bolivia, Peru, Ecuador, or the other recently founded Spanish American republics—Santa Cruz had relatively great political autonomy. He began to build his power base when he assumed the Bolivian presidency in 1828. It seems that his endeavors to control opposition leaders through extraconstitutional means were highly successful. His control of the army was the key element that enabled him to intervene in the Peruvian civil war in 1835 in order to create the Confederation. After his military victories at Yanacocha (August 13, 1835) and Socabaya (February 7, 1836), Santa Cruz enjoyed an autonomy that allowed him to design the Confederation without any major constraint. Even so, though there was not much internal opposition, the external opposition proved too strong for the Confederation.

The bases of Santa Cruz's power were complex and varied: (a) a well-organized army; (b) his alliances with the *montoneros* (bands of guerrillas); (c) a well-organized state; and (d) a strong support among the elite of Southern Peru. First, it has long been agreed that Santa Cruz's army was one of the best in Latin America at the time; furthermore, it did not experience internal rebellions. According to contemporary sources, the army comprised some

12,000 soldiers and was divided into the armies of Bolivia and Southern and Northern Peru. It had a long series of victories before the final disaster at Yungay (January 20, 1839). The army was built around a system of political alliances established with montoneros—for example, that with the Iquichanos against Gamarra and Salaverry in Ayacucho—which were established through a complex system of patronage.[8] Santa Cruz's reputation is primarily based on his skill in administrating the state, an unusual skill in Latin America. The newly independent states were always in urgent need of funds to pay their executive authorities, scribes, clerks, judges, and congressional deputies, and above all, their military officers. Santa Cruz realized that a good, well-paid army ensured internal and external security in a time of constant conflicts. The Confederation organized effective political propaganda that broadcast his image as a great administrator. Finally, in Southern Peru the Confederation enjoyed strong support, especially in Arequipa, Moquegua, and Puno. The elite in those cities wanted to reestablish the connection with Bolivia and also understood that the Confederation reduced Lima's control over Southern Peru.

A NEW CONSTITUTION, A NEW ORDER

Constitutional debates raised the question of how to end the revolutionary tradition triggered by the wars of independence, one of the most important issues of its time throughout Latin America. In Peru, it was related to the desire to end military revolutions once and for all. Everybody realized that the state of constant revolution was tearing the country apart. Felipe Pardo y Aliaga wondered whether a revolution that had obtained power through violence could even found a republican state. Pardo concluded that this possibility existed so long as the constitution was changed and the caudillo in charge represented the best part of society. He was not the only one who pondered this matter.[9] This dilemma was one of the major concerns of all caudillos. Up to a point, every leader dreamed of writing a new constitution that would bring an end to political anarchy, and the era saw constant constitutional tinkering. Montesquieu's belief that each country needed its own laws (according to its mores, tradition, society, etc.) was a key concept among Latin American leaders. In this respect, the great task a legislator faced was to find the laws that fit his country best.[10] Santa Cruz believed in a new constitutional arrangement under his own personal leadership. But the need for the leader, a sort of founding father, was nothing new, and in this Santa Cruz was in no way original.[11]

Like Bolívar and others, Santa Cruz saw himself as a legislator who would change both the state and society. He envisioned himself in the tradition of the great legislators, like Solon in Greece or Moses in the Jewish tradition, who gave laws to their people without debate. In this way a country was set on the road to civilization. The other ingredient for ensuring success was leadership. A true leader knows how to guide his people. The adequate combination of law and good leadership was therefore a prerequisite for the construction of a prosperous nation-state.[12] According to his political propaganda, both qualities were combined in Santa Cruz and reflected in his constitutional arrangements. The prosperity of Bolivia since he had gained the presidency showed that he was in fact the right leader for the central Andean region, including Peru. And one could indeed find a significant difference when comparing Bolivia and Peru (or any other Latin American country): stability versus chaos. Santa Cruz's discourse emphasized order.

In the pro–Santa Cruz political propaganda for 1835–1836, his followers claimed that Peru needed a new political pact. Peruvian republican history showed a series of disasters: continuous revolutions, chaos, and anarchy. From the government of José de la Mar to that of José Luis Orbegoso, Peru had not had a year of peace because civil wars broke out again and again.[13] Bolivia was quite different. With Santa Cruz, political peace had come and anarchy had not recurred. According to the propaganda, the old Peruvian institutions had led to anarchy. What Peru therefore needed was for Santa Cruz to redesign its republican institutions and rule the country, thus giving rise to a new institutional arrangement that would establish a new compact.[14] It goes without saying, of course, that the new pact required the wisdom of Santa Cruz. He was the great legislator and administrator who would found a new state and control society.

Santa Cruz's public image was designed to portray him as a father figure and founder of a new state. The titles he bore in 1836 show how important his persona was for him, and how he portrayed himself as Caesar: "Capitán General, Presidente Restaurador de Bolivia, General de Brigada de Colombia, Gran Mariscal Pacificador del Perú, Jefe Superior del Ejército Unido, Protector del Estado Sud Peruano, encargado de su administración &&."[15] In the end, the new pact (the Confederation) was not only related to new legislation but also to Santa Cruz himself. His project, like many others, could neither create nor envision a new legality that worked without the caudillo.

Santa Cruz's constitutional ideas were far more complex than those of José María Pando, Felipe Pardo y Aliaga, and others.[16] He not only believed in the need for new laws but also envisioned a new nation-state: the Confederation of Peru and Bolivia. Like Bolívar and his Andean Federation before him, Santa Cruz had to answer why, and in what terms, Peru and Bolivia would be united. Santa Cruz combined constitutional issues, national identities, and territory since he favored the creation of a new political entity. He was certainly not the only one who thought in this way—but he was the only one able to reunite both countries for at least a few years. Others had similar dreams but were unable to make them come true, as in the case of Santa Cruz's one-time friend and later nemesis, General Gamarra.

Santa Cruz's followers justified the division of Peru into two new states (Southern and Northern Peru) with the argument that citizens or, in contemporary terminology, the *pueblos,* had the right to reject an old pact (the state of Peru) if they were unhappy. Sovereignty could revert to the people or pueblos, if the people or pueblos disliked current conditions. This conception was far removed from the colonial political tradition, its contractual tradition notwithstanding.[17] The neoscholastic understanding of the right to rebel was far more conservative. For one thing, it respected the status quo. Pacts had to be solid and subjects had to obey the king. For instance, Suárez and other neoscholastic thinkers believed that subjects had the right to break the pact if the sovereign took to tyranny as his way of ruling. It was not enough for the king to commit some tyrannical acts; it had to be a constant behavior.[18] We can nonetheless trace some connections between neoscholastic ideas and the idea that the people or pueblos can rewrite the constitution.

According to the argument presented by the Santa Crucistas, Peru's failure in the construction of a stable regime owed to the artificial nature of its territory and its unitarian character. Southern Peru had never received its due in the union of the Peruvian republic, whereas it was the southern taxes which paid for the government salaries in Lima. In this way the Peruvian capital profited from the union. In addition, Bolivia and Peru belonged to the same human community, shared the same culture and history, and had to be reunited. Meanwhile, from an economic perspective, the separation of Southern Peru and Bolivia had given rise to artificial customhouses, which reduced commerce. This affected the economy of both Southern Peru and Bolivia in a negative way, for commerce, as Adam Smith and his followers proclaimed, brings progress.[19] As we saw, the Santa Crucistas used not only economic but also cultural and identity-related reasons to defend the need for a new pact, which is why citizens had the right to establish one. It was, according to Santa Cruz's propaganda, a pact born out of tradition and mutual interest and justified by contractual thought.[20] But at the same time it was justified in terms of history and tradition. Both will and tradition were united in defense of the new pact.

The arguments of the Santa Crucistas were based on constitutional and contractual thought. We therefore need to explain how the Confederation was consolidated step by step. The first step was to justify the intervention of the Bolivian army, under the command of Santa Cruz, in the Peruvian civil war from late 1835 to early 1836. This was related to the debate on the legality of the treaty (*Tratado de Auxilios*) signed on June 15, 1835, by Casimiro Olañeta, the Bolivian minister of foreign affairs, and General Anselmo Quirós in representation of José Luis Orbegoso, president of Peru.[21] Orbegoso needed the aid of Santa Cruz in order to contain Salaverry in Northern Peru and Gamarra in Cuzco, Puno, and Huamanga.[22]

Santa Cruz opted for Orbegoso instead of Gamarra because he found in him a weak president and a person he could easily control. A further reason was of a constitutional order: Orbegoso had been elected provisional president by congress, and thus had constitutional legitimacy. At that moment, Orbegoso had received extraordinary powers from congress, which gave him considerable autonomy of action; he could, for example, undertake extreme measures, such as declaring a state of emergency. But Orbegoso had a curious reading of his extraordinary powers. He understood that these powers allowed him to sign a treaty with Santa Cruz and, even worse, to transfer his special powers to Santa Cruz as if they were his private property. This in fact happened in the treaty of Vilque on July 28, 1835. This way of understanding the *facultades extraordinarias* was not based on any constitutional provisions. Even so, in this way Santa Cruz received some kind of political legitimacy.[23] All this shows that in Peru, as throughout Latin America, caudillos were eager to have constitutionality as support: it was an essential part of the process of legitimizing their acts. And despite his contempt for the liberal state, Santa Cruz proved no exception to the rule.

The treaty with Orbegoso enabled Santa Cruz to enter the Peruvian civil war in late 1835 and to become the major political actor. He was named commander in chief of the United Army, which was really the Bolivian army. Its mission, as the pamphlets by Orbegoso and Santa Cruz described it, was to quell all rebellions. They stood for the constitution and against revolutionary leaders.[24] Santa Cruz reaffirmed his power successfully in the battles of Yanacocha against Gamarra on August 13, 1835, and Socabaya against Salaverry on February 7, 1836. With these achievements, he built his power and his political persona as "the Pacifier and Protector of Peru." In addition, he showed that he was not afraid of meting out punishment. He allowed the execution of Salaverry and some of his officers after their trials. Furthermore, Santa Cruz made Orbegoso spread favorable publicity throughout Peru. By decree, Orbegoso ordered that every municipality had to display the picture of Santa Cruz.[25] Political propaganda, based on Santa Cruz's image as a leader who maintained order, consolidated his position.

The treaty between Orbegoso and Santa Cruz also had another intention: the establishment of new state entities. It set goals for the future after the war.[26] The treaty stipulated that two deliberating assemblies would be called in representation of Southern and Northern Peruvian pueblos. The first one would meet in Sicuani (Cuzco), the second in Huaura (north of Lima). These assemblies had to decide whether they would continue with "the old Peruvian association" or accept instead a new type of state organization. In the end, however, neither assembly actually had much choice in the matter. The elections for the assemblies had not been very transparent, and Santa Cruz exercised firm control over each of them. In his best Bonaparte style, he sent his loyal General Ramón Herrera with a division of 3,000 soldiers to "protect" the northern assembly—and thus imposed his decision. Herrera shared these responsibilities with Orbegoso, president of the assembly and later president of Northern Peru. All this obviously hastened favorable decisions. Besides, many members of the northern elite deemed that it was impossible and dangerous to oppose Santa Cruz.[27]

Before the Bolivian army intervened in the Peruvian civil war of 1835, the priest and liberal politician Francisco Xavier Luna Pizarro saw in Santa Cruz the means to bring Gamarra's power to an end. Partly at the insistence of Luna Pizarro, the 1834 constitution dropped the article of the 1828 constitution stipulating that Peru could not be united with another country. This clause had originally been written as reaction to Bolívar's 1826 constitution, which had codified his plan to create the Andean Federation: Bolivia, Peru (divided into two), and Gran Colombia in one federation.[28]

The assemblies at Huaura and Sicuani—together with the congress of Tapacarí in Bolivia—gave Santa Cruz dictatorial powers (*suma de poderes*) to organize a new state, the Peru-Bolivian Confederation, and named him protector of the two Peruvian states and Bolivia. He received dictatorial powers to build a new constitutional arrangement, which enabled him simply to avoid elections. He did not receive the suma de poderes to end anarchy or fight an external war, as was the case in the classic Roman dictatorship, where a general on exceptional occasions had received dictatorial power to defeat an external enemy; his task done, he had to return power. Instead, Santa Cruz received dictatorial powers to change the constitution, which came closer to a revolutionary notion of dictatorship.[29] In this way he managed to escape the tradition (sparked by the Cortes de Cádiz) of calling for elections to a constitutional convention. The process of selecting representatives took place in secret, and the rationale behind the selection of representatives escaped the electoral logic.

According to the legislative assemblies of Huaura and Sicuani, Santa Cruz had to call for a constitutional convention that would give the final form to the general structure of the Confederation. In early 1838, this convention met in the city of Tacna, with its members hand-picked by Santa Cruz. Each state had three members in representation of the army, the church, and civilians. But it was not an ancien regime-type election, where each corporation chose its representatives. The selection shows which groups had power. Clearly, the army and the church held a lot of power. So it is not hard to understand why the resulting Pacto de Tacna of May 1, 1838, ended up as a most authoritarian arrangement (see below).

There was strong opposition in Bolivia, especially in Chuquisaca, for fear that Peruvians would control the Confederation: one vote (Bolivia) against two (Southern and Northern Peru). At the same time, in Northern Peru a great number of public figures saw in the Confederation a system that went against their interest or against Peruvian nationality. Santa Cruz felt obliged to call another convention in Arequipa on May 24, 1838, due to the protests that the pact had caused and the threat raised by the second Chilean expedition to defeat the Confederation. In what is certainly a sign of the decadence of his regime, Santa Cruz called for the election of a new congress which would take place immediately after the victory against the Chilean expedition. This, as we know, was never to happen because the Confederation was defeated militarily.[30] At this late point, then, Santa Cruz had to convince others that he could share political power. Analysis of the political events clearly reveals that he called for elections only when he was in a weak position.

THE CONFEDERATION

The Santa Crucistas favored confederation as a constitutional solution. They argued that federalism had created the prosperity of the United of States of America. In fact, the strength of the thirteen colonies was due to a federal system where each state received its share of benefits and responsibilities. This could also happen in South America.[31] The comparison with North America was of course most superficial. No other constitutional arrangements were reviewed. For instance, there was no discussion at all of the electoral system, or of the role the army had in the North American political system.[32] Even so, in Peru a comparison with the United States constitution was somewhat uncommon because attempts to establish a federation had been rare. José Faustino Sánchez Carrión was one of the few who in the early nineteenth century found a good example in the United States constitution. As for Pando and Pardo y Aliaga, they believed that a federal system would be tantamount to anarchy: many forces would simply escape control. Hence Peru needed a strong central state. This point of view was shared by many of the so-called liberals, like Luna Pizarro.[33] Santa Cruz argued exactly the opposite. Following the example set by the United States, a federation would bring peace because each state would receive its share.[34] Besides, Peruvian history had shown that unitarian constitutions created the necessary conditions for a revolutionary political culture.

Santa Cruz divided Peru into two states, partially following Bolívar. There were a number of reasons to divide Peru into two. First, there was an idea of a balance of power that should exist between the Confederation's states. Bolivia would lose its leadership with a united Peru. Everybody knew that Bolivia was powerful at the time because of the political anarchy that had turned Peru into a weak country, but Peru might rapidly recover its lost supremacy. Other ideas behind federation were related to the differences between the south and the north, particularly the conflict of interests between Lima and the southern cities (Huamanga, Cuzco, Puno, and Arequipa).[35] Finally, Santa Cruz knew that his allies came from Southern Peru, where many leaders favored the Confederation. Moreover, Santa Cruz often toyed with the idea of organizing a federation uniting Bolivia and Southern

Peru. In Santa Cruz's plan, Northern Peru was not as essential as Southern Peru.

The constitutional arrangements made by Santa Cruz were most peculiar. In the Pacto de Tacna we find the protector as the head of the Confederation who would rule in a highly authoritarian way for ten years and could be reelected by congress. The federal government was to be in charge of the army and foreign policy, just as in all federations, yet each state would retain its own coinage and flag. The protector had the right to intervene in both judiciary and legislative power. A senate and a house of representatives formed congress. Fifteen life-long senators were to be chosen by the protector from a list prepared by electoral colleges. The protector was responsible for choosing the president of each republic and the ministers of the supreme courts, from a list selected by each congress respectively. These constitutional arrangements had many similarities with the 1826 constitution prepared by Bolívar, not surprisingly, given that both sought to reduce elections and political participation and to concentrate power in the executive.

The Confederation was so focused on the figure of the protector that Santa Cruz displayed a peculiar understanding of the location of the Confederation's capital: the notion that the capital was wherever the protector was at any given moment. This was an idea similar to the old European kingdoms or the Inca empire, where the center moved whenever the king or the Inca moved. According to Santa Cruz, this was an efficient way to be close to the people and solve their problems.[36] In this way he avoided the discussions and strife that would ensue if any city were named capital, be it La Paz, Chuquisaca, Cuzco, Arequipa, or Lima. Moreover, this was a further way of centralizing power in the figure of the protector, who usually moved from one place to the other with a group of civilians and an army to ensure respect.

The protector's power actually originated in the army. Santa Cruz argued that the Confederation would put an end to all military revolutions. He therefore stressed the idea that the army should be an autonomous entity, thus avoiding political conflicts and rivalries among each state. There would only be one army, the army of the Confederation.[37] However, the hold Santa Cruz had over the army was not based on his own institutional arrangements, as he often explained. I concur with those historians who believe that his lucid policy of appointing foreigners like Trinidad Morán, Guillermo

Miller, Otto Felipe Brunn, and others to high command positions was a key element in his control of the army. Foreigners could not expect anything more than high positions in the army. None of them could dream of becoming president. Yet they had a respectable public image as warriors in the wars of independence. In this way Santa Cruz controlled the army.[38] There can be no doubt that the stability of his regime, like that of the regimes of Bolívar or Napoleon before him, was related to the control he exercised over the army.

CITIZENS

Santa Cruz believed in a semiauthoritarian constitution. Like Bolívar and Pardo y Aliaga, he reduced the number of citizens accorded the right to vote, but unlike them, Santa Cruz did not want to create an overly active civil society of *notables* (a select group of elite citizens marked more by family lineage and education than by wealth). He preferred a very quiet civil society. In contrast to Santa Cruz, Pardo y Aliaga believed that the best part of society (the elite) had a political role. He realized, for instance, the role a strong militia had in the cities as a way of reducing the importance of the army, a tactic that had just been used in Chile. Pardo therefore did not seek a silent and passive civil society in his political reforms but an active and politically oriented one formed only by the best—mainly Creoles and, to a lesser extent, mestizos from "good families." In Bolívar's 1826 constitution, for instance, 10 percent of the citizens were actively involved in politics. Their multiple roles included the election of the members of congress, presenting citizens' demands to congress, and the defense of public liberties.[39] In sum, Pardo and Bolívar believed in a small and active civil society. This was quite different from Santa Cruz's vision of a modest and silent civil society. Santa Cruz did not envision elite participation, much less any popular participation. His was just another version of an authoritarian government.

For Santa Cruz, popular participation was limited to civic festivities organized around himself. In civic festivities he was portrayed as the father and founder of the new state—for example, in the celebration of the anniversary of the declaration of independence in Cuzco, or in his triumphal entry in Arequipa in 1837. In Cuzco, the commemoration of independence organized by the government of Southern Peru started with a *Te Deum* mass in which the military, ecclesiastical, and civilian corporations took part. At different moments, church bells and cannon shots broke the silence in a city decorated for the occasion. After the Te Deum, Santa Cruz inaugurated the Hospital of the Holy Spirit. At the end of the commemoration, the government presented monetary awards to worthy citizens and institutions selected by the prefect: an honorable and great artisan, financial help to a poor father with more than six children, an honorable widow with more than two legitimate children, and a *beaterio* with financial problems.[40]

In Arequipa, the corporations welcomed Santa Cruz outside the city. The national guard escorted him to the Plaza de Armas. There, soldiers and the city's corporations commemorated the battles his army had fought. The bishop and the ecclesiastical chapter awaited him in the cathedral and held a Te Deum mass in his honor. At the same time, the people danced in the city. The next day, all the corporations once again visited Santa Cruz and gave speeches, requesting his protection as the great leader. No emphasis was placed on civic participation in the process of building the new state. Both celebrations were centered on the figure of Santa Cruz and—to a much lesser degree—on the army. The claim of high moral and heroic qualities of officers and soldiers was also noteworthy. And then came citizen participation, last and certainly least.[41]

The development of a modern citizenship like the one described by Benjamin Constant was not among Santa Cruz's priorities. For Constant, ancient liberty was based on citizens who sacrificed their private liberty in order to participate in public life and fight for the polis, while modern liberty is based on citizens focused on private life who participate in politics through a representative system. Ancient liberty encompassed a minority of the people of the polis. Slaves, women, and children could not participate in public life.[42] In the terms of the nineteenth century, ancient liberty was based on a system of notables. It can be said that Bolívar thought in Greek terms—and so did Santa Cruz at least to some degree: his concept of citizenship was far more related to participation in the army than to representation or participation in the political arena. It is obvious why both shared this view: in constructing their ideas about civic behavior they drew on their military experience.

Yet Santa Cruz also emphasized the preeminence of aristocracy in society. A review of his political allies in Peru shows that many of them belonged to the old viceregal nobility: José Mariano de la Riva Agüero y Sánchez Boquete, nephew and heir of the last colonial Marquis of Montealegre de Aulestia; Juán Pío Tristán y Moscoso, considered by some the last unofficial viceroy of Peru;[43] Orbegoso, heir to his family's *mayorazgo,* whose mother was the last Countess of Olmos; and Domingo Nieto, whose uncle was the Count of Alastaya, among others. At the same time, Santa Cruz attached much importance to the creation of the "Legion of Honor," which was modeled on the French order of the same name. The Legion of Honor was to reward key supporters and create a new aristocracy that would be based on merit and not on lineage. The legion was divided into two orders: civilian and military. Military leaders, businessmen, intellectuals, and others who demonstrated exemplary personal qualities and performed activities beneficial to state and society would be selected for membership. In its emphasis on public and personal qualities, the Legion of Honor expressed a modern notion of virtue. Like José de San Martín before him, who had founded a similar institution, Santa Cruz realized the importance of creating a new elite that would favor the new pact.[44] This elite would be loyal to the Confederation because in substantial measure its honor hinged on the very existence of the Confederation. Such a conception of the Confederation is far removed from that of Pardo y Aliaga, who construed (and criticized) it as the regime of the Andean underclass.[45] Yet it is clear that Santa Cruz firmly believed in aristocratic values and institutions.[46]

Santa Cruz was a man of his times. He did not have an overly democratic view of society, but he did not conceive an overly static one either, in which one's position was ascribed. He positioned himself and the regime he sought to build between both. He belonged to the Andean aristocracy, and aristocratic values often meant subscribing to a view of society in which everyone had a fixed place. Yet Santa Cruz could not escape his time, either: an era when constant displacements brought about considerable mobility. He had served as an officer in several armies (those of Spain, Gran Colombia, Peru, and Bolivia) and—as sociologists are wont to emphasize—armies are major vehicles for social mobility, particularly in times of war, as the best officers rapidly move upward. The Legion of Honor expressed both the notions of social climbing and of aristocratic values. It was a way of creating a society based on honor.

INDIANS AND CITIZENSHIP

Santa Cruz was a serrano who understood the political life of the Indian. He still believed in traditional institutions like the protector of Indians, the *kurakas* (village headmen), and the Indian *alcaldes* (mayors). In a more typical nineteenth-century understanding of how to improve the Indians' condition, Santa Cruz passed laws to protect them from abuse, although it is not clear how vigorously these were enforced.[47] Santa Cruz was aware of the abuses that Creoles and mestizos committed against Indians, and he believed that the latter needed some kind of special treatment given the way power relations were structured in the Andes.

By far the Confederation's most interesting laws relating to Indian institutions were connected to the colonial "Republic of Indians" which, to a certain degree, Santa Cruz sought to recover. He had a favorable understanding of the kurakas, an office abolished by Bolívar, and restituted their lands.[48] More broadly, in relation to indigenous authorities he visualized a chain of command descending from prefects to subprefects, governors, and Indian mayors, an institution within the sphere of the indigenous community. This was different from other imaginable chains of command. For instance, Gamarra's chain of command did not include the *alcalde de indios* as a legal institution.[49] Moreover, Santa Cruz reinstated the *protector de indios,* in charge of representing Indians in legal activities and paid by the municipalities. Yet on this issue he changed his mind in 1838, toward the end of his regime. He now saw the protector of Indians as a burdensome and expensive institution, which only ensured that lawsuits would never end.[50]

Like many members of the elite, Santa Cruz had a decidedly paternalist view of the Indians. He did not see them as autonomous individuals capable of making their own decisions. They needed to be protected by the state. This can be seen in his policy on indigenous landholding. As part of the liberal policies of Bolívar and Sucre between 1824 and 1828, community lands were supposedly divided in individual lots and given to each adult Indian.[51] Yet they could not sell them before 1855, as it was assumed that only then would Indians acquire a better understanding of the market. Santa Cruz shared this view and sought to enforce this law vigorously. Land that Indians had sold since 1825 had to be returned to them.[52] For Santa Cruz, an Indian could not make any autonomous, rational decision in the land market.

Santa Cruz combined modern and traditional institutions in various ways. He saw Indians behaving in corporate fashion. He did not share the liberal notion of a Westernized Indian as Bolívar and many liberals had envisioned him: the Indian as a Catholic farmer with European habits, manners, and language. Instead he wanted to perpetuate some colonial institutions, at least for a while. We should also recall that a preponderant share of the fiscal income of Southern Peru and Bolivia came from the *contribución general,* or head tax (at times including the castas).[53] As Tristan Platt has famously pointed out, the payment of tribute or contribución established a kind of pact between the indigenous community and the state, perceived as an exchange of tax payment for state protection of community lands and other resources.[54] All this reinforced a split of society into two spheres with respect to rights and duties. In this project there was no great concern for the development of a society based on citizens sharing equal rights and duties, or of political participation.

• • • • •

The army strongly shaped politics in the Andes. In the case of the Confederation, it helped to foster a kind of civil-military regime. This regime was based on a diminishing representative government marked by a limited electoral system. Compared to other constitutional visions of his time, Santa Cruz's regime consisted of a small number of people who could vote and a still smaller number who could be elected. We have seen how the protector heavily interfered with the judicial and legislative powers, and of course with the army. The Confederation created a public image which suggested that the chief of the army (Santa Cruz) and his officers and soldiers were the founders of a civilized and peaceful political entity. As they would have it, order was attained through a combination of a good constitution, a great leader, and a well-organized, invincible army.

Santa Cruz's project constituted a different approach to state building than that of many liberals. It does not belong in François Guerra's model of the nineteenth century, which is based on the conflict between modern institutions and traditional society. For Guerra and Anthony Pagden, many of the great politicians during that century of progress imagined and construed a state from which all native traditions had been uprooted. Their point of reference for state building came from the Greek tradition and from modern English, French, and Spanish constitutional thought.[55] By contrast, the Confederation was no tabula rasa. It was based on Andean traditions and notions of authority and power. It embodied a process of state building that was far removed from the designs of Bolívar, who likewise sought to recreate society and state. When Bolívar and Santa Cruz are compared, the former comes out a revolutionary, the latter a brilliant conservative. However, the term "conservative" is misleading, for it can make us see Santa Cruz as a man who sought to preserve the status quo. The truth is that he and his project lay squarely in between tradition and innovation. And we should not forget that this was the result of a break with the past: the wars of independence.[56]

NOTES

1. Changes in the national borders forced those who lived within the national territory to deal with different nation-state discourses, which included references to citizenship and nationality.
2. *El Telégrafo de Lima,* June 11, 1836 (no. 864).
3. *El Eco del Protectorado* (Lima), Nov. 9, 1836 (no. 24); *El Yanacocha* (Arequipa), Jan. 7, 1837 (vol. 2, no. 20).
4. Guerra, *Modernidad,* 138–44.
5. Crespo, *Santa Cruz,* 17–23; Parkerson, *Andrés de Santa Cruz,* 21.
6. Walker, *Smoldering Ashes,* chaps. 4–7.
7. Aljovín, *Caudillos,* chap. 6.
8. Méndez, "Rebellion without Resistance."
9. Zamalloa, "El pensamiento político" and "La Guardia Nacional."
10. Montesquieu, *The Spirit of the Laws,* bk. 19.
11. Aljovín, *Caudillos,* chap. 6.
12. *El Regulador de la Opinión* (Cuzco), Sept. 13, 1835 (no. 4).
13. *El Regulador de la Opinión* (Cuzco), Sept. 6, 1835 (no. 2); Sept. 23, 1835 (no. 4); *El Telégrafo de Lima,* April 19, 1834 (no. 513); Feb. 20, 1836 (no. 780).
14. *El Telégrafo de Lima,* Feb. 20, 1836 (no. 780); May 12, 1836 (no. 841); May 13, 1836 (no. 842).
15. *El Republicano* (Arequipa), July 20, 1836 (vol. 11, no. 31).
16. Baltes, "José María Pando, colaborador peruano" and "José María Pando, colaborador de Gamarra."
17. *La Aurora Peruana* (Cuzco), Aug. 25, 1835 (no. 1); Sept. 29, 1835 (no. 8); Oct. 16, 1835 (no. 10); Oct. 23, 1835 (no. 11); Feb. 25, 1836 (no. 28); Feb. 27, 1836; *El Eco del Protectorado* (Lima), Oct. 29, 1836 (no. 21); *El Yanacocha* (Arequipa), April 2, 1836.
18. Skinner, *The Foundations,* 2:154–78.
19. *El Yanacocha* (Arequipa), Nov. 21, 1835 (no. 6); *La Aurora Peruana* (Cuzco), Oct. 23, 1835 (no. 11); Nov. 18, 1835 (no. 14).
20. "Variedades," *El Republicano* (Arequipa), June 10, 1836 (no. 29).

21. Crespo, *Santa Cruz,* 142–43; Parkerson, *Andrés de Santa Cruz,* 95–100.
22. Circumstances were difficult for Orbegoso in late 1835; early in the year, Salaverry had rebelled against him and controlled Northern Peru, including Lima. At the same time, Gamarra, who had also staged a rebellion, controlled Cuzco, Ayacucho, and Puno. Furthermore, Gamarra was in the process of signing a treaty with Santa Cruz. Orbegoso and some loyal officers were in a desperate situation and only controlled Arequipa, some southern provinces, and a small part of the army. The conclusion was easy: without help, Orbegoso could not control the situation. In this context, Santa Cruz appeared as arbiter of Peruvian affairs. As commander in chief of the Bolivian army, he could decide who would win the civil war. In the end, Santa Cruz opted for Orbegoso. Parkerson, *Andrés de Santa Cruz,* 87–110; Crespo, *Santa Cruz,* 113–45.
23. Oviedo, *Colección de leyes,* 2:192–93; also see the various numbers of *El Intérprete* (Santiago de Chile), 1836–37.
24. *La Aurora Peruana* (Cuzco), Feb. 25, 1836 (no. 28); *El Boliviano* (Chuquisaca), July 23, 1837 (vol. 4, no. 38).
25. *La Aurora Peruana* (Cuzco), March 30, 1836 (no. 34).
26. Crespo, *Santa Cruz,* 143.
27. Parkerson, *Andrés de Santa Cruz,* 127–29.
28. Aljovín, *Caudillos,* 245.
29. Bobbio, *Democracy and Dictatorship,* 158–66.
30. *El Iris de la Paz* (La Paz), March 25, 1838 (vol. 5, no. 44); Sept. 27, 1838 (vol. 5, no. 97).
31. *El Telegráfo de Lima,* June 11, 1836 (no. 864); *El Despertador público* (Cuzco), Nov. 20, 1835 (no. 1).
32. *El Yanacocha* (Arequipa), March 25, 1837 (no. 38).
33. Aljovín, *Caudillos,* chap. 2.
34. General Herrera advised Santa Cruz that the federation should conceal a unitarian government. For political reasons, Herrera wanted a strong, centralized state with a federalist form; cf. Parkerson, *Andrés de Santa Cruz,* 128.
35. *La Aurora Peruana* (Cuzco), Oct. 16, 1835 (no. 10); Oct. 23, 1835 (no. 11); Nov. 18, 1835 (no. 14); Feb. 2, 1836 (no. 28).
36. *El Victorioso* (Ayacucho), April 23, 1836 (no. 23); *El Eco Nacional* (Ayacucho), Nov. 17, 1838 (no. 5); *El Yanacocha* (Arequipa), Nov. 28, 1836 (no. 8).
37. *El Eco del Protectorado* (Lima), Nov. 9, 1836.
38. Cf. Parkerson, *Andrés de Santa Cruz;* Crespo, *Santa Cruz.*
39. Bolívar, "Discurso . . . constituyente de Bolivia," 300–301.
40. *La Estrella Federal: Extraordinaria* (Cuzco), March 18, 1837.
41. *El Yanacocha* (Arequipa), Sept. 13, 1837 (vol. 2, no. 82).
42. Constant, *The Liberty,* 309–28.
43. Although he never assumed office after the battle of Ayacucho.

44. La *Aurora Peruana* (Cuzco), March 5, 1836 (no. 31).
45. Porras Barrenechea, "Don Felipe Pardo y Aliaga," 237–304.
46. For a contrasting position, see Méndez, *Incas sí, indios no.*
47. *El Telégrafo de Lima,* Nov. 29, 1836 (no. 973).
48. Personal communication from Pablo Macera; Langer, "El Liberalismo," 61–64.
49. *El Mercurio Peruano* (Lima), May 8, 1830 (no. 758); "Andrés de Santa Cruz, Capitán General [1837]."
50. *La Estrella Federal* (Cuzco), Sept. 15, 1838 (vol. 2, no. 24).
51. I am not aware of how far this policy was actually enforced.
52. *Iriz de la Paz* (La Paz), February 2, 1838 (vol.5, no. 36).
53. Sánchez Albornoz, *Indios y tributos,* 187–218.
54. Platt, *Estado boliviano,* 100–10.
55. Pagden, *Spanish Imperialism,* chap. 5; the justification of the wars of independence was taken from other sources in the neoscholastic tradition; see Giménez Fernández, "Las doctrinas populistas," 517–666; Stoetzer, *Las raíces escolásticas.*
56. Pardo, "Prólogo," xv–xviii.

THE TAX MAN COMETH

LOCAL AUTHORITIES AND THE BATTLE OVER TAXES IN PERU, 1885–1906

Carlos Contreras

During the mid-1880s, a serious attempt to introduce liberal reforms was undertaken in Peru.[1] It was hoped that these reforms would transform a nation weighed down by a dual social structure and militaristic-authoritarian politics into a democratic republic in which the separation of powers and the rights and duties of the citizens were clearly established and freely practiced. This reform drive formed part of the spirit of "regeneration" that jolted Peru after the traumatic defeat in the War of the Pacific (1879–1883). Peruvians launched into bitter condemnations of the past and seemed disposed to examine and change many aspects of national institutions and life. As one can easily deduce from today's vantage point, those reforms failed, if not totally, at least in great part. Even so, they had important consequences for the organization of the Peruvian state and for the political culture of the inhabitants of the republic.

In this essay, I propose to portray the fate of one of those reforms: the separation, in the governance of Peru's interior, of political and "treasury" functions, or, put differently, of purely political administration and revenue collection and public expenditure. Since the colonial era, these functions had been fused in one office.

This reform was launched in 1886 as part of President Andrés Avelino Cáceres's project of fiscal decentralization. Twenty years later, it reached a clear form, yet one entirely different from the initial proposal. We might say that the reform failed, faced with powerful obstacles arising from various interests and power constellations in the interior of the republic. Nevertheless, the reform accomplished the objective of separating the political and treasury functions of governance. However, it did so at the enormous price of further centralization, which created as many new problems as it was supposed to solve.

THE LOCAL POLITICAL AUTHORITIES

From the beginning of independence until the end of the nineteenth century, the prefects in Peru were, at one and the same time, the highest representatives of the central government and directors of the treasury in their departments. For political administration of local populations and societies the republic, since its first constitution of 1823, relied on a pyramidal system of authorities inherited from the Bourbon era of colonial rule. The minister of government stood at the apex of the pyramid. His jurisdiction covered the entire national territory. Appointed by the president, he could be removed by him at will. Below the minister came the prefects who held sway in the departments (successors to the colonial intendancies, although over time new departments were created); below these, subprefects ruled over provinces (successors of the colonial *partidos*); and below them, governors were in charge of districts. At the bottom of the pyramid came the deputy governors, appointed as authorities in hamlets and villages.

In accord with the republic's centralist model, these authorities were not elected by the inhabitants of their jurisdictions but appointed by the government. The minister of government appointed the prefects and subprefects (these latter chosen from a list of three candidates proposed by the prefects) while the governors were appointed by the prefects (from a list of three candidates submitted by the subprefects); the subprefects in turn appointed the deputy governors.[2] Prefects and subprefects received a salary established in the national budget, but governors and deputy governors did not. Their offices were considered of a civic nature, an obligation that did not need to be remunerated and from which one could not resign.[3] Until shortly after the War of the Pacific, prefects and subprefects were commonly recruited among army officers: prefects from the ranks of colonels and lieutenant colonels, and subprefects from among lieutenant colonels and majors.[4] Thus they usually were strangers in the jurisdictions to which they were appointed. They belonged to a kind of caste of mobile public functionaries whose true home base was the army. By contrast, the governors were local figures, chosen primarily for their knowledge of Spanish and also for their potential loyalty to the government of the day.[5] Local authorities did not have a definite term of office; it came to an end whenever they were removed by superior authority.[6]

According to Article 73 of the Law of the Interior Organization of the Republic of 1857, prefects were in charge of "the economic administration of public funds in their respective departments." In plain language, this meant that they were responsible for the collection of the revenues established by law as well as for their expenditure. It was this accumulation or fusion of functions in the authorities of the interior (on top of their extensive other executive powers) that became the target of reform efforts of the national elite during the late nineteenth century. Of colonial origin, such fusion of functions can in a way be considered a trait of ancien regime governments.[7]

To collect the various taxes, the prefects put in motion the pyramidal machine of authorities below them. Subprefects and governors were the linchpins of the system: the former because they were obligated to deposit a bond in the public treasury for a sum equivalent to one semester's tax collection in their province, which made them eager to undertake a thorough collection effort; the latter because their proximity to and knowledge of the taxpayers gave them undeniable advantages. A typical rural district contained perhaps some 500 families, allowing a quasi-personal contact among all residents. Only in a few regions did subprefects at times rely on tax collectors specifically appointed for that purpose.[8]

The abolition of the head tax on Indians and *castas* (persons classified as being of mixed descent) by the 1854 revolution of Ramón Castilla came nearly at the apogee of the fiscal bonanza based on guano exports. This meant that direct taxation in the interior dropped to an insignificant level. In the years 1860–63, for example, when the budget of the republic reached between 20 and 23 million soles annually, direct taxes collected by the local political authorities in the entire country amounted to only 156, 572 soles; that is, less than one percent of the national budget.[9] Sporadic attempts to restore some type of general direct tax, which would replace the abolished head tax, failed. The general pattern of minimal direct taxation remained unchanged for the three decades after 1854. Not even the desperate fiscal measures of 1879 became reality, first because of the Chilean occupation, and later because of the virtual collapse of the Peruvian state until 1885.[10]

Even though the local authorities held the double jurisdiction over political and fiscal administration in their territory from independence until the War of the Pacific, after 1854 their treasury functions had become very weak, at least with regard to revenue collection. Basically they depended on funds remitted from Lima or one of the major customs agencies to sustain as best they could the necessary public expenditures in their territory. This affected the pattern of how the rural population and state authorities had related to each for the past three centuries: through an exchange of tributes for autonomy. Such an ingrained pattern of exchange had produced a profound impact on the understanding that the indigenous population and the Creoles in control of the state had formed about their rights and obligations.

This situation underwent drastic change with the reconstruction of the state and its fiscal apparatus after Chile terminated the occupation of Peru in 1883. Given the loss of the old mainstays of public revenues, guano and nitrates, the reconstruction of the state necessarily implied dusting off old taxes and creating new ones that could minimally sustain national budgets. Among the old taxes dusted off, property taxes (*contribuciones de predios rústicos y urbanos*) and license taxes on various crafts, businesses, and professions (*contribución de patentes, contribución de industrias*) were especially important. Assessments were increased to 5 percent of net income from property, a trade, or business and were to be based on new appraisals. Among the taxes newly put on the books, a general head tax (*contribución personal*) stood out. It was levied on every male inhabitant between the ages of twenty-one and sixty years, at the rate of four soles for residents of the coast and two soles for residents of the *sierra* (Andean highlands). Even though this new tax came to make up about one half of the revenues in the budgets of average departments, and two thirds in those of departments in the southern highlands, this was still considerably lower (both on a per capita basis and as a share of overall departmental revenues) than the indigenous head tax before 1854.[11]

As a result of the fiscal reform, the departmental taxes in the budget proposal for 1887 reached 1.8 million soles, and 2 million soles for that of

1888. This represented almost one fourth of the national budget, fixed for the two-year period at 8.1 million soles annually.[12] After three decades during which government revenues depended almost entirely on export trades, the "interior" seemed to reemerge as an important fiscal arena for the state. To be sure, this shift represented nothing else than an ad hoc response to the desperate financial situation. Nevertheless, an increase of domestic direct taxes from 150,000 to 2 million soles in a brief time span required much more than a few well-meaning legal resolutions.

Dozens of tax commissioners (*apoderados fiscales*) were recruited among the seasoned personnel of the ministry of finance and empowered to elaborate new tax registers with the express purpose of raising collections. The apoderados received a "bonus" proportional to the increase of assessments in the registers. But once the registers were completed, the question became: "who would hang the bell on the cat?" That is, who was going to collect taxes in the interior after thirty years of near inactivity? The departmental treasuries, created by the law of fiscal decentralization of 1886, depended on the *juntas departamentales,* which were to exercise oversight, but were not conceived as administrative agencies. Consequently they were not given the function of tax collection. Existing laws and the powerful force of habit suggested that the political authorities should once again be responsible for tax collection. The identification of the tribute collector with the political authority representing the state on the local level went back for several centuries to the *corregidores* of the early colonial period, when even the indigenous lords were co-opted to aid in the collection of *tributo.* Moreover, the political authorities controlled the few gendarmes and policemen, who could back them up at the time of collection.

Nevertheless, elite groups with exotic and progressive ideas raised their vigorous opposition to this return to old habits. They aimed to separate the function of political administration from that of tax collection. They based their central argument on the "extortions" that had occurred in the past because of the fusion in the same hands of the power to rule and the power to collect taxes. In the debate on the law of fiscal decentralization of November 1886, Deputy Patiño Zamudio, presented this point of view as follows: "To collect *contribución personal,* it is necessary that the government designate special employees for this purpose; otherwise, bitter experience has taught all the towns and villages that the presence of the subprefects with the authority of tax collector, produces the same impression, as Mirabeau used to say, as a hawk in a chicken coop."[13]

This current of opinion also argued that if the subprefects were once again put in charge of revenue collection, they would once again have to post a bond in the amount of one semester's taxes of their province. They would ask traders or other powerful local figures for that money, the only people in the province with sufficient funds to finance such outlays. This financial nexus would make the subprefects dependent on the local elites and would not allow them to make autonomous and impartial decisions on issues of concern to those elites.

The effort to exclude local authorities from fiscal administration can be understood as part of the attack on the political influence of the military, which, until then, had controlled those administrative positions. The reformers sought to build a body of professional bureaucrats who would be more docile than the local mestizo and indigenous oligarchies. Moreover, indigenous rebellions, such as that led by Atusparia in Huaraz in 1885, had convinced the Limeño elite that central state control over the exactions demanded of peasants was fundamental in order to guarantee internal governance and peace of the republic.

The polemic between principled reformers and the "pragmatists" who insisted on the advantages of continuing with the prewar system of tax collection spread from congress to the press and to the very functionaries of the government. The alignment of social and political forces in this debate is not entirely clear. The *civilistas,* a party that no longer held the majority in congress during the 1880s and 1890s, still enjoyed a kind of intellectual hegemony in its chambers. They stood for a Europeanizing liberalism of notables, in defense of the separation of powers and the rights of the individual against tradition and the power of the state. It appears that this party defended the principled reform position and managed to push through congress the principle of appointing specialized tax collectors, under the supervision of the juntas departmentales.

THE APODERADOS FISCALES

These tax collectors were to be the apoderados fiscales, an office established in December 1886 as a provision complementary to the Law of Fiscal Decentralization. Such functionaries had existed in the past, as expert tax appraisers, or in charge of preparing the tax registers, while the actual collection of taxes was left in the hands of the subprefects. According to the new provisions, the apoderados were to be appointed by the central government for each province, on the presentation of candidates by the junta departamental or the prefect who served as its president.[14] They were required to post bond at the departmental treasury in the amount of one semester's tax revenue, up to a maximum of 6,000 soles.[15] Like prefects and subprefects, they did not have a fixed term of office and would serve until their replacement by the central government. In the case of their absence, or a vacancy of the office in a particular province, their functions were to be carried out by the subprefect.

The apoderado fiscal had to draw up new tax registers every five years and correct them annually between April and May. For this work he would receive a fixed fee, plus a commission in proportion to the increase in revenue generated by the update. He was prohibited from collecting taxes without giving each taxpayer an official receipt prepared by the departmental treasury and was required to turn over the amounts collected to the treasury at the end of each month. This rule was intended to avoid the prewar practice of subprefects and governors who, according to Christine Hünefeldt, kept the collected taxes for several months as "working capital."[16] The apoderados could request police or military support for their collection efforts. Besides the specific payments for the preparation of the quinquennial registers and the annual rectifications, the agents would receive a commission of 4 percent of the taxes they collected.

The new provisions entrusted numerous other responsibilities to the embattled apoderados: to report about the national assets in their province, to inform about the best manner of stimulating its trade, agriculture, and mining, and to represent the government's interest in inheritance cases. There is little doubt that the state had decided to entrust a vast array of its provincial-level functions and interests to these new "superfunctionaries." At the same time, it prohibited them from getting mixed up in "electoral and partisan battles" in order to safeguard their character as civil servants acting as neutral experts in a context of charged partisan politics. The reform project of the apoderados fiscales expressed the desire to form a technical bureaucracy that would emancipate state finances from the "barbarism and dangers" entailed by local bossism and from the ballast of "cultural atavisms" of the "indigenous race." In the imagination of the national elites, the tax collector should cease to be a powerful local lord or an indigenous leader legitimated by tradition. He should simply become a functionary of the state. In 1888, for example, Minister of Finance Antero Aspíllaga, one of the politicians most committed to the fiscal reform program, spoke of the "urgent need in public administration to form a professional body of civil servants dedicated to the formation of tax registers and the collection of revenues."[17]

But the apoderados fiscales failed to fulfill the expectations that were placed on them. If it was thought that they would be the matrix of a specialized fiscal bureaucracy, disillusionment must have set in within a few years. During the early 1890s, the alliance between the Civilista Party and the Cáceres regime unraveled, and an opposition majority took charge in congress. As a result, in 1893 congress abolished the office of apoderado fiscal, for both technical and political reasons.[18]

Why did the system of apoderados fiscales fail, and what were the consequences of this failure? First, it failed because their salary basically consisted of the 4 percent commission on the taxes they collected. In the poorer provinces of the interior, the taxes were too meager to make the collection effort lucrative on this percentage basis. In the modern senses of the words, neither commerce nor industry existed there. Property existed, but the income it generated was small, or difficult to estimate in monetary terms. For the apoderado this left only the incentive of the commission on contribución personal. However, this tax quickly proved to be enormously difficult to collect. Not even the increase of the commission to 6 percent in 1888 motivated potential candidates to want such a position.[19]

Such exiguous taxes that were so difficult to collect left many provinces, and even entire departments, without apoderados fiscales.[20] There were provinces where the sum collected barely amounted to a few thousand soles. A commission of 4 percent, therefore, even in the improbable case that all the assessed taxes could be collected, left the apoderado with a remuneration of only slightly more than 100 soles per year, a salary smaller than that of a doorman in a government office.[21] On top of this, it was assumed that the commission would cover such costs as transportation, printing of receipts, and other expenses.

Moreover, the social and economic upheaval caused by seven years of war and civil war had brought fiscal discipline to a low ebb. Each leader of the opposition to the current government initiated his assault on the power holders with a call for the nonpayment of taxes in the interior provinces.[22] The countryside was well stocked with firearms as a consequence of the wars, and it had become relatively easy to form a group of bandits or start a local tax revolt. It was also a fact that in past decades the country had lived on the receipts from the exportation of guano and nitrates, and secondarily from customs revenues. Thus hardly anybody had cared to note that there were entire provinces where the tax laws of the nation were not applied, hence they had become something like "liberated territories." The prefect of the department of Huanuco reported to the Ministry of Government in January 1886, for example, that his authority in truth "only extends to a few pueblos of the province of Huanuco."[23] And congressional Deputy Ruiz of Ayacucho in 1887 flatly claimed that three provinces in his native department "are impossible to govern or maintain tranquil," and there "even the idea of authority has disappeared."[24]

Perhaps because they found themselves deeply involved in the national defense during the war against Chile, the population of the interior believed they did not have to pay taxes for an indefinite period of time.[25] Or perhaps they resisted payment, as many people thought and publicly stated, because the country acquired the bad habit of not paying taxes during the years of guano and nitrates. Whatever the reason, collecting taxes turned out to be a thankless and often futile drudgery for the apoderados fiscales.

It was foreseeable that the political authorities and treasury officials would blame each other for the miserly collections. The prefects accused the apoderados of lack of zeal in their labors. Those in his department worked "slowly and carelessly," opined Teodorico Terry, prefect of Ica.[26] The prefect of Huancavelica noted that the failure in collecting contribución personal was due "not so much to the resistance in complying with this legal tax, but rather to the negligence of the officials called upon to enforce the law."[27] Meanwhile, the apoderados complained about the lack of police support on the part of the prefects and subprefects, and about their low commissions. The tension between political authorities and apoderados fiscales climaxed in a bitter exchange between the ministers of government and finance in 1887. The latter demanded more "prudence" from local political authorities to facilitate the effective collection of taxes and allow new registers to be drawn up.[28]

The critique of apoderados fiscales by the political authorities was self-interested, as it masked their aspiration to recover the tax collection authority they had held in the prewar era. In reports and official communications, prefects recognized that police support was insufficient. They knew that a vicious cycle was blocking progress in making taxation effective: without adequate police forces, tax collection would diminish, and, with less collection, there would be even fewer policemen, since funding would be even shorter.[29] Entire departmental police contingents consisted of a few dozen gendarmes, stationed only in the capital of the department and in some of the provincial capitals. District governors lacked any police forces.[30]

But even a harmonious coordination between apoderados and prefects did not guarantee a fully compliant tax collection, as the archival record amply demonstrates.[31] One might think that, as a deputy to congress from Ayacucho suggested, "extremely bitter conditions" and the "utter and most atrocious poverty" might account for low compliance rates with taxes in many provinces. Yet one has to wonder whether in the waning decades of the colonial era, when indigenous tribute payments brought in twice the amount produced by the contribución personal in 1887 and were apparently collected in full, people from Ayacucho, Huancavelica, or Cuzco were less poor. Could it be that the republic was extending tax collections to territories or settlements that had not been controlled by the Spaniards? Beyond the often-cited disuse into which tax obligations had fallen over the preceding decades, one further explanation for the difficulties of fiscal control likely rests in the scant legitimacy of the government, and of its fiscal agents. Elaborating Tristan Platt's notion of a "compact" between the Creole state and the Andean ayllu, Mark Thurner has stressed the apparent departmental as opposed to national nature of the collection apparatus for the contribución personal, and the neglect of community involvement and recognition in the design of this tax. Thus the notion that payment of the tax would guarantee the state's protection of the lands and resources of indigenous communities was considerably weakened in the minds of indigenous peasants.[32] Even hacendados closed ranks with their labor tenants to resist paying the tax.[33]

The attempt to separate collection of taxes from the functions of political governance failed completely. The local authorities, on the front lines of these battles, were among the first to realize this. One notion that frequently appeared in their correspondence was the divorce between the "legislative mentality" and the prevailing reality in many localities, one that the legislator ignored but which governors and subprefects confronted day after day. With tiresome frequency, the prefect of Apurímac noted in his annual report for 1892, "the legal prescription clashed with the obstacles posed by the pueblos' nature [*calidad*]."[34]

After a lapse of three decades, the idea proved illusory that collection of direct taxes could be restored through the formation of a professional corps of fiscal agents. "Extortions" by local authorities could not be stopped. This had been one of the main purposes of fiscal decentralization and the establishment of juntas departamentales, elected city councils, courts, and apoderados fiscales. These measures only diminished the legitimacy and effectiveness of the old authorities. In the past their power and prestige was based on their role in the redistribution of resources coming from Lima. Now that the capital had little to distribute, both the central state and the local authorities had to look for new sources of legitimacy. This turned out to be a difficult transition process. The Cáceres regime had the habit of issuing solemn declarations to the political authorities in the departments, provinces, and districts. Writing in a personal style to the higher-level authorities and in a paternalistic style to the district governors, the president entreated them to fulfill their civic duties in this hour of national reconstruction. He admonished them to undertake frequent inspection tours through the entire territory under their control, and to listen personally to the complaints of the population about local authorities, including those of the Church. Annual reports of prefects and subprefects attest that some inspection tours were actually carried out. But in many areas, the authorities did not comply with the president's exhortations. They had too few resources to undertake the inspection, lacked interest in doing so, or were inhibited by the hostility of the population which had learned that behind the hand of friendship extended by the political authorities the iron claw of the apoderado fiscal would appear demanding taxes.[35]

The political and cultural bases that had sustained the revenue system of the ancien regime since the colonial era lay in shambles. Yet the ties of national identity and solidarity which could nourish a modern fiscal compact, devoid of the crutches of ethnic lineage and local bossism, were still too weak for the population to accept the figure of the expert treasury bureaucrat.[36] A strong and centralized state, such as the Bourbon regime during the last half-century of colonial rule, would probably have achieved a better tax collection result. In fact, it did, once the intendants and subdelegados had been appointed and did their yeoman's labor as treasury officers.[37] The Cáceres regime was different. Here the state was weak and promoted a decentralization project in which the promise of reciprocity in exchange for tax compliance became less convincing.

Since no other bonanza commodity appeared on the horizon, from which the state might have monopolized and drawn rich public revenues, the government lacked funds to confront the needs of interior administration. If this situation continued much longer, the state apparatus could collapse or the country might disintegrate territorially. Few people doubted that Peru was facing a life and death crisis.

THE RETURN OF THE SUBPREFECTS

In light of the scant efficiency of the apoderados fiscales and their repeated abandonment of their positions, many subprefects reassumed the collection of taxes. If the apoderado failed, a subprefect was not going to leave the police garrison without pay or his own family without bread. Many apoderados resigned, or were fired for corruption, and replacing them often proved impossible. Yet the subprefects did not have to post the corresponding bond, since it was thought that they discharged these duties only on an interim basis. Moreover, subprefects as well were frequently replaced and reassigned before they could deposit the collected taxes. Sometimes they lacked time to gather taxes collected by the district governors, on whom they relied.[38]

Local political authorities, and on occasion police, no longer received their salaries from the departmental treasury, as conceived by lawmakers in Lima. Rather, they collected their salaries directly from the population they administered, as in the era of the corregidores.[39] For the actual collection, the subprefects depended mostly on the district governors. They gave them blank receipts to fill out according to type of tax and amount paid. "The subaltern collectors yield to some ancient habit," wrote the subprefect of Puno in May of 1888. "They receive five, ten, or twenty centavos weekly from each taxpayer; in this way it takes them at least five months to complete their collection every semester."[40] Collection of taxes thus became the governors' principal and most delicate task and left them "no time to assume other [duties]."[41] "Your Honor does not ignore that the governors' time is spent in the difficult task of collecting taxes," wrote the subprefect of Lampa to the prefect of Puno in 1887.[42] And the prefect of Apurímac confirmed that this was a task "in itself more than enough to occupy all the time available to a man."[43]

Subprefect and governor, working hand in glove, enjoyed greater recognition and legitimacy than the apoderados among the rural population. First, they were authorities with a long tradition that in some form had existed for centuries.[44] Second, because other authorities, above all those of the judicial system, were lacking on the local level, the governor acted in multiple roles, as judge and whatever else was necessary.[45] Most importantly, it was a rural tradition to pay the taxes to the governor, which helps explain the failure of the apoderados fiscales. As Deputy Agustín Tovar proclaimed in congress in 1886, "One can observe that whenever tax collectors have been appointed they have found it impossible to make the collection. The Indian will only pay his governor. This happened when Mr. Solar was the chief of the southern departments, and at other times as well. In the face of these facts there are no arguments."[46]

The peasant population personalized their tax payment vis-à-vis the officeholder they considered their principal mediator with the state. If they depended on the governor for the outcome of a court case, for land distribution, or to avoid conscription into the army or other public services, they wanted to pay their taxes to him, not to another person or office. They rejected the project of separating state functions pushed by the Cáceres regime. Instead, they embraced a model of concentrating powers in one hand. As Nelson Manrique has shown for Cuzco, the governors in turn relied on the traditional indigenous authorities, elected or designated annually by their communities, to carry out the tax collection.[47]

These communal authorities, also known as *varayoqs* (Quechua for "staff bearers"), carried out functions of mediation between the governors and the peasant population. They organized the recruitment of men for communal tasks (such as garbage collection, messenger, or jail guard), or for other local public works projects. These communal offices constituted the last refuge of the ancient lineages of ethnic lords, who found themselves in an ever more degraded situation.[48]

The subprefect-governor pair faced one particular problem when they took charge of tax collection again. If the governor truly was the linchpin of the tax collection campaigns, then he should receive some compensation for his efforts. Recall that this officer did not formally receive any salary from the government. The prefect of Junín, José Rodríguez, complained about the lack of incentives to serve as governor:

> Citizens of well-known competence and social rank should occupy the offices of governor and deputy governor because they are charged with carrying out superior orders. The ones that are

> qualified refuse such an office as it imposes heavy responsibilities; however, the same office is sought after by unscrupulous citizens seeking personal profit, undertaking speculations that become known to the authorities after it is too late.[49]

Under the circumstances of postwar penury, it was impossible for the national treasury to pay a regular salary to the almost 1,000 governors serving throughout the republic. A modest yearly salary of a 1,000 soles (equivalent to that of an army captain) would have meant an expenditure of nearly one million soles, about one-fifth of the republic's budget, and almost half of the direct taxes to be collected in the departments. Under these circumstances it was hoped that the social prestige of the office would be a form of compensation. It was also well known that the closeness to the district's residents and knowledge of their resources provided governors with the possibility of acquiring—informally or even illegally—tangible benefits that the fiscal system could not extend.

In the past, one benefit had been the retention of the collected taxes for several months before delivering them to the treasury.[50] This ended during the period of the apoderados fiscales, whom the governors were supposed to help but from whom they received nothing in return. When the subprefects reassumed the responsibility of tax collection and handed the actual work over to the governors, the latter were in a position to negotiate retention of the legal commission of 4 percent (6 percent in the case of contribución personal) since they had physical control of the taxes. Such negotiations over commissions must have led to severe tensions with subprefects.

The governors received other benefits, such as control over specific lands set aside for the authorities by the communities and "free services" (corvée labor drafts) of local residents. For example, in the department of Puno, these lands were called *aynas* or *yanasis.* They probably represented the legacy of the ancient custom of leaving specific plots of land for the use of the *curacas* of *ayllus* or communities. In 1888, the subprefect of Puno, Octavio Diez Canseco, explained that in districts "where these plots of land do not produce a considerable income a sensible person will not assume the governorship; it is therefore necessary to accept the incompetent services of sincere simpletons for this office."[51]

Corvée labor services consisted of work the local peasant population was supposed to perform under the rubric of "civil tasks" or service: bridge building, repair of roads or public squares, but also service as messenger, assistant to the governor as *alcalde vara,* constable or community councilor. It could also include service on ad hoc police forces put together by a governor to pursue bandits or other types of "outlaws."[52] But local authorities did not limit themselves to such quasi "legal" services. Following long-established custom, they used the peasants to work the yanasis plots or on purely personal business ventures. Some of the most persistent and forceful attacks against the custom of corvée labor services came from the pioneers of *indigenismo,* who exaggerated its horrors in order to eradicate the practice.

Admittedly, it could prove difficult at times for the governors and their deputies to distinguish between personal and official business. For example, if in order to attend an official duty the governor had to neglect his planted fields, was it legal for him to rely on corvée laborers to avoid crop losses? Such dilemmas must have occurred frequently. Let us not forget that the office of governor itself was of a "civil" nature (just as the corvée labor services), without any budgeted police support, or, in all likelihood, any reimbursement for office expenses. From the governor's perspective, it seemed only fair to receive help, free of charge, from the residents of his district for the fulfillment of his duties.[53]

However, in the postwar period, with the influx of liberal and positivist ideas in Peru, new and exotic notions about governance spread among the social groups ruling the country.[54] One notion was that despite the abysmally different social and economic conditions under which the citizens of the republic lived, all Peruvians should be equal under the law. Therefore, no one should be obligated to work for free. The accusing finger was pointed toward the local authorities, judges, and the parish priests of the interior. Witness, for example, the terse condemnation of "the trinity that brutalizes the Indian: the priest, the judge, and the governor," hurled against the local elites by Manuel Gonzalez Prada.[55] A supreme decree of October 15, 1887, prohibited the occupation of Indians in corvée labor drafts to which the other citizens of a district were not also subjected, "an abusive custom that violates existing regulations."[56] Although the decree remained somewhat ambiguous, since it did not expressly prohibit corvée labor services for the private benefit of local authorities, it was employed to attack such abuses. In this way it contributed to growing condemnation of the corvée labor services in public opinion, stiffening the resistance of peasants to fulfill such obligations, and even inhibiting some local authorities from demanding them.

With the "ideal of justice" served and the humanitarian feelings of the Lima elite satisfied, a troubling question arose at this juncture. Who would still want to be a governor, with all the office's onerous duties, but without the customary benefits? Because of such maladjustments, the prefects complained about having to depend on illiterate governors and justices of the peace in the districts. "With such qualifications, they can hardly carry out their duties based on highly complex laws, such as that on interior organization of the republic, the organic law of the municipalities, the regulations about the justices of the peace, and others that require an advanced knowledge in jurisprudence to understand their goals and objectives."[57]

THE JUNTAS DEPARTAMENTALES IN ACTION AND THE REVOLUTION OF 1895

Without benefits for the governors and without bonds posted by the subprefects, it did not take long to prove that the return to the old tax collection system—the "hawk in the chicken coop" model—was a complete failure as well. In August of 1893, congress transferred the responsibility of collecting taxes to the juntas departmentales.[58] That same year, congress, already on a collision course with the president, passed a law excluding the prefects from the presidency of the juntas, which became more autonomous from the government. There would no longer be apoderados fiscales accountable to the central government, but tax collectors appointed by and responsible to the juntas departmentales, who, in turn, would answer to the central government.[59]

Small wonder that this system of tax collection failed as well. The means at the juntas' disposal were no more effective than those of the apoderados fiscales or the subprefects. In fact, the new legal provisions merely reflected the breakdown of the alliance that earlier had supported the Cacerist regime, and the open battle now raging between the executive and legislative branches of government. The republic's interior administration had never been as underfinanced as it was in 1893 and the following years.[60] The situation was becoming unsustainable. The Cacerist regime, in power since the end of the civil war in December 1885, had tried every possible solution to advance its program of fiscal decentralization, the linchpin of its project to "regenerate" the republic: apoderados fiscales, subprefects, juntas departamentales. Retaining the subprefects and governors as tax collectors seemed to be the most effective approach. But this solution was also the one most reviled by the modernizing ideas publicized by the *civilistas* who had passed to the ranks of the opposition in 1892. It implied that these authorities would continue to seek compensation through illicit means. In practical terms, any idea of reviving the office of cacique, the ethnic lordships and their alliance with the state that had assured tribute collection during the colonial era seemed hardly feasible. More than six decades had passed since the formal abolition of the caciques and those who held on to the vestiges of this ancient Andean institution enjoyed little support and prestige in the 1890s. Moreover, such a project would automatically raise the most determined opposition of all those groups in the country who deemed themselves "modern" and "progressive": the urban elites, intellectual groups of various tendencies, and even sectors within the Catholic Church and the military.

The confusion and paralysis that befell the "reconstruction" project became more apparent as a consequence of the global economic crisis after 1893 when prices for Peru's export commodities declined. The contraction of foreign trade led to diminished government revenues, by now highly dependent on customs collections. The subsequent decrease of public expenditures worsened the crisis. When Nicolás de Piérola organized his *montoneras* (irregular troops) in mid-1894, to launch a national uprising against the Cacerist regime, the fiscal crisis had spread from the departmental treasuries of the interior to the budget of the national government.[61] The success of Piérola's revolution in March of 1895 consequently brought down an already weakened and confused regime. The Cacerists had failed to find an intermediate position that could bridge their initial democratic and decentralist aspirations with the archaic, authoritarian and terribly impoverished reality that confronted them.

The Cacerist project thus unleashed a conflict between two distinct political cultures then vying for dominance in the country: that of the enlightened Limeño elite pursuing its project of constructing a "republican" order inspired by idealized Europe and North America;[62] and that of the people in the provinces especially of the Andean interior who conceived of the concept of good governance (*buen gobierno*) primarily as an adeqaute exchange of services between the elites and popular groups, rather than a system controlled by faceless bureaucrats. Once in power, the triumphant Piérola resolved the conflict between democratic and fiscal objectives by abolishing the contribución personal, the principal source of income (at least on paper) for the departmental treasuries. The juntas departamentales remained in charge of collecting local taxes and fees. Salaries of political authorities, police forces, provincial judges, and their court employees did not have to be defrayed any longer by the ever slimmer revenues of the departmental juntas, but reverted to the central state's responsibility. In the following years, the national treasury's income grew sharply because of revitalized export trades and new or increased sales taxes on tobacco, alcohol, opium, and salt.

Although the juntas departamentales now had considerably diminished responsibilities, their performance in collecting the remaining local taxes was still "not satisfactory," as Minister of the Treasury J.V. Larrabure wrote in 1900. Many departments had failed to send their annual accounts, and among those that had sent them, tax collection was less than half of projected revenues.[63] In 1906, the collection of departmental taxes was finally entrusted to the Compañia Nacional de Recaudación, which had been founded in Lima a decade earlier with private and public funds. The problem was thus resolved through an entirely centralist solution. Now that tax collection was entirely removed from the responsibilities of local authorities, these ceased to come from the ranks of the military, and began to be recruited from the local elite. All sides were able to claim a victory of sorts: the Lima elite achieved the separation between political and fiscal administration in the provinces and districts, the regional elites in the interior came to control the prefectures, and the rural population successfully threw off the burden of ancien regime taxes, which it perceived as prejudicial. An ever more powerful centralism raging beyond control was the price paid for such "triumphs of modernity."

NOTES

1. I would like to thank Nils Jacobsen for comments on a previous version of this chapter; translated from Spanish by Robert Sanchez and Nils Jacobsen.

2. On the history of Peruvian centralism see Planas, *La descentralización,* and Zas Friz, *La descentralización ficticia.*

3. By 1879 there were 17 prefects, about 100 subprefects, 1,000 governors, and 5,000 deputy governors in the entire country.

4. Use of military officers as political authorities saved the government money, since, by law, no one was allowed to draw more than one public salary.
5. On the importance of local authorities for Ramón Castilla's political system during the 1850s, see McEvoy, *La utopía republicana,* chap. 1.
6. See the "Ley de Organización Interior de la República" of Jan. 17, 1857, in Aranda, *La Constitución,* 73–87. This law has not been repealed up to the present, even though many of its provisions have changed; cf. Zas Friz, *La descentralización fictícia,* 89.
7. Cf. Ardant, "Financial Policy."
8. Hünefeldt, "Poder y contribuciones" and "Contribución indígena"; Peralta, *En pos del tributo;* and Contreras, "Estado republicano"; according to Hünefeldt, tax collection served as the basis of the commercial system in the interior provinces; see her "Contribución indígena," 538–48.
9. Rodríguez, *Estudios financieros,* 250.
10. On fraudulent tax collections and theft of taxes during the War of the Pacific, see the report by U.S. Minister, dispatch no. 142, Aug. 20, 1886, National Archives and Records Administration, U.S. Diplomatic Correspondence, microfilm T52, role 43.
11. Contreras, "La descentralización fiscal," 221–22.
12. Dancuart and Rodríguez, *Anales,* 17:194-A, and 18:152.
13. Cámara de Diputados, *Diario de debates, 1886,* 229.
14. *Reglamento de Apoderados Fiscales,* Dec. 20, 1886, 276.
15. The average salary of a midlevel civil servant was 1,000 soles annually (depending on the specific province, a subprefect might earn 1,440 soles annually).
16. Hünefeldt, "Contribución indígena," 537.
17. Dancuart and Rodríguez, *Anales,* 18:413.
18. See Silva, *Legislación,* 303 ff.
19. Dancuart and Rodríguez, *Anales,* 18:436a.
20. Cf. annual report by the prefect of Ayacucho for 1890, Biblioteca Nacional del Perú [hereinafter BNP], MS D5564/1890.
21. The subprefect of the fairly affluent province of Tarma collected 7,000 soles in taxes each semester and earned a premium of 280 soles; after collection expenses, he was reportedly left with nothing; BNP, MS D3978/1888, Memoria del Prefecto de Junín, José Rodríguez y Ramírez, June 1888.
22. Cf. annual report by the prefect of Apurímac, Heraclio Fernández, for 1892, BNP, MS D4581/1892, suggesting decline of this practice.
23. Antonio Zapatel to Director de Gbo., Jan. 10, 1886, BNP, MS D3852/1886.
24. Camara de Diputados, *Diario de debates, 1887,* 609.
25. Mallon, *Peasant and Nation,* 216 ff.
26. BNP, MS D4509/1893, Memoria del Prefecto de Ica, Dec. 31, 1892.
27. BNP, MS D4507/1892, Memoria del Prefecto Felipe Ruíz, June 15, 1892.
28. Antero Aspíllaga, Minister of Finance, to F. Denegri, Minister of Government, Nov. 18, 1887, BNP MS D8654/1887.
29. BNP MS D3891/1886, Memoria del Prefecto del Cuzco, Nicanor Somocurcio,

May 19, 1886, and MS D8460/1888, Prefecto de Huancavelica, Tomás Patiño, al Director de Gobierno, July 14, 1888.

30. In the national budget for 1890, total police forces in the country included 907 gendarmes (on average 9 per province) and 1,734 civil guards (not mounted), concentrated in the larger urban centers; Archivo General de la Nación [hereinafter AGN-P], H-6-0857, Anexos, 1890.

31. Prefect of Lambayeque, Pedro Ugarteche, to Director de Gbo., Chiclayo, Aug. 23, 1887, BNP, MS D4022/1887; BNP, MS D7171/1887.

32. Thurner, *From Two Republics,* 118–19.

33. For a case from Chota province, see *El Comercio* (Lima), March 14, 1888.

34. BNP, MS D4581/1892, Memoria del Prefecto de Apurímac, Heraclio Fernández, Nov. 1890–May 1892.

35. For an example of hostility against local authorities, see the case of the Castrovirreyna rebellion of 1887–88, BNP, MS D7171/1887, Apoderado Fiscal, Emilio Lozano, to prefect of Huancavelica, Dec. 2, 1887, and prefect of Huancavelica to Director de Gbo., Dec. 8, 1887.

36. On the rise of the modern treasury system in Europe, see Ardant, "Financial Policy."

37. Nils Jacobsen, personal communication, suggested comparison with Bourbon regime.

38. BNP, MS D4558/1887, prefect of Puno to Director of Gbo., June 16, 1887.

39. The ministry of finance tried to combat this practice, as well as the use of customs revenues for departmental expenses, apparently with little effect.

40. Octavio Diez Canseco, subprefect of Puno, May 30, 1888, BNP, MS D4569/1888.

41. Subprefect of Sandia, Bruno Lazo, July 18, 1887, BNP, MS D4240/1887.

42. Julio Arguedas to prefect of Puno, July 26, 1887, BNP, MS D4240/1887.

43. BNP, MS D4581/1892, report by prefect of Apurímac, Heraclio Fernández.

44. Guerrero, "Curagas," 343–49, suggested for the region of northern Quito that the lineage groups of the caciques often filled republican governorships; there is less evidence of this for Peru in the period studied here.

45. See statement by José Rodríguez y Ramírez, prefect of Junín, June 1888, BNP, MS D3978/1888.

46. AGN, H-6-1416; Cámara de Diputados, *Diario de Debates, 1886,* 229.

47. Manrique, *Yawar Mayu,* 152–54, 170–71; for the period before the abolition of *contribución de indígenas* in 1854, see Thurner, *From Two Republics,* 36–39; see also Guerrero, "Curagas," 343–49.

48. Cf. Guerrero, "Curagas," 349–58.

49. BNP, MS D3978/1888, report by prefect of Junín. José Rodríguez y Ramírez, June 1888.

50. Hünefeldt, "Poder y contribuciones," 385, 391.

51. BNP, MS D4569/1888, report by subprefect of Puno, Octavio Diez Canseco, May 30, 1888.

52. Manrique, *Yawar Mayu,* 152–56; for an interpretation of these services as a "compact" between communities and the state to safeguard communal lands, see Jacobsen, *Mirages,* 275–76.
53. See the annual report by the prefect of Apurímac, Colonel Heraclio Fernández, for 1892, BNP, MS D4581/1892.
54. Cf. Forment, "La sociedad civil," 202–30.
55. Gonzalez Prada, "Discurso en el Politeama [1888]," in Gonzalez Prada, *Pájinas libres,* 55.
56. *El Comercio* (Lima), Jan. 16, 1888.
57. Annual report by the prefect of Apurímac, Heraclio Fernández, for 1892, BNP, MS D4581/1892.
58. Silva, *Legislación,* 303 ff.
59. Ibid., 296 ff.
60. In 1893, all juntas departamentales collected only 57 percent of the budgeted taxes; the following two years must have been even worse due to the civil war and the chaos in departmental finances, although information is lacking.
61. McEvoy, *La utopía republicana,* 342.
62. "Republican" in the sense that McEvoy has developed it in several studies, see especially ibid.
63. Report of Minister Larrabure about the *Cuenta Nacional* for 1899, AGN-P, H-6-0958.

"UNDER THE DOMINION OF THE INDIAN"

RURAL MOBILIZATION, THE LAW, AND REVOLUTIONARY NATIONALISM IN BOLIVIA IN THE 1940S

Laura Gotkowitz

In 1945, Bolivia's National Congress debated one of the most interesting if least remembered reform proposals of the country's prerevolutionary era.[1] Termed "special justice," the resolution would have established indigenous juries to conduct oral trials in native languages, in line with local "uses and customs." The measure was proposed on the heels of the 1945 Indigenous Congress—a five-day event that brought together delegates from large estates and communities of every region—and just before one of the most intense cycles of rural revolt in the country's modern history. The reform's sponsor was none other than Hernán Siles Suazo, cofounder of the MNR (National Revolutionary Movement) and future president. Initially, Siles said that the special tribunals should restrict themselves to petty crimes among peasants or Indians (*indígenas*).[2] Towards the end of his congressional address, he suggested that the indigenous tribunals should not only hear crimes among peasants/indígenas but those involving peasants and rural powerbrokers. The "white mestizo," "exploiter of the indian's labor," Siles concluded, must also submit to peasant juries and thus to the "jurisdiction of the national majority."[3]

That the leading member of a party committed to ideals of national unity and incorporation should propose a system of indigenous juries in and of itself is extremely noteworthy. That he did so at the height of indigenous demands for the return of usurped communal land, the reincorporation of evicted *colonos* (labor tenants on haciendas), and an end to abuses by landlords and local authorities makes this proposal all the more compelling. In part, Siles justified the measure with an appeal to an age-old fear of "race war." Continual recourse to ordinary courts by peasants/indígenas often ended in conflicts, he warned. Those conflicts could push the nation to a civil war more destructive than one in an ethnically homogeneous nation because it would be rooted in "racial hatred." Siles also articulated a second compelling reason: he considered the measure for "special justice" a means to fortify the nation.[4] A stronger nation, he implied, would be achieved not only by expanding the state's hispanicizing institutions to rural areas but also via the opposite: by recognizing indigenous language, law, and custom.

Focusing on the proposal for special justice, the 1945 Indigenous Congress, and the rural uprisings that followed the 1946 overthrow of populist military President Gualberto Villarroel, this essay explores the relationship between indigenous political projects and populist state making in the years leading up to Bolivia's 1952 revolution. With special attention to conversations about the law, it first emphasizes the ambivalent but integral connections between the 1940s revolutionary-populist project and indigenous mobilization. The dominant image is that the MNR always embraced an assimilationist project rooted in Hispanicization, private not communal property, and *campesino* not Indian identity. Incorporation was certainly one strategy conceived for establishing a "culture of legality" that would integrate indigenous peoples into state institutions and the national economy.[5] For example, many MNR leaders endorsed an agrarian labor code based on uniform rules and standards for all rural properties. But the MNR's program was flexible and eclectic. In these early years, differentiating the rights of Indians and non-Indians was also considered a viable means to create a modern legal order. In short, tensions between integrationist and anti-integrationist conceptions of the nation typified the MNR populist project initially articulated under Villarroel's short-lived regime (1943–46). The essay attempts to show, secondly, how these tensions in the Villarroel-MNR program, and the regime's ambiguous attention to indigenous rights and guarantees, could become the basis of indigenous leaders' subversive action once Villarroel was overthrown and his promises were negated.

Disputes over indigenous rights and guarantees were a central locus of Bolivia's prerevolutionary political culture. Such contests were not restricted to elite interlocutors but had to contend with interventions by indigenous leaders, in word and action. This fundamental element of the prerevolutionary political terrain has not been fully appreciated. Instead most studies emphasize the assimilationist and/or class-based elements of prerevolutionary populist politics. Anti-oligarchic political projects of the late 1930s and early 1940s did indeed reject segregationist tendencies of Bolivia's exclusionary past and promoted an integrated nation along corporatist lines, partly substituting "social" for "racial" discourse and classification.[6] Rather than a clear transition, however, I suggest that this period of heightened rural and urban mobilization was marked by ongoing tensions and debates over conceptions of rights and race. Many of the most outspoken reform politicians of the 1940s championed productive property owners and fair labor contracts, downplaying the interests of Indian communities, which they sought to modernize. Others, however, supported *indigenista* positions.

Like their counterparts in other Latin American countries, Bolivian indigenistas—intellectuals, lawyers, and politicians—drew on currents common throughout the region but adapted them to their own political realities. In most general terms, indigenismo constitutes a field of dispute over national identity, regional power, and rights which places "Indians" at the center of politics, jurisprudence, social policy, and/or study. A fundamental element concerns the granting of special status to Indians or Indian communities, but such recognition has no univocal meaning. At its heyday (c. 1910–1940s), indigenismo throughout Latin America was marked by a diversity of political positions and modes of racial thinking. Some indigenistas advocated fundamentally integrationist aims, others centered on racial purity.[7] Indigenismo in 1940s Bolivia represented neither extreme. Rather, it was typified by constant vacillation between the endorsement of separation and of incorporation. This was not nostalgia for a purified Inca past, as exemplified by Peru's leading indigenista, Luis Valcárcel. Nor was it necessarily a program for integration without de-indianization, as Mexico's Manuel Gamio advocated. Integration was highly valued by Bolivian indigenistas, but many considered it an impossible or even dangerous goal.

Siles's proposal for a system of indigenous courts typifies Bolivia's ambivalent prerevolutionary indigenismo. An even more powerful instance is the 1945 Indigenous Congress. At this unprecedented gathering, President Villarroel not only promised support for indigenous delegates, he partially endorsed demands for special legal guarantees and explicitly validated community authority structures. From the government's perspective, the overarching goal of the Congress was to institutionalize power in the hands of the state, create a legal order, and incorporate Indians into one national culture. Key members of the governing coalition assumed, however, that culturally differentiated laws and authorities were the most appropriate means to achieve these universalizing ends.

As for indigenistas in Peru and Mexico, education and the modernization of agriculture were crucial state projects for Villarroel and the MNR, the military president's principal ally. Social well-being and the creation of a legal order were equally central goals. If any objective was paramount, it was to extend the state to a rural hinterland viewed as stateless. And in certain respects the countryside was just that. A legal structure—a primary "effect" of the state—did not exist as an abstract formal arrangement in prerevolutionary Bolivia; there was not the slightest illusion that the law existed above social practice, that it stood separately from society as part of the state.[8] Of Villarroel's many projects, the most fundamental was to effect that arrangement, to impose the law on a lawless countryside. The most oft-repeated symptom of unrule was the fact that landlords controlled the courts. Yet the remedy of choice was not so much institutions (courts), or even agents (judges), but the law itself. In a speech to the National Convention, Villarroel claimed that the key goal of his revolution was not to violently transform institutions but to give "juridical form to a constant and gradual transformation of the state, to grant the state more vigor, efficiency, and technical capacity for its many activities."[9] It seems that Villarroel considered the law the most powerful force in society, which he insisted would last even if he himself were killed.[10]

This essay first examines the origins and objectives of the 1945 Indigenous Congress and its relationship with rural political movements. Claims regarding land and "community" did not diminish after the Chaco War with Paraguay (1932–35), as often argued; they remained central to rural mobilization in the 1940s. I attribute the force of such demands to supralocal political networks that linked rural indigenous leaders with urban labor organizations and offices of legal assistance designed, ironically, to direct such claims through state channels. These rural-urban connections were crucial for the circulation—and miscirculation—of ideas about labor, land, "community," and the law. The second section of this essay examines the rebellions that followed the Indigenous Congress. Rather than on labor rights per se, my analysis of the Indigenous Congress and its aftermath places central emphasis on struggles over the law. Dialogues about the law were the terrain where tentative alliances could be forged, and the place where they would unravel.

THE 1945 INDIGENOUS CONGRESS: LAND, LABOR, AND THE LAW

Bolivia's 1945 Indigenous Congress was undoubtedly influenced by indigenista congresses convened during the same period in Mexico and Peru. In contrast to those events, the principal impetus behind the Bolivian assembly was not the state but forceful indigenous movements. Indeed the regime was accused of convening the Indigenous Congress "out of fear."[11] When Villarroel came to power in December 1943, his closest circle of advisors convinced him of the need to sponsor a national congress of Indians.[12] Before the regime actually offered its sponsorship, however, local leaders grouped in the "Bolivian Indigenous Committee" had already begun to plan the Congress. Despite increasing government control, and the inclusion of members of the landowners association (Sociedad Rural) on the organizing committee, the Villarroel regime could not fully suppress the more radical proposals endorsed by indigenous leaders.[13]

If the government's very participation was compelled by the pressures of rural mobilization, once committed, the Villarroel regime used the Congress to promote its own reform program, attract new political allies, and counter political inroads in the countryside made by the leftist opposition. Indeed the Indigenous Congress is forceful evidence of political ties Villarroel and the MNR sought to forge with rural communities in the 1940s. Along with the MNR, this decade saw the rise of two other influential anti-oligarchic parties: the PIR (Partido de la Izquierda Revolucionario) and the POR (Partido Obrero Revolucionario). Of the three, the MNR was the least indigenista; its most closely targeted supporters were mineworkers, urban labor, and the middle class. Through events like the Indigenous Congress and the measure for special justice, it is clear that the MNR also sought rural indigenous support, yet the party's manifestos made no explicit call to mobilize Indians. Individual MNR affiliates provided legal assistance or sought political contacts with indigenous leaders in the 1940s. Right-wing members of the party nevertheless opposed the participation of Indians or peasants in the party's revolutionary actions.[14] In short, the MNR pursued rural indigenous allies in an effort to control a volatile political situation, but that pursuit was fraught with ambivalence and tension.

In agreeing to convene the 1945 Indigenous Congress, Villarroel and the MNR were clearly concerned with regulation and control. The mix of alliance and ambivalence that characterized MNR-Indian relations in the prerevolutionary era militated, however, toward the opposite. Rather than incorporating loyal, dependent allies, the Villarroel-MNR regime buttressed the autonomous agendas of local leaders. Two points should be stressed in this regard. First, the Villarroel regime considered indigenous authorities crucial for the very process of state regulation and control. In his inaugural speech to delegates at the Indigenous Congress, the president not only called caciques and *principales* (indigenous authorities) of "haciendas, communities, and ayllus" his representatives, he entrusted them to keep order and peace.[15]

Second, Villarroel's policies heightened opportunities for such representatives to organize across regions. Villarroel encouraged rural leaders' longstanding requests to authorize their own schools, endorsed the expansion of offices of free legal assistance for indígenas (Oficina Jurídica de Defensa Gratuita de Indígenas), and even offered a slate of favorable decrees. Though the juridical office was designed to bring more independent actions under the purview of the state, it enhanced opportunities for contacts within and between rural and urban leaders. Indeed lawyers affiliated with the institution apparently endorsed some of the key demands advanced by rural leaders. A preliminary program for the Indigenous Congress prepared by two such attorneys argued that the overarching goal should be to incorporate Indians into the national economy and polity. To achieve this end, however, the lawyers called for special legislation that would officially recognize Indian communities, land rights, and authorities (*caciques, jilacatas, alcaldes, curacas*).[16]

Although the Villarroel regime ultimately controlled the official agenda of the Indigenous Congress, it could not manage the *unofficial* agenda such organizational contacts facilitated. Villarroel sought to control the composition of the delegates and even allowed landlords and state authorities to handpick some of them. Nevertheless, many representatives were wellknown leaders who had gained local prestige precisely through continual trips to lobby for local interests in La Paz. Although most of the claims rural delegates brought to the table were not approved, the Indigenous Congress represented a powerful—and for many a threatening—recognition of indigenous authority. The government provided a forum where local leaders could publicize their demands.

Along with rural mobilization, the government's reform initiative, and the MNR's ambivalent quest for allies, urban labor was a crucial element in the genesis of the Indigenous Congress. Two meetings of Quechua-speaking "indígenas" that preceded the more massive 1945 Congress illustrate the interconnections between rural and urban movements. These were convened in 1942 and 1943 with the support of Bolivia's first national labor federation, the CSTB (Confederación Sindical de Trabajadores de Bolivia), and other organizations of workers and students. Both meetings endorsed a worker-peasant alliance, argued that haciendas be taken over by peasants, and demanded that the free services colonos were required to provide for landlords be abolished. In addition, the 1942 event called for a review of communal land boundaries, the principal demand of indigenous leaders in the years between 1910 and 1930.[17] The very idea of holding a national indigenous congress may have even emerged at the first of these encounters between rural indigenous leaders and the national labor federation.[18] There is also evidence that Oruro's local labor federation played a key role in calling for the 1945 Congress.[19]

Labor's role in the genesis of the Indigenous Congress and its emphasis on urban and rural "workers" did not, however, lead to the suppression of indianness as a political identity. The burgeoning labor movements of the 1940s coalesced with and gave new impetus to longstanding struggles by indigenous leaders for land, education, and citizenship. Those earlier movements—the 1920s networks of caciques apoderados—were greatly transformed during the tumultuous Chaco War years, but they were not fully suppressed.[20] One of the most important changes was a far more pronounced integration of rural and urban political networks. Rather than the definitive shift from one distinct project or identity to another, from land to labor or from indio to campesino, post–Chaco War movements merged the very category "worker" with the category "Indian." If hacienda labor grievances became central, community land claims hardly vanished.

The 1945 Indigenous Congress, first and foremost, was the product of significant pressure and ingenuity from individuals who embodied this state of affairs, and who literally shuttled between rural and urban worlds. The earliest concrete instance of preparations for the event was a September 1944 meeting between Villarroel and members of the Comité Indigenal Boliviano. Comprised of fifteen representatives from all over the country, this committee emerged in late 1943. Although sponsored by the Villarroel regime, local leaders were responsible for organizing the group and its activities.[21] The committee's principal spokesperson was Luis Ramos Quevedo, son of a *piquero* (smallholder) from Cochabamba's Valle Bajo and a longtime rural organizer affiliated with Oruro's labor federation (Federación Obera Sindical, FOS).[22] Ramos had been incorporated into the labor federation as a "Secretary of Indigenous Issues." The role he and others like him played—as rural organizers affiliated with labor federations—confirms that the growing rural-urban interface was not simply a top-down process whereby labor organizers or middle-class sympathizers fanned out to rural hamlets in search of new adherents. Instead "rural" leaders were also conduits of "urban" ideas.

Before the Villarroel regime was fully committed to convening the Indigenous Congress, Ramos circulated an "independent newspaper" with a photograph of himself and other members of the Indigenous Committee posed next to Villarroel at the presidential palace, announcing an upcoming Indigenous Congress. This circular apparently alarmed Villarroel, who had only agreed to contemplate the idea of such a congress but not yet offered to sponsor it.[23] Next, and before the government even had a chance to prepare and publicize its own program, the "Bolivian Indigenous Committee" led by Ramos elaborated a twenty-seven-point agenda, which was reprinted in the national press. Of the many demands in this richly detailed program, the most notable include: "That the indian be free, secure in his life and work, and respected the same as everyone; that there be special laws and authorities for the indian; and that there be Committees of lawyers paid by the government to defend the indian." Not coincidentally, the list begins and ends with the longstanding claim that all the land "belong to the indians"—that it be "returned to the Community" and belong to "those who work it . . . the indian."[24]

If controversial demands for land and justice were paramount to the Indigenous Committee's program, there is also a second set of very different claims in the long list: appeals to civility, order, progress, and modernization. The authors offer to "civilize" themselves in exchange for land, respect, and fair wages. Thus the Committee's program interspersed demands for land and labor rights with promises to "serve Bolivia better" through education, sports, military service, and the modernization of agriculture. It urged respect for indigenous cultures while professing love for the patria. It not only requested justice and land but that "male and female indians" be taught the "good customs of the city . . . that the indian be taught Spanish while perfecting the use of native languages . . . be provided with machines and instructed in their use . . . that the state assist with women's and men's change of dress and clothing."

Were such appeals to modernization and national unity instrumental and strategic, designed to appease state authorities obsessed with order and "progress"? Or were they, more than strategic expressions of genuine convictions? It is quite likely that the Indian Committee's very incursion into the national arena masked substantive local differences; disagreements between leaders who favored multiethnic alliances and those who favored autonomy may have been glossed over when particular delegates appealed to state authorities with this majestic synthesis. Such local differences notwithstanding, this particular document clearly reveals points of agreement *and* points of disagreement between local projects and state projects. The program suggests room for convergence but also manifests fundamental differences. Thus it cannot simply be considered an instrumentalist ploy, designed to appease government ears. The authors do not suppress Indianness or communal land claims. Nor do they reject "modernization" or bilingualism in favor of "pure" indigenous cultures. The Bolivian Indigenous Committee requests changes in dress and clothing but does not specify for which contexts or encounters. Was the point to transcend the negativity projected on Indians' clothing—and Indians—by city people?[25] The document is ambiguous, but no irreversible conversion is announced.

As the date of the Indigenous Congress neared, rural strikes intensified and landlords' true and untrue denunciations of subversive activity got louder. In this increasingly tense context, government officials abandoned their support for Luis Ramos Quevedo and identified him as the principal agent of an elaborate antigovernment program. By the end of April 1945, Ramos and five other "agitators" were in jail. The approximately 1,500 rural delegates who attended the May Congress nevertheless arrived expecting a discussion of the demands endorsed and circulated by those jailed leaders. News articles published after the Indigenous Congress confirm that many of those items were in fact discussed—even though they no longer figured in the government's official agenda.

Indeed the final organizing phases can be read as the government's unrelenting effort to reign in the meeting, to control the program, and to manage the composition of the delegates. With regard to the program, the Villarroel regime was successful; it created an official committee, comprised primarily of representatives from government ministries, which drafted and approved a formal agenda. At the Congress itself, four additional committees were convened, each including representatives of colonos and comunarios from all regions. Their recommendations resulted in a series of decrees endorsed by the Villarroel government on the final day of the Congress.[26] These called for the suppression or remuneration of free services rural laborers were required to provide to landowners (mail delivery, weaving, etc.); the abolition of *pongueaje* and *mitanaje* (forced turns of service in the landlords' home); the establishment of schools on rural properties (but with no reference to schools for Indian communities); and the preparation of an agrarian labor code.

The underlying concern of all four measures was the need to bring the law to a lawless countryside. An article in one of the decrees criminalized the fraudulent sale of "copies of legislative initiatives, [and] other dispositions or material containing counterfeit property titles or other propaganda." The consideration here was twofold. Rural leaders were frequently accused of exchanging false property titles for funds—*ramas*—they collected among rural followers. But the measure also criminalized the sale of proposed laws, presumably because they were passed off as real ones. This clause was similarly directed at rural "agitators," but they may not have been the only target. Bolivia's National Congress itself was accused, in April 1945, of selling Indians legalized copies of parliamentary documents registering decisions that benefited them. The chief of the congressional editorial staff indignantly denied the allegation and demanded a full investigation.[27] Even if untrue, the charge reveals the depth of anxieties about the law and what was perceived to be a widespread trafficking in legislative initiatives and property titles.

The majority of the items listed in the Indigenous Committee's twenty-seven-point agenda did not figure in the official program or government decrees. Most notably, the items about land had been eliminated. Indeed an official circular sent to prefects of all departments explicitly stated that there would be no return of communal lands.[28] A close look at the proceedings of the Congress reveals, however, that the question of land was not entirely suppressed. By the time the Indigenous Congress was convened, MNR leaders affiliated with Villarroel had themselves made statements favoring some kind of land reform. Specific proposals they advocated in congressional sessions of 1938 and 1944 were defeated, largely due to protests by the Sociedad Rural.[29] Villarroel also stressed the importance of land, and in certain contexts he focused special attention on the usurpation of communal property.[30] At the Indigenous Congress itself, Hernán Siles, speaking in the name of the MNR party, declared that "the land should belong to those who work it."[31] This is precisely what the Bolivian Indigenous Committee claimed. After the Congress was finally convened, the minister of labor reported that the delegates had presented numerous points of importance, including the demand for "the return of lands that, according to the colonos, have belonged to them since the colonial era and had been seized from them by the landlords."[32] To conclude that the Indigenous Congress only considered labor issues, as most studies do, overlooks these subtle but influential subtexts.[33]

Given the demands and expectations of the delegates, the four formal decrees were fairly modest gains. Even so, they inspired the rage of the landowners association. Some landlords sought to intimidate delegates, block the decrees, and punish so-called agitators.[34] The same labor requirements as always continued to be imposed on many properties, now simply under different names. New and old authorities charged with implementing the provisions of the Congress failed to do so. Bolivia's National Congress could not settle on an agrarian labor code, as the Indigenous Congress stipulated. Nor did it formally ratify the four presidential decrees.[35] The National Congress did not possess effective mechanisms to enforce them anyway. Thus the law remained ever more forcefully in the hands of landlords and local authorities. There was, however, one significant shift. Delegates returned with the knowledge of more favorable decrees and the president's explicit backing. In at least one case, and probably in others, a colono was ordered by the minister of government to deliver duplicates of the new rulings to local authorities.[36] Of course making colonos direct conduits of the law wholly contradicted the institutionalizing mission of the Indigenous Congress.

Up to a point, the government itself had acknowledged that the decrees were not particularly new or revolutionary. The articles outlawing servitude, for example, were presented as the fulfillment of Bolívar's 1825 edict. What made Villarroel's proclamations historic was the locus of enunciation. Their force resided not so much in the content but in where and to whom they were announced and who would be authorized to convey them. In theory, the decrees were to be transmitted to and through representatives of the state. If effectively established, such mechanisms of communication between local and national authorities might have ensured greater governability.[37] But that goal was not achieved. Rather than resolving a perceived crisis of the law by professionalizing, codifying, and institutionalizing legal practice as planned, the Indigenous Congress exacerbated the turmoil by empowering delegates themselves to be agents of the law.

Over the course of the year following the May 1945 Indigenous Congress, sit-down strikes became common on haciendas in many regions, with hacienda colonos themselves trying to enforce compliance with the May decrees.[38] Just as before the Congress, local leaders and "outsiders" were accused of copying and distributing proposed laws and fraudulent land titles.[39] As rural social conflict intensified in the months after the Congress, police presence in the countryside was greatly augmented.[40] It was in this context of political agitation and expectation that Bolivia's National Congress debated Siles Suazo's proposal for "special justice."

First it should be said that this unusual measure breathed only a very short life. Initially criticized, temporarily approved, and then repeatedly modified, it was finally transferred to the "Commission on Indigenous Affairs," which amounted to a relatively swift legislative death. Many practical objections were raised, about jurisdictional limits, for example, and whether court resolutions should be in writing. Whether or not customary justice violated human rights, a key criticism of similar measures proposed in the 1990s, was not an issue then. Instead the obstacle that most thoroughly buried this unprecedented measure for indigenous justice was the inability to decide whom it was for: Indians? Peasants? Indigenous peasants? The indigenous race? Indian and mestizo peasants? A race, or a class? The National Congress could not agree on terms.

There had been legislative proposals for special laws and even a Patronato Indígena along Peruvian lines during the early twentieth century. To a certain extent, Siles's recommendation resembled those straightforwardly protective and paternalistic plans. The 1945 measure for special justice departed from the earlier model, however, by appealing not simply to special protections but to indigenous language, law, and custom. At least implicitly, debates over the initiative also recognized that indianness was not confined to rural spheres but was very much an urban identity. Indeed, the blurring of racial/spatial boundaries made it impossible for lawmakers to come to any agreement about just whom special justice would be for.

If both law and society had changed dramatically, debates about the 1945 proposal reveal that its backers had not shed the paternalistic vision that motivated their 1920s counterparts. Like 1920s proposals, the 1945 measure for special justice ultimately presumed an indigenous population that lived outside the law, beyond the state's courts and decrees. It presumed that Indians were innocent, uneducated beings who needed protection from mestizos and other "urban dangers." The debate over Siles's tabled proposal can thus be summed up as a forward-looking recognition of indigenous rights, and a backward glance at special protection. For Siles could simultaneously affirm indigenous justice and praise colonial law; he said at one point that the laws of colonialism were superior even to those just passed by the Indigenous Congress. And one of his colleagues could declare Bolivia an indigenous nation but lament the lack of unity, the inability to "mix" Indians with whites and mestizos. And Siles could recognize indigenous authorities but slip and call their historic encounter with the president a "Peasant Congress."[41] The recognition of indianness—in the legal realm—was fraught with tension. Indians should be bearers of the law; indigenous language, law, and custom should be elements of the nation's legal order. If such ideals were to be realized, however, Indians had to be people safely secluded in rural realms, "remade" in their "racial proper place."[42] Along similar lines, the "Juridical Office for Indígenas" not only sought to eliminate abuses by local authorities but to prevent the displacement of Indians to cities.[43] Indigenista thinking of the forties was in flux. "Incorporation" was a goal, but a vague and distant one often combined with a call for rural seclusion. As some legislators implicitly acknowledged, the latter was not only a new mode of colonization but utterly unrealizable.

"EVERYONE WILL BE COMUNARIOS": THE POST-1945 REBELLIONS

The period of acute political conflict and violence that followed the 1945 Indigenous Congress is best known for the brutal lynching of Villarroel during an urban uprising in July 1946. Ensuing governments insisted that peasants did not have the constitutional right to organize, and landlords refused to heed the murdered president's decrees. In addition to this conservative backlash, Villarroel's death triggered a cycle of rural rebellions. Spanning the departments of Cochabamba, Chuquisaca, La Paz, Oruro, and Tarija, and heterogeneous in their methods and demands, the uprisings were uniformly and aggressively repressed.[44] One of the most important was the Ayopaya uprising of February 1947. Ayopaya province, located in the department of Cochabamba, included a small number of Indian communities (*comunidades originarias*) but was essentially dominated by large estates.[45] Centered in the Hacienda Yayani, the Ayopaya rebellion encompassed numerous other properties in the area and reportedly involved anywhere from three to ten thousand individuals. In fundamental ways, the rebellion was linked to wider disputes over the law engaged by the Indigenous Congress and the measure for indigenous tribunals. The Ayopaya rebels not only appropriated and redefined the state's rhetoric, they enacted their own vision of justice and the law.[46]

Drawing on extensive oral histories and transcripts from the trial of the rebellion's leaders, Dandler's and Torrico's important study demonstrates the close connections between the Ayopaya rebellion, the 1945 Indigenous Congress, the decrees against pongueaje, and Villarroel's personal commitment to indigenous rights and justice.[47] Focusing on the trial, I develop a somewhat different interpretation that links an imaginary law for revolution with Villarroel's real decrees against labor obligations. Witness after witness in the Ayopaya trial makes reference to laws and decrees. Many recall leaders traveling to La Paz in search of guarantees against pongueaje or authorizations to create schools, and make allusions to Villarroel and the Indigenous Congress. They identify the leaders of the uprising as individuals who attended the Congress, or those who went to La Paz in search of "guarantees." Their references to the "law" nevertheless center on a rather surprising and certainly implausible thing: a law passed by a revolutionary government that called for the murder of landlords, the redistribution of all the land, and that everyone become comunarios.

The trial transcript indicates that a most immediate catalyst of the rebellion was landlords' refusals to comply with Villarroel's decrees against service obligations. Two of the principal leaders, Hilarión Grájeda and Antonio Ramos, painstakingly obtained government "guarantees" to enforce those decrees, to no avail. A second, critical factor was an apparently chance meeting between Grájeda, Ramos, and Gabriel Muñoz, the "mineworker comrade," whom Grájeda first met at the 1945 Indigenous Congress.[48] Muñoz reportedly told Ramos and Grájeda that "the press and the authorities had declared civil war in the nation and that an order had been issued to kill all the landlords and that all the land would then be distributed among the indians, because it was the indians' land, and that [the indians] should no longer work on the haciendas."[49] Grájeda and Ramos apparently achieved a very broad diffusion of this striking declaration, for numerous defendants repeated it. Sometimes it was called a law, other times an order, occasionally a rumor. One crucial detail absent in the above rendition appeared in almost every other reference: all the land would be "converted into communities."[50]

Many of the accused linked the "law" they repeatedly invoked with not only political movements and parties but also a government presumed to be in power. Most referenced the MNR, its leader Víctor Paz Estenssoro, or the head of the mineworkers union (FSTMB), Juan Lechín. A few instead mentioned the PIR or the "communists."[51] For some, a party's orders played no role at all; they had acted to revenge *their* president's murder (Villarroel).[52] In its decision, the court fixed responsibility for the uprising on Lechín and Paz Estenssoro. Whether or not the Ayopaya movement was actually linked with the MNR's post-1946 attempted insurrections remains an open question.[53] In either case, the court's ruling clearly fit with the government's broader effort to fully discredit the FSTMB and the MNR.[54] Some of the interrogated did indeed present evidence that "outsiders" had forced them to participate in the uprising.[55] Yet the associations that many witnesses made between political figures and the "law" suggests that the emphasis on external forces was more than coercive cover or even simple evasiveness. The accused were not just hiding behind the MNR, Paz, or Lechín, the "mineworker comrade" (Muñoz) or the Indian "ringleader" (Grájeda). They conjured up a "law" a local leader had described to them or even read from a newspaper. That law merged the official and unofficial agendas of the 1945 Indigenous Congress. It linked decrees against pongueaje with the demand that all the land be returned to the "Community." Such merging of messages is most apparent through loose inference or juxtaposition. For example, witnesses frequently said that the mineworker, Muñoz, told them that "we would all be comunarios, because the laws favor us and were decreed for us and not for the landlords."[56] Another witness explicitly connected the two themes. Asked about the origins of the uprising, he referred to the "law passed last year," which Grájeda had told them about. That law suspended all the services colonos were required to provide for landlords and, he said, meant that "finally we would be comunarios."[57] The force of the law is further evidenced by participants' descriptions of their own actions; even after the attack on the house of the Yayani landlord some said they traveled to Oruro to learn about the laws that might exist in their favor.[58] A letter apparently sent by Grájeda and Muñoz to Juan Lechín (addressed as the "Vice President") substantiates Grájeda's own investment in the law. The letter first denounces failure after failure to heed the decrees against forced services. Then it reports that "luckily it has been publicly decreed that there be revolution against exploitation and misery and because abuses are committed; we have made a revolution in defense of our rights and the truth is that we do not abuse anyone without an order; just because we are blind does not mean that we do not understand what is the order of God and the *current true law* (my italics)."[59]

The Ayopaya trial transcript suggests that a very radical, unreal but palpable edict to make everyone comunarios and all the land a Community was one of the most important, albeit unintended, consequences of the 1945 Indigenous Congress. The similarities between the rebels' claims and the demands of the "Bolivian Indigenous Committee" that spearheaded the Congress are too great to be ignored. Both made the same magnificent request that all the land be returned to the "Community." What did that oft-repeated phrase conjure up? Did the rebels mean communal property, or a community of small property owners? Were their allusions to many communities, or just one? Who were the members?

The trial transcript provides no clarity or consensus about the meaning of such terms, but a few of the declarations give rough clues. Before the 1947 uprising, communities in the Ayopaya region insisted that Villarroel's decrees not only be enforced by existing authorities but implanted their own local officials. One witness said that Mariano Vera, another local leader, told the Indians of the area not to obey the landowners' orders because they were now "under the dominion of the indian."[60] Vera said that they should heed only the alcaldes' commands, as the alcaldes were higher than any other authorities in Ayopaya. He told the Indians "not to obey any authority appointed by law," because he and the other leaders were "primordial authorities," not "ringleaders" but " 'Alcaldes' mayores."[61] An office of colonial origin, the indigenous alcalde was situated both to serve local government—primarily in a judicial capacity—and to represent the community before outside powers.[62] The meaning attributed by Ayopaya's 1940s rebels exceeded both roles: as "primordial" authorities, Vera suggested, alcaldes were both separate from and higher than officials appointed by the state.

In their depositions to the court, landlords, foremen, and the *corregidor* complained that local leaders not only enunciated such claims but enacted them. The rebels had appointed their own alcaldes, and even the state's local representative, the corregidor. The "real" corregidor was only so in name and title; apparently he no longer held any authority.[63] If local power resided in Indians' hands, a few declarations by the accused allotted a clear space for whites' power and property. Antonio Ramos informed participants that a kind of equality of property rights would reign. "We would all be owners of the land, all the goods would be owned in common, in the countryside for the indians and in the town the stores and things for the whites, in common for everyone." This vision apparently had wide support: "It made us all so happy when he said this," one witness testified.[64]

Viewed together with this ritual of justice, the Ayopaya uprising not only represents a struggle against labor abuse and exploitation but a process of political empowerment and confrontation whereby the community substituted its own authorities for the state's local representatives. A second complaint waged by landlords in the year preceding the uprising adds further weight to this interpretation. They not only grumbled about colonos' demand that Villarroel's decrees be fully enforced. Their most forceful gripe was against constant requests that the decrees be publicly recited to the last letter. In short, leaders and followers insisted on the full performative force of the law, that every single stipulation be read to the public in the space of power (town square) by the properly authorized individual. Not only did they demand the new rights granted by Villarroel's decrees, they sought to fix the limits of local power.[65]

The causes of rural unrest in this tumultuous era, and the intellectual origins of the diverse political projects articulated, far exceeded the 1945 Indigenous Congress.[66] But the Congress was a crucial catalyst. It facilitated the transmission of laws, slogans, and prophecies between the government and rural communities; it also increased contact among rural communities themselves. These exchanges, appropriations, and misappropriations between rural and urban, state and nonstate entities were what led indigenous leaders to claim, incorrectly, that their subversive action was the law. The most threatening act, however, may not have been that violent culmination, when landlords and their homes were attacked. Before the rebels of Ayopaya ever took up arms, they insisted on complete affirmation of the law and imposed their own authorities, alcaldes. In doing so, they not only took Villarroel's command to ensure order at its word. They exposed the state's absolute inability to control its own laws, institutions, and lawmakers.

◆ ◆ ◆ ◆ ◆

Over the course of the early twentieth century, both Indians and non-Indians endorsed special protections, institutions, and guarantees, but they did not invoke the same meanings. In the 1920s, government officials explicitly used special rights to maintain or refurbish structures of separation and inequality. In the 1940s, there were more tensions and ambiguities: Some even viewed indigenous rights as a means to unify the nation.[67]

There are many reasons why vacillation between assimilationist and antiassimilationist norms so deeply marked anti-oligarchic political projects of the prerevolutionary era. One crucial factor was precisely the unique strata of indigenous political and intellectual leaders who continuously intervened in the public sphere to contest and define the meanings of citizenship and nationhood.[68] That public sphere had changed and expanded significantly by the 1940s. Powerful public dialogues marked this decade. Greater ideological diversity characterized debates, and many new political entities participated in them. What had been isolated, private conversations between indigenous leaders and elite politicians in the 1920s could now be public discussions convened in national arenas and broadly publicized by the press. In pursuit of competing aims, powerful and not-so-powerful allies endorsed indigenous claims for land and justice to an extent not previously witnessed. As the debate over "special justice" shows, indigenous rights and guarantees, in the 1940s, were clearly a strategy of rule rooted in hierarchical concepts of race. Yet it would be wrong to consider such concepts a tool of domination alone. The language of special rights and guarantees was a multivocal one also engaged by leaders of local resistance.[69] State authorities were patently unable to control the circulation of messages about such rights, even when the state's own institutions, like the Office of Free Legal Defense, were the source. This continuous force of autonomous indigenous mobilization, through which the "effects" of the state were barely visible, is a peculiarity of modern Bolivia. It helps explain why indigenous rights and guarantees were such a powerful impetus, and why some elite politicians thought they could be—had to be—a means of national unity. Bolivian political leaders, in a sense, were also "under the dominion of the indian."

Twentieth-century indigenismo was undoubtedly a paternalistic movement that generally implied the negation of Indian agency. Yet the specific alignment of political forces is what ultimately gives meaning to such doctrines. In 1940s Bolivia, indigenistas sought to control and regulate rural peoples and communities in the interests of "modernization," but they did not manage to suffocate Indian agency. Nor could they simply reinforce images of Indians as illiterate or "backward" beings, as obstacles to "progress." This is not to suggest that indigenista projects such as those advanced in the 1940s affirmed the agency of rural peoples. Indigenista advocates did not evince respect for their right to choose if and how they wished to "modernize." Yet they were unable to completely stifle the public interventions of rural-urban interlopers like Ramos who insisted that indianness was compatible with literacy, legal expertise, technical innovation, and Bolivianness. In its quest for political allies, the Villarroel regime inadvertently publicized these messages and even helped foster Ayopaya's radical call for no landlords, only "communities."

Bolivia's twentieth-century indigenous leaders repeatedly invoked two key terms: the "community" and the "law." The distinct uses of these words attests to competing political codes, visions, and moralities infused by decades of battles and memories. Their recurrence also points to a common field of symbols and images with disputed meanings. This field of interface, between the state and local communities, could be the basis of clever exchange or profound miscommunication.[70] Both things together made it possible for the rebels of Ayopaya to profess the truth of an untrue law. Those two things were also the rebels' undoing.

NOTES

In addition to the participants at the conference on Political Cultures in the Andes, I thank Cristóbal Aljovín, Marisol de la Cadena, Nils Jacobsen, Brooke Larson, Deborah Poole, Cynthia Radding, and Joanne Rappaport for their insightful comments and suggestions on earlier drafts. In the title and in the text, capitalization within quotes follows the Spanish-language original.

1. República de Bolivia, *Redactor de la Convención Nacional de 1945*, La Paz, 2:727–43.

2. Siles used these words interchangeably and maintained that the term "indígena" necessarily referred to "the man who works . . . and lives in the countryside." *Redactor*, 1945, 2:737.

3. Ibid., 743.

4. Ibid., 2:757–58.

5. Comaroff, "Foreword," ix–x.

6. On anti-integrationist thought and policy in Bolivia, see Larson, this volume; on exclusionary principles of Bolivian legal codes, see Barragán, *Indios, mujeres y ciudadanos.*

7. See de la Cadena, *Indigenous Mestizos,* 63–68; Knight, "Racism, Revolution, and Indigenismo"; Mendoza, *Shaping Society,* 49–55; Poole, *Vision, Race, and Modernity,* 182–87; Wade, *Race and Ethnicity,* 32–35.

8. Mitchell, "The Limits," 94.

9. Tcnel. Gualberto Villarroel, *Mensaje a la H. Convención Nacional de 1944* (La Paz, 1944), 61.

10. Dandler and Torrico, "From the National Indigenous Congress," 354.

11. *El País,* May 23, 1945.

12. Lehm and Rivera, *Los artesanos,* 81.

13. Federación Rural de Cochabamba, *Memoria,* 29.

14. Klein, *Bolivia,* 213; Klein, *Parties,* 338–42; Malloy, *Bolivia,* 123–64; Rivera, *Oprimidos,* 73–75; Dunkerley, *Rebellion,* 25–37; Albó, "Andean People," 797–98.

15. *La Razón,* May 11, 1945.

16. *El Nacional,* February 8, 1945.

17. Antezana and Romero, *Los sindicatos,* 86–88, 91–92; *El Nacional,* February 1, 1945; Lehm and Rivera, *Los artesanos,* 81; Choque, "Las rebeliones indígenas," 39–40; U.S. National Archives (USNA), Record Group (RG) 166, Box 48, September 7, 1942.

18. *La Calle,* August 13, 1942, cited in Antezana and Romero, *Los sindicatos,* 86–88.

19. USNA, RG 59, 824.402/2-1545, Thurston to Secretary of State, February 15, 1945, 3.

20. See Rivera, *Oprimidos,* 36–65; Mamani, *Taraqu,* 127–60; Ticona and Albó, *Jesús de Machaqa,* 89–165; Albó, "Andean People," 781–83; and Choque et al., *Educación indígena.*

21. Dandler and Torrico, "From the National Indigenous Congress," 344.

22. Ibid., 341–42; and Rivera, *Oprimidos,* 63.

23. USNA, RG 59, 824.00/4-2345, April 23, 1945; Antezana and Romero, *Los sin-*

dicatos, 102; Dandler and Torrico, "From the National Indigenous Congress," 341–42; see also Choque, "Las rebeliones," 42–43.

24. *El País,* February 16, 1945, 5.

25. Abercrombie, "La fiesta del carnaval," 289–91, 313–14.

26. "Primer Congreso Indígena Boliviano, Recomendaciones y Resoluciones. Acta de la Sesión Preparatoria, Apendice," La Paz, May 10–15, 1945, mimeograph, in USNA RG 59, 824.401/5-3045.

27. Archivo Histórico del Honorable Congreso Nacional (AHHCN), Box 300, Letter from the Jefe de Redacción to the Oficial Mayor de la H. Convención Nacional, April 27, 1945.

28. Choque, "Las rebeliones," 44.

29. C. Whitehead, "Cochabamba Landlords," 44–61; Klein, *Parties,* 284–90.

30. USNA, RG 59, 824.00/4-1145, "Conversation of Members of Embassy Staff with President Villarroel," April 11, 1945.

31. Ibid.

32. *El País,* May 15, 1945.

33. For exceptions, see Rocha, *Con el ojo,* 182–206; and Choque, "Las rebeliones."

34. Thurston to Secretary of State, May 29, 1945, 11, USNA, RG 59, 824.401/5-2945; Dandler and Torrico, "From the National Indigenous Congress," 356–58.

35. Ibid., 360.

36. *Pregón,* June 29, 1945.

37. On local authorities' state linkages, and performative powers of the law, see Guerrero, "The Construction," 586–90.

38. Dandler and Torrico, "From the National Indigenous Congress," 360–61.

39. *El Diario,* September 10, 1946; Oficio contra Virgilio Vargas y otros, Varios, February 14, 1947, Archivo de la Corte Superior de Justicia de Cochabamba (hereafter ACSJC), AG #791, Segundo Partido Penal.

40. Klein, *Parties,* 357–58, 360.

41. *Redactor,* 1945, 2:750–51, 756.

42. de la Cadena, *Indigenous Mestizos,* 66.

43. *El Nacional,* February 8, 1945.

44. Rivera, *Oprimidos,* 66–75; Dunkerley, *Rebellion,* 34; see also Antezana and Romero, *Los sindicatos,* 123–68.

45. Rivera, *Los terratenientes,* 70–72.

46. My analysis draws much inspiration from Sergio Serulnikov's work on collective violence in Northern Potosí. See "Disputed Images of Colonialism" and his chapter in this volume.

47. Dandler and Torrico, "From the National Indigenous Congress."

48. Margarita vda. de Coca vs. Hilarión Grájeda y otros, ACSJC, AG# 1202, Segundo Partido Penal, Varios Delitos, 1947, Tercer Cuerpo, fols. 89–89v (incomplete trial record); on Grájeda's previous activities, see also Archivo de la Prefectura de Cocha-

bamba (APC), Expedientes, "Hilarión Grájeda et al, indígenas de Yanani, al Sr. Ministro del Trabajo y Previsión Social," 1942.

49. ACSJC, AG# 1202, fol. 7.

50. Ibid., fols. 15–15v, 72–72v, 85v, 103v, 107.

51. Ibid., fols. 7v, 10, 73, 84, 91, 103v–104.

52. Ibid., fols. 106v–107, 108.

53. Gordillo, *Campesinos,* 204–5.

54. On such efforts, see L. Whitehead, "Bolivia," 141–42; on mineworkers-MNR relations, see also Dunkerley, *Rebellion,* 6–18, Klein, *Parties,* 373–76.

55. ACSJC, AG# 1202, fol. 10v, for example.

56. Ibid., fol. 85v.

57. Ibid., fols. 109–109v.

58. Ibid., fols. 152–152v.

59. Ibid., fol. 101v.

60. Ibid., fols. 189v–190.

61. Ibid., fol. 190.

62. Thomson, "Colonial Crisis," 53–62; Rasnake, *Domination,* 76–80.

63. ACSJC, AG# 1202, fol. 192v.

64. Ibid., fol. 179v.

65. Ibid., fol. 191–192v; Serulnikov, "Disputed Images," 218; on juridical rituals, see also Langer, "Andean Rituals"; and Rivera, *Oprimidos.*

66. On continuities between rebellions before and after the Congress, see Gordillo, *Campesinos,* 194–209.

67. *Redactor,* 1945, 2:750–51.

68. Similar movements were fully suppressed in Peru by the 1920s; see de la Cadena, *Indigenous Mestizos,* chap. 2.

69. Comaroff, "Legality, Modernity, and Ethnicity," 269.

70. See Abercrombie, *Pathways,* xxiv, 416, 422.

PART TWO

ETHNICITY, GENDER, AND THE CONSTRUCTION OF POWER

EXCLUSIONARY STRATEGIES AND THE STRUGGLE FOR CITIZENSHIP

Issues of ethnicity and gender have had a powerful impact in Andean political cultures, especially during periods of crisis and transition. In fact, the central Andean countries are among the most "ethnicized" nations in Latin America, easy game for stereotyping or essentializing about "Indians" or "dark-skinned masses" by foreign interlocutors and domestic elite intellectuals and politicians. It is of course true that for centuries the majority population of Ecuador, Peru, and Bolivia have been native Andeans and that of Colombia mestizos or mulattos. But what this meant, how they were defined and defined themselves, how they intervened in the economy, in politics, and the cultural sphere shifted between epochs, as well as between states and even regions.

Recent anthropological research has demonstrated that ethnicity is always produced in fields of power. The cultural delimitation of the referent group from the "other" nearly always serves to establish or fortify exclusive rights to material and symbolic goods. It relies on state laws or decrees, public rituals and representations, violence, or appeal to customary rights. The referent group and the "other" have different access to such laws, rights, rituals, or violence. Such an understanding of ethnicity also presupposes that it is not an "essential" category—i.e., it does not inhere unchangeably in individuals and their descendents. The discourses, norms, and practices of ethnic differentiation can be produced on the local level, in the nation-state or internationally (e.g., through colonialism, neocolonialism, or imperialism). The categorization schemes for ethnicity and race deployed on these levels can vary significantly. The fixation of such categories by Latin American nation-states through tax lists, censuses, immigration laws, or laws aimed at protecting subordinated groups thus has often been at variance with the understanding and practices concerning ethnic differences at the local level.

The salience of nationally defined ethnic or racial orders increased in Latin America between the 1880s and the mid-twentieth century, parallel to the strengthening of the nation-states themselves. The rising concern among dominant groups over national unity and effectiveness found expression in elite projects aiming for ethnic/racial homogenization. But, as the chapters in this section make clear, *mestizaje* was viewed more skeptically in the central Andean nations than in Colombia. Moreover, throughout Latin America the relative hardness or flexibility of ethnic hierarchies continued to be influenced through specific local power, socioeconomic, and demographic structures. In regions where a closed, self-defined white dominant group had exercised all-encompassing authority for many decades or even centuries over broad majorities of subordinated ethnic groups, as in the Chocó region of western Colombia with its slave-based gold-mining complex, or the southern Peruvian highlands with their harsh large landholding and commercial regime incorporating indigenous peasants, ethnic hierarchies remained more closed. The situation tended to be different in rural areas where neither slavery nor hacienda complexes with harsh peonage regimes had shaped power constellations; and of course it was different in the cities. Here mestizaje had been an ongoing process for centuries, and persons belonging to subordinated ethnic groups had a greater chance, on an individual basis, to improve their social position (through education, and the labor and housing markets) and participate in the political process.

But what did mestizaje mean within specific regional or national power constellations (or racial orders), and how did those pulled into the vortex of biological or cultural miscegenation experience it? It was long seen as a solvent overcoming or at least diminishing rigid oppression or exclusion based on race especially when compared to the polarized U.S. race order. But in recent years critical race theory has castigated the "myth of the mestizo" as a particularly insidious white elite strategy designed to erase the cultural identity and difference of blacks and indigenous peoples and to undertake their cultural whitening under the guise of constructing a race-neutral national community. According to Carol Smith, mestizaje comprises three distinct processes: "1) the social process . . . used to procreate, socialize and position people of mixed biological heritage . . . ; 2) the personal identification of an individual or community . . . with mestizo communities or the mestizo national subject . . . ; and 3) a political discourse in which people argue about the racial, cultural, and political character of the mestizo in relation to other identity types."[1] For Smith these three processes are interlinked and have never appeared in isolation from each other in Latin American historical formations. Yet it is precisely the different contextual meanings, subaltern strategies, and elite projects in and through which distinct social, identity, and political processes of mestizaje occur that produces such varied outcomes in terms of power and political participation.

While never totally transcending racialized power hierarchies, there are numerous cases in Andean history in which subaltern groups embraced mestizo identities even when the white elites excoriated "mixed races." There are also cases, as in twentieth-century Cuzco, where mestizos insisted on indigenous cultural identities while fully participating in the "whitened" public and political spheres. And there are cases—especially in cities but even in rural settings, as Margarita Garrido demonstrates—where mestizos and mulattos became vital participants, together with blacks and/or native Andeans, in "plebeian cultures" that contested elite norms and exclusionary rule. Clearly mestizaje has frequently been employed in the political arena by Hispanized elites as a tool to denigrate cultural otherness and to disempower nonwhite majorities. Yet it carried within it the potential—at times even the reality—of destabilizing exclusive power structures and pursuing rights and political projects significantly different from those of the Hispanized elites.

It is now a commonplace of theoretically informed literature on social, cultural, and political histories of Latin America that the three dimensions of ethnicity/race, class, and gender at times overlap and at times conflict with each other. But they always exert mutual influences in the renegotiations of power. Thus the representation of gender has routinely been shaped by the ethnic/racial and class positions of the specific groups of men and women being represented and of those doing the representing. Elite constructs of women during the era of nation-state formation have clustered around two ideal types: the maternal woman, heavily influenced by Catholicism (especially the Marian cult), and the emancipated woman, with equal access to rights and privileges in society. It appears that the maternal ideal type has been particularly powerful and long lasting in the Andean societies. Throughout the nineteenth century and the first half of the twentieth, liberal, nationalist, and even many socialist movements have tended to assign distinct roles for women, defined around notions of purity and the moral function of raising children to become upright citizens. In combination with class and ethnic/race hierarchies this has meant that popular (lower-class, dark-skinned) women needed to be reformed, controlled, and given limited rights until they were deemed to fully embody that morally pure, maternalist ideal. The chapter by Derek Williams discusses such an ideologically hybrid instrumentalization of women for the creation of an "Ecuadorian Catholic people" by Garcia Moreno.

At the same time, different women from different class and ethnic backgrounds fought for expanded rights in distinct arenas of activities, at times utilizing elite gender models, and at times subverting them. Just as in the case of ethnic/racial hierarchies, distinct notions of honor or respect could be employed to establish arenas of power or influence for lower-class or Indian, mulatto, mestizo, and black women in local settings and social networks. And just as it has proved too simple to construct a linear model for the Andes moving from a corporatist caste society to one overwhelmingly ordered by class distinction, there was no linear change from a model of subjected maternal women to emancipated women. Different classes and ethnic groups of women experienced redefinitions of their power and inclusion in specific arenas (the household, business, the public sphere) and nationally and locally distinct historical conjunctures.

Margarita Garrido's chapter focuses on the negotiation of rights and privileges of the "free men of all colors" (largely mulattos and blacks) in the Atlantic coast region of Nueva Granada (Colombia) during the late-colonial period. The key concept at stake was honor that previously had served to naturalize ethnic hierarchies of rights and power. By insisting on their honor as virtue, *libres de todos colores* both confirmed and undermined the normative bases of the colonial regime. While local Spanish authorities and notables resisted the redefinition of the honor and privileges of the libres de todos colores, the Bourbon reformers were forced to make concessions to them because they needed them for the defense of the empire. Garrido places these changes in the context of the formation of a plebeian culture among Nueva Granada's castas.

Aline Helg's chapter deals with much the same groups, the free people of color on Nueva Granada's Atlantic coast, in the context of the struggle for independence and alliance formation with the region's Creole elites. While Creoles needed the castas to free themselves from Spanish rule, the castas hoped to gain equality from this alliance. Although the issue of race was central to regional power structures and for the process of alliance formation itself, the racial order was never explicitly challenged during Nueva Granada's "first independence" (1810–15). The castas accepted a subservient position in the alliance with the Creoles as long as their citizenship was recognized, in part because of the atomization of the region and the failure to bring together a broad-based casta movement. This failure on the coast to change the racial order allowed both the royalists and later the elites in the eastern Cordillera (Bogotá) to dominate the Caribbean coastal region and define Nueva Granada as Andean, white, and mestizo.

Derek Williams's chapter analyzes the gender and ethnic/racial components of President García Moreno's project to forge an Ecuadorian Catholic people and nation between 1861 and 1875. The president, combining ultramontane Catholicism with faith in scientific progress, used the Church and the teaching of Catholic morality to extend the influence of the state among indigenous peoples and women. His program was rather successful in extending education to women and native Andeans, in fact more so than those of most contemporary liberal regimes who proclaimed education as fundamental for creating a rational citizenry. García Moreno's approach to women and native Andeans was overtly paternalist: under state tutelage they would become crucial for forging a virtuous, industrious Ecuador. Williams shows how this project relied on a selective use and denial of stereotypes of these strategic subaltern groups. While highly authoritarian, the project clearly helped to incorporate women and native Andeans into the nation. They, in turn, appropriated the Catholic-nationalist discourse of the regime and used it for their own goals.

Brooke Larson's chapter presents a fine-grained analysis of the representation of race and nation in the work of four influential Bolivian intellectuals of the early twentieth century. They were concerned with designing a racial order for the nation capable of overcoming what they saw as the degenerate, corrupt, and chaotic Bolivian republic of the nineteenth century. In the context of the early, timid, and patronizing incorporation of mestizo/cholo lower-middle-class groups into the elite-dominated political process, all authors agreed that these groups exerted a corrupting influence and that the pure Indians had to be protected and uplifted. But, significantly, they disagreed on the methods by which this should be achieved. Some intellectuals believed that it was to be done by the "white" landholding oligarchy, while others emphasized the expanding role of the state. In either case, they visualized the citizenship of the indigenous wards as highly limited: they were to become dependable workers, soldiers, and taxpayers. Larson concludes that such projects were aimed at neutralizing and pushing back the growing networks of indigenous and lower-class political activism.

NOTE

1. Carol Smith, "Myths, Intellectuals, and Race/Class/Gender," 150; we owe this quote to a paper by Daniel Gutierrez, graduate student in anthropology at the University of Illinois.

"FREE MEN OF ALL COLORS" IN NEW GRANADA

IDENTITY AND OBEDIENCE BEFORE INDEPENDENCE

Margarita Garrido

This chapter focuses on a significant population that has been invisible in much of the historiography on late-colonial New Granada: the so-called free men of all colors. I explore questions about their notions of obedience and authority, as they relate to their own identity and to an incipient plebeian political culture. New Granada society, as that of other Spanish American colonies, was based on a representation of order according to which the *ethnic* hierarchy corresponded to a *moral* hierarchy. This hierarchical order was derived from the Spanish conquest and subsequent racial mixing and largely coincided with economic, social, and political hierarchies. It was thought of as a *natural* order, and therefore obedience to authorities that were supposedly superior in all these dimensions, should also be thought of as *natural.* The notion used to express the place of people in society was *honor,* understood mainly as privilege and status, but also as virtue. Social superiority corresponded to moral superiority, or, put differently, status corresponded to greater virtue. Laws and religious sermons legitimized this order and vision.

The position of individuals in the community was related to birth, character, and behavior. With regard to birth, the most important aspect was ethnic origin, followed by the merits of ancestors, which in some cases included allusions to nobility, and in all cases related to the question of legitimacy or illegitimacy. The family's or individual's economic assets and power of disposition over people and goods also strongly influenced one's position in the community. Second, those aspects related to character concerned social and political prudence (not making a scene, not being an impudent prattler, not causing a riot, not being quarrelsome, not using bad or dangerous language) and courtesy (showing respect and good manners). Third, moral qualities were associated with a tacit code of good behavior on which most residents in a given neighborhood could agree. The existence of such a code can be deduced from the reports of good behavior written by priests for members of their community, or from judges' characterizations of witnesses and other participants in court cases. Good behavior was associated with honesty, fulfillment of one's duties as a family member and as a neighbor and parishioner (including collaboration with charitable projects), and obedience. The importance of occupation for one's position in the community varied according to the context.[1] The composite weighting of all these aspects making up one's social standing varied greatly from one town to another. A person's social standing was constructed locally. While there was agreement throughout the colony (indeed, throughout Spanish America) that ethnic and moral hierarchies were largely identical, the filling of those categories with meaning varied from place to place.

That position was expressed in terms of honor, a key notion of the common discursive framework by which an individual gauged his or her own worth and was appraised by society.[2] According to Pierre Bourdieu, the sense of honor is the engine of the "dialectic between challenge and response, between one's own endowments and faculties and those of others." [3] Honor was the operative concept enshrining all those categories explained above, related to birth, character, and behavior that shaped the position of individuals in the community. It articulated everyday practices of domestic, labor, social, and cultural exchange in the community; it calibrated the recognition as equal by equals and as superior by those considered inferior. As Lyman Johnson has noted, "social place and identity were slippery questions [in colonial Latin America], but they were central to notions of honor."[4] In spite of this ambiguity—or perhaps precisely because of it—the sense of honor and the set of elements related to it constituted the *symbolic capital* of every person and family. Inherited or acquired, it could be exchanged, invested, or lost in daily social relations.[5]

Honor also governed the relationship between authority and obedience. An individual's honor was shown not only in the treatment she or he received from others in civil society but also and especially by the treatment received from authorities. Speech and gesture became more delicate and strategic in the individual's relations with authorities. Exchanges and conversations between an individual and an officeholder in position of authority implicated notions of self and the other as well. Obedience was dependent on whether subjects had found a satisfactory image of themselves reflected in the public treatment at the hands of authorities. This satisfactory image confirmed the social identity and place of an individual. For this reason, a strong relationship obtained between secure identity and obedience. If in any way the subject did not clearly comprehend and articulate her own position and that of her ruler, or the ruler did not recognize this vision of their relative positions, this could result in an interchange of defiance and rejoinder, and eventually in disrespect and contempt. In essence this constituted a type of repositioning by those feeling they had been pushed from their original social standing. When the ruler committed injustices, he not only revealed his own lack of moral courage but also did harm to his subjects' feelings.[6]

In the second half of the eighteenth century, New Granada society was unlike the rest of the Andean world in at least one regard: people of mixed race made up of Indians, whites, and blacks had largely replaced the Indian population.[7] The fact that 46 percent of the population in New Granada was made up of free castas, and that in the rest of Andean America 46 percent of the population was Indian, highlights this difference.[8] Multiple cultural and racial mixing over several generations had made it impossible to classify individuals according to different percentages of admixtures of blood. Thus, at the end of this century, use of the term "free men and women of all colors," initially coined for the military battalions of the reforming Bourbons, became generalized.

During the same era, a peculiar form of settlement appeared in vast areas of New Granada, especially in the Cauca and Magdalena river valleys, which has been considered sui generis by some. I am referring to the settlements of free men and women of all colors, which in some areas were recognized as parishes, villages, or towns. In other areas they were known as rural shanty settlements (*rancherías*), which were considered by authorities as unruly zones (*rochelas*), beyond the reach of police order and the sound of the church bells. In the central area of the viceroyalty a process of Hispanization and cultural miscegenation accompanied the transformation of Indian villages into "white" parishes. All these demographic and settlement processes contributed to changes in ways people were living together (*convivencia*) and in the underlying discourses constitutive of the ethnic, social, and political order.

The position of the various mixed ethnic groups was ambiguous in the late-colonial socioethnic hierarchy. The very term "free men and women of all colors" (*libres de todos los colores*), encompassing *mulatos, zambos, mestizos, pardos,* and *montañeses* in military recruitment, denoted the increasing difficulty of classifying individuals according to race and also signaled exclusion/inclusion. It was presumed that those who were "of color" should not be free, because at least some of their ancestors had been slaves. In the original design of colonial society, freedom was a precious privilege reserved for the Spanish settlers and their descendants. Those classed as "free men and women of all colors" had managed to achieve freedom, either through prohibited racial mixing and consequently their own illegitimacy, or as a result of migration and uprooting which meant ascent for some in the social hierarchy and descent for others. Freedom signified independence from a cacique, a slaveowner, or a lord, autonomy to leave the town, to labor in different places, or to support oneself by one's own industry. Recognition as free men or women signified an inclusion among non-Indians and nonslaves, although the qualification "of color" alluded to a stain, which justified exclusion from whites. In sum, the libres de todos los colores found themselves in an intermediate position that was ambiguous and slippery.

They or their close ancestors were *self-made men and women,* who had "invented" themselves in the course of difficult life histories. These were not the self-made men of today where all kinds of circumstances facilitate the multiplication of the possibilities of free choice, and where most discourses explicitly reward the choices of those who seek to go beyond the type of life they inherited. Those of the colonial society were men and women who had to construct their honor from scratch, in other words, from a situation replete with negative prejudices about racial mixing, with talk about the stain of corrupted races, illegitimacy, and outsiders (*forasteros*). This was more challenging still in the case of the free women of all colors, due to prejudices concerning "the weakness of their sex" and their "problematic honor." The libres de todos colores were thought to be disobedient, restless, and of low moral standards. By means of special measures they were denied the recognition as free people that they expected, as well as access to education and higher public offices. Following the pioneering work of Jaime Jaramillo Uribe, scholars have confirmed that the people of mixed race in New Granada were objects of a disdainful gaze on the part of Hispanic colonial elites.[9]

Yet we still know very little about the libres de todos colores' view of themselves, of others and of the society they lived in. The issue that seems to have caused them most difficulties in their relationship with others and with authorities was the separation of ethnic origin and skin color from the value of honor. In this chapter I explore some aspects of political culture, particularly with regard to the values that shaped the notions they held about obedience and authority. The cases of disobedience and disrespect analyzed here will help us to understand aspects of the interchange between rulers and subjects, the limits of obedience, and the intertextuality in which these were inscribed. I will present details of different cases in two small villages on the Caribbean coast, Valencia de Jesús in the province of Santa Marta and Tolú, in the province of Cartagena.[10]

RECOGNITION AND OBEDIENCE IN THE MILITIA

In the struggle to ascend the social hierarchy and achieve an honorable social position, some of the libres de todos colores found recognition of their moral qualities and loyalty through designation as a militia captain, while others had to content themselves with the deference accorded them by their home community. Some found serious opposition to the recognition of their merits by the local authorities.

Let us first look at the case of a pardo called Simón Córdoba who was appointed Militia Captain of Valencia de Jesús by the governor of Santa Marta in 1750. His leadership capacity was challenged by some of the traditional local authorities, including the mayor and the probate judge, who thought that a man of low social origins should not be a captain.[11] They managed to convince two militiamen to disobey him, then refused to allow the captain to punish these men for their disobedience and in turn accused *him* of disobedience for failing to answer their summons. For his part, Captain Córdoba argued that he did not present himself when called by the authorities because "as a man, and although being pardo, I feared that I would be subject to some kind of injury to my person." Tried for disrespect and disobedience, Córdoba was condemned to prison and stocks and fined thirty-one pesos. After some time in prison, the captain complained about the injustice of his punishment and requested his freedom. He said that his behavior had been correct, as he was carrying out his duties as captain according to regulations and customs dating back from time immemorial and he "wanted to suffer no longer the bad reputation of being a trouble-maker, a rebel, and arrogant."

In this case, it seems, the two local authorities, representatives of the Creole and Spanish establishment, shared certain prejudices, fears, and interests. Apparently the probate judge wished to test his ability to command the obedience of the mixed-race militiamen against that of the pardo Córdoba. The judge was concerned that Córdoba was removing himself and the militiamen under his command from his traditional sphere of influence and clientelism. The newly formed militia units of freemen of all colors had been granted the *fuero militar,* that is to say, protection by the military code including certain immunities and exemptions. Moreover, their officers were given badges and jurisdictional rights emblematic of their legitimate command authority. Captains of Spanish militia companies along with the established civil authorities begrudged such privileges awarded to free men of color. To a certain extent this removed mixed-race militia captains from their power and control, granting them a degree of autonomy and opening the doors to social mobility.

In the debates about the formation of mixed-race militias, similar voices disapproving of this innovation had been heard. The viceroys feared the consequences that arming the populace could have for domestic security. However, Spanish ministers and colonial viceroys ultimately had to accept the Americanization of the colonial army. The share of American officers rose from 34 percent in 1740 to 60 percent in 1800, while American troop contingents increased from 68 percent of total troop strength in 1740–57 to 80 percent in 1780–1800. For the Creoles of New Granada in particular this meant having to accept the "mulatization" of the militias.[12]

In the context of the colony's hierarchical socioracial order, how should we understand the privileges granted to newly commissioned militia officers of mixed-race backgrounds? Along with the reinforcement of standing army battalions, the formation of militia battalions was part of the military reforms, which, among other Bourbon innovations, were intended to improve the defense of the Spanish imperial nation, and of the colonies in particular. They did not aim to introduce the type of social changes that today would be labeled as democratization of society or reduction of social divides. Nevertheless, some of these measures, aimed at greater economic, commercial, financial, political, and military efficiency, did imply social change.

The case considered here occurred very early in the process of organizing militias in New Granada, which only reached its definitive legal form in 1773. By 1781 the new militia battalions had become sufficiently widespread and effective as to play an important role in containing the *Comunero* insurgents. The 1778 inspection reports on these new military units had made it evident that the ethnic composition of militias in New Granada could not follow the Cuban model, that is, battalions clearly differentiated by their ethnic composition (whites, mixed-race, and blacks), all with white officers. In spite of many battalion names denoting a specific category of racial mix given by Lieutenant Colonel Anastasio Zejudo to the militias of Cartagena (there were battalions of pardos, of zambos, of morenos, of pardo-morenos, and of cuarterones), the confusing presence of all castas in each of those battalions led Governor Pimienta to propose the following simplification in 1778: there should be one battalion of whites which would include mestizos with indigenous ancestry as well as those "who having left the obscurity of blackness approach the status of quadroons and the like," and one pardo battalion that would include mulattos and zambos. Later, the regiment of the free men of all colors was incorporated into the white battalion.[13]

But the new situation of those of mixed race granted privilege and power did not put an end to longstanding ambiguities. On one hand, they still had to contend with discrimination by whites. On the other, they wished to distinguish themselves from the plebe, seeking to avoid any kind of gesture or activity that might associate them with people of their ethnic category and the negative traits they represented for the colonial elites. In the case discussed above, Captain Córdoba expressed, on the one hand, his fear that white notables would cause "some injury to my person"; on the other he was eager to present affidavits affirming that he was "esteemed for his good behavior, by both notables and plebeians."

The honor that he was defending was derived, first and foremost, from virtue (good behavior), which had garnered him social recognition (credibility, general esteem). Second, it was derived from the military rank to which he had been appointed. This officially reinforced his distinction from the populace as a subject of exceptional merit. His complaint about being imprisoned and the seizure of his goods was made in defense of his "person." His protest about the disapproval, at the hands of a couple of notables, of his punishment of the two disobedient militiamen was meant to defend the authority and jurisdiction conferred on him.

Men of mixed race such as Captain Cordoba deployed "honor" in such a way as to emphasize their virtue and the merit of their services to the crown. Only when they obtained the recognition of an official rank could they cautiously insist on the acceptance of their superior honor, begrudged them by a local Creole elite that felt its own standing and power threatened. The notion of "person" that men like Cordoba had in mind appears to refer to a certain sense of dignity (respect due a human being), which disturbed an order in which people of all colors were not respected in the same way that whites were. The term still implied a certain sense of being exceptional, as it was not yet applied to all human beings. We should thus not underestimate the exemplary nature of the demeanor and comportment of men like Cordoba, which showed that choosing an orderly life and ostensibly being a loyal defender of the established order was a viable option for many, in spite of their skin color.

RECOGNITION AND OBEDIENCE IN THE RANCHERÍAS

Some free men and women of all colors decided to live in unsettled territory (*monte*), beyond the control of towns, and there establish rudimentary homesteads both individually and as couples and families. Their relationships with the neighboring town, with the priest and the mayor, were generally difficult. The latter often tried to get them to adhere to the authority of the Church, to attend mass, and to participate in town life. The people who lived in the monte were able to frankly reject this control or tacitly ignore it. In any case, those who lived in the monte had different ways of interacting among themselves and their neighbors, which openly challenged ethnic differences and the narrowness of social and moral codes.

Since mayors and corregidores saw it as their duty to keep the population "civilized" and within earshot of church bells, they tended to mistrust and fear those poor settlers living scattered in rural areas. They considered these settlers to be transients, not subject to strong ties, without much to lose, and ready to earn a living in any way they could. Their frequent complaints about robbery and cattle theft are connected with this persecutory attitude, which often led the authorities to commit abuses, answered with disobedience by the libres de color.[14] Robbery and cattle theft, common among just a few settlers, led to the spread of negative prejudices about new settlements of free men and women of color on the Atlantic Coast, as well as in the Cauca region.[15]

References to settlements of such *arrochelados* (squatters) are fairly well known to historians, yet very little is known about how they defended themselves and what their ideas were about their chosen lifestyle. In 1789, Benito Blanco was arrested while returning from the market.[16] A former slave who had received his freedom for loyal services, Blanco now lived with other free men and women of all colors in the hills of Quilitén, near Tolú, in the province of Cartagena, dedicated to the cultivation and sale of crops. In his trial, it was revealed that the mayor of the town of Tolú had sought to round up all the settlers in Quilitén, considering them squatters, and made them promise to lead decent lives. The mayor was going to charge them for the cost of this preventive operation. But Blanco was not among those rounded up since he had gone to market. As he was the only one with sufficient funds to pay, the mayor decided to seize Blanco's goods and charge him the cost of the operation, accusing him of living indecently with the wife of Justo Amaya, another settler.

According to Justo Amaya, the freedman Blanco was a farmer like himself with whom he shared his table and daily life "in good harmony and union," "helping each other with farm tasks," following moral rules and a decorum, which they referred to as "good conduct and correct behavior." Blanco's behavior had not injured him personally or his honor but had expressed friendship, mutual respect, and solidarity. In Amaya's version, there was no hint of resistance or rebellion.

Blanco considered the actions of the mayor and soldiers as injurious to his person, credibility, and reputation as a man of good conduct.[17] In presenting his complaint, he made it clear that in the town of Tolú he could not receive a fair trial due to his "unhappy status of an African-born freed black man." Blanco requested the return of his money so that his own reputation and the honor of Candelaria Oliva and her husband would be restored.[18]

Contemporary crown and Church officials throughout the provinces of the Caribbean coast frequently condemned what town residents considered to be the crimes and reprehensible lifestyle of the squatters of the rancherías of Quilitén. In his pastoral visit to Tierra Adentro and Tolú from 1778 to 1781, the bishop of Cartagena, José Fernández Lamadrid, referred to "the universal laxity and corruption of the habits of the faithful." His misgivings about such disorders became all the greater on discovering that the free blacks were living in a state of spiritual abandonment. "Since they dwell very far from the towns, they do not recognize their priests, nor follow the teachings of the Church, thus living without law or obedience and in a state of total dissipation."[19]

In his travel diary of 1787–88, Father Joseph Palacios de la Vega also recounted how horrified he was at discovering the discordant, uncivilized customs in many of the rancherías of Indians, blacks, and those of mixed race in the provinces of Cartagena and Santa Marta.[20] The persecution of these arrochelados and the attempts to reduce them to living under urban authority, within earshot of the church bells, had not only civilizing and religious purposes but also the aim of allaying the fears of their attacks and the menace of destabilizing the hierarchical order. In the case at hand, we can see that the squatters of the Quilitén hills did not deliberately intend to oppose the authority of Church and of royal justice. Rather, they chose an autonomous lifestyle that reflected a certain coolness and indifference toward complying with formal religious and civil precepts, an attitude not limited to this group.

POLITICS AND MORALS

The two cases discussed above have their origin in the notables' failure to recognize the achievements of libres de todos colores. Their social ascent was considered contrary to the natural order of things in which skin color corresponded not only to social status but to moral quality and one's place in the hierarchy of command. Militia Captain Simón de Córdoba and Benito Blanco, a farmer and small trader, were individuals of color who had achieved a certain degree of autonomy in different places and spheres of society. They had found avenues for going beyond the narrow confines of life opportunities normally imposed on those of their "class."

The defense of the militia captain of pardos emphasized the affirmation of his personal honor and dignity achieved by merit of his position: that of the black freedman focused on portraying his different manner of leading an honorable life. Both values, the dignity of the person, and the sense of an honorable living, were closely linked with the construction of identity. Each of these moral standards linked the entire life of a person to the relationship with others, as they provided a means of social recognition. Both standards concerned central dimensions of their honor and, therefore, an important part of the symbolic capital that these individuals had accumulated during their lives. Local authorities harassed these men precisely because their achievements threatened the representation of the established ethnic, economic, social, and political hierarchical order. Yet, on the surface, in both cases the authorities objected to their behavior not on political grounds but on moral grounds. One was accused of being unjust to the militiamen and the other of living in an indecent state with a married woman. In both cases, their defenses were also based on moral appraisals. Thus these cases exemplify the struggles precipitated by the breakdown of barriers and ways of achieving inclusion and recognition.

In both cases the subjects affirmed that their ethnic origin was preventing their being recognized as virtuous. They thus felt compelled to seek the contemporaries' recognition of their honor through emphasizing virtuous *behavior*, in spite of their ethnic origin. Their behavior and character were matters of ethical choice, in contrast to the constitutive elements of ascriptive identity inherited by birth (family, ethnicity, and gender). If we accept Charles Taylor's notion that personal identity (individuality) should not be separated from the concept of good (morality), we can understand how these free, albeit colored, men felt that they *were* their behavior, and that their identity was directly related to their customs and lifestyle. For this reason, they made reference to their morals as the basis of their own identity.[21]

In the testimony of captain of pardos Simon Córdoba, of Benito Blanco, of his friend Amaya, and of numerous other witnesses, we can discern a vision of good that is closely tied to corresponding practices. These were defined by a pattern of "do's" and "don'ts" very similar to those we know as central to Spanish colonial society: living without causing scandal, showing obedience to one's superiors, being appreciated by all, living in order and harmony, respecting the wife of the other, doing one's work with dedication, and extending help to one's neighbors. It is thus not surprising that some witnesses even gave more details than asked for regarding the plaintiffs' customary behavior and their habitual harmony with neighbors and friends.

Clearly the contention over the honor of our two libres de todos colores protagonists from late-colonial New Granada was inscribed in a larger process of redefining honor that has been observed in many places in the Western world during the waning centuries of the ancien regime. In seventeenth-century Europe, the ideal of honor understood as privilege was losing influence while the ideal of an ordinary virtuous life accessible to everybody was gaining currency. Protestantism fostered this process through the heightened valuation of labor and family, in addition to spiritual devotion. The literature of the Spanish *siglo de oro* praised the gentleman's honor as well as that of the rustic commoner on the grounds that they were old Christians and honest people. During that era, new possibilities for constructing individual lives had arisen in Spain quite distinct from the conventional lives as defined by corporate groups or kinship lineages.[22] For other parts of Western Europe, the change in the notion of honor has been understood as a double process of generalizing and spiritualizing honor.[23] Progressively, honor was accessible for more people and it could be related to virtues and feelings and not only to birth. Many historical studies show struggles over the bases of identity formation in waning old-regime societies.[24] For the Andean region, the excellent work of Sarah Chambers on Arequipa between the late-colonial and early republican era has demonstrated the transformation of the honor code, from status to virtue. [25]

Nevertheless, the pattern of do's and don'ts for free men and women of color does not appear to coincide exactly in every detail with that of other contemporaries, especially with that of some of the authorities. The key issue in Captain Córdoba's case was that a person of mixed race was commander of a group of persons that formerly was under the sole authority of the local white notables. Although he followed the regulations guiding the treatment of militia troops by their officers, the local authorities felt certain that he should not be in charge of troops at all because of his lowly status. The underlying problem consisted in the dislocation of the social order, so that the ethnic order no longer corresponded with the political order.

The arrochelados of Quilitén declared that they lived in an orderly and pious manner, in mutual respect and dedicated to useful pursuits, as was evidenced by the amount of products they took to the market. But the residents of the town thought that "as they do not know what is right, they do not respect it." Clearly, "knowing what is right" meant living within the social order of the town. Their disagreement was mainly about the squatters' autonomy. For the latter, their autonomy was what they cherished most, what was most meaningful in their lives, and thus worth fighting for.

AMBIGUOUS CULTURAL AND POLITICAL IDENTITIES

This issue becomes clearer if we understand, as historians of Europe have stated, that the idea of social identity is in many cases profoundly ambiguous. According to E. P. Thompson, "often it is possible to detect identities that alternate in the same individual, one deferential and the other rebellious." He goes on to refer to what Gramsci called contradictory consciousness, or two theoretical consciousnesses: one related to praxis and the other to the inheritance of the past, which is taken on board without a critical sense. Thompson proposes to understand the two theoretical consciousnesses as derived from two aspects of the same reality: on the one hand, the conformity to the status quo necessary in order to survive and to adjust to the realities of the world; on the other hand, a "common sense" derived from the experience of exploitation, scarcity, and repression shared with fellow-workers and neighbors. This common sense continuously exposes the text of the paternalist image of order to critique through irony and, much less frequently, revolt. [26]

In the cases discussed above, the free men of color uncritically accepted the inherited discourse of a society stratified according to racial origin and its correspondence to the entire social, political, and moral order. This inspired their deferential practices and their respect toward authorities and order in general. On the other hand, their life experience with others sharing patterns of work and leisure led them to reject accusations of being disloyal, dishonest, or immoral and to vehemently defend their social and ethnic customs as worthy and honorable. In this way, their actions appear to be subversive of order, rebellious.

Although the libres de todos colores mostly accepted the colonial society's principles of morality, they were not prepared to compromise on either their acquired power (the case of the militia captain's modest office) or their autonomy from elite urban control (the case of the freedman). In the testimony of Blanco and the witnesses in his favor, what was being defended was a plebeian culture that could not be simply reduced to a traditional culture or classified strictly as a rebel culture. As Thompson has said of England's eighteenth-century plebeians, "the norms which they were defending . . . were not the same as those proclaimed by the Church or the authorities."[27] Perhaps it is appropriate to speak of a mode of resistance-assimilation.

From a broad historical perspective, the relationship between these new attitudes emerging among libres de todos colores and the changes introduced by the Bourbon reforms are especially important. It is obvious that once the crown opened the ranks of the militia officer corps to persons of lower status in the socioracial hierarchy because of strategic defensive considerations, it had to recognize corresponding privileges for those free men of all colors receiving an officer's commission. This partly explains how challenges to the old hierarchical order originated. The judge's ultimate support of the captain's complaint signaled recognition of his authority as derived from the king, but perhaps also recognition of his everyday virtuous life. The fact that by the late eighteenth century quite a few judges ruled in favor of complaints by freedmen and libres de todos colores suggests the strengthening of a notion of honor as virtuous living vis-à-vis the older notion of honor in the sense of hierarchy and relative worth. This was a shift which local notables remained long unwilling to accept.

There is a well-known case of a pardo militia captain who did not encounter resistance from the Creole elite to his newly found authority and status.[28] José Antonio Valenzuela, son of prosperous half-breed traders, was appointed Alferez de Milicias de la Compañía de Pardos of the city of Antioquia. For his excellent services as alferez against the tobacco harvesters' uprising in Sacaojal in 1781 and 1798, Valenzuela obtained a *real cédula* in 1796 "because of his white color, his good manners, his upbringing and good habits, to which could be attributed the good treatment and attention he gave to everyone of importance in that city." For this reason, "he was able to remove this stain [his identification as pardo] which greatly afflicted him." In Popayán, province of Cauca, Don Melchor López, Guarda Real de la Real Audiencia, complained before the judge because Juan Manuel Pérez had called him pardo. Surprisingly, the judge declared that "since the color of one's skin is an accident, it does not allude to the quality and nobility of individuals."[29] Closely related to these changes, it has been pointed out that the title of *don* to address white people in colonial Nueva Granada "was undergoing a process of deterioration that indicates the progress of leveling forces and the undermining of lineage as the basic element of social status."[30]

A second case has to do with the Bourbon civilizing project aimed at controlling popular culture. As many historians have shown for Spanish colonial societies, concerns over impious and potentially subversive behavior of the lower classes motivated the Bourbon social and urban project.[31] In Chambers's examination of Arequipa in a later period, she notes that "growing elite concerns over disorder and immorality made cultural practices a key terrain of conflict and negotiation during the transition from colonialism to republicanism."[32] Charles Walker also draws our attention to the disregard of rules by the lower classes as a "weapon of the weak" against the Bourbon civilizing project. But he warns us against automatically considering such strategic behavior as resistance. Still, even if disregard of rules was not resistance in most cases, it could turn into resistant behavior whenever the intervention of authorities seriously affected important aspects of such popular groups' lives. The cultural debate over autonomy, or, put differently, over the defense of popular forms of sociability (*coexistencia*) as righteous, marked the crossroads of politics and morals within the discursive framework of honor.

But why did higher authorities at times support some persons from the lower strata of the socioracial hierarchy? During the second half of the eighteenth century, the Real Audiencia of Santa Fé adjudicated a growing number of cases of abuse or insult committed by local authorities.[33] At the same time, cases of disobedience, defiance, and unlawful challenge of authority were also on the rise.[34] This increase of legal complaints from individual commoners and neighborhood and squatter groups spurred Bourbon authorities to assert control over local politics. One way to do so consisted in supporting plebeian authority when challenged by a disobedient local notable, another in helping victims of abuse by mayors. In some cases lawyers did not limit their defense of plebeians solely to asserting an honor for their clients proportional to their position but reminded offending notables that their behavior also must demonstrate virtue proportional to their status lest they wished to lose that status.

With the coming of independence, the category of libres de todos colores disappeared. At an early stage they were included in the catchall category of pueblo as part of a discourse designed to blur differences and foster equality.

In the new constitutions there was a formal recognition of citizenship for free men, including Indians but not slaves. The first law against slavery was issued in 1821 for the freedom of newly born persons (*libertad de vientres*), but complete abolition came only in 1851. This carried with it the obligation of patriotic duties, including, for adult men, that of serving as soldiers. One purpose of granting universal citizenship to men was to underscore the contrast with the colonial period, when people were categorized as vassal or subject and many suffered major legal inequalities. Nueva Granada's republican censuses stopped classifying people by race, an important difference from other Andean countries.[35]

The title of citizen, which became generally used, especially by those who were involved in patriotic struggles, is an example of this discourse of formal equality and inclusion. However, it did not have any effect on the right to elect or to be elected. The republic inherited the prejudices that existed toward different racial groups and free men and women of all colors. The right to vote was limited to those who had property or a certain minimum income and were free men able to read and write. This meant that members of some socioracial groups remained totally excluded from suffrage, while free men of all colors obtained only conditional inclusion as active citizens.[36] Thus there was a change from explicit exclusion to ambiguous inclusion. Even though it is evident that it was an abstract and formal inclusion rather than a reality, the proclamation of citizenship for all and the elimination of ethnic categories in the census opened a legal space which was decisive for the country's future.

• • • • •

In the late-colonial period, the conception of society as an ethnic, social, economic, political, and moral hierarchy was evidencing certain signs of crisis. Not all ruling positions corresponded to this hierarchy, the forms of obedience were not restricted to those derived from the traditional order, and the identities of individuals were no longer completely consistent with their ethnic origins.

The free people of all colors believed in the dignity of a person who lived honorably, respected the rules, and behaved without scandal. They believed that the authority of all officeholders derived from the king and that royal authority came from God. But they also believed that those holding office were obliged to behave morally and to recognize and treat their subjects according to their position and honor. They also defended their hard-earned autonomy. Free people of all colors, a population that had long been invisible, strove to gain social recognition. In this they relied on the ethical norms of their position and honor, which they viewed as symbolic capital, while they downplayed their relative exclusion based on their ethnicity. They wrested the notion of honor from the exclusive appropriation of Creoles and stressed its meanings linked to virtue. For this reason, many conflicts with authorities were expressed in terms of morals. The Bourbon attempt to control popular culture revealed a surprisingly broad space in which politics and culture coincided, competed, and clashed.

The lives of libres de todos colores in late-colonial Nueva Granada evidenced elements of both assimilation and resistance. The main traits of this group's incipient plebeian political culture may be summarized as follows: acceptance of the existing power constellations, a certain internalization of obedience, the hope of holding a local office, the ideal of reaching greater autonomy, and recognition as an honorable subject and a man of virtue. The partial opening of new spaces for the free people of all colors in New Granada during the late-colonial period lost its meaning with republican political changes. However, the previous experiences of recognition, autonomy, and defiance in processes of negotiation of identity and obedience had some effect on the memory of individuals and groups. The possibility of extending the notion of honor as virtue to all, whatever their ethnic origin, was an achievement of major significance.

NOTES

1. According to Helg, "The Limits of Equality," 15, in Cartagena "there was a clear hierarchy of professions corresponding to the color hierarchy"; see also Helg's chapter in this volume.
2. Pitt Rivers, "Honour and Social Status," 19–97.
3. Bourdieu, *El sentido práctico,* 175.
4. Johnson and Lipsett-Rivera, "Introduction," 13.
5. For the concept of *symbolic capital,* see Bourdieu, *El sentido práctico,* 189–204.

6. See Veyne, "El individuo herido," 9–24.
7. Tovar Pinzón, "Introducción."
8. Esteva Fabregat, *El mestizaje,* 230–31. At present, modern genetic measurements of different countries seem to show traces of their colonial makeup, with some changes. In Colombia, a majority of the population is mixed-race, composed of *mestizos* (45.3 percent), followed by whites or *Européidos* (30 percent), blacks and mixed-race (*mulatos, zambos*) (23 percent), and finally Indians (1.59 percent). In comparison with the eighteenth century, the percentage of mixed-race (*mestizos*) has not changed, the percentage of whites is a little higher, and the percentage of blacks is much higher than those classified as slaves or as Indians, whose numbers are greatly reduced. Even if these classifications are dubious, it is interesting to have them as reference.
9. See Jaramillo Uribe's essay, "Mestizaje y diferenciación en el Nuevo Reino de Granada en la segunda mitad del siglo XVIII," in his *Ensayos.*
10. This essay is based on my recent research into cases of disobedience, disrespect, or resistance to the local authorities. Some of these cases were resolved in provincial courts, and others were taken to the *Real Audiencia.* Between 1700 and 1810, we find 70 cases noted of disobedience, and 30 of disrespect to authority, which were taken to the *Real Audiencia,* totaling 100 cases. Some of the documents of these cases are better preserved than others, and in some cases the outcomes are known, whereas in others there is no record of the final outcome. Archivo General de la Nación (AGN) Sección Colonia, Fondo Juicios Criminales.
11. AGN, CJC, tomo 76, fols. 340–419; quotation from fol. 359.
12. Lynch, *El siglo XVIII,* 307. The effects of the war against England in 1762—mainly the loss of Cuba and Manila for a year, and the loss of Florida until 1781—combined with the stronger territorial, commercial, and naval position of England in the Caribbean, made defense of empire the number one priority. First in the Viceroyalty of New Spain, then in that of Peru, and later and less powerfully in that of New Granada, regular battalions were created. Militias were organized in strategic areas of New Granada.
13. Pimienta, Reporte de Inspección, Cartagena, March 26, 1778 (AGN, MM, tomo 40, fols. 152–65), as cited by Kuethe, "Flexibilidad racial," 177–91; in the Vicariat of Valencia de Jesús, which included the city and five other places, according to the census of 1778 there were only 8 ecclesiastics, 272 whites, 1,199 Indians, 1,777 free men and women of all colors, 402 slaves; the city's population was 1,939 inhabitants and the total in the Vicariat was 3,658; Tovar Pinzón, *Convocatoria al número,* 507–19.
14. Conde Calderón, "Castas y conflictos"; Palacios de la Vega, *Diario de viaje;* Zuluaga, "Conformación," 231–37; Caicedo and Espinosa, "'Públicos ladrones,'" 91–108.
15. See Colmenares, "Región-nación," for a lucid discussion of difference between the free men and women of all colors who settled spontaneously outside city and

village boundaries on the Atlantic Coast and in the River Cauca valley. In the Cauca region, they eagerly sought official recognition as site, village, or town, as well as the delimitation of their jurisdiction and the right to their own parish priest and local authorities. In contrast, on the Atlantic Coast, making the most of a vast interior frontier and partly harassed by independent Indians, they settled on mountain slopes and along rivers. For this reason, they were treated as shanty settlers (*arrochelados*) and subjected to intermittent persecution by authorities.

16. AGN, CJC, tomo 107, fols. 851–82.

17. In 1789, the same year in which Benito Blanco complained about persecution by the mayor of Tolú, the governor and commander general of the city and province of Cartagena, Don Joaquín de Cañaberal y Ponce, published rules for the whole population, entitled *El Deber de Vivir Ordenadamente para Obedecer al Rey,* republished by Mora de Tovar in *Anuario Colombiano,* 109–31; paragraph 88 established that when someone was apprehended, without specifying the crime, s/he should be taken to prison, "as under arrest and within doors, without the mayor being able to demand prison fees, or any other payment, until the law decided on formal arrest or release." The mayor of Tolú ignored this ruling.

18. AGN, Colonia, Juicios Criminales, tomo 107, fols. 853–54.

19. "La universal relajación de las costumbres de los fieles . . . ," published by Bell Lemus, *Cartagena de Indias,* 152–61; see also Conde Calderón, "Castas y conflictos."

20. Palacios de la Vega, *Diario de viaje,* passim.

21. Taylor, *Las fuentes del yo,* 220.

22. Ibid., 227–31; Maraval, *La literatura picaresca,* 301.

23. Spierenburg, "Violencia," 116–51.

24. Baumeister, *Identity,* chaps. 3 and 4, offers a good review.

25. Chambers, *From Subject to Citizens,* 160–87.

26. Thompson, *Costumbres en común,* 23–24; my own retranslation into English.

27. Ibid., 21

28. Patiño Millán, *Criminalidad,* 213.

29. Archivo Central del Cauca, Colonia J-I 11, Juicios Criminales, sig. 8009.

30. Jaramillo Uribe, *Ensayos,* 196.

31. See Walker's chapter in this volume.

32. Chambers, *From Subject to Citizens,* 13.

33. Garrido, *Reclamos y representaciones,* chap. 2.

34. AGN Catalogue of Colonial Criminal Lawsuits.

35. For a good treatment of the theme, see König, *En el camino,* 274–313.

36. Patiño Millán, "Indios, negros y mestizos."

SILENCING AFRICAN DESCENT

CARIBBEAN COLOMBIA AND EARLY NATION BUILDING, 1810–1828

Aline Helg

Since its independence from Spain in 1821, Colombia has promoted itself as an Andean, white, and mestizo nation. Colombia, however, is also a Caribbean country and has the largest population of African descent among the Spanish-speaking nations of the Western Hemisphere. This chapter examines the historical roots of Colombia's neglect of its Afro-Caribbean identity by exploring the processes and political cultures of Caribbean Colombia during its "first independence" (1810–15). It argues that during these crucial years, both the elite and the lower classes in the region took a pragmatic approach to the new circumstances since they needed each other to advance: the Creole elite to gain power, and the men of color to gain equality. Race was an omnipresent factor, because the small white minority could not survive without the support of the overwhelming majority of African descent, and because what people of color meant by equality was equality with whites. However, both groups tacitly agreed not to make race an issue, as it would have threatened their society with violent destruction. Yet their shared silence also meant that during its first independence, Caribbean Colombia lost a major opportunity to assert its singularity and its importance vis-à-vis Andean Colombia.

Based on sources in Colombian and Spanish archives and on published collections of archival documents, this chapter begins with a description of Caribbean Colombia's political cultures and processes of independence and reconquest by Spain during the years from 1810 to 1815. Notably, it compares the cities of Cartagena and Mompox, which favored independence early, with Santa Marta, which remained royalist. The second part of the chapter analyzes the various factors in the region's political cultures that prevented the consolidation of its first independence and facilitated its subordination to Andean Colombia after 1821. In particular, it focuses on the role of elite whites as well as free and slave people of African descent and on the meanings each of these groups attached to the mobilizing concept of equality during this key period of Colombian history. It concludes by reflecting on Caribbean Colombia's place in the Gran Colombian experiment (the united republic of Venezuela, Colombia, and Ecuador, 1821–30) and the impact of its failure on the construction of Colombia as a white and mestizo Andean nation.[1]

In 1808, the abduction of King Ferdinand VII by Napoleon and the formation of regional juntas in Spain created a new context that widened the options of Spanish American colonies. The juntas introduced the principle of the sovereignty of the people, and in some colonies, such as New Granada (Colombia's name until 1863), leading Creoles began to view their region as an autonomous province within the Spanish kingdom. Not only did they form juntas, they also rejected the authority of the regency council to rule for the king.[2] New Granada's embrace of autonomy, and later independence, was far from being countrywide, however. It was an elite-led movement limited to certain cities and areas, whereas other cities and villages remained faithful to Spain. The process was thus conflictive, not only dividing New Granada as a whole but each region into royalist and autonomist (later, pro-independence) areas.[3]

During the colonial period, New Granada had not been an integrated viceroyalty but a loose structure of distinct regions, principally the eastern cordillera of the Andes, the southern province of Popayán, the Caribbean provinces, and Antioquia. Although political and administrative power was centralized in its capital, Santa Fé de Bogotá (hereinafter Bogotá), located in the eastern cordillera, the Caribbean port city of Cartagena monopolized its legal foreign trade, leading to tensions between the two cities. The enormous difficulties of travel and transportation between them—a journey of between one and five months—complicated relations between the Caribbean and the Andean regions.[4]

Representative of the weakness of the colonial state and police forces, large portions of Caribbean New Granada were still controlled by unsubdued indigenous communities; other areas were inhabited by runaway slaves, fugitives, and illegal settlers. As the crown did not promote the cultivation of tropical crops for exportation in the region, the countryside witnessed little state and Church interference. White elite *hacendados* and ranchers dominated large fiefdoms where they employed slaves and free people of African descent to produce sugar cane and cocoa and to raise cattle for regional markets. Most villages and small towns were inhabited by *libres de color* and had only a handful of civil servants and church officials; a few were *pueblos de indios.* In addition, the Caribbean coast sheltered numerous ports dedicated to contraband, especially the export of gold dust from the Pacific coast and the import of manufactured goods from Britain.

Despite these characteristics, Caribbean New Granada was not perceived by Spanish officials as a region prone to rebellion. It had remained immune to the 1781 Comunero revolt, in which a coalition of peasants and Creole elite in the tobacco-producing eastern cordillera area of Socorro rebelled against the Bourbon fiscal reforms, even contributing militiamen of color to its repression.[5] After the Haitian revolution, policymakers continued to view Caribbean New Granada as a stronghold of the Spanish monarchy. Although a few incidents momentarily raised fears among Spanish officials and Creole aristocrats that the revolution might spread to the region, in general whites remained confident in the loyalty of the free and slave population of African descent, on whom much of the coast's defense rested.[6]

On the face of it, elite confidence seems misplaced. In every Caribbean New Granadan city, town, village, and rural area, whites (a category including the *blancos de la tierra,* persons reputed to be white) were a small minority. According to the 1777–80 census, the population in the three provinces of Cartagena, Santa Marta, and Riohacha totaled 170,404 inhabitants: approximately 63 percent of them were free people of color, 17 percent "civilized" Indians, 11 percent whites, and 9 percent slaves.[7] However, the free population of African descent was scattered across a vast territory that resembled a patchwork of rival cities, small towns, villages, and haciendas, often several days of travel distant from each other. The unconquered Indians in the periphery were separated by huge distances and cultural differences. "Civilized" Indians were divided by ethnicity and assigned to specific pueblos de indios. Many slaves in the cities lived independently of their masters, whereas rural slaves worked in isolated haciendas and ranches. Such fragmentation and dispersion were not conducive to large-scale collective revolt. As Viceroy Pedro Mendinueta noted in 1803, trouble was less likely to occur in the countryside than in the more "civilized" cities.[8]

Indeed, Caribbean New Granada's anti-Spanish movement was launched in the two most populated and developed cities of the region: Cartagena and Mompox. In 1809, the *cabildos* (town councils) of both cities, comprised of Spanish and Creole merchants and hacendados, began to resist the imposition of new Spanish authorities: in Cartagena, the new governor for the province, Brigadier General Francisco Montes; and in Mompox, the town's new military commander, the Lieutenant Colonel and Engineer Vicente Talledo. In Cartagena, the Creole hacendado and lawyer José María García de Toledo capitalized on popular anti-Spanish discontent to organize a force able to neutralize the pro-Spanish fixed battalion known as the Fijo and other troops garrisoned in the city. Notably, he entrusted one wealthy mulatto, Pedro Romero (a Cuban-born master blacksmith in the arsenal and owner of a foundry), with the formation of the unit of the Patriotic Lancers in the black and mulatto suburb of Getsemaní.[9] On June 14, 1810, armed men from this new force helped the cabildo to depose the governor.[10] The cabildo then formed two battalions of "patriot volunteers to conserve the august rights of Ferdinand VII," one labeled "of whites," uniting Spaniards and Creoles in order to prevent clashes among them, the other "of *pardos*" (mulattos), for free men of African descent.[11]

In Mompox, anti-Spanish ranks included several leading Creole families, the majority of the cabildo, free blacks, mulattos and *zambos* (of mixed African and Indian ancestry), and some slaves under the command of their master. In late June 1810, as the city's cabildo approved Cartagena's deposition of Montes, an insurgent crowd, led by the zambo José Luis Muñoz and the black Luis Gonzaga Galván, forced Talledo into hiding. Shortly thereafter, Talledo secretly left Mompox for Bogotá, with the hope of returning with troops to suppress the rebellion, but the viceroy ignored his demand.[12]

Mompox and Cartagena followed similar paths until July 20, 1810, when

Bogotá established a "supreme junta" to govern New Granada in the name of Ferdinand VII. The supreme junta was to be autonomous from the council of the regency but, much to Cartagena's chagrin, kept the viceroyalty's power structure centralized in Bogotá. When the supreme junta summoned the provinces to send delegates to Bogotá for a general congress that would form a centralist government, Cartagena refused, proposing instead a congress in Medellín to establish a federalist government.[13] In contrast, Mompox's cabildo formally recognized the supreme junta of Bogotá, signed an act of independence, and sent it on to the juntas of Cartagena and Bogotá for approval. The hacendado and cabildo member, Vicente Celedonio Gutiérrez de Piñeres, freed his slaves, an act reportedly imitated by some other patriots.[14] In August, the cabildo decreed the organization of two battalions of volunteers to defend the city, one composed of whites and the other of pardos, but both commanded by white officers.[15]

In open defiance of Bogotá, in August 1810, Cartagena's cabildo established its own supreme junta, which enabled the provincial capital to appear to respond to Bogotá's July 20 revolution, while simultaneously securing its domination in the Caribbean region.[16] Presided over by García de Toledo, the new junta made two significant steps toward democracy. First, the free men of Cartagena, regardless of color, were called to select their city's six deputies. The inclusion of the lower classes of color in the selection process was a major sociopolitical change, even if the selection was done through public demonstrations that could easily be manipulated and produced only white elite Creole deputies.[17] Second, the interests of the rest of the province were given limited recognition with five delegates representing the region's other important cities. In the new context created by the July 20 revolution in Bogotá, however, such an overture was too modest to satisfy Mompox's radicals.[18]

Tensions between the two cities reached a climax after Cartagena issued a manifesto against holding a supreme congress in Bogotá.[19] On October 8, 1810, Mompox's cabildo voted to separate the city from the jurisdiction of Cartagena and to raise it to the status of capital of a new province, a decision ratified by an open cabildo on October 11.[20] The self-proclaimed independent province of Mompox formed a "patriotic junta" presided over by Vicente Celedonio Gutiérrez de Piñeres, and promulgated a republican and democratic constitution, a document that has since disappeared.[21]

In contrast to Cartagena and Mompox, Santa Marta was not subjected to new Spanish authorities in 1809, but continued to be ruled by the governor in place since 1805. Thus, only in August 1810, as news of the establishment of autonomous juntas in Cartagena, Mompox, and Bogotá arrived in the city, did a portion of the Creole elite mobilize a crowd and demand that a junta govern the province autonomously from the regency. The governor responded to the popular pressure and met with the city's cabildo. They agreed to entrust the male heads of households, regardless of race, with the selection of a junta to be presided over by the governor. As in other cities, only aristocrats were selected. The junta included autonomists, among them Colonel of the Militia José Munive, elected vice-president, as well as strong supporters of the regency. Most in the lower classes of color backed Munive's push for a government similar to Cartagena's and repeatedly demonstrated in the public square to force a reform of the junta. However, as an increasing number of Spanish and Creole royalists took refuge in Santa Marta to escape from the revolutions in Venezuela and New Granada, the balance of power shifted to the supporters of the regency.[22] On December 22, 1810, a crowd headed by a mulatto contractor, Narciso Vicente Crespo, made a last attempt to impose an autonomous junta.[23] Massed in front of the building where the junta was in session, they demanded that the people of Santa Marta be allowed to elect their own representatives to the junta, as in Cartagena, and that Munive be elected as the deputy of the province to the Cortes of Cadiz (parliament of the Spanish empire). The junta responded that such an election on the spot would be "invalid because a great part of the noble people and other plebeians were absent from the crowd." But it agreed to have "the *vecino* heads of family, nobles as well as plebeians," elect six deputies to a new junta. Simultaneously, the junta declared its president, the Spanish governor, "perpetual," thus not on the ballot.[24] With Munive elected representative at the Cortes, the new junta tipped toward the royalists. The regency sent a new Spanish governor and soldiers to the city. The voices for change were silenced definitively in June 1811 when, following pro-Spanish demonstrations and an expeditious vote in which only some sectors of the capital were consulted, the junta was replaced with the old form of government comprising the governor, his lieutenant, and the cabildo. "All commotion, tumult, or reunion of many persons, under the pretext of representing and demanding what they judge convenient to their right," was strictly prohibited.[25]

In the second half of 1810, various other Caribbean New Granadan towns and villages also rebelled, but there was little coordination among them. Some rose up against the authority of Cartagena or Santa Marta; others, against an abusive local government; still others, against Spanish direct government. In the process, some localities stood up for independence; others, autonomy; and still others, the Spanish monarchy. Several aligned themselves to one or the other side according to changing contexts. In addition, although still officially tied to Spain, Cartagena was progressively breaking away. When, in November 1810, the regency tried to send a new governor, the *cartageneros* of color took up arms and randomly attacked Spaniards and pro-Spanish Creoles. A crowd massed around the governor's palace to make sure that the cabildo would not allow the new governor to disembark.[26]

In December 1810, Cartagena's supreme junta democratized the province's electoral system into one of indirect semiproportional representation. All male parish citizens, "whites, Indians, mestizos, mulattos, zambos, and blacks who were heads of a family or a household, or lived off their own labor" could participate in the election of parish electors. "Only vagrants, those who had committed a crime leading to infamy, those salaried in actual servitude, and slaves will be excluded from [elections]."[27] Indians were granted full rights of citizenship, and there were no restrictions on who could become a people's representative based on race, place of birth, or property. Due to the secession of Mompox, however, no election took place.[28]

Furthermore, the supreme junta of Cartagena declared a war against Mompox. In January 1811, it sent 400 well-equipped veterans of the Fijo battalion against Mompox's battalions of pardo and white volunteers. Under the banner of "God and Independence," but with few arms and ammunitions, the *momposinos* resisted the attack for three days before evacuating the city. Cartagena's troops occupied Mompox and destroyed its revolutionary institutions. A new cabildo and new authorities were sworn in, many of whom were Spaniards and firm supporters of Spanish rule. Dozens of revolutionary leaders fled to other provinces, while many others were captured and imprisoned in Cartagena.[29]

The brutal repression of revolutionary Mompox fed hopes among Cartagena's pro-Spanish population that they could still turn the tide of events. On February 4, 1811, a few days after returning from its military attack against Mompox, the Fijo, backed by supporters of the regency, attempted to take over the governor's palace. Denounced by lower-rank officers, the conspiracy fell apart before any shots were fired.[30] Nevertheless, the lower classes took to the streets. Over a period of several days, hundreds of armed blacks, mulattos, and zambos attacked Spanish homes, arrested Spaniards, and imprisoned them in the barracks of the Pardo Patriots.[31]

After the conspiracy of the Fijo was thwarted, it became increasingly difficult for the supreme junta of Cartagena to maintain its loyalty to Spain as the popular classes and the radical portion of the elite demanded independence. United behind Gabriel and Germán Gutiérrez de Piñeres, supporters of independence also denounced the junta's fierce repression of Mompox's revolution that their brother Vicente Celedonio had promoted. Indeed, the occupation of Mompox initiated a personal feud between García de Toledo and the Gutiérrez de Piñeres brothers that rapidly evolved into a political conflict with socioracial overtones. Schematically, it opposed *toledistas,* representing the reformist elite interested in autonomy, and *piñeristas,* comprising more radical patricians and leaders and their lower-class, darker followers, who advocated independence.[32]

Piñerista pressure for independence increased, notably with a petition to the supreme junta signed by 479 vecinos from Cartagena. The junta refused to declare independence, arguing that the petition did not represent the general will of the province and that broader consultation was necessary.[33] But on November 11, 1811, the radicals forced the junta's hand. The Patriotic Lancers of Getsemaní and the Pardo Patriots took up positions on the walls and turned the artillery against the barracks of the Fijo and the White Patriots to prevent them from intervening. Gabriel Gutiérrez de Piñeres and Pedro Romero assembled lower-class men and artisans in Getsemaní. The crowd entered the city, seized arms in the arsenal, and invaded the palace of the junta.[34] Among their demands were absolute independence from Spain, "equal rights of all the classes of citizens," a government divided into three powers, appointment of pardo and black commanders in the battalion of pardos and the artillery, and the exclusion of "antipatriotic Europeans" from public office.[35] The armed populace assaulted García de Toledo and forced the full junta to sign the act of independence of the province. Later all the military corps, public officials, and ecclesiastic authorities (excepting the bishop) swore loyalty to independence.[36]

On November 11, the demonstrators in Cartagena also successfully demanded an end to the occupation and repression of Mompox. Vicente Celedonio Gutiérrez de Piñeres and his allies returned to power.[37] Thus, by early 1812, the piñeristas won over the toledistas in Cartagena, and the revolutionaries in Mompox had regained control, abandoning their project of forming an independent province. The whole region's male heads of family, regardless of race, designated the electors who then chose the deputies to a constituent convention. At least one of the thirty-six elected deputies, Romero, was of partial African descent.[38]

The 1812 constitution of the State of Cartagena de Indias developed the principles put forward by the 1811 act of independence. It was representative, republican, liberal, and stressed the fundamental rights of free individuals. It granted the right to vote for each free man, regardless of color, who was "resident, father or head of a family, or head of a household, who live[d] off his rents or labor, without depending on another person." It stated the importance of the Catholic religion to preserving public morality, seen as a necessary complement to the people's freedom. The constitution supported the decline of slavery but did not mention abolition. Inapplicable in the conditions of war and upheaval that followed its adoption, it was rapidly superseded by a series of regulations that gave extraordinary powers to the executive branch.[39]

Rather than initiating a period of region building and better conditions for all, Cartagena's act of independence in November 1811 triggered fragmentation, war, and destruction. From 1812 to 1814, the piñeristas controlled politics in Cartagena and Mompox. Now in power, they kept the capital's black, mulatto, and zambo lower classes in check, although the toledistas strongly resisted piñerista rule. Several, notably García de Toledo, retreated to their estates in the countryside. Through their network of haciendas and patronage in such towns as Barranquilla, Mahates, and Sabanalarga, they progressively built up an important opposition movement. In the words of the province's president, "in the midst of so many calamities, in the midst of so much suffering, civil war raises its head in the very heart of the state."[40]

The traditional rivalry between Cartagena and Santa Marta due to Cartagena's monopoly of the colonial foreign trade escalated into a war over the issue of independence versus Spanish colonialism, and for political and commercial control of the region.[41] In addition, Cartagena could not prevent its province from disintegrating. In September 1812, rallied by their priests, the small towns and villages in the vast southern area of Sincelejo and Corozal rebelled against the corregidor imposed by Cartagena and declared their allegiance to Ferdinand VII.[42] Troops from Santa Marta entered the province of Cartagena to back them and inflicted heavy losses on Cartagena's army, which was already hampered by "desertions and insubordination."[43]

The military fate of Cartagena only briefly improved at the end of 1812, after the arrival of some 400 Venezuelan and French refugees from the defeated pro-independence army of Venezuela. Among these officers and soldiers eager to keep fighting was Simón Bolívar, who regained most of the Magdalena region south of Barranca to the control of Cartagena. A French professional officer, Pedro Labatut, headed Cartagena's patriot troops in the reconquest of most of the lower Magdalena area and the triumphal occupation of Santa Marta in January 1813, leading to the mass exile of the city's royalist leaders and followers.[44] However, rather than building support for independence, Labatut forced the remaining inhabitants to approve the constitution of the province of Cartagena, imposed exorbitant war contributions, and pillaged the city and its surroundings. As a result, two months later neighboring Indians and escapees from the city expelled him and his troops, and Santa Marta returned to royalist control.[45]

From this brief account of Caribbean New Granada's early struggle for independence, what can we conclude about the region's political culture in the early nineteenth century? In Cartagena, Mompox, and Santa Marta the popular movements of 1810 did not question the colonial socioracial hierarchy and corporatist order. The movements' intellectual directors were all hacendados, merchants, lawyers, and clergymen. Powerful black, mulatto, and zambo professionals and contractors of some means linked them to the lower classes of color, whom they mobilized in mass demonstrations to pressure for change. In all the cities, in 1810 the popular mobilization was bloodless. Yet its outcome varied. In Cartagena and Mompox, the movement led to the eviction of Spanish officials and to independence. In Santa Marta, the small autonomist elite and its followers in the population of color were silenced by the growing number of royalists.

Important factors explain the different outcome in each city. First, Santa Marta had remained isolated from the currents of enlightenment and economic liberalism, and sustained only a tiny lettered elite beyond a handful of priests. Those who supported autonomy, rapidly marginalized by wealthy royalists seeking refuge in the city, were forced to embrace the cause of Spain or to escape. In contrast, several reformist elite leaders in Cartagena and Mompox had graduated in law or theology in Bogotá, had taken part in political discussions there, built long-lasting relations with the intellectual elite of Andean New Granada, and closely followed the debates of the Spanish Cortes. In addition to the three Gutiérrez de Piñeres brothers linking Cartagena and Mompox, many shared family ties.[46]

Second, both Governor Montes in Cartagena and Commander Talledo in Mompox were new to the region and lacked the experience to handle the Creole challenge. By contrast, the governor of the province of Santa Marta, in office since 1805, managed the situation with an expert hand, seeming to give in to the popular will while retaining absolute power for himself as president of the junta.

Third, regardless of the city's position toward Spain, in the elections to the 1810 juntas the ruling authorities enfranchised all men who were heads of household and earned an independent living, regardless of race. Such an enfranchisement violated the decision by the Cortes in Cadiz to limit the exercise of citizenship to "natives derived from both hemispheres, Spaniards as well as Indians, and the children of both" and to exclude by default Africans and those of full or partial African descent.[47] No doubt this decision was dictated by the region's demography: even the governor of Santa Marta was aware that to deprive blacks, mulattos, and zambos of the vote could result in rebellion. After 1810, Santa Marta's return to the old form of nonelected government removed the issue of the black vote from the agenda. In the case of Cartagena, however, the late-1810 decision by the Cortes to deny proportionally equal representation to Americans and Spaniards became the piñeristas' principal justification for demanding independence from Spain.[48] Although the Cortes's denial triggered anti-Spanish movements in much of Spanish America, in Caribbean New Granada there was an additional urgency. Disenfranchisement of the great majority of the population of full or partial African ancestry would have deprived Cartagena's elite of a deputy to the next Cortes to promote its interests against those of the Andean interior. As argued by the anonymous letter of "a Creole" to Cartagena's first weekly, *El Argos Americano,* in a rare mention of the issue of race, the free "castas" deserved the right to be represented as much as the "ignorant Indians obedient to the priests."[49]

Last but not least, only in Cartagena and Mompox did the elite and the intermediate leaders organize lower-class men of color in the militia and distribute arms to them. This armed mobilization, given the cities' demography, inevitably neutralized the royalist minority. In contrast, in Santa Marta the free population of color opposed to Spain remained amorphous and unarmed. There the men of African descent in the colonial militia of all colors did not take advantage of being the city's only military force to challenge their officers, all white and members of the junta. In brief, independence established roots only when a powerful nucleus in the local elite was committed to reform and when, together with leaders of African descent, they mobilized and armed lower-class men of color.

Coming after the Haitian revolution, the cross-class and cross-racial movement against Spain that took place in Cartagena and Mompox had few equivalents in other Latin American cities with large populations of African descent. For example, the first Venezuelan republic established in Caracas in 1811–12 was racially and socially exclusive and limited political participation to the landed aristocracy.[50] It should be noted, however, that in Cartagena and Mompox, elite leaders and the popular classes joined forces without upsetting the colonial socioracial order. Each group pursued different goals behind a common republican discourse: freedom from the restrictions imposed by the metropolis for the elite, racial equality for the lower classes.

Several characteristics of the political culture and the socioracial fabric of Caribbean New Granada explain why the first independence could not firmly establish itself in the region. First, division among the leading anti-Spanish Creole elite was based more on family feuding than on ideological or organizational differences. Still, piñeristas and toledistas did disagree on the nature of the relationship of their province with Bogotá. The toledistas advocated strong federalism and rejected the leadership of the New Granadan capital, whereas the piñeristas, often themselves not native cartageneros, did not oppose some centralization in Bogotá in order to secure victory against Spain. Nevertheless, in spite of favoring racial equality among the free, both groups were anxious to keep the people of African descent who had brought them to power in check. As a result, the ideological similarities between piñeristas and toledistas prevented the polarization of the movement into two opposing projects of society: one of social revolution empowering the lower classes and one more conservative and socially exclusive. Simultaneously, both the piñeristas and toledistas channeled lower-class men of color into their movement, thus neutralizing the latter's autonomous socioracial challenge.

Like most pro-independence leaders in Spanish America, the toledistas and piñeristas were unable to question the colonial territorial organization and imagine a new nation with different boundaries and a democratically integrated territory. In early 1811, Cartagena's Creole leaders waged a war to reimpose colonial subordination on secessionist Mompox. Throughout the period, rather than using the constitution of 1812 as a tool of propaganda, they fought to impose Cartagena's hegemony on Santa Marta. They struggled to maintain their domination over the villages, towns, and territory they considered to be in Cartagena's jurisdiction by any means, including military occupation, the destruction of villages, and the rejection of Simón Bolívar's supreme leadership in New Granada's war for independence. They were unable to conceive of new, less centralized relations of power that might have forged broad regional support for their cause. Therefore, they failed to address one of the principal problems of Caribbean New Granada: its territorial fragmentation in rival hacendados' fiefdoms, villages, small towns, and cities. In other words, they missed the historical opportunity to unite Caribbean New Granada behind a project of independence and regional identity vis-à-vis Andean New Granada.

Yet the toledista and piñerista aristocrats could agree on a project that did not upset the colonial socioracial order because free people of color and slaves did not collectively challenge them in their endeavor.[51] The white elite's alliance with the free men of color, unlike the French revolutionary clubs, remained highly hierarchical. In particular, in 1810–11 the popular sectors in Cartagena and Mompox conformed to the elite's decision to organize their urban defense along racial lines. Although in Cartagena such an organization corresponded to the racial separations established by Spain in the militia, in Mompox, where the colonial militia had been "of all colors," this introduced a new racial division. The reason for such acquiescence may be that under Spain the colonial militia had been the first institution to grant free men of African descent equality by extending the military *fuero* and some corporate privileges to the militia's officers and enlisted men, regardless of race.[52] In the new independent units formed in 1810, those traditionally subordinated because of their race gained further consciousness of their equality, grounded in their political, economic, and military participation in the struggle against Spain, which led to the acquisition of their political rights as citizens.

However, these racially based military units did not transform themselves into autonomous political organizations. Although armed and comprising the majority of the population, in 1810–12 the free men of color in

Cartagena and Mompox continued to entrust their political representation to the white reformist elite. This was partly due to their mobilization by leaders of African descent who were too entangled in vertical patronage networks headed by white aristocrats to become ideologically independent. The only exception, perhaps, was the zambo José Luis Muñoz in Mompox, described as "one of the directors of the town councilors," but unfortunately his ideas were never recorded.[53] This pattern of white patronage with intermediate leaders of African descent also explains why in Santa Marta the only armed unit in the city, the militia of all colors, did not rebel independently. As the city's swelling royalists forced the pro-autonomy elite to switch their allegiance to Spain or leave, the leaders of color had to undertake dramatic political realignments. Whereas some went to Cartagena, Narciso Vicente Crespo, for example, became a commander in Santa Marta's royalist army and led his lower-class followers to fight victoriously against Cartagena's pro-independence troops.[54]

Hierarchical alliances between white leaders and free men of color did not evolve into autonomous political organizations along racial lines also because men of African descent saw them as a major step toward their much desired integration into the new political system. Because a discourse on equality required silence on the question of race, the demand for equality was not made on the grounds of one's color but of one's personal value and services to society. This automatically limited the application of the concepts of equality and citizenship to the free adult male population with gainful employment or some financial means. As a result, the free men dissociated their cause from that of other disenfranchised members of society such as indigents, slaves, servants, women, and Indians. Moreover, by participating in some organizations, such as the patriot militias, that supported the new social order against anarchy, the citizens of color helped prevent unwelcome movements and slave unrest. Although many dark-skinned piñerista supporters united behind their leaders' message of independence and equality, they did not question the significance that racial categories such as *negro, pardo, zambo,* or *cuarterón* (quadroon) had in defining one's socioeconomic status and identity. Hierarchical status assignment between free persons of partial and full African ancestry continued, and therefore no racial consciousness uniting the free and slave populations as well as blacks, mulattos, and zambos emerged in this process.[55]

By not forming their own political movement in 1810–11, the free people of color lost a major opportunity to assert themselves and push for a distinct agenda. Although in Cartagena they briefly showed their capacity to act independently from the white leadership in the revolt against the conspiracy of the Fijo in February 1811, afterward they returned to their homes and barracks. When in November 1811 they were able to force some reforms on the supreme junta, their demand for equality of all citizens regardless of race merely repeated what had already been granted in 1810. They requested that "the battalion of pardos have its commander from the same class and be allowed to name its adjutants," and that "the militia of artillery have the same terms as the battalion of pardos, with officers from their class."[56] This confirmed their acceptance of colonial corporatist and racial categories, and they did nothing then to promote the end of slavery. By the time of the debates about the constitution in February 1812, the piñerista leaders had managed to end armed demonstrations by the populace and the Patriot Lancers of Getsemaní aimed at exerting pressure on the deputies. Later that year, newly arriving Venezuelans and Frenchmen took positions of command previously held by cartageneros, thus completing the process of political subordination of the city's free population of color. As the war with Santa Marta deepened, the separate units of men of African descent were dissolved and their soldiers were absorbed into racially and regionally inclusive armies. They had definitively lost the possibility of organizing autonomously around a distinct agenda.

Slavery did not become a major issue in Caribbean New Granada. Slaves maintained themselves at the margin of the independence process, and few, if any, took advantage of the breakdown of the colonial order to organize movements to gain their freedom and equality. Neither did the free population of color prompt an abolitionist movement in the province. In addition, if kinship and similar labor conditions sometimes linked slaves and poor free people of color, some free individuals of African descent owned slaves. Thus, no racial or class consciousness united them that could have produced a common movement. The reformist elite was free to draft social policies for slaves corresponding to their own interests as hacendados, merchants, miners, and slaveowners.

Yet after 1810, the number of slaves declined sharply in Caribbean New Granada to 7,128 (4 percent of the total population) in 1825, down from 14,067 (8.7 percent) in the late 1770s.[57] Much of this decline was due to factors unrelated to the war, such as the end of the slave trade, the low birth rate among slave women, self-purchase, and flight. But the general lack of order and the crisis produced by the war speeded up the process. Many slaves seized the opportunity to run away and settle in remote areas, quietly joining the ranks of the free population of color after the war.[58] The war also caused the departure or death of many slaves. Some emigrated with their masters. Others were exported to the Caribbean, particularly patriot conscripts captured by royalists; others again were confiscated as payment for fines and war contributions.[59] Finally, slaves residing in cities were the victims of wartime hunger and epidemics, notably during the deadly siege imposed on Cartagena by Spanish General Pablo Morillo in 1815.[60]

People of African descent in small towns, villages, and hacendados' fiefdoms reacted without regional vision or coordination to the struggle for independence. Allegiance to one or the other side often depended more on specific circumstances than on ideology.[61] In 1810, free people of color in several villages and small towns east of the Magdalena River took advantage of the breakdown of Spanish authority to momentarily seize power. In some places the "frail remnants of subordination that contained the people" vanished under the pressure of the lower classes of color, and "the evils of anarchy" reigned.[62] However, lacking coordination, leadership, and arms, these villages could not resist the forces sent by Santa Marta and were rapidly reconquered. Even the villages and towns in the plains of Corozal and Sincelejo that in 1812 rejected the jurisdiction of Cartagena and proclaimed allegiance to Santa Marta did not remain royalist strongholds. As a result of his abuses against the local population, the Spanish commander was driven out, and Corozal returned to the bosom of Cartagena.[63]

Throughout the first independence, neither royalists nor patriots were able to consistently rally Caribbean New Granadan communities to their cause. In reality, people struggled to survive. Villagers increasingly resorted to the tactic of abandoning dwellings and crops to the invaders and taking refuge in the woods to avoid abuse and enlistment. As misery, havoc, and forced conscription increased, more and more communities missed the loose domination that had characterized colonial rule before 1810. Although, ironically, this very looseness facilitated Spanish military reconquest in 1815, the crown's brutal policy of "pacification" blocked any rebuilding of support for colonial government.[64] By 1819, Simón Bolívar and Francisco de Paula Santander had begun to retake control of Andean Colombia. As a new war for the control of Caribbean New Granada began in 1819, few communities participated in the patriot advance or the royalist resistance. People were simply too exhausted to envision more than survival. Only a few communities, such as Barranquilla and Soledad, volunteered men and goods to the advancing pro-independence army. After strong resistance from neighboring Indians and royalist forces, Santa Marta surrendered in November 1820. As during Morillo's reconquest in 1815, Cartagena was the last city on the coast to fall to the patriot army, in October 1821, after a long siege.[65]

Tragically, the region that had been first in Colombia to declare independence and to grant equality and full citizenship to people of African descent regained independence last (with Pasto in the south) in 1821. Fragmentation, division, competition between cities and among elites, as well as the lower classes of color's inability to challenge the small white elite, frustrated Caribbean New Granada's unique alternative opportunities: either to lead the movement of independence in New Granada, or to form a separate nation with its own Caribbean identity. As a result, the Andean elite could blame much of the failure of the first independence on Cartagena and its resistance to the leadership of Simón Bolívar.[66]

When, in 1821, Caribbean New Granada became part of Gran Colombia, its economy and social fabric were much more damaged than those of Andean New Granada. Two sieges had initiated Cartagena's rapid decline. The region had lost most of its leadership in the Spanish reconquest and the war. As a result, in the 1820s the department of the Magdalena (comprised of the provinces of Cartagena, Santa Marta, and Riohacha) was headed by a Venezuelan general, and Venezuelan officers commanded many of its towns and villages. Among the most vocal delegates for Caribbean New Granada at the 1821 Congress of Cúcuta that debated and approved the constitution of Gran Colombia was the Venezuelan Pedro Gual.[67] The constitution was rigidly centralist, with Bogotá as Gran Colombia's provisional capital. It stressed protection of Colombians' "liberty, security, property, and equality" but actually did not include measures for eradicating inherited colonial racial inequalities.[68] However, the Congress of Cúcuta approved the law of October 11, 1821, that gave equality to Indians while laying the groundwork for the liquidation of their community lands.[69] Slaves were the focus of the law of July 21, 1821, which progressively abolished slavery while attempting to reconcile the contradictory constitutional rights to freedom, equality, and property. It declared that, from that point on, all children born of slave mothers would be free but would have to work for their mother's masters without pay until they reached the age of eighteen in order to compensate for their upbringing.[70]

Like the constitution of 1821, the first post-independence census, in 1825, did not mention race: it comprised only the categories of ecclesiastics, slaves, and free people.[71] Although this absence of racial labeling broke sharply with colonial practices, it did not mean that race had ceased to matter with the advent of the republic. In reality, it created a free space in which some Colombians began to portray New Granada as Andean and white, in contrast to Venezuela where "free pardos" dominated, and Ecuador where Indians were the absolute majority. Typical of this view were the estimates of Gran Colombia's population by country and "caste" given in 1824 by the white *antioqueño* minister of the interior José Manuel Restrepo, who also was the director of the 1825 raceless census and one of the principal architects of the 1821 constitution:

CASTE	VENEZUELA	NEW GRANADA	ECUADOR	TOTAL
Whites	200,000	877,000	157,000	1,234,000
Indians	207,000	313,000	393,000	913,000
Free *pardos*	433,000	140,000	42,000	615,000
Slaves	60,000	70,000	8,000	138,000
TOTAL	900,000	1,400,000	600,000	2,900,000[72]

In order to whiten New Granada's population, Restrepo simply eliminated the category of mestizos and assimilated them to whites. As a result, Andean New Granada appeared as the white, civilized center of Gran Colombia against the pardo Venezuela and the Indian Ecuador. Yet Restrepo still attributed 140,000 free pardos to New Granada, mostly in La Costa, where he sensed the same danger of pardo takeover as in Venezuela.[73]

This construction of Andean New Granada as white and superior occurred as tensions between Bolívar and Santander increased. As early as 1821, Bolívar had accused Santander and his fellow "*caballeros*" (gentlemen) in the eastern cordillera of living isolated from "all the savage hordes from Africa and America that, like bucks, cross[ed] the wilderness of Colombia" and composed most of its pro-independence army, and of envisioning a liberal government incompatible with this reality.[74] Only an authoritarian and centralized government could unite and rule over Gran Colombia's diverse population. As Bolívar's strongest supporters tended to be high-ranking Venezuelan officers, often in government positions in Caribbean New Granada, Bolívar's discord with Santander evolved into a nationwide political conflict with socioracial connotations. It confronted the educated white elite of the Andean cities and their mostly mestizo inhabitants with the "rough" Venezuelan military and Venezuela's and Caribbean New Granada's population of mixed African descent. Moreover, in 1827, in an affront to Santander, several cities in the Caribbean region demanded that Bolívar assume dictatorial powers.[75] As Venezuelan provinces began to withdraw from Gran Colombia at the end of the decade, anti-Bogotá feelings and separatist ideas were on the rise in the Caribbean region.[76] As a result, New Granada's early nationalism not only exalted the Andes, it was also constructed against Venezuela and, by extension, against Caribbean New Granada.

Major changes within Caribbean New Granada were contributing to decreasing the region's importance vis-à-vis Andean New Granada. In the 1820s, the region was in crisis and its share of New Granada's total population declined. The three rival cities of Cartagena, Mompox, and Santa Marta did not regain their key colonial position but began to face the growing competition of the Caribbean port of Sabanilla near Barranquilla. Decimated by war and reconquest, the regional elite lacked vision, and its most prominent members chose to pursue their careers in Bogotá. Neither did the free population of color recover the political importance they had in 1810. In a few villages and cities some leaders reportedly agitated pardos against whites, yet no significant revolt or confrontation took place.[77] Free men of African descent also lost their leading role in Caribbean New Granada's military defense. Before 1810, defense principally rested on self-supporting blacks, mulattos, and zambos readily joining the status-earning militias. But after 1821 army enlistment became increasingly violent and served to punish vagrants, petty criminals, and noncompliant peasants and workers, generally of African descent. In 1810, militiamen of color gained citizenship and racial equality for their role in the overthrow of the Spanish authority, but by 1828 most soldiers had been disenfranchised by Santander on property grounds.[78]

The most enduring characteristic of the political culture of Caribbean New Granada's first independence was the cross-class and cross-racial alliances linking the white elite to the popular classes of color without challenging the socioracial hierarchy. These alliances continued in the movements attached to Bolívar and Santander in the 1820s, and would form the backbone of the two-party system Colombia adopted in the 1840s.[79] Like these alliances, the Conservative and Liberal parties did not have fundamental ideological differences, which precluded the conceptualization of two rival projects of society. Moreover, as Conservative and Liberal leaders were able to channel lower-class men of color under their respective banner, they neutralized autonomous socioracial challenges. As the two parties integrated local and regional constituencies into the Colombian nation, they also prevented the Caribbean region's united challenge to the Andean center. This enabled the highlands' elite to construct the Colombian nation as Andean, white, and mestizo, and to minimize its Afro-Caribbean identity.

NOTES

1. On pre-independence free people of color in New Granada, see Garrido's chapter in this volume.
2. Lynch, *Spanish American Revolution;* Rodríguez O., *Independence;* Hamnett, "Process and Pattern."
3. McFarlane, "Building Political Order"; Tovar, "Guerras de opinión"; Earle, *Spain.*
4. Nichols, *Tres puertos,* 39–41; Fidalgo, "Expedición Fidalgo," 76 n; Consejo Regional de Planificación de la Costa Atlántica, *Mapa cultural,* maps on 51, 85; McFarlane, *Colombia,* 39–40.
5. Phelan, *People and the King,* 26; McFarlane, *Colombia,* 232–71; Kuethe, *Military Reform,* 86–87.
6. Pedro Mendinueta to José María Alvarez, May 19, 1799, Archivo General de Indias, Seville (hereinafter cited as AGI); Archivo General de Simancas (hereinafter cited as AGS), Guerra 7247, no. 26, May 19, 1799, fols. 147–48; Helg, "Fragmented Majority."
7. McFarlane, *Colombia,* 353; these figures do not include the thousands of unsubdued Indians and free people of color living on the periphery.
8. Mendinueta, "Relación," 55–56.
9. Corrales, ed., *Documentos,* 1:127, 413.
10. Ibid., 1:81–90, 127–28, 385–89; Antonio de Narváez y la Torre to Virrey de Santa Fe, June 19, 1810, AGI, Santa Fe 1011.

11. Corrales, ed., *Documentos,* 1:94–95.
12. Ibid., 1:119–21, 149–50; Salzedo del Villar, *Apuntaciones,* 93–94.
13. On Bogotá, see McFarlane, "Building Political Order," 17–20.
14. Corrales, ed., *Documentos,* 1:87–89; Salzedo de Villar, *Apuntaciones,* 100.
15. Corrales, ed., *Documentos,* 1:187–89, 206–7; Salzedo del Villar, *Apuntaciones,* 100, 117–18.
16. "A todos los estantes y habitantes de esta Plaza y Provincia," November 9, 1810, AGI, Santa Fe 747.
17. Jiménez, *Los mártires,* 1:147–48, 238–39; Corrales, ed., *Documentos,* 1:82.
18. Ibid., 1:199, 226.
19. See Junta de la Provincia de Cartagena de Indias a las demás de éste nuevo Reyno de Granada, September 19, 1810, AGI, Santa Fe 747.
20. Corrales, ed., *Documentos,* 1:198–210, 232–33.
21. Ibid., 1:219; Salzedo del Villar, *Apuntaciones,* 112.
22. Corrales, ed., *Documentos,* 1:136–40.
23. Romero, *Esclavitud,* 86–88.
24. Corrales, ed., *Documentos,* 1:184–85; see also Restrepo Tirado, *Historia,* 499–507.
25. Corrales, ed., *Documentos,* 1:338–42.
26. Ibid., 1:390; Jiménez, *Los mártires,* 1:149–53.
27. Corrales, ed., *Efemérides,* 2:48.
28. *El Argos Americano*, suplemento, Dec. 24, 1810.
29. Salzedo del Villar, *Apuntaciones,* 113–18; Arrázola, *Los mártires,* 180; Corrales, ed., *Documentos,* 1:205, 218, 370, 372.
30. *El Argos Americano*, Febr. 4, 1811, March 18, 1811; Miguel Gutiérrez to Capitán General de la isla de Cuba, March 3, 1811, AGI, Santa Fe 747.
31. Corrales, ed., *Efemérides,* 2:67–68; "Alegato del gobierno de Cartagena," Febr. 8, 1811, AGI, Santa Fe 747.
32. *El Argos Americano*, April 15, 1811; Jiménez, *Los mártires,* 1:192, 238–44, 260–63.
33. Corrales, ed., *Efemérides,* 2:72–73; Corrales, ed., *Documentos,* 1:368.
34. Ibid., 1:412.
35. "Proposiciones presentadas por los diputados del pueblo y aprobadas y sancionadas el 11 de Noviembre de 1811," in "Carta del comandante general de Panamá a ministro de justicia," Nov. 30, 1811, AGI, Santa Fe 745.
36. Corrales, ed., *Documentos,* 1:351–56, 365, 371, 394–95; Copia de la correspondencia entre la Suprema Junta de Cartagena de Indias y el obispo Fraile Custodio, June 1, 1812, AGI, Santa Fe 747; Jiménez, *Los mártires,* 1:238–81.
37. Arrázola, *Los mártires responden,* 183–84, 196.
38. Jiménez, *Los mártires,* 1:281, 285–86.
39. Corrales, ed., *Documentos,* 1:485–546.
40. Ibid., 1:557.
41. Ibid., 1:259–73.

42. Ibid., 1:445–47; Restrepo, *Historia,* 1:242–43.
43. Gabriel Gutiérrez de Piñeres to Pantaleón Germán Ribón, Oct. 16, 1812, in Archivo Histórico Nacional de Colombia (Bogotá), Archivo Histórico Restrepo, caja 1, fondo 1, rollo 1, fols. 116–17.
44. Corrales, ed., *Documentos,* 1:561–74; Castro Trespalacios, *Culturas aborígenes,* 79.
45. Corrales, ed., *Documentos,* 1:595–601; Ortiz, *Franceses,* 103–8.
46. Cf. Uribe-Urán, *Honorable Lives,* 60–65.
47. Cf. O'Phelan Godoy, "Discurso y etnicidad."
48. Americans were allowed one deputy per 100,000 inhabitants, but peninsulars one deputy per 50,000 inhabitants; only Spaniards, Indians, and their mixed descendents could vote; King, "The Colored Castes," 33–64; Anna, "Spain and the Breakdown," 242–72.
49. *El Argos Americano,* Jan. 28, 1811.
50. On Venezuela, see Hamnett, "Process and Pattern," 317–19.
51. On indigenous challenge during the process of independence, see Helg, "Liberty and Equality," chap. 4.
52. Corrales, ed., *Documentos,* 1:187–89; Salzedo del Villar, *Apuntaciones,* 117–18.
53. Corrales, ed., *Documentos,* 1:53.
54. Ibid., 1:595–96.
55. Posada Gutiérrez, *Memorias,* 2:195–209; Corrales, ed., *Efemérides,* 2:64–70.
56. "Proposiciones presentadas por los diputados del pueblo," Nov. 30, 1811, AGI, Santa Fe 745.
57. McFarlane, *Colombia,* 353; Tovar Pinzón, '*Convocatoria,*' 93–96.
58. Francisco de Paz to gobernador político y militar, Sept. 20, 1816, AGI, Cuba 715; Bell, *Cartagena de India,* 80–95.
59. Corrales, ed., *Documentos,* 1:310, 571–72.
60. Ibid., 2:272–90; Bossa, *Cartagena,* 24–26.
61. For a similar pattern in Guerrero, Mexico, see Guardino, *Peasants,* 48–54.
62. Corrales, ed., *Documentos,* 1:270.
63. Ibid., 1:592.
64. Earle, "Popular Participation," 87–101.
65. Correspondencia del gobernador militar de Mompox, Sept. 1819, AGI, Cuba 746; Alarcón, *Compendio,* 90–105; Sourdis Nájera, "Ruptura," 181–89.
66. Restrepo, *Historia,* 2:6–30.
67. Restrepo Piedrahita, *El congreso,* 48 n.
68. Uribe Vargas, ed., *Las Constituciones de Colombia,* 2:707–38.
69. Colombia, *Codificación nacional,* 1:16–18.
70. Ibid., 1:14–17.
71. Tovar Pinzón, "*Convocatoria,*" 90–98; an appendix listed "the tribes of independent and uncivilized indigenous" with their estimated numbers.

72. Restrepo, *Historia,* 1:19.

73. Ibid., 1:15–18, 40–44.

74. Bolívar, *Obras completas,* 1:565.

75. Maingot, "Social Structure," 311–20; Sourdis Nájera, "Ruptura," 193–96.

76. Bell, "Conflictos regionales," 43–44; Bushnell, *Making of Modern Colombia,* 51–73.

77. For example, Causa criminal contra Valentin Arcia, Majagual, 1822, AHNC, República, legajo 61, fols. 1143–1209 and legajo 96, fols. 244–322; "Disturbios en Mompox," 1823, AHNC, República, legajo 66, fols. 804–11; Alarcón, *Compendio,* 181.

78. Uribe-Urán, *Honorable Lives,* 90.

79. Fals Borda, *El presidente Nieto,* 65B, 70B-72B.

THE MAKING OF ECUADOR'S PUEBLO CATÓLICO, 1861–1875

Derek Williams

In late 1873, an assembly of Church dignitaries in Quito offered the Ecuadorian "nation" to the "sacred and most loving heart of Jesus." Upon approval by congress some weeks later, Ecuador became the first and only republic in Spanish America to dedicate itself to the cult of the Sacred Heart.[1] Ecuador's unusual consecration marked the climax of an equally extraordinary national-Catholic project under the government of Gabriel García Moreno, the country's earnestly religious and resolutely authoritarian president (1861–65, 1869–75). In 1862, as one of his first executive acts, García Moreno negotiated a concordat with the Vatican, bolstering clerical autonomy against customary state patronage and intervention. Seven years later, he drafted a constitution that made Roman Catholicism a prerequisite for citizenship, conformed to Pope Pius IX's anti-liberal *Syllabus* of "errors," and pledged to make "political institutions" conform with "religious beliefs." Between 1861 and August 1875—when García Moreno was assassinated—Ecuador's government-Church coalition laid an impressive legal and administrative foundation for the construction of a "truly Catholic nation."[2]

The Garcian government broadened public education, passed comprehensive legislation, and developed a state policing apparatus to vigorously repress immorality and impiety.

This essay studies the process by which the Garcian government "catholicized" civil society and political culture, and what this meant for the creation of an inclusive national community and the strengthening of state power. It examines government strategies to make piety, morality, and hard work the essence of Ecuadorian identity and the ultimate source of legitimate political claims.[3] It specifically analyzes state initiatives in the areas of education and the repression of vice, assessing the utility of gender, race, and class understandings that informed García Moreno's nation- and state-making enterprises. I contend that while the ideals of official discourse were sporadically realized, the Garcian project of reinforced Catholicism generated impressive achievements. On one level, it elevated and potentially empowered certain sectors of the national population, most demonstrably a reformed clergy, but also women and indigenes—two groups portrayed as future embodiments of an authentically Catholic community. At base, however, national-Catholic politics was authoritarian, formidably seeking to subordinate all Ecuadorians—men and women, white and indigene, citizens and would-be citizens—to a state-defined culture of religiosity.

THE GARCIAN PROJECT

Ecuador's ultra-Catholic experiment seemingly runs counter to broader Latin American "modernizing" ideological currents, which after midcentury justified the nationalization of Church wealth, questioned Catholicism's customary "official sanction," and defined civilization in increasingly secular terms.[4] Yet the making of a "truly Catholic" Ecuador was to be a decidedly modern project—infused with progress-minded, state-building and nation-making imperatives. First, Garcian advocates believed that a regenerated religiosity would lay the basis for a "Catholic modernity"—a model of development that judged Christian morality to be the basis of genuine and lasting economic progress.[5] And the interventionist central government was committed to rapid material development, particularly the incorporation of regional economies into world markets, the construction of a modern transportation network, and the formation of a national technical elite.[6] Second, the Garcian government's tight connection with the institution of the Church never implied the abandonment of secular political authority. Although the central government protected the property and prerogatives of the Church, it substantially reformed and subordinated the clergy, strategically intervening in the Church's administrative infrastructure to extend state vigilance and repression into the provinces.[7]

Finally, while García Moreno tightened links to transnational Roman Catholicism, he clearly understood the utility of strong religiosity for building a *national* identity.[8] However, unlike its ultimately tactical relation with the Church, the Garcian government's dual commitment to "*religión y patria*" was by all accounts authentic.[9] Indeed, García Moreno's piety cannot be reduced to "a means to a secular end"—a rhetorical gambit for a larger state-building enterprise.[10] Although religion served to legitimate and consolidate central governance in Ecuador, García Moreno was genuine in his advocacy of progressive and practical—if hierarchical and repressive—Catholic morality for the Ecuadorian people. In the end, his political and religious purposes were inescapably intertwined, both integral parts of an ambitious authoritarian national project.

García Moreno's nationalism was aptly expressed in the notion of "*pueblo católico*"—an inclusive community of pious, moral, and industrious members, open to men and women, to all races, to every class.[11] This national collectivity captured Catholicism's universalizing imperative "of incorporating subaltern classes" in the march of progress—what its proponents considered a fundamental advantage over the "solely individualist" focus of the "liberal Protestant world."[12] To be sure, the Garcian Catholic community retained customary hierarchies, and as such was an effective means of social control for a country riddled with racial, class, and gender inequalities. Still, the collective-popular emphasis of the project was powerfully deployed and had the effect of tempering individual liberties and citizenship rights, both of which were subordinated to a state-defined Catholic morality. Indeed, civil society in Catholic Ecuador was to be restricted and carefully regulated by the central government's antivice police agents and Church allies. Legitimate politics was tied to a culture of Catholic religiosity and morality that was narrowly defined by a dictatorial government.

EDUCATING THE ECUADORIAN PUEBLO

Widely disseminated and standardized state schooling is a powerful tool for inventing, reshaping, or perpetuating national identities. While education systems rarely do what governments claim or hope, they remain an effectual, if contested, means for constructing homogeneous communities.[13] The García Moreno government actively sought to establish a centralized public school system that could form moral and industrious national subjects. During the Garcian era, annual school funding jumped eightfold and by 1874 had topped $400,000—an impressive 14 percent of government revenues. Elementary school enrollment rose steadily in the 1860s to reach 15,000 in 1871, then exploded to 32,000 in the following four years.[14] Education became funded directly from treasury funds—bolstered by flourishing cacao export revenues and an increased state tithe share.[15] García Moreno strove to make public instruction more Catholic, practical, accessible, and uniform. In the new centrally administered national system, Catholic doctrine was considered the "only basis" of instruction, inspiring every aspect of schooling.[16] At the same time, however, the government pioneered technical and scientific training, and education was increasingly judged on its demonstrable utility to national progress.[17]

García Moreno's education policy was notable for its broad scope—from a polytechnic school in Quito to well-funded music and fine arts institutions. Above all, however, it prioritized free and compulsory elementary schooling in Catholicism and Castilian literacy.[18] For leadership in primary schooling, as in other areas of education reform, the government turned to Europe. In 1863, the Christian Brothers arrived from France, bringing with them their state-of-the-art "simultaneous" pedagogy. Based in the teachings of the order's founder, Jean Baptiste de la Salle (1651–1719), instruction was to be rigorously Catholic, but also "practical, rational and progressive."[19] The La Salle curriculum linked Christian morality and virtue to habits of hard work and productive skills obtained through technical training.[20] The government promptly contracted the Brothers to set up schools in Cuenca, Guayaquil, and Quito, and other provincial capitals scrambled to raise funds to establish similar facilities. By the early 1870s, with centralized standards in place and the first official textbooks in circulation, Ecuador had the makings of its first national elementary education system.[21]

The classrooms of the new schools, of course, were filled largely with the sons of urban society's upper class. However, the Christian Brothers—renowned in Europe for educating the "working classes"—also taught a sector of Ecuador's "poor" urban children, who comprised over a quarter of their 870 students.[22] In this way, La Salle schools contributed to a more ambitious state project to extend education to the most "abject" sectors of society. At the start of his second term, García Moreno launched an eleven-year plan to eradicate illiteracy among all Ecuadorians born after 1870.[23] Most notably, the government channeled funds and energies toward schooling females and *indígenas*—society's most "neglected" but promising children.

SCHOOLING GIRLS AND INDIGENES

In the area of female education, the achievements of the Garcian government were considerable—"nunnish" perhaps, but substantial and progressive nonetheless. Reflecting the broader imperatives of the state, the education of Ecuadorian girls, while "essentially religious," prioritized as well feminine elements of "arts and sciences." The Sisters of the Sacred Heart, for instance, were contracted from France to train the daughters of the urban elite in reading and writing, basic geography and arithmetic, foreign languages and fine arts.[24] History and literature were also taught, though restricted to topics approved by activist Church censors.[25] For middle- and lower-class girls, the government funded a variety of Catholic institutions that more explicitly focused on "scientific" training in "manual arts." Dressmaking, lacework, and the manufacture of artificial flowers were among the "womanly tasks" that an urban middle-class girl was likely to learn. Girls in poorer neighborhoods, or those living in orphanages, were typically schooled in ironing, cooking, and laundering, skills required to become domestic servants.[26] In rural areas, the curriculum emphasized basic literacy and religion, with additional instruction in sewing, weaving, hygiene, and "home economics." To train young women to work as teachers in the countryside, urban secondary schools established "pedagogic divisions."[27] To be sure, progress toward implementing universal female education was slow, a reality that particularly irked the president. Yet, despite its limitations, the state program backed up its promise to enlighten women with impressive advances in school attendance. The number of girls' schools quadrupled between 1857 and 1875. At the time of García Moreno's death, over 8,500 girls were enrolled in primary schools.[28]

Extending the benefits of education to the "destitute indigene class"—about half of Ecuador's roughly one million inhabitants—posed similar but specific challenges for the government.[29] For indigenes of the sierra, whose "repugnance to all innovation" was notorious, the government deemed a nationalizing curriculum and reforming pedagogy as secondary to creating a culture of school attendance.[30] To this end, legislation in 1871 making elementary education obligatory eliminated the unpopular customs of subsidizing rural schooling with special taxes or the sale of Indian lands. Sanctions against students' families for nonattendance were counterbalanced with incentives, such as exempting literate indígenas from customary public works obligations.[31] School timetables were rearranged so that Indian children could both attend classes and help their families with agricultural tasks.[32] The government raised teacher salaries, contracted local entrepreneurs to build basic schoolhouses, and enlisted parish priests and estate owners to encourage enrollment.[33]

In an unprecedented effort to improve rural education, the government contracted the Christian Brothers in 1865 to train indigene teachers in a uniform curriculum of basic literacy and religious ethics.[34] Generating a cadre of indigenous maestros to spread "enlightenment and progress" into the nation's "most remote villages" was seen as a practical solution for both chronic teacher shortages and trenchant parental resistance to schooling. In 1871, various Indian teenagers were recruited and began to train at a "normal school" in Quito.[35] Diverging from a strict assimilationist approach, the government pragmatically supported a pedagogy that built on an existing base of Quechua language and culture. An official teaching manual published in 1869, for instance, recommended that instruction for indígenas be conducted in the "language that they understand and speak." Teachers were told to keep their lessons clear and simple, using Quechua explanations and stories as a practical means to facilitate the teaching of Catholic morality and—eventually—literacy in Castilian.[36]

Despite reports about the intelligence and progress of the Indian teachers-in-training, the normal school's impact was disappointing. By 1875, four years after the school opened, just five Indian teachers had graduated, with only another ten still studying in Quito. Although teachers did return to their regions of origin, only two provinces appear to have ever received benefit from the program.[37] After García Moreno's death, the school declined and was eventually shut down. New rural schools would remain staffed for the most part by priests or other literate members of rural society. In the end, state initiatives in rural education never even approached the 200,000-children mark promised by the president in 1871.[38] Many local officials, faced with large populations of truant youths, advocated instead for obligatory training in manual arts.[39] Still, Garcian education policy in rural-

Indian regions was comprehensively conceived, substantially funded, and had a discernible impact. The 17,000 new students enrolled between 1871 and 1875 came chiefly from the towns and villages of Ecuador's highlands.[40]

WOMEN AND THE CONSTRUCTION OF A CATHOLIC NATIONAL IDENTITY

Despite important distinctions in the content of Indian and female education, the central government had parallel expectations for both groups within a new Catholic community and talked about them in strikingly similar ways. Education reform, like the broader cultural policies of García Moreno, was rooted in intersecting sexist and racialist discourses that identified "women" and "Indians" as minors. Both collectivities were infantilized, their souls deemed innately pure, and their minds open to both corruption and redemption. Dangerously unenlightened and "undiscerning" dispositions made them especially susceptible to immorality.[41] Yet, at the same time, the childlike docility and innocence made indigenes and females seemingly well suited to achieve Catholic virtue. Above all, they required vigilant paternal direction.

Such commonsense understandings of race and gender of course were not unique to García Moreno's Ecuador. Indeed, the same discourses validated the limitation of individual legal rights for indigenes and women across Latin America during the nineteenth century.[42] However, the Garcian government officialized—and strategically deployed—this knowledge toward the making of a genuinely Catholic national identity. Its rhetoric maintained that Ecuador's women and indigenes were especially inclined toward religiosity, self-sacrifice and hard work. Both groups had the right stuff—the potential, if carefully nurtured, to become formidable allies in the state-led nation-building enterprise.

Nineteenth-century Ecuadorian elites—like their counterparts elsewhere in Latin America—judged their women to be the "soul of society," a reflection of the country's level of civilization.[43] The emblematic significance of Ecuador's women was amplified, however, as part of the Garcian project to construct a rigorously Catholic and industrious community. Within a discourse that feminized Christianity as the "mother without equal,"[44] women could be portrayed as the household disciples of a great religious hierarchy. Indeed, conservative elites understood Ecuador's women to be the very embodiment of national Catholic values. "Attacks against Christianity" were judged to be "attacks against woman," and vice versa.[45]

As in other postcolonial contexts, the women of Garcian Ecuador were also cast as society's principal storehouses and transmitters of national culture. For the central government, women conveyed the piety and moral strength so necessary for a society on the verge of being "drowned by barbarity."[46] Similarly, Ecuador's women were celebrated as models of "hard work and economy," core values that it sought to instill in national society.[47] As mothers, women were the shapers of national "ideas and principles," the conduits through which "excellent citizens were delivered to the fatherland."[48] Yet, such heady expressions of women's ideal function in society clashed with laments that, historically, the "fair sex" had been "sadly neglected." Ecuadorian women, the well-worn simile intoned, were "like the soil of their country—fertile but uncultivated."[49] The potential fruits of women's "examples and lessons" for society were indeed great, but required—it seemed—the government's paternal direction and painstaking husbandry.

Linking the fate of national civilization to the enlightenment of its female population was of course standard rhetoric within nineteenth-century Latin America. As a high-ranking Garcian minister himself noted, the notion that "nothing contributes to the advancement of society like the education of women" was an axiom for all progress-minded factions and nations.[50] Similarly, in extending female education beyond the rich, outside of cities, and into technical fields, Ecuadorian policies differed little from those advocated by pioneering educators elsewhere in region.[51] However, addressing an incipient "woman question" in Ecuador was particularly urgent for the Garcian government as it sought to forge a progressive Catholic nation. Within a project that placed Catholicism at the very center of nationhood, women's "natural" capacity for piety and hard work was viewed as a crucial resource. Prevailing optimism about innate female religiosity was further buoyed by the estimation of Ecuadorian women as exceptionally moral within the South American context.[52] Such virtue, enhanced through an enlightened education, could give Ecuador a comparative national advantage among American nations.[53]

Beyond energizing the ideological project of the Ecuadorian "nation," Ecuador's women also fortified the Garcian *political* project. Whether swelling the crowds at religious processions or organizing to fend off liberal attacks on church prerogatives, virtuous mothers, daughters, and wives were mobilized as political allies of the central government. Both before and after the Garcian era, groups of women petitioned government or published broadsheets in support of the Church's civilizing work.[54] During the 1860s and 1870s, when the government linked itself so inextricably with religion, the support of self-identified "Catholic women" could only help to legitimate state policies and authority. A year after García Moreno's death, supporters claimed that his government had successfully transformed the Ecuadorian woman into "the handsome mosaic of the national edifice: on the side of piety [and] economic industry."[55] Perhaps. Yet they had become as well the very mortar holding together Catholic Ecuador.

MAKING PIOUS INDIGENES

Government attempts to represent Ecuador's Indian population as a useful component of the Catholic nation were decidedly more problematic. In contrast to the cultural construction of female religiosity, depictions of the "indigene class" as the epitome of national values of hard work, piety, and self-sacrifice were far from conventional. In fact, given widespread perceptions of drunken revelry, unbridled sexuality, and sacrilegious customs among indigenes, they seemed the class furthest removed from Christian morality.[56] Yet, akin to woman, the indigene's eternally adolescent character was deemed malleable, making him (or her) capable of achieving great virtue and becoming a valuable ally of the Catholic state-in-formation.

The strategic deployment of the Ecuadorian indígena as the embodiment of a new evangelized national identity was facilitated by the specific geography of Ecuador's "Indian question." Throughout colonial and early republican periods, state Indian policy had categorized Ecuador's Indian peoples into two distinct cultural groups: the sedentary, once-cultured peoples of the sierra and the nomadic "savages" of the upper Amazon or "Oriente" region. Governments had repeatedly shifted priorities of investing limited human and financial resources between the two regions. Immediately preceding the García Moreno presidency, an "anti-landlord" liberal government largely abandoned missionary activity in the Oriente, focusing its attention on the sierra indígena, particularly the abject conditions of estate debt peons.[57] Indian policy under García Moreno, however, reprioritized the spiritual conquest of the Oriente, renewing Jesuit missionary activity in the region. In part, the evangelizing enterprise promised to display the true strength of

Ecuadorian Catholic civilization—its ability to triumph over barbarism. But Christianizing and acculturating the Amazonian indigenes also could serve to foster economic "progress" and "patriotism"—creating a hardworking and manageable labor force and shoring up Ecuador's tenuous territorial claims.[58]

To be sure, the ambitious evangelizing program fell far short of its objective to convert and settle Ecuador's vast Amazonian hinterland. Missionary settlements never expanded beyond the Napo and Auca districts of the upper Amazon. In regions deeper into the Oriente, such as the *jívaro* territory of Gualquiza, catechizing efforts floundered, and the government contemplated a "North American" relocation-or-extermination strategy.[59] Even in zones where the Jesuits were well established, indígenas countered the imposition of the agricultural-settlement model through legal channels, tactical alliances with rubber traders, dissimulation, and flight.[60] Still, the tangible presence of the Jesuit missions heartened the central government as to an eventual incorporation of the "rich but wild" Oriente. In 1873, the president boldly asserted that the "civilization of the cross" had repenetrated Amazonian society, with "days of light and prosperity" soon to follow.[61]

While lacking the stark civilization-versus-barbarity dichotomy of the missionary enterprise, state discourse about the sierra indígena remained an important element of the government's broader national project. Rhetorical optimism for transforming the Oriente was actually facilitated by an idealized representation of the "civilized" sierra, whose "hard-working villages" of indigenes were to be a model for their Amazonian brethren.[62] Official documents portrayed the highland indígena as industrious and religious, the two key traits of the new national ethic. Such a depiction, however, required a highly selective construction out of conventional prejudices. It drew on only one half of the prevailing polarized perceptions of Indians: docile and hardworking, *not* insolent and lazy; spiritual and religious, *not* superstitious and pagan. Such one-sided representations were aided by affirming a lineage between the present-day Quechua indígena and her (or his) "more cultured" prehispanic ancestors. Even though the contemporary highland indígenas had lost the greatness of the tenth-century "kings of Quito" or the Inca empire, the regeneration of their civilization was imaginable.

In theory, the long-term outcome of Catholic modernity was to be the transformation of indigenes into citizens.[63] Yet, for the moment, the Garcian government sought to include indígenas in the national community not as republican citizens but as a moral and industrious "class." Thus, while local authorities and European travelers continued to decry Indian idleness and laziness,[64] the central government increasingly valued indígenas for their productive roles in agriculture, church construction, and road building. Indeed, as Indian children were being corralled into adobe schoolhouses, their parents were mobilized to great effect in the construction of national highway projects.[65] The Ecuadorian indígena was praised as well for her or his craftsmanship and creativity in manual arts—such as weaving and hat making—an economic sector considered to have tremendous growth potential.[66] Predominant understandings of Ecuador's indígenas as "inoffensive, good natured, and easily manageable"—especially in comparison with their counterparts in neighboring republics—further heartened statesmen as to the productive potential of this population.[67] Thus, by the time the first official primary-school catechisms were published in 1875, "humble" and "hardworking" literally had become textbook definitions of Ecuador's "indigene class."[68]

In proclaiming the utility of its Indian population, the government echoed sentiments heard elsewhere in Latin America. Optimistic statesmen across the continent envisioned Indian populations as practical contributors to society—whether as soldiers, farmers, artisans, or road-builders.[69] More remarkable, however, was the Ecuadorian government's assertion that its functional indigene class was also well disposed toward religiosity and morality.[70] Ultra-Catholic intellectuals—while bemoaning Indian "superstition"—argued that such "religious sentiments" could be "enlightened and ennobled" under proper tutelage.[71] To be sure, indígenas were not considered as religious as Ecuadorians of European ancestry. But they ranked above the mestizos or *cholos,* mixed bloods that lacked the redeemable qualities of either half of their racial ancestry.[72] They also compared well to the Anglo-Saxon race, routinely disparaged as a materialistic, lazy, and immoral force threatening Catholic civilization. Indeed, Catholicized Amazonian indígenas were viewed as a potential accessory to—even substitute for—European immigration.[73]

THE "EMPIRE OF MORALITY"

The Garcian nation-making project was marked by an overarching generational divide. Ecuador's children (regardless of region, race, or gender) were to be the moral and hardworking "leaders of the family, state, and Church"—

the future of the pueblo católico.[74] Government rhetoric was never so optimistic, however, about transforming the present pueblo whose tendency toward vice and impiety was considered widespread and deeply etched. Expectations for the adult-age population were correspondingly distinct—more about repression than enlightenment, short-term regulation rather than long-run reform. As the nation waited for its "citizens of tomorrow" to come of age, then, the government and its Church allies set out to "reestablish the empire of morality."[75] While confronting everything from raffles to sex crimes, government vigilance and repression focused particularly on three areas: public drunkenness, fiesta sacrilege, and extramarital sexuality.

For the righteous conservative-Catholic coalition, drunkenness was considered a generalized vice among men, crossing regional and racial boundaries, a "demon" that needed to be exorcised from Ecuadorian society.[76] As had Quito's colonial officials, Ecuadorian postindependence authorities considered alcohol the root of all immoral behavior, particularly among the lower classes and indígenas, from dancing and sexual impropriety to gambling and street brawls.[77] In 1871, the central government reacted to what it deemed ineffective local police codes with a national ban on the consumption of alcohol in taverns, chicherías, or town plazas.[78]

The criminalization of public drinking complemented initiatives aimed at extirpating "scandalous" spectacles and "pagan" rituals during religious celebrations. Government disdain targeted particularly the *corrida de toros,* an enormously popular spectacle in rural and urban fiestas, and carnival masquerading, a pre-Lent celebration "bastardized" by revelry and impropriety.[79] Advocates of Catholic progress, like other self-styled modernizers of the day, disdained popular culture and sought to eliminate (or strictly regulate) it so that Ecuador could join the ranks of "civilized nations."[80] However, the Garcian government acted with unparalleled boldness to prohibit plebeian festivities. In the early 1860s, for instance, the president converted Quito's main plaza into a tree-lined park, explicitly to discourage the distasteful bullfights.[81] In 1868, after the event had relocated to nearby Plaza de San Francisco, the government completely banned corridas, outlawing masquerading in the same legislation. It hoped to replace them by promoting moralizing theater and offered incentives to municipalities to construct stages and script dramatic compositions.[82]

Celebrations of religious feasts in the indigenous countryside of the sierra were considered even more problematic. Officials routinely lamented that religious processions and other acts of worship were nothing but "accessories" to the weeklong "*paseo*" celebrations.[83] For both civil and ecclesiastical authorities, Indian paseos were filled with sin and profanity—at best an excuse for ridiculous masquerades, barbaric bullfights, "and other inventions to satisfy sensuality."[84] At worst, however, the events displayed behavior wholly antithetical to Catholicism, not simply scandalous but sacrilegious. Ritual dancing performed by men, for instance, freely mixed Catholic symbols with pagan customs. Dancers borrowed priestly vestments to costume themselves, or paraded around elaborately dressed images of saints.[85] For the state, such unabashed displays of profanation were painful, perennial reminders of the superficiality of Christianity, and an indictment of its long-standing inability to control Indian redeployment of Catholic doctrine.

While unsuccessful in remaking rural holidays into purely religious events, the state-Church alliance of the 1860s and 1870s did manage to regulate and sometimes eradicate "offensive" Indian fiesta behavior. Church edicts and political pressure, for instance, led to the banning of all paseos during the festival of San Juan in Otavalo, among the country's largest and most spectacular feast-day celebrations.[86] The central government strictly prohibited bullfighting in the Indian sierra throughout the 1870s, and violations were thoroughly investigated. In 1873, Quito's Archbishop could credibly boast that sacrilege during fiestas had "very much declined" under García Moreno, and that Ecuador was well on its way to detaching the pueblo from its "most ancient customs."[87]

In step with papal directives, the government also devoted considerable energies toward eradicating extramarital sexuality and reasserting the sanctity of marriage.[88] In 1869, it criminalized concubinage and set up a centralized network of surveillance to enforce compliance with orthodox Catholic morality.[89] Much of state-Church efforts were directed against prenuptial "concubinage" among indígenas, a widespread cultural practice throughout the sierra.[90] Drawing on commonplace tropes of animal sexuality among indígenas, Church officials decried the "exaltation of passions" and "unbridled" sexual improprieties.[91] Armed with their petty officials, parish priests put the anticoncubinage dispositions into practice, exercising state juridical and enforcement functions. In the Church's version of a shotgun wedding, accused indígenas were obliged to choose between marriage and corporal punishment.[92]

The central government was even more vigilant about the sexual behavior of Creole women. In its anticoncubinage laws, for example, the government reiterated longstanding double standards that defined extramarital sexuality for women in broad terms.[93] Education reform similarly was infused with a puritanical concern to avoid scandals. Schools were strictly gender segregated, and male teachers were forbidden to teach girls without a female chaperone—policies that inadvertently restricted the expansion of female schooling in the impoverished countryside. Similarly, special attention was given to ensure that women teachers, once "freed from all vigilance," were morally equipped to work in rural regions.[94] Even the most progressive initiatives, such as obstetrics training in Quito, were shot through with concerns about female honor, the dissemination of practical knowledge a secondary consideration. Thus, while women saw their national status raised as captains of religiosity, their "dangerous" potential came under the repressive scrutiny of a national government obsessed with the moral purity of its female representatives.

That the central government's antivice campaign targeted the customs and practices of females, indígenas, and, more generally, of the pueblo should not surprise.[95] Policing customs was quite openly an exercise in social control, a bald attempt to reinforce class, racial, and patriarchal hierarchies. And after a "disorderly" decade of popular-liberal reforms in the 1850s, such reordering of society had particular resonance.[96] Gender ideologies and policies in Garcian Ecuador reaffirmed the cult of domesticity—deeming women "passive and incapable in the public world . . . [and] denying them direct input in economic and political affairs."[97] Catholicism, from a class perspective, was esteemed precisely because it was the "most gentle and efficacious means" for repressing "the licentiousness of those who obey, [and] prescribing . . . the submission of the people." Only it could mediate between "order and liberty, giving morality better rule over the hearts" of the people. Popular sectors and females were to remain subaltern, their advancement left to the paternal direction of an "enlightened, patriotic and religious Government."[98]

Yet Ecuadorian women and indigenes were more than semantic pawns in the new national culture of Catholicism. To varying degrees, members of both groups critically engaged Garcian ideals, sometimes advancing their respective group interests in the process. For women, the linkage between religion and nation potentially widened the scope for legitimate involvement in politics. Without challenging the notion that politics was the "patrimony of man," women could conceive their duties within the "domestic sphere" to extend beyond the family—into matters affecting religion and the "fatherland."[99] Regional groups of elite white women, for instance, embraced their "duty" to advocate the patriotic cause of Catholicism. At the same time, they called on national society as part of the "Christian world" to make good on its rhetoric to "esteem and respect" the female gender. As the government looked to harness women as a national civilizing force, some "Catholic women" pushed to "take possession of their rights" to validate broader involvement in the "activity of society."[100]

The "indigene class" also engaged the religious imperatives of the state, often exploiting it for individual or community benefit. Certain Indian authorities, for instance, had their status raised in recognition of the "important services" they provided in Christian indoctrination.[101] At the same time, the new culture of morality encouraged indigene commoners to frame complaints against "despotic" Indian authorities in moralizing terms, by highlighting scandalous behavior.[102] Similarly, the Garcian distinction between uncorrupted Catholic faith and corruptible Catholic authorities (see below) was particularly useful for indigenes in day-to-day relations with clergy. They astutely exploited state-Church rifts to curb "arbitrary punishments" meted out by local priests.[103] Indian communities could depict themselves as good "Catholic Christians," while freely denouncing abusive clerics or challenging customary Sabbath-day labor obligations.[104]

THE POLITICAL CULTURE OF GARCIAN CATHOLICISM

The central government's concern regarding society's "dangerous" subaltern sectors was part of an all-encompassing campaign to control social and political behavior. Recasting the notion of "fraternity"—one of liberalism's "magic words"—the state-Church alliance envisioned an "evangelical" community that incorporated "all men, great or small, learned or ignorant, poor or rich, to share in the same rights, same favors, [and] same graces, through the practice of the same virtues."[105] Indeed, the moralizing campaign was most radical in that it sought to regulate the comportment of *all* Ecuadorians, plebeian sectors *and* upper class, Indian *and* non-Indian, female *and* male. Temperance and anticoncubinage initiatives, for example, were broadly policed against members of all social classes. In the end, the making of a "truly Catholic nation" (with citizenship restricted to "true believers") was a political project that sought to restrain individual rights—including those of white, propertied men—and to centralize political decision making.

Despite its direct access to the Church's formidable administrative power, the government was limited in its efforts to rigorously enforce an elevated standard of morality among the *entire* citizenry. However, García Moreno's efforts to harmonize "political institutions" and key sectors of civil society within a Catholic framework were considerably more fruitful. Indeed, the central government was remarkably successful in establishing a standard of Catholic morality among those who aspired to formal political power in society. Those who wished to participate in the "public" sphere—whether as police chiefs or publishers, schoolteachers or parish priests—would be held to a higher standard of religiosity and morality.

García Moreno lived an exemplary life of sobriety, moderation, and piety and had little tolerance when civilian and church officials failed to embody similar values. Most famously, the government's anticoncubinage policy targeted the clergy, especially its domestic "regular" members.[106] Temperance and antigambling policies were also useful means to "depoliticize" maverick monks and priests who opposed the government's authoritarian-Catholic project. Declaring clergy the captains of a national Catholic revolution empowered local clerics in disputes against local temporal authorities. Yet, at the same time, it allowed the central government to justify heavy-handed intervention in Church matters, purging "immoral" priests and multiplying the ranks of "upstanding" foreign clergy.[107]

Moralizing statecraft also entailed strict adherence of all public servants to Catholic teachings. The president purged his government of many habitual drunkards and scandalous womanizers. He used private persuasion with friends and public humiliation with adversaries to ensure that government embodied morality and good customs. In several high-profile instances, he threatened to depose state employees who were living in concubinage and refused to marry.[108] García Moreno strictly legislated compulsory Church attendance for an unprecedented array of public officials during holidays.[109] A symbolic demonstration of Church-state harmony, this also ensured that local authorities were practicing—if not devout—Catholics. In order to detect impious behavior and to identify malcontents and "subversive" elements among local politicos, the government actively promoted a surveillance network consisting of priests and low-level government agents. Temperance and antigaming rhetoric was strategically deployed against recalcitrant regions and individuals. The province of Azuay, whose local officials were notoriously at odds with Garcian centralized rule, was depicted as a region of iniquity and routinely targeted in moralizing state rhetoric. Concurrently, the president deposed police and civilian officials for failing to respect the "prerogatives" of the Catholic Church.[110]

The process by which the state's Catholic-moral discourse intersected with local cultures was contested and negotiated, and ultimately García Moreno's ambitious national objectives remained unrealized. Yet, the Church-state alliance was more successful in disseminating a common discursive framework that obliged local elites to couch their politics in terms of its spiritual benefits and to speak about economic progress as a function of religious advancement.[111] Municipal councils in both sierra and coast were pressured to support national moralizing initiatives even when these ran counter to dominant local interests. For example, a sierra-wide campaign to switch market days from Sundays to Saturdays—to restore the sanctity of the Sabbath—was broadly successful despite often running counter to landlord interests. Similarly, municipalities gave up key revenue streams by collaborating with the central government to moralize feast days or to ban Indian labor recruitment during Sunday school meetings.[112] In this way, the national project to instill Catholic morality, despite its limitations, powerfully shaped the framing and pursuit of political claims.[113] By the early 1870s, municipal councilmen increasingly justified legislation in terms of bringing temporal interests in line with moral ones. They scrambled to repackage their local public works or education initiatives in terms of their relevance to religious and moral advancement. Even when Catholic discourse was used disingenuously, the net result was the same: religiosity had been prioritized within local political discourse.[114] Such a culture of doing politics subordinated regional, class, and ethnic interests to the government's agenda of creating new boundaries for national community.

ORDER, PROGRESS, AND CATHOLIC MORALITY

The Garcian government's use of Church to extend state power and of Catholicism to legitimate authoritarian governance is reminiscent of Latin America's "classically conservative" dictatorships, such as Carrera's Guatemala or Rosas's Argentina.[115] Yet, García Moreno was also an order-and-progress caudillo, akin to Colombia's Nuñez or Mexico's Diaz, combining positivist spirit with authoritarian means to pursue technical and economic development.[116] Indeed, his government left an impressive legacy of public-works projects, from its state-of-the-art astronomical observatory to one of Latin America's first modern penitentiaries. García Moreno's commitment to build a modern road network was perhaps unmatched by any of his contemporaries, a noteworthy achievement given Ecuador's utter failure to attract foreign investment. In the area of educating and incorporating subaltern sectors of society, García Moreno achieved much more than Liberals in most Latin American countries, despite their strong rhetoric in favor of popular schooling.

Yet, the Garcian government's progressive, "liberal-positivist" achievements ultimately cannot be separated from its political project of Catholic nation-making. García Moreno's religiosity was never simply a rhetorical ploy or tactical maneuver for *larger* aspirations of economic development or state building. García Moreno insisted on the indivisibility of material and *moral* progress and pursued a modernity grounded in "authentic" Catholicism. His impressive consolidation of state authority was tied up with the institutionalization of a *national* Catholicism. Only strong and centralized public authority in "harmony" with Catholicism, García Moreno wrote in 1869, could bring the "order, progress and happiness" that Ecuador deserved.[117] Indeed, the Garcian project was most deeply marked by faith that religion and authoritarianism were Ecuador's best, if not only, resources for the construction of a modern nation.

NOTES

1. Legislative Decree, Oct. 18, 1873, in *Leyes,* 354–55; as quoted by Hartup, "Artists," 83–84.

2. García Moreno, June 2, 1871, as cited in Tobar Donoso, *Instrucción pública,* 249.

3. On how cultural understandings legitimate politics and shape community identity, see Baker, "Introduction," xii.

4. Halperín Donghi, *Contemporary History,* 124–28; Aubert et al. *The Church,* 269–72.
5. Maiguashca, "El proceso," 388–90.
6. Ibid., 389.
7. King, "Ecuadorian Church," 385; Williams, "Empire of Morality," 157–58.
8. Demélas and Saint-Geours, *Jerusalen y Babilonia,* 147–55; Maiguashca, "El proceso," 383–90.
9. García Moreno, "Contestación" (Aug. 10, 1869), in *Escritores políticos,* 359; for explicit conflating of Catholic "morality" and "nation," see Menten, "Discurso," 13–15.
10. *Pace* King, "Ecuadorian Church," 383.
11. León, *Discurso . . . de 1865,* 8; "*pueblo católico*" connotes both a "Catholic population" and a "Catholic people"; cf. Eyzaguirre's contemporaneous notion of a "Christian society" that was "formed and sustained by the maxims of the Gospel" and comprised of "active, hard-working and intelligent members"; Ezyaguirre, *Los intereses católicos,* 2:39–40. The notion also evokes "*la plebe Cristiana,*" a Jesuit ideal that advocated "Catholic democracy"; Lievano Aguirre, *Los grandes conflictos,* 265–300, esp. 268, 276.
12. Maiguashca, "El proceso," 388.
13. On interaction between "local practices and beliefs" and government schooling initiatives, see Rockwell, "Schools," 173–74.
14. Tobar Donoso, *Instrucción pública,* 205, 219n; Garcian schooling statistics (roughly 36 students per 1,000 people) should be viewed skeptically; still, they appear to rank favorably within the South American context (c. 1875), ranking far below Argentina (72), but comparable to Chile (44), and well above figures (compiled twenty-five years later!) for its Andean neighbors—Colombia (20), Peru (14), and Bolivia (11); for Argentina, see Vedoya, *Cómo fue la enseñanza,* 84–85, 126; for Chile, see Campos Harriet, *Desarrollo educacional,* 30; for comparative pan-American statistics (c. 1900), see ibid., 34.
15. Paredes Ramirez, "Economia y sociedad," 120–28; Rodriguez, *Search for Public Policy,* 84.
16. Tobar Donoso, *Instrucción pública,* 212.
17. García Moreno, "1871 Mensaje," cited in Noboa, *Recopilación,* 3:112–13.
18. Law of Nov. 3, 1871, in *El Nacional,* June 12, 1872 (no. 179); annual spending on primary education jumped from $15,000 in 1861 to $100,000 during the 1869–75 period; Tobar Donoso, *Instrucción pública,* 216, 219.
19. Ibid., 212.
20. Menten, "Discurso," 8 [511]; Circular of Oct. 28, 1865, *El Nacional,* Nov. 4, 1865 (no. 202); for strikingly similar neo-Bourbon justifications for technical training in Colombia, see Safford, *Ideal of the Practical,* 13, 17.
21. "Reglamento," *El Nacional,* July/August 1872 (no. 191).

22. Yon-José, "Informe," April 1, 1873, Ministry of Interior (hereinafter Min. of Int.), *Informe*; and *El Nacional*, May 27, 1862 (no. 76).
23. Tobar Donoso, *Instrucción pública*, 202.
24. Executive Decree of Oct. 27, 1874, in *El Nacional*, Oct. 30, 1874 (no. 375); Guerrero, *La música ecuatoriana*, 44–45.
25. For the 1871 ban on publication or importation of imprints deemed contrary to "morality and Catholic religion," see *El Nacional*, Dec. 27, 1871 (no. 124).
26. Tobar Donoso, *Instrucción pública*, 243, 246, 250.
27. "Informe . . . de enseñanza primaria," May 21, 1872, in *El Nacional*, June 12, 1872 (no. 179).
28. García Moreno, "Mensaje . . . 1875," in Noboa, *Recopilación*, 3:134; between 1857 and 1875, over 120 girls' schools were constructed, for a total of 164; Tobar Donoso, *Instrucción pública*, 238; for calculation of only 48 girls' schools in Peru (1861), see Regal, *Castilla educador*, 191.
29. For 1858 estimate of 462,400 highland "indios," see Villavivencio, *Geografía*, 164.
30. "Informe . . . de enseñanza primaria," May 21, 1872, in *El Nacional*, June 12, 1872 (no. 179); *El Nacional*, Nov. 29, 1871 (no. 116).
31. Law of Nov. 3, 1871, in *El Nacional*, June 12, 1872 (no. 179).
32. Tobar Donoso, *Instrucción pública*, 408.
33. *Segundo Sinodo . . . Quitense*, chap. 4, arts. 18–20; García Moreno to León Mera, May 24, 1873, cited in Tobar Donoso, *Instrucción pública*, 259–60.
34. León, *Discurso . . . de 1865*, 8; Law of Nov. 3, 1871, in *El Nacional*, June 12, 1872 (no. 179).
35. *El Nacional*, Nov. 29, 1871 (no. 116).
36. Salazar, *El método productivo*, 78–79; for similar directives for preaching to Indian and mestizo soldiers, see Min. of State to Bishop of Ibarra, Feb. 20, 1872, Archivo de la Curia (Ibarra) (hereinafter: AC/I), 17/15/1/c.
37. Yon-José, "Informe," April 1, 1873, in Min. of Int., *Informe*.
38. García Moreno, "1871 Mensaje," cited in Noboa, *Recopilación*, 3:111.
39. See "Informe . . . de Tunguragua," Archivo Nacional de Ecuador (Quito), Gbo. 92, doc. "8-IV-1867"; and Tte. Político of San Luis to President of Municipal Council, Otavalo, May 17, 1875, Instituto Otavaleño de Antropología, Serie Municipal (hereinafter IOA: SM), 32c.
40. For near doubling of rural school funding in the Canton of Cotacachi between 1865 and 1871, e.g., see "Acuerdos . . . hasta el año 72"; "Presupuestos . . . de 1862," etc., Archivo Municipal de Cotacachi; in the same period, seven new schools were established in the Canton of Otavalo, Municipal Accord, Otavalo, March 5, 1867, IOA: SM 38: 38, fol. 2.
41. Guerrero, "Ventriloquist's Image," 562–66.
42. On women's struggles for full adult legal status in nineteenth-century Latin America, see Dore, "One Step Forward," 17–25; on maintaining a "distinctive cate-

gory of Indians" in the nineteenth-century Andes, see Harris, "Ethnic Identity," 361, 363.

43. Wilson, *Ley del progreso*, 75–77; for an influential example of Latin American thinking on women, see Sarmiento, *Educación popular*, 120.

44. Gomez, "¡García Moreno!," 13.

45. Martinez et al., *La voz del deber*.

46. García Moreno, "1875 Mensaje," cited in Noboa, *Recopilación*, 2:134; O'Connor, "Dueling Patriarchies," 105–6; on multiple ways that women are implicated in national processes, see Yuval-Davis and Anthias, *Women-Nation-State*, 9; Chatterjee, *The Nation*, 126.

47. Wilson, *La Ley del progreso*, 75–77.

48. Municipal Accord, Otavalo, 13 Nov., 1867, IOA: SM 38, fol. 9; see also Menten, "Discurso," 518.

49. Hassaurek, *Four Years*, 91; see also León Mera, *Ojeada histórico-crítica*, cited in Robalino Dávila, *García Moreno*, 372–73.

50. Min. of Int., *Informe*, 72; cf. Rocafuerte, "Mensaje . . . de 1837," cited in Paladines Escudero, *Pensamiento pedagógico*, 219; and Sarmiento, *Educación popular*, 119–26.

51. For the case of González de Fanning in Peru, see Valcárcel, *Breve historia*, 186–87.

52. Hassaurek, *Four Years*, 89.

53. León, *Discurso . . . de 1865*, 9; see also O'Connor, "Dueling Patriarchies," 105.

54. Martinez et al., *La voz del deber*; Urbina et al., "Otra igual . . .," 20.

55. Gustavo de Almenara, c. 1876, cited in Moscoso, "Las imágenes," 95.

56. For trenchant notions of highland indigenes as superstitious "semi-Catholics," see Eyzaguirre, *Los intereses católicos*, 2:38–40; Hassaurek, *Four Years*, 107.

57. Williams, "Popular Liberalism."

58. "Ecuador y la civilización cristiana," in *El Nacional*, Dec. 30, 1874 (no. 393); on the link between territorial claims and missionary activity in the Oriente, see Eyzaguirre, *Los intereses católicos*, 49–50; on missions forming "bonds of nationality," see Moncayo, *Cuestión de limites*, 13–24.

59. García Moreno, "1871 Mensaje," in Noboa, *Recopiliación*, 3:109; by 1873, the government abandoned its *jívaro* missions, focusing solely on the Napo River region; see García Moreno, "1873 Mensaje," in Noboa, *Recopiliación*, 3:124.

60. Muratorio, *Life and Times*, 80, 83–84, 89.

61. García Moreno, "1873 Mensaje," in Noboa, *Recopilación*, 3:124.

62. "Ecuador y la civilización cristiana," *El Nacional*, Dec. 30, 1874 (no. 393).

63. On turning Indians and peasants into "citizens," see Eyzaguirre, *Los intereses católicos*, 2:9–50; León, *Discurso . . . de 1865*, 8–9.

64. See, e.g., André, "América equinoccial," 827.

65. Williams, "Negotiating the State," chap. 6.

66. On potential of textiles and "Panama" hats as lucrative export goods after Ec-

uador's success at the Paris exposition of 1867, see "Ecuador," in *El Nacional*, July 11, 1868 (no. 331).

67. Cevallos, *Resumen*, 155; Hassaurek, *Four Years*, 107.

68. León Mera, *Catecismo*, 51.

69. For upbeat rhetoric on "industrious" and "apt" Indians in nineteenth-century Peru, see Gootenberg, *Imagining Development*, 95, 194–95.

70. "Ecuador y la civilización cristiana," *El Nacional*, Dec. 30, 1874 (no. 393).

71. Ezyaguirre, *Los intereses católicos*, 11.

72. León Mera, *Catecismo*, 51; see Brooke Larson's chapter in this volume.

73. "Ecuador y la civilización cristiana," *El Nacional*, Dec. 30, 1874 (no. 393); on García Moreno's longing for Catholic European immigrants (particularly Germans), see ibid.

74. Wilson, *Ley del progreso*, 6.

75. García Moreno, "Mensaje," April 2, 1861, cited in Robalino Dávila, *García Moreno*, 307–8.

76. García Moreno to León Mera, Jan. 4, 1874, cited in Pattee, *García Moreno*, 401.

77. Cevallos, *Resumen,* 86, 151; "El demonio Alcohol," *El Nacional,* Feb.-Mar. 1875 (nos. 407–13); for a less damning assessment of drinking, see "Informe . . . de León," *El Nacional,* March 8, 1871 (no. 26); for a link between Indian drunkenness and domestic violence, see O'Connor, "Dueling Patriarchies," 110–14; on colonial perceptions of Indian and popular drinking, see Minchom, *The People of Quito*, 88, 96, 217–19.

78. Presidential Decree of July 18, 1871, in IOA: SM 8, 5, f. 15; see also Bishop of Riobamba, "Informe," March 29, 1873, in Min. of Int., *Informe*.

79. On bullfighting and carnival rituals, see Cevallos, *Resumen*, 118–28; Hassaurek, *Four Years*, 95–99.

80. Cevallos, *Resumen*, 128–30.

81. Hassaurek, *Four Years*, 99.

82. Legislative decree of Jan. 31, 1868, in IOA: SM 14: 3, 23.

83. For vivid descriptions of *paseo* festivities during the 1860s, see Hassaurek, *Four Years*, 151–64.

84. Archbishop Checa y Barba, "Informe," April 22, 1873, in Min. of Int., *Informe* (1872–73); Hassaurek, *Four Years*, 149; Cevallos, *Resumen*, 153–54.

85. *Primer Concilio . . . Quitense*, decr. IV, art. 5; *Segundo Sínodo . . . Quitense*, ch. VII, art. 6.

86. Williams, "Empire of Morality," 164–66.

87. Archbishop Checa y Barba, "Informe," April 22, 1873, in Min. of the Int., *Informe*.

88. The papal *syllabus* of 1867 devoted ten of its correctives to the issue of Christian marriage; see Pius IX, "Syllabus of Modern Errors."

89. Executive Decree, May 15, 1869, in *Leyes*, 167–69.

90. "Informe . . . de León," *El Nacional,* March 8, 1871 (no. 26); Herrera, *Monografía*, 264.

91. Bishop of Riobamba, "Informe," March 29, 1873, in Min. of Int., *Informe*.
92. Jefe Político [hereafter, J. Pol.] to Vicario Foráneo, Otavalo, June 30, 1875, AC/I, 2995/7/19/c.
93. Moscoso, "Discurso religioso," 55.
94. *El Nacional*, Oct. 24, 1874 (no. 375).
95. Archbishop Checa y Barba, "Informe," April 22, 1873, in Min. of Int., *Informe*.
96. Williams, "Popular Liberalism."
97. O'Connor, "Dueling Patriarchies," 107.
98. Noboa, *Sermón . . . de 1861*, 10.
99. Martinez et al., *La voz del deber*.
100. Ibid.
101. Circular of Governor of Imbabura [hereinafter Gov. of Imb.], March 2, 1871, IOA: SM/8: 5, fol. 5.
102. Vicario Capitular to J. Pol., Otavalo, Nov. 20, 1876, IOA: SM 26a: 4.
103. For evidence of increased government response to complaints of immorality among priests in the province of Imbabura during the Garcian era, see Min. de Int. to Administrador Apostólico, Ibarra, Oct. 29, 1866, AC/I: 7/15/1/c; see also Gov. of Imb. to Vicario Capitular, Dec. 22, 1869, AC/I: 235/27/1/C; and Gov. of Imb. to Bishop of Ibarra, April 11, 1870, AC/I: 236/34/1/C.
104. "Simón Ysama . . ." IOA: Jefetura Política 1a, caja 41, doc. 1096; Gov. of Imb. to J. Pol., Ibarra, Jan. 22, 1866, Archivo del Banco Central (Ibarra) 667/176/13/M.
105. Noboa, *Sermón . . . de 1861*, 9–10.
106. See, e.g., Hassaurek, *Four Years*, 173–74.
107. Williams, "Negotiating the State," chap. 5.
108. Gálvez, *Vida de Don Gabriel García*, 348.
109. Executive Decree, April 12, 1872, *El Nacional*, April 12, 1872 (no. 158).
110. Williams, "Negotiating the State," chap. 5.
111. For implications of a "common discursive framework" for conceptualizing hegemony, see Roseberry, "Hegemony," 364.
112. Williams, "Empire of Morality," 164–65.
113. Baker, "Introduction," xii.
114. Williams, "Empire of Morality," 166.
115. On Church-state alliances under Carrera, see Sullivan-González, *Piety, Power*, 81–119; and Woodward, *Carrera*, 258–71; on Rosas, see Lynch, *Argentine Dictator*, 183–86.
116. On Nuñez's "positivist-conservative" program of "regeneration," see Bushnell, *Modern Colombia*, 140–48; on Porfirian "scientific politics," see Hale, *Transformation*, 96–97, 139–68, 205–44.
117. García Moreno, "1869 Mensaje," in Noboa, *Recopilación*, 3:105–6.

REDEEMED INDIANS, BARBARIZED CHOLOS

CRAFTING NEOCOLONIAL MODERNITY IN LIBERAL BOLIVIA, 1900–1910

Brooke Larson

This essay isolates a pivotal decade in the racial formation of Bolivia's exclusionary political culture.[1] I refer to the contested process by which Bolivian intellectuals and policymakers articulated racial ideologies and practices in an effort to reorganize power, map the contours of political culture, and redefine citizenship under the modernizing liberal state. The early 1900s proved to be an interpretive turning point as Bolivian intellectuals began to distance themselves from imported European racial theories, to reexamine their own multiracial heritage, and to prescribe reforms to improve the Indian races and the nation. For a tiny group of Paceño intellectuals thrust into the progressive vanguard of liberalism, modernity, and nation making, the first decade of the twentieth century was a peculiar historical moment of collective hope and despair. On the one hand, Bolivia was on the crest of a sustained tin-mining boom; the latifundia frontier was rapidly advancing across the northern altiplano; and the Liberal Party had finally routed the Conservatives of Chuquisaca and come into power in 1900. On the other hand, the nation was recently wrenched by the most violent indigenous rebellion in more than a century. The internecine Federalist War of 1899 had opened a space for indigenous-*criollo* alliances, which had later deteriorated into a putative "race war" replete with all sorts of barbarities. It also had brutally demonstrated the raw power struggles that still roiled Bolivian political life after nearly a century of endemic political instability. On the cusp of a new century and new political era, yet still haunted by the specters of race war and caudillo politics, Bolivia's Liberal vanguard was plunged into a collective exercise of national introspection and moral self-critique about the failed Bolivian republic, its racial heritage, and its future prospects. At stake here was the question of national identity and belonging—of how to improve and where to position the Indian and mestizo races within the parameters of Bolivia's political culture and nation-state.

In this essay, I explore the production of modern Bolivian race-thinking in the ethnographic, literary, and prescriptive writings of prominent intellectuals and statesmen at either end of this critical decade of liberal nation making. I begin with a consideration of the ethnographic and philosophic writing of Bautista Saavedra and Manuel Rigoberto Paredes. Tempered a little by the passage of time, the second pair of *pensadores,* Alcides Arguedas and Franz Tamayo, transcended the earlier writers by folding the so-called Indian question into a nationalist discourse. Race served as a springboard for constituting a national memory and identity, which embedded in it their respective agendas for cultural and political reform. I argue that collectively these writers shaped a "cult of anti-mestizaje," which served as a gloss on the dangers of unbridled republican liberalism and aggressive subaltern politics gone awry. As Florencia Mallon has argued, Mexican projects of "hegemonic mestizaje" found little resonance in the Andes during the early decades of the twentieth century.[2] Indeed, Bolivia's enlightened elites consolidated negative notions of mestizaje to forge a political language of authoritarian paternalism and exclusion in the heyday of Liberal Party rule.

The consolidation of anti-mestizaje discourses combined imported European imperial elements of race science (particularly French theories of crowd psychology and racial degeneration) with deeply embedded assumptions about Andean-colonial hierarchies. In their effort to tap the environmental, biocultural, and historical roots of Bolivia's racial heterogeneity, however, these Paceño intellectuals revisited older bipolar constructions of Indian/mestizo in the context of republican history and modernity's mandates. Furthermore, this emerging racial discourse marked an important departure from late-nineteenth-century theories of Indian decadence, attrition, and death through social-Darwinian processes of natural selection and survival of the fittest.[3] After 1900, the literary vanguard of La Paz neither predicted nor advocated ethnocide through "natural" or "unnatural" causes but instead viewed the Indian Race as a permanent and, indeed, necessary fixture of the rural landscape.[4] As the self-appointed architects of nationhood, their reformist mandate was to redeem and remake the Indian Race into a rural laboring class that would contribute to Bolivia's booming tin-mining economy, expanding labor markets, and rapidly spreading latifundias.

Deeply embedded colonial-racial ideologies, then, in combination with the "practical" necessities of improving the labor force and securing the social peace on the altiplano produced a neocivilizing narrative. Its main protagonist was, of course, the "white" civilizing vanguard—those very writers and reformers who ordained themselves experts on the "Indian problem." Their mission: to uplift the Aymara, now deemed civilizable and useful to the nation. No less crucial to this narrative were the mongrel demons of backward provinces and urbanizing cities. This moral meditation on mestizaje produced interlocking villains of Andean modernity: the provincial mestizo (the product of Indian/white breeding, uncivilized, economic parasites, political despots, etc.) and the urban *cholo* (the product of Indian/mestizo breeding, semiacculturated, semiliterate, semiurban, politically volatile, socially and/or sexually transgressive, etc.). Both racial stereotypes functioned as foils for the "white" civilizers. They had to rescue the Indians from the grip of their feudal-colonial "mestizo" overlords and place them under the jurisdiction of the liberal-positivist state. At the same time, they rushed to impose restrictions on the expanding cholo hoards, who were migrating to La Paz and invading the political, cultural, and spatial domain of the "white" lettered elites. In short, I argue that this racial project forms the basis of Bolivia's emerging political culture of paternalism, authoritarianism, and exclusion. It remapped the racial and spatial segregation of modernizing Bolivia under the contradictory impulses to civilize the Indians, contain the urbanizing mobilizing masses, and redefine citizenship around restrictive notions of whiteness.

DEFINING NEOCOLONIAL MODERNITY AGAINST MESTIZAJE

I begin my discussion by focusing on the writings Bautista Saavedra and Manuel Rigoberto Paredes, whose critical voices framed the fundamental social and moral issues of their day. They established themselves as prominent authorities on the "Indian problem" during the early 1900s, in the immediate aftermath of the Mohoza trial. They used the 1899 Aymara rebellion on the altiplano, and the subsequent Mohoza trial condemning hundreds of Aymara men for the murder of white Federalist soldiers, to advance a scientific/ethnographic discourse on the biocultural and environmental causes of Indian behavior. Saavedra and Paredes were drawn to their tasks of interpreting the Indian problem from very different sources of concern and authority. Bautista Saavedra was a lawyer and a member of the political elite of La Paz who eventually became president of the nation in 1920. He was catapulted into public life in the year 1901, with his appointment of defense attorney for the Aymara rebel leaders during the Mohoza trial. His first writings on the question therefore emanated from his ambivalent role as interlocutor of the accused Indians and as moral and scientific interpreter of the "savage atrocities" committed against the Indians' Liberal allies. This contradictory self-positioning comes to light in his combined deployment of geneticism, tellurism, and social environmentalism. Like so many other race theorists of the day, Saavedra diagnosed the "primitive character" of the Aymara Indian as one that oscillated between a surface submissiveness and a deeper savagery. Marshalling the techniques of anthropometry during the Mohoza spectacle, Saavedra invoked the idea of natural selection and adaptation to adduce the Aymara's defensive and erratic behavior, particularly the Indian's radical mood-swings between total passivity and spasmodic fury. He also borrowed Lamarckian biocultural assumptions about the inheritance of acquired characteristics, arguing that the Indian character was an inherited condition of a race that had become "an abject and miserable beast of burden."[5]

Thus Saavedra stood at the interface of biocultural and environmental determinism, which allowed him to combine his blunt and official indictment of Indian brutality and bestiality, on the one hand, with his defense of the Indian as a victim of wretched social conditions, on the other. It is precisely this conceptual wavering between race science and incipient social critique of the ancien regime that began to turn the Indian Race from criminals into victims of Bolivian history and biology.[6] Although Saavedra deployed various populist tactics to advance his own political career, his greatest legacy was his anti-Indian rhetoric and policies. He ultimately accused his Aymara defendants of premeditated murder and insurrection born of inbred Indian hatred for white people. Except for occasional populist or paternal gestures to bind indigenous clients to his growing anti–Liberal Party movement (formalized through the founding of the Republican Party in 1914), Saavedra expressed a lifelong antipathy toward indigenous struggles to defend or recover ayllu lands and communities. In *El ayllu* (1904), his most serious sociological tract, Saavedra advocated a state policy of Indian removal—full-scale assault on the "anachronistic ayllu."[7] Almost twenty years later, when he served as president of the republic, Saavedra acted on those sentiments, unleashing his military against the peasant protesters in Jesús de Machaca in the most brutal massacre of the era.[8] Shortly thereafter, Saavedra pronounced ayllu self-governance to be inherently reactionary "because it maintains an ominous status quo which impedes all attempts at reform and progress and maintains, in latent forms, the ancient hatred of the Indian against the white race which it accuses of usurpation and oppression."[9] In that sense, I agree with Marie Demelas's assessment that Saavedra's writings represented the apotheosis of social Darwinism.[10] But we can also see in his early writings the glimmerings of a more subtle social critique of the crushing burdens that "predisposed the Indians to commit crimes."[11] And his incipient concern for the agrarian "roots of rebellion" encouraged a new critical scholarship on the interior ethnic frontier.

Writing race into this emerging critical ethnography was best accomplished by a provincial intellectual, critic, and politician. Perhaps alone among his contemporaries, Manuel Rigoberto Paredes authorized himself as an expert in contemporary Aymara culture and society on the basis of his own ethnic identity and rural experience. Born of mixed parentage in the town of Carabuco on the shores of Lake Titicaca, Paredes came from a long line of Aymara caciques. Bilingual, educated, and conversant with the political and scientific theories of the day, Paredes acquired firsthand knowledge of provincial life as the subprefect of the province of Inquisivi during the turbulent years of 1900–1904.[12] But like Saavedra, he was also appalled and threatened by the specter of "race war" and, perhaps more profoundly, by the persistence of Bolivia's backwardness, which he adduced to the degeneration of the Indian Race. Thus, Paredes advanced the assumption that the Indian Race was a victim of history and biology. "Two successive conquests, one by the Incas and then one by the Spaniards, followed by long periods of domination, have crushed the character of the *colla,* dimming the lights of his intelligence and conditioning him for only mechanical, agricultural, or pastoral labor."[13] Inca and Spanish despotism robbed the Indian Race of its free will and "spirit of progress," thus in effect depriving it of the essential attributes necessary for participation in projects of modernity and nation building. Thus explained, the Indian Race was written out of the nation.

Yet Paredes took the Indian-as-victim analysis further than did Saavedra. For he brought to it an intimate knowledge of and concern for Aymara communities in Inquisivi and elsewhere, which were under siege by liberal divestiture policies, fraudulent lawsuits, and hacienda encroachment on all sides. The land question lay at the center of his social critique, for he did not abide by liberal land-reform policies. But perhaps his most vivid ethnographic insights came in the form of his catalogue of the informal abuses against Aymara peasants in the villages and towns of Inquisivi and neighboring provinces, perpetrated, above all, by corregidores, priests, and *patrones.* Explaining the Mohoza massacre, he pointed to the abuses of local officials who had provoked Aymara savagery.[14] Adding fuel to those "structural causes" of Indian violence were two catalysts: alcohol and the influence of "mestizo agitators." Here, then, we begin to perceive Paredes's understanding of race relations between Indians and mestizos. If he was advancing the theme of Indian-as-victim, he was also honing a Darwinian view of these subaltern races engaged in perpetual struggle and mutually transformed through symbiosis, conflict, and the struggle for survival in a harsh and forbidding land. In this respect, Paredes both borrowed from the earlier writings of Gabriel René Moreno and anticipated the later treatise of Alcides Arguedas in making a case for the mestizo-as-victimizer. In his taxonomic scheme, the Mestizo Race did not bridge or fuse Indians and whites but instead embodied the worst of both: the audacity, arrogance, adventurousness, and fanaticism of the Spaniard and the passivity, primitiveness, and pusillanimity of the Indian. In other words, miscegenation wiped out the redeeming qualities of these "pure" races while perpetuating the debased characteristics of the conqueror and the conquered. Thus the hybrid Mestizo Race incarnated a volatile mix of "vulgarity," "servility," and "audacity" which added up to an "ungovernable" mass of people.

The main culprit in Paredes's study was the provincial mestizo, whose drunken, violent, exploitative lifeways had brutalized the Indian Race since colonial times. Thus, while this author brought intimate ethnographic knowledge to his analysis of agrarian power relations, he framed it in broader terms of the degeneration and demoralization of the body politic through centuries of mestizaje. What is particularly interesting here, I think, was his effort to locate the Mestizo Race vis-à-vis the market and the nation. On the one hand, the mestizo-as-victimizer construct cast mestizos as social parasites. As exploiters of Indians, they lived not through their own hard work and initiative but by the sweat and toil of Indians. Mestizos thus lived on the margins of the modern market economy, possessing none of the bourgeois virtues that would promote progress. Instead, they threatened to diffuse their "racial poisons" (alcohol, venereal diseases, etc.) throughout Indian society. On the other hand, the provincial Mestizo Race had acquired a certain kind of "vulgar intelligence" enabling them to make political mischief and sabotage the institutional workings of the republic. Paredes noted their peculiar cleverness for provincial politics and law. If Paredes casts "parasitic mestizos" out of the arena of the modern marketplace, he located them very much inside the public political domain. This rhetorical strategy, borrowed from René Moreno, of denying the mestizo the bourgeois virtues of the *homo economicus*, yet essentializing him as a litigious man of political intrigue, corruption, and demagoguery, turned the Mestizo Race into the symbol and source of national decline and decadence. Bolivia's failure to forge a unifying, orderly society was pinned therefore on the political machinations of power-grabbing mestizos who had dominated political life during the dark age of the republic. Like René Moreno, Paredes deployed his degenerative race ideology to repudiate the "mestizo epoch" of nineteenth-century republican rule and to plot the nation's escape from it. As we shall see, Alcides Arguedas's *Pueblo enfermo* represented the apotheosis of moral pessimism that courses through Paredes's more prognostic ethnography.

Paredes's ambivalent stance toward Aymaras and his unmitigated contempt for provincial mestizaje sparked in his political imagination a modernity that was at once paternalist, nativist, and assimilationist. As Sinclair Thomson has recently argued, Paredes was concerned about the loss of Aymara lands and the restoration of a precarious social peace on the altiplano. This compelled him to search for short-term remedies for the routine abuses that provincial administrators heaped on Indians, as well as long-term, more radical solutions to the land/community question that so vexed indigenous/state relations in this period. Alone among his peers, Paredes called for a solution to the growing immiseration of Indians through the "nationalization and socialization of the land, that is, a return to the incaic regime."[15] The restoration of communal lands—i.e., rolling back the latifundia frontier, liberating "captive communities," and reorganizing economic life on the altiplano around the ayllu—isolated him as a bold, perhaps utopian, nativist who stood up against the anti-ayllu policies and practices of the day. And yet, as Thomson makes clear, Paredes was also a progressive modernist who advocated a program of institutional and cultural reform to bring the Indians into the fold of civilization, if not the nation. Thus, for example, he advocated coaxing Indians toward civilization by requiring them to wear European-styled dress; colonizing the province of Inquisivi with civilized immigrants who would improve the ethnic mix of its inhabitants; and promoting new settlements and industries on the altiplano.[16] Flourishing ayllus amid advancing modernity: Paredes's vision seemed to reflect his own fragmented identity in this neocolonial society on the cusp of capitalist expansion.

But context has a strange way of entangling racial genealogies, even among Paceño intellectuals who shared many of the tenets of evolutionary racism, not to mention their common class interests and racial anxieties. Briefly, the decade witnessed a conjunctural shift in the balance of power that disillusioned many Paceño intellectuals and statesmen who found themselves out of favor with the ruling Liberal Party. Increasingly they worried about political patronage, corruption, and violence that tightened the grasp of the Liberal Party over the parliament and the presidency. Party tactics turned Manuel Rigoberto Paredes into a bitter critic of Liberalism. Before the ink had dried, Paredes turned from his monograph on Inquisivi to write a scathing critique of the bully tactics used to amass an "electoral mob" in order to fix the elections and pack the parliament in the election year of 1907. Both Arguedas and Tamayo were public critics of liberal-republican values, and a few years later, even Bautista Saavedra defected in order to form the opposition Republican Party in 1914. Race-thinking was permeated by partisan politics and, in turn, legitimated the conservative-aristocratic reaction to liberal-republican rhetoric. At a structural level, liberal assaults and hacienda expansion across the altiplano backlands of La Paz had unleashed migratory waves of "expelled Indians" thrown off communal lands recently absorbed into private landed estates.[17] On the edges of La Paz whole barrios of Aymara migrants sprang up and spread down the slopes into the bowl of the city. Although these patterns of popular and peasant incursion into the city and politics were to intensify in later decades, they were already a source of anxiety to intellectuals and politicians, especially those in political disfavor. Mapping Indianness and mestizaje in this deteriorating political and moral climate had assumed national significance by the end of the decade.

HONING HYBRIDITY, CENSORING CHOLOS

The writings of Alcides Arguedas and Franz Tamayo presage an emerging, conflictive hegemonic discourse on Bolivian race(s), history, and nationality. Arguedas's rich, encyclopedic *Pueblo enfermo* (1909), along with his celebrated novel, *Raza de bronce* (1921), and his lesser-known and later historical tomes, and Tamayo's more pedestrian reflections and editorials, collected and published in 1910 as *Creación de la pedagogía nacional,* were cultural and political landmarks in Bolivia. They began to reconfigure the preexisting "Indian-mestizo" dichotomy into a broader moral-ethnographic-philosophical quest for the essence and possibilities of Bolivian race evolution and national identity. Indeed, their efforts to encompass issues of nationality are reflected in the very titles of their respective works.

The intellectual formation of both Arguedas and Tamayo was firmly rooted in the salons and townhouses of privileged Paceño families. They belonged to the landholding oligarchy and wrote of rural life and Indian labor from the position of paternal masters to the colonos inhabiting their own haciendas. Both writers also traveled in high political and diplomatic circles. It was Paris as much as La Paz that nurtured Arguedas's intellectual formation. He was a cosmopolitan, indeed expatriate, intellectual, whose early writings (particularly *Pueblo enfermo* and *Raza de bronce*) were celebrated in high-literary circles across Latin America. Tamayo, on the other hand, was a local writer and policy advocate who never produced a work of international acclaim, although later generations of Bolivian scholars have given *Creación de la pedagogía nacional* appreciative attention. But as he ground out his newspaper articles on the transcendent issues of race, national character, and politics, as well as on the pragmatic issues of educational reform, Tamayo shaped political, ideological, and institutional debates about Bolivia's capacity for "order and progress" and its prospects for moral and eugenic improvement. It is true that Arguedas and Tamayo subscribed to opposing eugenic theories. Arguedas, the pessimist, adhered to the fashionable doctrine of "racial degeneration," while Tamayo, the optimist, ambivalently embraced the idea of "racial regeneration" through racial assimilation, that is, the absorption of indigenous peoples into the superior white-mestizo races. Yet what I want to argue here is that both writers forged a negative national symbol of *cholaje* to signify Bolivia's degenerative history of racial hybridity, moral decline, and political chaos. Departing from different premises about race mixture, both writers fastened on the cholo as the essence of the other and of the past, of "Them" and "Then." Race and history were conflated into one negative symbol, against which to redefine and reconstruct a paternalist project of modernity and nationality.

Before I turn to the underlying social and political implications of their ideas, let me map briefly the contours of their respective ideas about the "Indian Race" in relation to mestizaje and, more specifically, cholaje in the modernizing polity. Alcides Arguedas's *Pueblo enfermo* is a stark example of descriptive ethnography married to moralistic, conservative doctrines of racial decline and decay. Arguedas drew inspiration from a wide circle of European and Latin American race theorists, ranging from Gustave Le Bon and Count de Gobineau to Euclides da Cunha and Carlos Octavio Bunge.[18] As much as anyone, it was the conservative Argentine writer, Bunge, who provided Arguedas with the theoretical premises and metaphor of social illness to use in his own study of Bolivia's biomoral pathology. Like Bunge, Arguedas believed that hybrid races were characterized by psychological imbalances and moral deficits, and that contemporary Bolivia—and, to a certain extent, all of Latin America—was suffering from the consequences of race mixing, which had begun with the conquest. But it was not only the mestizo (and other hyphenated races) that was the source of Bolivia's racial contamination and decline. Arguedas argued that the roots of racial degeneration were traceable to the inferior hybrid stock of Spanish-Arab colonizers, who interbred with Indian and African peoples, further debilitating their own racial stock and that of the Indians.[19] Arguedas's pessimism derived, in part, from the assumption of criollo racial inferiority and its incapacity to absorb and improve the racial stock of inferior Indian and mestizo races. In contradistinction to the evolutionists who had prognosticated the disappearance of the Indian Race in their optimistic preface to the 1900 Bolivian census, Arguedas set out to take a hard, critical look at the "abnormalities" and "peculiarities" inherent in Bolivia's character. His subject varied: sometimes he essentialized a composite Bolivian psyche (" the diseased people" or, "the Indo-Spanish character"). But he was interested primarily in disaggregating the racial, regional, and class components of Bolivian society in order to stereotype their essential attributes within a hierarchical racial order and trajectory of eugenic regression. Applying this doctrine, Arguedas examined the crucial elements of Bolivian "exceptionalism": the mountain geography that had molded its original indigenous inhabitants; its heritage of two Indian civilizations (Tiwanaku and the Incas); the survival and presence of the Aymara and Quechua "races" in spite of the extinction of their civilizations; the minimal infusion of "white" European blood (due to the lack of European colonization); and Bolivia's long, deep history of racial miscegenation.[20] And he did so from multiple vantage points that reveal an astonishingly intimate and encyclopedic knowledge of Bolivia. Much more than a diatribe against the social ills of Bolivia, *Pueblo enfermo* is a vivid ethnographic, historical, muckraking composite of national self-discovery, encased in an implicit allegorical narrative of Bolivia's fall and redemption.

Although Arguedas's redemptive rendering of the Indian Race revisits many of the themes and assumptions that framed the earlier study of Inquisivi by Paredes, tellurism looms larger in his work. More than biology, history, and social conditions, the mountains molded the physical and psychological character of Bolivia's Aymara and Quechua races. From the outset, Arguedas structures his analysis of Bolivia's Indian Race around binary oppositions between Aymara/Quechua, mountains/valleys, and masculinized/feminized psychological traits. Accordingly, the cold, harsh climate of the altiplano, crowned by towering snow-capped mountains, had yielded the solitary, impenetrable, taciturn, defensive, bellicose Aymara Indian; whereas the inter-montane valleys and eastern slopes of Bolivia had cradled the passive, emotive, lyrical, accommodating Quechua race.[21] In this schema, the Aymara Indian belonged to the purer race, having been more disposed by geography and psychology to resist biocultural contamination and domestication by Spanish and mestizo society.[22] Isolated, diffident, reserved, the Aymara existed outside and beyond the bounds of Western civilization. The more vulnerable and open-minded Quechuas, in contrast, evolved "feminine virtues and vices": a love of poetry but also a tendency to dissimulate, connive, and deceive people.[23] From this dichotomous model, the Aymara Indian emerged the "nobler savage." Both biologically and culturally purer, and therefore slightly superior to the "domesticated," "contaminated" Quechua race, he was also potentially more dangerous.

As a Paceño landowner writing not even a decade after the 1899 Zárate Willka rebellion, Arguedas undoubtedly felt the urgency and immediacy of diagnosing and interpreting the Aymara psyche and soul to other members of the Bolivian landed oligarchy. His construction of Indian race and regionalism, in fact, moves almost in tandem with his social and moral critique of the brutal rural conditions under which Aymara Indians lived and worked. In his chapter on "the psychology of the Indian Race," Arguedas attempted to decriminalize the Aymara Indian by imputing "ignorance" and "lack of conscience." He also cast Indians as victims of the brutalizing system of *pongueaje* and other barbarities perpetrated by the usual trilogy of exploiters—patrones, priests, and corregidores. Indeed, Arguedas's redemptive Indian and impugned provincial parasites are forcefully evoked in his classic indigenista novels, *Wata Wari* and *Raza de bronce.* The latter novel turned Arguedas into Bolivia's most powerful social critic of the latifundista regime in the early twentieth century. Like Rigoberto Paredes whose work he found inspiring, Arguedas decried local coercive labor practices such as leasing Indian laborers and using them as beasts of burden in an age of telegraphs and railroads. But clearly there is no redistributive agrarian agenda hidden below the telluric powers of the land. Nor does Arguedas indulge in the kind of rhetorical nativism that Paredes flaunted in advocating the restoration of the ayllu and return to Incaic lifeways.

On the contrary, as Marta Irurozqui has argued, Arguedas positioned himself as a social critic of the feudal-colonial order to promote enlightened seigneurial protection and separation of the pastoral Indian.[24] Consistent with his suppositions about degenerative mestizaje and his biomoral profile of the Aymara Indian race, Arguedas allowed no possibilities for indigenous inclusion in an imagined national culture or polity. Arguedas extolled the Indian civilizations, particularly Tiwanaku, as Bolivia's noble Indian heritage whose material vestiges had been destroyed by the brutal and ignorant Spanish colonizers. He interrogated the geographic, social, and historical conditions of Bolivia's Aymara and Quechua races in order to build a psycho-sociological framework for understanding their gendered virtues and vices. And, not least, Arguedas lambasted the landed oligarchy, provincial elites, and the whole political-professional establishment for their pathological mental habits and customs. He left no stone unturned. But he did *not* advocate the incorporation of indigenous peoples into the economic or political life of the nation, and he did *not* engage the issues of cultural pluralism in a postcolonial project of nation building. Quite the contrary, Arguedas essentialized and redeemed a pre-political Aymara subject, who was destined to remain outside the imagined political community. He naturalized the Aymara Indian in telluric terms: as a cold, aloof, oblivious, barely sentient being perfectly adapted to life on the harsh and forbidding altiplano; in short, a being situated well beyond the boundaries of market, nation, and civilization.

In Arguedas's mental landscape, the Aymara race had no material interest in modernity. Barbed wire fences, railroads, the steam ship on Lake Titicaca held no value. The Aymara always avoided cross-cultural contact and retreated before the threat of acculturative forces. "The Aymara never puts a price on his own labor nor wants to learn the language of the white merchant (*comprador*); instead, he obliges the merchant to learn his own."[25] And this, he noted, is his "greatest virtue!" Arguedas imagined a modernity of enlightened seigneurial patriarchs who protected and improved the Aymara colono populations inhabiting their haciendas. The restoration of paternal pacts of reciprocity between landlords and peasants would thus ensure the social peace on the altiplano, protect the noble Aymara from further cultural contamination, and improve agricultural production. Clearly, Arguedas's moral pessimism was put to narrow neocolonial ends: he staked his interests in the rehabilitation, not of the Indian, but of the seigneurial oligarchy entrenched in La Paz.

By contrast, Franz Tamayo's cultural nationalism revoked the idiom of pathology to celebrate the authenticity of Bolivia's indigenous races. In fact, he set himself the task of constructing a counternarrative to discredit Arguedas and other writers who made careers of cataloguing the vices of "our race" and heaping calumny on the Bolivian national character.[26] He urged intellectuals (particularly educators) to engage in national self-discovery. They should " study all the virtues and forces of the race, the mysterious and divine warp and woof of efforts and activities, interior actions and reactions, that constitute the very life of the nation."[27] Tamayo heeded his own call to arms in his 1910 weekly newspaper essays, published in a collected volume, *Creación de una pedagogía nacional.* But he did so through abstract philosophical and moral musings, rather than through investigative reporting or ethnographic/sociological analysis. Consequently, Tamayo's rambling, often disjointed essays remain curiously aloof from the vivid social realities and complexities of everyday rural life and politics in Bolivia. Yet Tamayo broke with Arguedas and his fellow moral pessimists by creating an Indian subject that was civilizable and educable and therefore capable of eventual incorporation into the nation. In this sense, Tamayo was more influenced by the idea of "constructive mestizaje" that had captured the imagination of influential Porfirian *científicos* like Justo Sierra and Andrés Molina Enríquez. Long before the revolutionary Mexican state had sanctioned mestizaje as its official ideology, liberal-positivist politicians and intellectuals in Mexico had advanced the mestizo concept of nationality.[28] As Alan Knight makes clear, the proto-indigenistas (and even official, postrevolutionary indigenistas) "tended to reproduce many of the preceding assumptions of [progressive] 'Westernism,' which [they] opposed."[29] Pro-mestizaje indigenismo operated within a racist paradigm, but those authors argued that "acculturation could proceed in a guided, enlightened fashion such that the positive aspects of Indian culture could be preserved, the negative expunged."[30]

Tamayo subscribed to this view and called for the "creation of a national pedagogy" to execute it. His institutional project was predicated on the assumption that the Indian Race was worthy of education and integration into the Bolivian nation. Tamayo therefore took his redemptive campaign beyond the limits set by Arguedas and other negative eugenicists. Not only did he validate the Indian Race but he proclaimed it to be the "repository of the nation's energy." The key to order and progress was to tap into, and channel, that source of manpower for the good of the nation. Tamayo believed the Aymara Indian was eminently educable since he had proven to be an "autodidact" in spite of centuries of despotism, oppression, and poverty. His contemporary Indian Race may have lacked the intelligence that its ancient ancestors possessed in abundance during the height of their empire, but it revealed other positive attributes (endurance, stoicism, energy, and bravery), which could be tapped by the Bolivian nation. The solution to the Indian problem was to recognize the "comparative advantages" of the Indian Race, rehabilitate its redeeming cultural characteristics, and design a civilizing project that forged them into subaltern citizens serving the state in their "natural capacities" as rural laborers, artisans, and soldiers.[31] Tamayo conceived of Indian assimilation as a long-term, incremental process to be mediated and controlled by the moral-intellectual guardians of the nation's internal ethnic borders. The nation's educator-civilizers would improve the Indian Race, but Indians would have to earn their entry into the nation-state through productive labor, patriotic service, and civic virtues. Thus Tamayo envisioned a social compact between Indians and the state, one which vaguely promised citizenship in exchange for the conversion of Indians into a Hispanized underclass of rural laborers. In the meantime, he issued a call for educational policies capable of resolving the injustices of the past, of alleviating the burdens and abuses that made daily life so miserable for rural Indians, of cultivating civility among the elite and middling groups, and of forging an ethical national character. A national pedagogy, tailored to Bolivia's different races, was to be the panacea.

The unifying motif of these competing projects of Indian redemption was the vilified "hybrid races"—mestizo and cholo. Both Arguedas, who equated racial hybridity with psychological instability and degeneracy, and Tamayo, who left open the possibility of constructive mestizaje as Bolivia's bridge to the future, counterposed the immoral and dangerous mestizo to the victimized and redeemed Indian. We have already visited this construct of Indian/mestizo antinomy in the earlier work of Saavedra and Paredes, and of course the genealogy of this Manichean construct runs deep into the colonial past. But perhaps for the first time, the Indian/mestizo opposition was redeployed in an emerging discourse of national authenticity and authoritarian paternalism. Whereas the virtuous Indian served the symbolic needs of cultural nationalism, reformism, and authenticity, the vicious mestizo provided the foil for enlightened civilizing projects that would separate, protect, and civilize the hapless Indians.

But these writers also redeployed race categories to make sense of modernity and its discontents. As I have argued elsewhere, the cholo proved especially useful to these critics of the Liberal Party and its republican values and caudillo practices.[32] Whereas the mestizo of Saavedra, Paredes, and Arguedas embodied the colonial, feudal, and caudillo anachronisms of the past, the transgressive cholo/chola was made to embody the ills of migration, urbanization, and electoral democracy. Such social ills encompassed the breakdown of traditional codes of deference and authority in the countryside, as well as the rise of mass politics in the towns and cities, particularly those liberal-populist pacts which had bolstered Liberal Party power and their sham elections. As these writers and intellectuals grew disillusioned with the Liberal Party and its clientelistic strategies, and as they faced massive economic and social upheavals in the city and countryside after 1910, they worried less about predatory, recidivist mestizo *gamonales* in the provinces than they did about urbanizing cholos flooding into the cities. Increasingly, therefore, racial discourses cast the Indian/cholo dichotomy in explicitly political terms: the silent, passive pre-political Indian (uncorrupted by Liberal politics, pacts, and policies of universal suffrage and literacy) juxtaposed to the vice-ridden, unstable political cholo, the semiliterate rabble that formed President Ismael Montes' so-called electoral mobs.[33]

But *cholaje* proved elastic enough to accommodate multiple meanings and purposes. The multivocal cholo could signify variously the degraded colonial past (the amorphous mestizo/cholo as the provincial tyrant and blood-sucker); the depravity of anarchic republicanism (the "cholo caudillo"); the polluting dangers of race mixture and interethnic relations ("chola" as sexual, social, and spatial transgressor); and the multifaceted threat posed by acculturating Aymara migrants "contaminating" the exclusive criollo domain of the "lettered city." Yet at base, Bolivian race theorists and cultural nationalists deployed an anti-cholo discourse to redefine the liberal project along more exclusionary and authoritarian lines. As popular politics proliferated and the crisis of the Liberal Party deepened after 1914, its enemies went to battle on multiple fronts. They fired off racist ammunition to crush popular and plebeian political cultures, the stirrings of urban labor mobilization among the Indian parishes and artisan and anarchist associations of La Paz, and Andean resurgence in the courts, the streets, the printing presses, and government ministries in their escalating social movement to reclaim stolen ayllu lands and revitalize ethnic communities.

Ironically, this incipient agenda is enunciated in Tamayo's proto-indigenista call to arms for the construction of a "national pedagogy." Tamayo's deep racial anxieties surface in those essays once he abandons his platitudes about the generic Latin American Mestizo Race to focus more sharply on the specific biocultural-moral attributes of the Bolivian cholo.[34] Tamayo's contempt derives from his very concept of cholo as a subaltern transgressor of race, class, and citizenship boundaries. To be a cholo, in Tamayo's mental world, was to be a social parasite who did not contribute to the nation's economic progress and thus could lay no claim on citizenship rights. He had not fulfilled the social pact that Tamayo had in mind for the redeemed Hispanized Indians as the quid pro quo for citizenship rights. Yet the cholo by definition was literate and enfranchised. He was, and had been historically, able to "carry out his absurd will to the extent that it [weighed] heavily upon the solution to the gravest problems facing the nation."[35] Tamayo lay the wreckage of the nation, torn by a century of civil and caudillo wars and Indian rebellions, at the feet of a misguided model of universal education, which had proved to be dangerously inappropriate for Bolivian racialized reality. Indiscriminate schooling and lax literacy requirements, he argued, had created an electorate of 30,000 cholos "all [of whom] were ill from the same political unawareness, the same parasitic spirit, the same laziness, and the same immorality."[36] This had doomed the nation to an age of despotism and demagoguery. The Liberal government's goal of universal literacy, as opposed to a race-differentiated pedagogy for rural Indians, was proving disastrous. And what emerged as the product of these misguided Liberal ideals (universal literacy, military service, and suffrage)? The cholo—a deracinated, upwardly mobile, Hispanized Indian who abandoned his customs and acquired all the social vices that came with a little literacy, knowledge, and power. In the end, the nation was poorer and more backward for having dissipated the "natural energy" of the Indian race and converted it into a parasitic semiurban plebe empowered by its own unearned enfranchisement.

It does not take much subtlety of mind to discern a political mandate here! Tamayo's project of Indian redemption, protection, and mediated integration into the nation moved in tandem with his desire to suppress, if not reverse, popular "cholo" literacy and politics. At a deeper level, the proto-indigenistas wanted to banish Bolivia's peasant and cholo sectors from the public/political sphere and displace local "cholo" political authorities and mediators in order to insert their own authority to represent and mediate Indian/state and Indian/society relations in the new nation-state. Thus, while Tamayo formally distanced himself from Arguedas's blatant anti-mestizaje discourse, he smuggled the colonial Indian/mestizo dichotomy back into his diatribes against "cholo" vulgarity, low-classness, and political transgressions. It was Arguedas, however, who effectively transposed this theme to the historical canvas.[37] By racializing (or should I say cholifying?) the republican epoch, Arguedas consolidated an antirepublican master narrative of Bolivia's "barbarous," "anarchic" nineteenth-century past. In 1910, following one hundred years of "cholo caudillismo," the new oligarchic nationalists saw themselves as the cultural vanguard of modernity charting the passage from the decayed cholified republic of the past to the modern white nation of the future.[38] And they imagined a nation that would "reduce" Indians, banish cholos, and authorize the enlightened "white" reformers to police the boundaries of the public sphere.

• • • • •

By way of conclusion, I want to raise several points concerning the deeper ideological and institutional implications of this emerging racial formation in the construction of Bolivian modernity.

In this most "Indian" of postcolonial Latin American nations, elites and popular sectors struggled to reconcile the divisive colonial-caste legacy with Eurocentric notions of nationality, political identity, and homogeneity. As a cultural artifact, a nation creates bonds of identity and community, helped along by the diffusion of cohering ideas and images through print capitalism, as Benedict Anderson long ago suggested.[39] But equally powerful components of nation building are the cultural practices and representations that precipitated racial, class, and gendered others who were located on the margins of, or outside, the boundaries of national belonging. Notions of identity and alterity, after all, are mutually interactive and self-defining processes grounded in the specific historical interplay of language, culture, power relations, and material practices.[40] In the ethnically plural postcolonial nations of Latin America, of course, the mapping of a nation's interior racial-ethnic boundaries was of immediate concern. Thus racial discourses took on transcendent importance in postcolonial political imaginaries: how was the white/mestizo/Indian/black continuum to be sliced, what "sub-races" were to be precipitated, and, above all, which of these "races" were to be included in the nation, and by what means?[41]

For predominantly indigenous societies like Bolivia, the "Indian problem" of inclusion/exclusion must have seemed almost intractable. The "whitening"/colonization option, premised on the idea of the biological triumph of the superior white race, was supposed to be hastened by the rapid infusion of white immigration. But by 1910 it had proved impossible to realize, in spite of official predictions of the 1900 census that Bolivia's Indian populations were gradually being overtaken by the rising mestizo populations. On the other hand, Indian extermination modeled after the Argentine military assault on its Araucanian populations was also deemed untenable. After all, Indian labor sustained the haciendas, the workshops, and the mines of Bolivia, and throughout the country local elites continued to extract all manner of gratuitous labor and tributes from indigenous peoples. Power and productive relations rested on the bulwark of racial-ethnic division. And yet, the turn-of-the-century mining and agricultural booms, growing elite hunger for productive lands and disciplined laborers, and the latent threat of indigenous mobilization all conspired to demand a new social-political order that would assure the passage toward modern nationhood. Indigenous rights to land were perhaps the crux of the problem, although perhaps not in the way historians have tended to pose it. We know that intensifying agrarian battles led to massive litigation and political campaigns by indigenous authorities and their intermediaries. Indigenous peoples acted on these weak structures of the liberalizing state in manifold ways, pressing their various colonial, republican, and/or citizenship claims and generating a whole petty officialdom that mediated (and often exploited) their struggles with the liberalizing criollo state. Beneath the political surface raged another struggle over the rights of self-representation. Responding to the postcolonial particularities of this society, then, Bolivian nation-builders sought a peculiar kind of *neocolonial modernity.* It would subjugate and transform Indians into a disciplined and patriotic labor force and soldiery. Furthermore, it would reinscribe race-ethnic divisions in order to preempt the possibilities of "dangerous" Liberal-populist pacts by containing the spread of literacy and suffrage among Montes's "electoral mobs." Under this competing neocolonial utopia, Bolivia would steer a middle course between the extremes of racial assimilation and extermination, between Indian inclusion and exclusion. It would do so by transfiguring virtuous pre-political Indians into wards of an enlightened seigneurial class or secular civilizers of the modernizing state *and* by expelling subaltern political (cholified) subjects from the nation's political sphere. The emergent Indian/cholo antithesis thus effaced Bolivia's long, deep history of indigenous political, litigious, and discursive traditions of struggle and adaptation under colonial and republican rule, as well as argued in favor of severely restricted popular sovereignty, literacy, politics, and political-ethnic mobility. Barbarizing cholos—either through race theory or antirepublican historiography—was intrinsic to oligarchic longings for racial order and hierarchy consonant with Bolivian modernity.

Like most such projects, Bolivia's vanguard of neocolonial modernity clearly envisioned a multifaceted agenda of political repression, social control, and moral reform. But, judging from Arguedas and Tamayo, they disagreed on the site and agents of Bolivia's would-be cultural renovation. Arguedas privileged the seigneurial sector, while Tamayo called for an ambitious statist project of nationalized education. Clearly, the ruling Liberal Party was unwilling to leave the Indian question to the whim of landlords, and they increasingly looked to education as the key to social control and moral reform. Between 1910 and 1920 government policymakers and intellectuals debated the nature and purposes of rural (i.e., indigenous) education in Bolivia. Tamayo had turned pedagogy into a symbolic site of competing nationalisms. Gradually his campaign against a universal, race-blind pedagogy carried the day. In 1920, the Ministry of Education began to craft a nonacademic curriculum for Bolivia's indigenous schools.[42] Literacy was deemed useless and inappropriate for the indigenous majority. There were other, equally divisive aspects of neocolonial modernity that merit more research, because it required attacks on all fronts. Criollo civilizers, regardless of their partisan stripe, needed to respond to the structural needs of the incipient capitalist order. They needed to turn an unruly peasantry and plebe into disciplined workers, soldiers, and tax-payers; to impose municipal control over public space, and invasive popular economies; to rid the nation—and especially the cities—of superstition, crime, and vice; and to extend control over the forms of family organization, sexual practices, and moral and hygienic instruction. By these various means, the modernizing state would police the social boundaries of race and class, modernize social life, and better secure the elites' power and authority in times of terrible flux and change.

Thus, in the years between 1900 and 1920, Paceño intellectuals and politicians became crucial agents in the formation of a representational project of racial and national identity. Not only did they construct a semiofficial discourse of postcolonial modernity, specifically tailored to Bolivia's intractable "cholo problem" and to the perceived legacies of anarchic republicanism and unbridled individualism. They also authorized themselves to interpret and mediate interethnic relations between Indians, the state, and civil society, as well as to prescribe policies of Indian protection, moralization, and control. In this way, they hoped to marginalize traditional subaltern or middling intermediaries who continued to advance ayllu claims and broker cultural relations. In times of crisis, these indigenous authorities, activists, and intellectuals were branded by politicians, journalists, and writers as "rebellious Indians" or, later, as "subversive communists." But in the context of broad structural transformations in the countryside, and moments of intense political tension within the liberal-oligarchic camp, the white civilizers deployed *cholaje* to condemn plebeian forms of low-classness and proscribe perennial political troublemakers, such as "the pettyfoggers" (*tinterillos*) and corrupt politicos (*traficantes en política*).[43]

Through their self-appointed cultural authority and imagined modernity, then, the criollo vanguard went a long way toward censoring the growing network of local and ethnic authorities and intermediaries, who were mounting their own political and discursive projects *from below* to engage or contest liberal-oligarchic political discourses and practices. No less important, their taxonomic categories did violence to the variety, complexity, and historicity of rural and urban indigenous/popular cultures and to peasants' and cholos' rights of self-representation in early-twentieth-century

Bolivia. Thanks to recent research on indigenous politics and culture by Bolivian scholars, we now have a rich historiography on indigenous and popular politics in all their variety and complexity.[44] They deal with such topics as the ongoing legal and discursive struggles of *comuneros* to recuperate or defend their communal lands, the emerging national network of *caciques apoderados* demanding rights to land, literacy, and citizenship, and the intensifying municipal battles that raged in the center of La Paz and Cochabamba over the rights of petty mestiza marketing women and pubkeepers to pursue their everyday activities of livelihood in the streets of the city.[45] It is precisely in the context of this ethnically plural, tumultuous political landscape that we must interrogate the deeper political implications of the proto-indigenista racial discourses for the making of an exclusionary political culture in early-twentieth-century Bolivia.

NOTES

1. For the concept of "racial formation," see Omi and Winant, *Racial Formation,* 48–76.
2. Mallon "Indian Communities," 36–41 and ff; however, for the Bolivian case Mallon correctly draws the sharp regional distinction between the highlands of La Paz, where the "unifying mestizo model of hegemony" never caught on, and the valleys of Cochabamba, where distinctive historical processes rendered positive meanings and uses of mestizaje for the purposes of regional and national identity-making; on the politics and discourses of race, ethnic, class, and regional identities in Bolivian history and historiography, see Larson, *Cochabamba, 1550–1900,* 322–47.
3. Demélas, "Darwinismo a la criolla," 55–82.
4. In this chapter "Indian Race" will be capitalized throughout to denote the racial terminology of Bolivia's early-twentieth-century intellectuals.
5. Irurozqui, *La armonía,* 151.
6. Ibid.
7. Saavedra, *El ayllu,* 13–14.
8. Choque and Ticona, *Jesús de Machaca,* esp. chap. 4.
9. As quoted by Klein, *Politics and Political Change,* 70.
10. Demélas, "Darwinismo," 70–71, 80.
11. As quoted by Irurozqui, *La armonía,* 150–51.

12. Thomson, "La cuestión india," 92.
13. Paredes, *Provincia de Inquisivi,* 77–78.
14. Thomson, "La cuestión india," 95.
15. As quoted in ibid., 103.
16. Ibid., 104.
17. Mamani Condori, *Taraqu,* 43–54.
18. Otero, "Temperamento," 100–103.
19. Arguedas, *Pueblo enfermo,* 62 ff., 87; Helg, "Race in Argentina and Cuba," 40–41.
20. Arguedas, *Pueblo enfermo,* 87 and passim.
21. Ibid., 51.
22. Ibid., 46.
23. Ibid., 51.
24. Irurozqui, *La armonía,* 165; see also her most recent book, "*'A bala, piedra y palo.'* "
25. Arguedas, *Pueblo enfermo,* 146.
26. Tamayo, *Creación,* 24–25.
27. Ibid., 25.
28. Hale, *The Transformation,* 260.
29. Knight, "Racism," 87.
30. Ibid., 86.
31. Ibid., 112.
32. Larson, "National Pedagogy"; see also Irurozqui, "La amenaza chola," 357–86.
33. See esp. Paredes, *Política parlamentaria,* 1–7, 194–204; Paredes, *La altiplanície,* 177–93; on the relationship between race and "crowd psychology" in French conservative thought, see Nye, *The Origins.*
34. Tamayo, *Creación,* chaps. 16, 20.
35. Ibid., 55.
36. Ibid.
37. Arguedas, *Historia general,* 3:159–202 and 5:265–342.
38. See also Paredes, *La altiplanície,* 177–93; Saavedra, *La democracia,* 22–25, 180–96, 250–51, 315–17; Romero, *Las taras,* 192–206, 233–36.
39. Anderson, *Imagined Communities,* 41–49.
40. Much work in the field of cultural studies has dedicated itself to the representational interactions of self and otherness, autonomy and difference, within the cultural domain of nation making, specifically postcolonial nationalist projects. But see especially the brief and lucid discussion in Chatterjee, *The Nation,* 3–13.
41. Cf. Wade, *Race and Ethnicity,* chap. 3; Knight, "Racism," 86–87. A new historical literature on contested Creole and indigenous discourses of nationalism and modernity in the Andes inspires much of the thinking in this chapter; in particular, I am indebted to Thurner, *From Two Republics;* Mendez, *Incas sí, indios no*; Muratorio, "Nación"; Mallon, *Peasant and Nation;* and Urbano, ed., *Modernidad;* see also the

splendid new studies of race-making in modern Peru by Poole, *Vision,* and de la Cadena, *Indigenous Mestizos.* For a recent interpretive synthesis of nineteenth-century Andean projects of race- and nation making, see my own study, "Highland Andean Peasants."

42. Larson, "Race" and "National Pedagogy;" Stephenson, *Gender and Modernity,* 111–57; Gotkowitz, "Race and Education."

43. Pérez Velasco, *La mentalidad chola,* 62–72.

44. See, for example, Mamani Condori, *Taraqu;* Condori Chura and Ticona Alejo, *El escribano;* and Choque et al., eds., *Educación indígena.*

45. See esp. Mamani Condori, *Taraqu,* 55–96; Rivera, "Pedimos la revisión," 603–52; Choque et al., eds., *Educación indígena;* Gotkowitz, "Within the Boundaries," chap. 2.

PART THREE

THE LOCAL, THE PERIPHERAL, AND THE NETWORK

REDEFINING THE BOUNDARIES OF POPULAR REPRESENTATION IN THE PUBLIC ARENA

Until recently, it has been common to imagine the formation of nation-states in Latin America as proceeding from the center to the periphery. Dominant classes, political elites, and intellectuals were portrayed as struggling over the design of the institutions, administrative procedures, and social-control mechanisms that were to span the entire national territory. From this perspective, the geographic and socioethnic contours of the nation were clear-cut from the beginning, and all that happened during the centuries of nation-state formation was to fill out this preexisting frame. Inevitably, such a view privileged political debates in the capital and among national elites. Even when conflicts with popular classes such as peasants or workers were taken into consideration they tended to be viewed from a national perspective. In the Andean region this centralist vision of nation-state formation has been most prevalent for Peru, and—for obvious reasons—least common for Colombia. But even for this northern Andean republic, the centrifugal forces from the distinct regional centers of power have often been naturalized as constitutive elements of a national state that had at least some unchanging essential characteristics (for example, as Aline Helg demonstrated earlier, being a white/mestizo Andean nation).

The three chapters in this section contribute to a more localized, decentered vision of the conflicts and negotiations through which the webs of power, institutions, and opinions underlying state- or nation-formation were constructed. While none deny the crucial role that elite-dominated central state structures and projects obviously played in such processes, they highlight the different meanings, representations, and projects for the body politic that could arise on local and regional levels. For widely varying social and ethnic settings and dimensions of public activity they demonstrate that notions of good government, networks of social and political ties and of opinion-formation arising on the local level, could differ notably from their counterparts pushed from the center by national elites. What is at issue is the degree to which local contests over power, resources, and representation interacted with and influenced national-level state-formation processes and the mechanisms by which they did so.

Finding convincing answers and adequate research methodologies for this issue is one of the most important challenges facing cutting-edge scholarship on Latin American political cultures today. It entails pinpointing the transmission spaces, the organizational ties, the rituals, the brokers, and the media of communication through which different local groups interacted with institutions, authorities, and influential individuals on the regional or national levels. Some of the connective tissues knitting together actors in the local and supralocal political arenas have diminished in importance over the two core centuries in the process of Andean nation-state formation, while others have maintained their potency and new ones have emerged. Caciques and priests, for example, belong to the first group, while union leaders, teachers, journalists, and perhaps military officers belong to the last-named group. Similarly, religious festivities have arguably diminished in importance while civic rituals—from independence-day parades to electoral rallies and popular demonstrations—have assumed a growing role for connecting local and national political visions. Moreover, different types of "connective tissues" between the local and the national had distinct implications for the construction of political cultures during the long phases of nation-state formation. Caciques, gamonales, and party or union bosses were likely to strengthen the hierarchical, clientelistic filaments connecting local groups with regional and national authorities and institutions. Grassroots associations of various types—from rural communities to mutual-aid societies and women's associations—could build more horizontal, networklike ties on the regional and national levels through a wide variety of communications channels. Vertical and horizontal connective tissues existed side by side, and there was no automatic, linear development from the one to the other.

Of course, the connection between the local and the national always depended on the material conditions through which communication could take place: horse, railroad, automobile, letters, telegraph, print and electronic media, to name a few. Within this changing material frame of communications, however, moments of crisis allowed local groups to reevaluate and reconfigure the nature and intensity of their ambiguous and malleable ties to supralocal political actors and institutions. This could lead to rejection or renegotiation of ties to brokers of long standing, reinterpretation of old pacts, or fashioning of new ones. The following three chapters explore this malleability of ties between local groups and regional or state-level political actors and suggest how local, especially subaltern, groups bring different meanings of the common good, public opinion, and the nation itself into supralocal political arenas.

Sergio Serulnikov offers an intriguing political-cultural interpretation of how different local constellations of power, social structure, and political imaginaries shaped different modes of insurrection during the Great Rebellion of the late 1770s and early 1780s in the Southern Andes, with massive consequences for broader regional political structures. In contrast to the older literature, he describes the insurrections as experiences of political and cultural empowerment and emphasizes ideological continuities between longer-standing nonrevolutionary projects and the insurgents' more radical, revolutionary stances at the height of the insurrections. In Norte de Potosí this radicalization occurred through processes of contestation around ancient rights claimed by the ayllus. In the region of La Paz the old brokers (caciques) lost power in the communities and the insurgency radicalized under nontraditional leaders who emphasized the ethnic/racial divisions of the late-colonial order.

For mid-twentieth-century Antioquia, Colombia, Mary Roldán demonstrates how the discourse and program of the progressive populist Jorge

Eliecer Gaitán was understood quite differently by his diverse Liberal Party constituencies. In the context of increasing political violence and the breakdown of the department's customary bipartisan elitist governance, this contributed to the reconfiguration of alliances and power constellations within Antioquia's Liberal Party. As the middle- and upper-class Liberal bosses abandoned party leadership in Medellín at the height of the Violencia, working-class Liberals put into effect a more revolutionary *Gaitanista* version of party strategy and practices. This crisis of Antioquia's regional and Colombia's national political culture also lead to rearrangements of patronage ties, with alienated working-class Liberals in Medellín and peripheral mining districts of the department bypassing departmental authorities in favor of direct links to Bogotá.

Nils Jacobsen's exploration of the formation of public opinions in late-nineteenth-century Peru suggests that the liberal, Tocquevillian notion of a clear separation between "modern" channels of communication fostering rational deliberation of citizens and "traditional" spheres of opinion, based on custom and social hierarchies, is not very helpful in deciphering Andean postcolonial public spheres. Modern means of opinion-formation, such as print media and associations, tended to be controlled by the elites and assumed a centralizing, civilizing mission of subjecting diverse social, regional, and ethnic groups to one particular, elite-dominated vision of the nation. Moreover, there were many overlaps between "modern" and "traditional" spheres of public opinion. And it was precisely in these overlapping spaces where localized popular and often illiterate groups could interact with public opinion on a national scale.

ANDEAN POLITICAL IMAGINATION IN THE LATE EIGHTEENTH CENTURY

Sergio Serulnikov

This essay explores the manifold expressions of Andean political consciousness and practices during the age of the great insurrections of the early 1780s. I will pursue two general lines of analysis that contribute to our understanding of this key event in the history of the region. The first is that the advent of the movement is better explained by a process of cultural and political empowerment of indigenous peoples than by revolutionary programs. Most of the political conceptions underpinning insurgent actions were indeed traditional and lay the ground for different kinds of cross-racial alliances. It was a shift in the field of political and symbolic power, before and during the insurrection, which turned those ideas into vehicles of anticolonial expectations and violence. Second, I argue that there were ideological continuities between revolutionary and nonrevolutionary conflicts, between community revolts and large-scale insurrections. Parochialism was not a necessary feature of local routines of protest. Centralized systems of government and surplus appropriation, peasant social autonomy and physical mobility, and homogenizing juridical notions of Indianness often endowed village protests with quite radical undertones. Given the nature of Spanish rule, Andean peasants needed to address broader structures of colonial domination, even when acting locally.

Before turning to these issues, I will summarize the distinctive regional characteristics of the pan-Andean uprising focusing on what the editors of this volume refer to as the different patterns of engagement between indigenous peoples and colonial governance. The center of my attention will be focused on the movements led by Túpac Amaru in Cuzco and Tomás Katari in Northern Potosí, the areas in which outright challenges to the colonial order began. The La Paz and Oruro insurrections will be mentioned only to highlight the contrasts and similarities of the anticolonial upheavals throughout the area.

ANDEAN REBELLION IN COMPARATIVE PERSPECTIVE

Political unrest took on distinct forms in each of the three major centers of rebel activity during the early 1780s, a cycle of social upheaval whose massiveness and ideological radicalization bear no comparison to any other period in the history of the Andean world. Historical literature, over the last twenty years, has unanimously shown the shortcomings of earlier Cuzco-centric interpretations of the event. Although Túpac Amaru eventually became the most recognizable symbol of insurgency across the Andes, this was not a single homogeneous movement but the conjunction of several uprisings with a history and dynamic of their own. Anticolonial consciousness varied significantly between regions in both its ideological content and the paths leading to its formation.

In the Cuzco area, two distinctive features shaped interracial relations. One was the increasing visibility of Inca imagery and Andean cultural motifs in elite and popular artistic expressions as well as in public ceremony in which most Cuzco social groups took part as performers or spectators. The colonial government greatly contributed to keeping precolonial memories vibrant and meaningful. It continued to endow the Indian aristocracy with privileges or taught it the "Incaic tradition" in the *colegios de caciques*, like the college of San Francisco de Borja in Cuzco whose walls were covered, in the course of the eighteenth century, with images of Inca figures.[1] Second, in Cuzco society the Indian aristocracy enjoyed high social standing among both indigenous communities and white settlers. The shared celebration of the pre-Columbian heritage was, in this sense, part of a larger pattern of cultural and economic interaction between the Andean nobility and Creole groups. Most indigenous lords were bilingual, literate mestizos and developed social and kinship networks with regional elites. Some caciques owned private haciendas and mines and engaged in commercial and financial ventures with Spanish officials and entrepreneurs as partners rather than as subordinate agents.[2] Several prestigious Cuzco noble families even had some of their members admitted into the priesthood.[3] At the same time, in sharp contrast to other regions, Indians of noble birth remained in control of most native chieftainships. These hereditary ethnic lords exerted a relatively undisputed authority within their rural towns, at least judging by the low levels of overt indigenous dissension.[4] Taken as a whole, the Cuzco native lords enjoyed a degree of social prestige unknown elsewhere in the Andes.

The public recognition of Inca historical legacies and the full integration of the indigenous nobility into colonial society echoed the tensions and ambiguities embedded in the Spanish colonial project. This complexity translated into the stark ideological ambivalence of the Túpac Amaru movement. Several layers of tension shaped insurgent practices and discourses. To begin with, the notion of Inca restoration was infused with millennial and messianic beliefs, including cyclical visions of history, circulation of prophesies announcing imminent cosmological and social cataclysms, and myths about the resurrection of the last Inca emperor.[5] Yet Túpac Amaru could also translate his political aspiration into the language of the ancient Spanish *pactismo,* namely, the reconstitution of the balanced relation between the king and the political communities or kingdoms that comprised the monarchy.[6] It is open to debate whether this traditional claim was ultimately meant to redefine the terms of the colonial pact or to terminate it altogether. In either case, Túpac Amaru did not define this Andean political community as merely indigenous but as composed of diverse American social groups.[7]

This initial appeal to both Indian and white people born in Peru may be pointing to the incipient formation of a discrete interracial "imagined community." Although unrelated to later liberal concepts of nationhood, this notion of political community underscored Andean elites' and Creoles' sense of cross-cultural identity as Americans, rather than merely as members of the Republic of Spaniards or the Republic of Indians.[8] Bourbon absolutism played a major role in subordinating racial antagonisms to a broader clash between imperial projects and local interests. The fiscal and institutional reforms undertaken by the Bourbon administration to transform its overseas possessions into full-fledged colonies provided a cross-section of local society with a common source of resentment and, for a short while at least, a sense of common destiny as well.[9] To be sure, Andean leaders and Creoles held divergent understandings of the aims of the movement. The former might have expected nonindigenous peoples to recognize the new balance of power emerging in the wake of Inca political revival, and the latter might have hoped to manipulate Indian unrest to halt the ongoing program of reforms. Still, their spontaneous, albeit short-lived, support of social upheaval of this magnitude suggests that Túpac Amaru's appeal to the Inca heritage was a language they understood and shared. In fact, Creoles and mestizos staffed the highest ranks of the insurgent command, and the revolt initially gained the sympathy of numerous members of the clergy.[10]

Ideological ambivalence also pervaded peasant-kuraka relations. The strength of the ascendancy of Andean lords over their communities passed the test of widespread political unrest: unlike in other centers of rebel activity, indigenous groups in the Cuzco area tended to abide by their ethnic chiefs' decision either to support or to oppose the Túpac Amaru insurrection. But those commoners who joined the upheaval understood their endeavor in an entirely different light than the indigenous aristocracy. Rank-and-file rebels saw the uprising as an opportunity to redress longstanding economic grievances against colonial officials, haciendas, textile mills, and white overlords in general. Collective mobilization was structured along traditional community lines, but from the peasants' standpoint, the distinction traced by the Indian leaders between Europeans and Creoles appeared to be pointless and vain.

In Northern Potosí, the other area where mass rebellion developed autonomously, we find a different dynamic in terms of the role of ethnic lords, the implications of state policies, the process of political radicalization, and the meaning of neo-Inca claims. The single most important contentious issue during the process leading to the outburst of mass violence was the control of native chieftainships. The protest grew out of intense battles over illegitimate ethnic chiefs, regardless of whether such chiefs came from noble lineages, were mestizo, or both. Protests also focused on the Spanish provincial functionaries backing such dubious lords, and the threats to community economic and political values that abusive authorities represented. The movement was therefore much less hierarchical, and much more organized from the bottom up than in Cuzco. On the other hand, as social conflicts revolved around customary modes of exploitation by civil, ethnic, and ecclesiastical authorities, Bourbon absolutism appeared to Indian communities as less of a central motive of discontent than a political resource to be manipulated for their own ends. The language of contention evolved from the enforcement of specific corporate privileges and the fair administration of justice to a redefinition of the power relations between the king, local colonial rulers, and the Andean communities. Such a redefinition of power relations along the lines of Tristan Platt's "pact of reciprocity" was Northern Potosí's version of the Andean utopia.[11] Entailing the reorganization of engrained systems of colonial and ethnic power, it proved to be as radical as any other utopia. Distinctions between Creoles and peninsular Spaniards were notoriously lacking from the concerns of leaders and common peasants alike. The basic antagonism here was located between indigenous and nonindigenous people within the rural world, rather than between local interests and imperial policies.[12]

Since ethnic identities in Northern Potosí were supported by local deities and rituals, with no pan-Andean or Inca undertones, the path to subversion differed from that in southern Peru. The formation of webs of political solidarity and cooperation among various communities and ethnic groups had grown through a long process of contention that led to the articulation of a common language of indigenous corporate rights. This in itself expressed the rise of a radical political awareness. Insurgency in the Cuzco area was set in motion by a conspiracy, an open act of violence that came as a total surprise to the authorities: the capture and public execution of the Tinta corregidor by a purported descendant of the last Inca. Though Túpac Amaru claimed to follow the king's instructions to purge the kingdom of corrupt rulers, the seditious nature of this action must have escaped no one.[13] Widespread peasant uprisings ensued. As Flores Galindo has noted, the general mechanism of expansion of the movement was less that of the advance of a rebel army than the establishment of contacts in the rural areas in order to encourage local revolts.[14] Mobilization in Northern Potosí ran in the opposite direction: anticolonial radicalism stemmed from a gradual process of contention. Collective violence escalated progressively. Every open confrontation between authorities and Indians was foreseen and announced in advance: from the small clashes provoked by Tomás Katari's several arrests

(March 1778–June 1780) and the bloody battle of Pocoata (August 1780), to the mass killings ensuing the leader's murder in late 1780. In short, for Cuzco rebels outright challenges to the colonial order represented the starting point, and for their peers in Northern Potosí the closing one.

In addition, Northern Potosí Indians' allegiance to Túpac Amaru in late 1780 had nothing to do with the restructuring of the relation between the Spanish monarchy and the Kingdom of Peru but with the embracing of an alternative source of sovereignty. By the time news from Túpac Amaru began to reach the area, the relationship between colonial authorities and Northern Potosí communities had already collapsed and social unrest ran rampant. Túpac Amaru came to occupy the vacuum left by the profound legitimacy crisis of the Spanish government in the region. Whereas in Cuzco the ideological strains lay in the variety of outlooks and expectations brought to the movement by the different participants—the native nobility, the Creoles, and the peasant masses—in Northern Potosí the main source of tension derived from the extraordinary trajectory of the conflict. The final engagement in nativist anticolonial projects coexisted in a rather difficult way with the much more modest initial agenda of the protest. The tensions between the original motivation and the outcome of the movement was always there and surfaced in a divided and weak leadership and contradictory set of goals during the last stage of the conflict. Thus, Nicolás Katari, one of the rebels who had commanded the killing of tens of Indians and non-Indians blamed for the murder of his brother Tomás in late 1780, refused to participate in the siege of the city of La Plata in February 1781. He argued that he "neither was able to nor wanted to mobilize the people, because he had wife, children and a king, to whom he had paid his tributes for nineteen years."[15] Dámaso Katari, the main leader of the assault on the city, did not hesitate to proclaim his loyalty to Túpac Amaru and his desire to "drink chicha in the skulls" of the Spaniards. Yet his last testimony also reflected the path the conflict might have taken. Had his brother Tomás's petitions been attended from the beginning, Dámaso said, "he [Tomás] would have not been stigmatized as a rebel and trouble maker, nor persecuted by his enemies until tragically losing his life, leaving his brothers with such agonies as inheritance."[16]

The case of La Paz presents several contrasts with its counterparts in the Charcas and Cuzco regions. In the first place, the rebellion led by Túpac Katari was not the result of endogenous political mobilization, either a conspiracy turned into massive upheaval (Cuzco) or a gradual process of radicalization (Northern Potosí). It was born out of a full-scale revolutionary situation both south and north of Lake Titicaca. Insurgent activities began in late February 1781, when mass mobilization was well under way in Cuzco, Charcas, and Oruro. Yet the La Paz region had not remained unaffected by the widespread social unrest prior to 1780. On the contrary, Aymara communities in the altiplano provinces had an unparalleled record of collective violence and open resistance, especially against provincial magistrates (two were killed in Pacajes and Sicasica in the early 1770s), illegitimate caciques, and the forced distribution of commodities. The city of La Paz itself had also witnessed one of the most notorious tax revolts against the establishment of a customs house for the collection of the *alcabala* (sales tax).

As we will see later, this historical experience of contention and the egalitarian ideas shaping Indian local protest help to explain the distinctive meaning La Paz peasants attributed to the pan-Andean upheaval. From its inception, the movement adopted a radical racial agenda. There were no illusions about cross-racial alliances against imperial policies, as in Cuzco, or about the reenactment of an ideal ayllu-state reciprocity pact against rural overlords, as in Northern Potosí. In addition, the organization and leadership of the movement did not present the traditional community power structure of the Cuzco rebellion. Nor did it evidence the kind of informal and loose quality—i.e., a social protest turned into anticolonial war—of the Northern Potosí uprising. While in La Paz, as in southern Bolivia, the kurakas played no major role in the organization of the uprising, the paceño leadership had a definite military style, at least at the top. Túpac Katari and his assistants exerted firm control over the Indian troops and had the will and power to discipline hostile peasants and competitors for the rebel command, especially members of the Túpac Amaru entourage. Unlike its counterpart in Cuzco, the Aymara communities conducted a caste war that left no room for future historical constructions as a protoindependence movement.[17]

ROOTS OF INSURGENCY: PATTERNS OF CULTURAL AND POLITICAL EMPOWERMENT

The conceptions of Indian-white relations, the political utopias, and the structure of leadership differed in each area of rebel activity. In this section I shall explore two lines of analysis that point to some general roots of Indian insurgency in the Andes. The first argument is that the pan-Andean upheaval of 1780 grew out of a long-term process of cultural and political empowerment of Andean peoples. This common trend presents, as should be expected, regional variances. In the case of Cuzco, John Rowe and Alberto Flores Galindo, among others, have demonstrated the eighteenth-century renaissance of Inca culture. It found expression in canvas and mural painting, textile designs, clothes, queros, public representations, dances, or the wide circulation of works like Garcilaso de la Vega's *Comentarios Reales.*[18] By the eighteenth century, it was fashionable for Andean lords to have themselves portrayed in Inca garb and insignia of power. Even Christian deities, according to the Bishop of Cuzco, were dressed in Inca costumes during the celebration of Corpus Christi and Santiago the Apostle. Leon Campbell noted that "an active cult of Inca antiquity had flourished in Cuzco from at least mid-century, carried on by both Creoles, who adopted Inca dress and furnishings, and caciques who proudly exhibited the ancient symbol of the Sun God and of the Incas in public ceremonies."[19] Although little is known about the impact of this process of cultural renewal on ordinary members of the Andean communities, their active participation in those dramatic representations, along with noble Indians and white elites, is beyond doubt. It has even been suggested that for the indigenous people theater replaced ritual as the main vehicle of community identity.[20]

Two aspects of this well-known phenomenon need to be emphasized here: its historical singularity and its connection to the outbreak of massive Indian insurgency. In the first place, an argument could be made that the Cuzco of the years immediately preceding the Túpac Amaru rebellion represents the moment in the history of Peru with the highest level of equivalence ever achieved between the Andean nobility and the Creole elites, in terms of social standing, economic power, and cultural prestige. Alberto Flores Galindo's assertion that by the eighteenth century "an [indigenous] Cuzqueño aristocrat . . . was considered as honorable as a Spanish aristocrat" could be something of a hyperbole.[21] Yet it may be pointing to an extraordinary historical trend in the patterns of interracial relations in the Andean world that the political cataclysm of 1780 (and then the defeat of the Pumacahua rebellion of 1814–15) turned into archeological ruins. In effect, in contrast to nineteenth-century Peruvian Creole nationalism (or Creole readings of the ancient Mesoamerican civilizations in colonial Mexico), the celebration of the Tawantinsuyu (the Quechua term for the Inca empire) was not meant to function as mirror image of the irredeemable backwardness of contemporary Andean peoples. Nor was it a paternalist discourse imposed on the natives, like twentieth-century *indigenismo.*[22] Cuzco colonial society, unlike postindependence caudillos such as Agustín Gamarra or Andrés Santa Cruz who also invoked the memories of the Incas, recognized tangible continuities, both cultural and political, between past and present. Unlike indigenismo, Indian peoples themselves were directly involved in the growing prestige and visibility of Andean traditions. Flores Galindo has aptly summarized this growing sense of cultural and economic self-reliance:

> In the plastic arts, as in any other field, indigenous culture is not despised; it is respected. . . . Thus the power of the Incaic aristocracy is not a mere gift from the Spaniards for their role as local authorities, but derives in part from the fortunes that they themselves managed to accumulate through involvement in trade, as in the case of Túpac Amaru, and the ownership and management of agricultural and mining enterprises, as in the cases of the kurakas of Acos, Acomayo or Tinta.[23]

A second critical question is how we construe the relation between this gradual process of empowerment and the advent of neo-Inca sovereignty claims. No doubt the celebration of the Inca past and the symbolic prestige and economic success of the Andean lords had ambivalent connotations and was by no means bound to evolve into nativist utopias. The celebration of the preconquest past was a hybrid and ambiguous device providing a type of historical narrative to which disparate members of colonial society could relate. Memories of the Tawantinsuyu were not automatically associated with a questioning of the legitimacy of the European conquest, nor were public dramatizations of the capture of Atahualpa and the Spanish conquest necessarily interpreted as a celebration of the fall of native imperial traditions. They must have just reminded people of the mixed origins of the civilization emerging out of the colonial encounter.[24]

Actually, the majority of kurakas and communities in the Cuzco area remained royalist during the rebellion. Ideas and representations of the Inca past were not radical per se; the fact that they seemed to produce a nativist revolution is indeed one of the outcomes of the revolution itself. The larger point, however, is that an engrained sense of cultural pride and social prestige, rather than deprivation and marginality, bred the growing radicalization of important sectors of Cuzco's indigenous aristocracy. As Andean cultural traditions became vested with swelling symbolic power, they ceased to function as marks of subalternity. By unwittingly undermining notions of racial inferiority, this process made the envisioning and diffusion of radical utopias possible. The slow evolution in the appraisal of the precolonial past, and the status of the representational practices (public theater, religious processions, parades, painting, etc.) through which this past was recast vis-à-vis the European invasion, points to the *cultural* rather than the *intellectual* origins of the Túpac Amaru revolution. As Roger Chartier said of the cultural origins of the French Revolution, the process brought about "changes in belief and sensibility that would render such a rapid and profound destruction of the old political and social order decipherable and acceptable."[25] The astonishing readiness with which thousands of Andean peasants in southern Peru followed the leadership of Túpac Amaru can only be understood through this unique historical trend. Of course, common Indians must have dreamed of an egalitarian society, instead of a hierarchical imperial system, and of a *pachacuti,* a complete reversal of the existing order, rather than of a coalition with Creoles and other power groups. All in all, Andean insurgency seems to be rooted in a process of cultural empowerment, rather than in indigenous anxieties about "their ability to culturally survive."[26]

This cultural trend was matched by equally significant changes in relations of political subordination. The increasing number of popular riots in cities and rural villages throughout the Andean region nurtured a climate of contention and unrest that proved the feasibility of outright assaults on colonial government. Antifiscal movements in cities like La Paz, Arequipa, Cochabamba, and Cuzco, Juan Santos Atahualpa's millennial upheaval in central Peru, abortive conspiracies in Huarochiri and Cuzco in 1750 and 1780, as well as the spreading of rural revolts across the Andean world, must have demonstrated the vulnerability of colonial rule. Ward Stavig has rightly noted that the large number of local protests could create a statistical mirage since each individual area tended to experience just a few episodes of political violence. Yet the multiplication of these episodes produced "a climate in which violent protests were more likely to occur."[27] Compliance to authority, in other words, should have no longer appeared as a fact of life.

This process of political empowerment is particularly noticeable in the case of Northern Potosí. Recent works show that the rebellion led by Tomás

Katari was preceded by an exceptional conjuncture of political turmoil in the course of which Indian communities achieved considerable success in their disputes with provincial magistrates, parish priests, and ethnic chiefs.[28] Though the cultural and social trends we found in Cuzco were mostly lacking here, the distinct dynamic of those political struggles could account for the unique role of Northern Potosí as the first, and largely autonomous, focus of insurgency outside of southern Peru. Thus, for instance, in 1776, only one year before the beginning of Tomas Katari's activities, the ethnic group of Pocoata (neighbors of Katari's ethnic group of Macha) had accomplished the removal of an illegitimate cacique appointed by the corregidor after almost two years of collective protests. These included dozens of petitions before Potosí and Charcas courts, as well as open demonstrations of force against rural authorities. While elsewhere in the Andes village revolts tended to fail, the Northern Potosí upheaval grew out of the triumph of an intense process of mass mobilization. Rebellion was not a desperate response to failure: it was largely the result of successful previous challenges to local power relations. For reasons distinct from those of the Cuzco Indian nobility, Northern Potosí peasants also had motives for defiance and self-confidence.

The empowerment of indigenous peoples is not only related to their undeniable capacity for cultural resilience and political mobilization. It can also be traced to colonial rulers' gross miscalculations resulting from the very nature of eighteenth-century Spanish colonialism in the Andes. Northern Potosí communities could persistently defy local authorities because of the ostensible strife among colonial elites: for example, conflicts between civil and ecclesiastical magistrates over church fees, between treasury officials and corregidores over tribute embezzlement, between the newly created viceregal court of Buenos Aires and the audiencia of Charcas over jurisdiction on Andean affairs. During and after the rebellion, enlightened bureaucrats blamed abusive rural authorities for stirring social unrest, and rural authorities blamed high courts for eroding power relations in the rural villages. Nevertheless, nothing could prevent rural elites from abusing their power (part and parcel of the structure of colonialism), enlightened magistrates from undermining rural elites' claims to peasant resources (a measure at the heart of Bourbon policies), and Andean communities from taking advantage of intra-elite disputes to regain command over their social and economic resources.[29]

In the case of Cuzco, Michel de Certeau's metaphor of the "beauty of the dead" may serve us well to highlight the paradoxical effects of the promotion of Inca memories. De Certeau argues that popular culture has entered the realm of elite representations only at the price of losing all of its original subversive meanings, only when it became "ruins . . . something preceding history, the horizon of nature, or paradise lost."[30] By the eighteenth century, the Spanish administration seemed to assume that by bolstering the prestige of the indigenous aristocracy its sense of subordination and loyalty would be reinforced, not the memories of its long-extinguished political prominence. It also must have assumed that the frequent public dramatizations of the defeat of Atahualpa helped instill the discourse of conquest, rather than the reversible nature of the European invasion. Where colonial rulers saw beauty in these cultural elements, because these were assumed to be death relics, Cuzco native peoples saw a potent ideological weapon: they believed (quite literally, it seems) that the dead might be resuscitated after all. Not surprisingly, in the aftermath of the insurrection, colonial rulers tried to address some of the main explicit objectives of the protest, notably the abolition of *repartos,* the elimination of corregidores, the reduction of tax pressure, and the establishment of a new audiencia in Cuzco.[31] At the same time, they sought to root out the historical forces that had quietly contributed to blurring the signs of Indian subalternity. In the Cuzco area, hereditary chieftainships were suppressed, the paintings of Inca emperors removed from public view, and the use of old Andean garments forbidden. Visitor General Antonio de Areche also made a point of banning theatrical representations of the Inca past or the conquest and even outlawed the use of native languages. In retrospect, Cuzco's Bishop Juan Manuel de Moscoso considered that allowing the display of such "gentile" practices and symbols had been a "capital error."[32]

The undermining of notions of racial and cultural superiority on which European rights to rule were predicated lay at the heart of Indian insurgency once mass mobilization gathered strength. A "purposive image" of the process by which revolutions develop—the idea that revolutionary movements begin with "revolutionary intention"—may mislead us in our efforts to grasp the causes and dynamics of the pan-Andean upheaval.[33] The initial socioeconomic and political programs of the rebellion were peripheral, if historically significant in other respects, to what made Indian collective actions so deeply subversive. The point is not merely that the ideas and collective violence became more radical as the rebellion evolved, which was unmistakably the case.[34] More importantly, Indian actions subverted the established order regardless of the particular agenda of their participants. Thus, when examined closely, the trajectory of the conflict in Northern Potosí almost naturally obviates teleology, "one of the besetting sins in analyses of revolution," as Charles Tilly warns.[35] Tomás Katari's demands stand out for their moderation rather than their radicalism. His strategy of struggle reminds us of the profound, lasting imprint of Spanish justice in peasant consciousness and political action. Just as some Creole groups initially lent their support to the Cuzco uprising, high officials of the Audiencia of Charcas, the royal treasury of Potosí, and the viceregal court of Buenos Aires genuinely believed, during the 1770s, that peasant complaints against rural civil, ecclesiastical, and ethnic authorities in Northern Potosí deserved to be backed. Yet the relentless pursuit of redressing popular grievances through legal channels turned the protest and its leader into an intolerable menace to colonial relations.[36] As I have argued elsewhere, such legal campaigns to redress grievances encouraged, rather than prevented, the deployment of popular violence. Local and regional power groups had insisted that the Northern Potosí communities sought to break their subjection to king and Church. Andean communities in turn reaffirmed their subordination to the crown by their continuous appeal to Spanish courts and their compliance with their basic economic obligations (mita and tribute). Ironically, in the end, Andean peasants did become increasingly rebellious, yet not for their rejection of Spanish institutions, as regional authorities had claimed all along, but by virtue of the same acts that, Indians believed, proved their allegiance to the colonial regime.

Nowhere were the consequences of the collapse of the colonial order more apparent than in the fate of the interracial relations within the rebel coalition. As already mentioned, the program of socioeconomic reforms pushed by Túpac Amaru was broad enough to lay the foundations for multiethnic alliances. Moreover, in opposing Bourbon absolutism, Túpac Amaru arguably articulated notions of colonial legitimacy that bear resemblance to traditional ideological claims of previous Creole conspiracies in Peru or the contemporary rebellion of the comuneros in New Granada.[37] Ideas might have similar roots, yet the meaning of their political enactment could still vary enormously. As conservative as those ideas might have been, in the context of a massive indigenous movement they became part of a counterhegemonic political practice undermining the core tenet of European colonialism: the notion that there was a definite linkage between power and culture, that political dominance was based on the inherent superiority of white (Spaniard and Creole) people. The challenge to this symbolic power in turn made the actual content of ideas both extremely unstable and ultimately inconsequential.

Indeed, the startling fluidity with which Túpac Amaru moved from ideas of monarchical legitimism to notions of Peruvian nationalism to Inca restitution claims has become an inexhaustible source of political and scholarly debate ever since.[38] As far as colonial elites were concerned, however, the content of those ideas was barely significant. As Creoles would learn very soon (and never forget thereafter), the rise of an Indian leader as a supreme authority and the autonomous mobilization of the Andean peasants were altogether incompatible with the perpetuation of colonialism in any guise or form. Once colonial hierarchies were dismantled, considerations concerning insurgent economic programs and political projects (whether separatist or royalist, exclusively indigenous or "Peruvian") became, for all practical matters, utterly irrelevant. As is well known, the vast majority of Creoles and members of the clergy withdrew their overt or tacit support to Túpac Amaru within the first weeks of confrontation.

The case of Oruro is in this sense instructive. Oruro was the only rebel territory where Creole groups held a firm command of the insurgent movement and Andean peasants lent explicit support to a cross-racial coalition. Led by Jacinto Rodriguez, city dwellers (Creoles, mestizos, and others) joined Indian communities to rise up against the constituted authorities and the peninsular Spaniards in general in the name of Túpac Amaru. Unlike other areas, Indian insurgents made here a conscious effort to distinguish Creoles from Europeans while Oruro elites treated Indian communities as formal allies. Despite these auspicious circumstances, interracial alliances could be sustained for less than a week. Andean peasants undertook a series of autonomous initiatives, from forcing all Oruro residents to dress as Indians and demanding the execution of the Europeans to asking for a redistribution of lands. The Creoles first tried to negotiate and then compelled the withdrawal of the Indians from the city. Eventually, the Creoles would ally themselves with the Europeans and abandon their allegiance to Túpac Amaru altogether. Like nonindigenous groups elsewhere, Oruro elites found out that no interracial cooperation could be sustained once the marks of social distinction and deference—which in a colonial society were based on caste hierarchy—collapsed.[39]

In conclusion, insurgent Indians across the Andes may have legitimized their collective protest by preaching their loyalty to the king, by expressing their attachment to corporative rights and judicial procedures, and/or by seeking to build cross-racial alliances with white regional elites. However, by defying de facto their subordinate place in the natural order of things, Indian collective mobilization precluded any potential common ground between colonizers and colonized. The analytical problem, again, is to shift focus from programs and ideas to the field of power relations within which programs and ideas take on actual social meaning. For instance, in his pathbreaking study of the Túpac Amaru movement, John Rowe reflected the following:

> The reader examining the decrees of the Inca leaders gains the impression that above all they pursued one program: to end some taxes which were much more bothersome to mestizos and Creoles than they were to Indians. The revolution would have had much more success if the whites of 1780 had taken rebel propaganda as seriously as whites do today.[40]

While in a sense this rings true, Creoles had powerful reasons not to take rebel programs seriously. Colonial white elites seemed to know that, once the insurrection gathered strength, the stakes of the conflict concerned something more fundamental than particular state policies or even the fate of Spanish domination. What was at stake here, regardless of what Andean peoples thought they were doing, was the entire system of colonial hegemony: the use of cultural difference as a signifier of racial inferiority, and the use of the notion of racial inferiority as a legitimate claim to rule. Only when the menace had seemingly vanished, and only at the expense of domesticating its subversive content, would republican rulers venture to retrieve the great Indian rebellions into their own historical record. Only then would they undertake to recast the eighteenth-century rebellion as an enlightened resistance to Spanish colonialism, to turn Túpac Amaru into a symbol of national identity, to find beauty in the Andean past once again.

THE PARISH, THE UNIVERSE, AND THE SPACE IN BETWEEN

The final point I want to address is the relationship between community revolts and regional insurrections. We must not dichotomize local and large-scale movements in terms of the ideological content of the protest. While regional upheavals, like the 1780 conjuncture, present obvious distinctive features with respect to village riots, we should think of these two forms of protest in fluid terms. Though often assimilated to the peasant revolts in the Mexican countryside analyzed by William Taylor, Andean village protests present distinctive features.[41] In the Andes, the scale of peasant mobilization did not always correspond to the ideological breadth of the protest or its range of political consciousness. Local disputes might have called for sweeping transformations insofar as the most common sources of discontent (*repartimientos,* scarcity of lands, taxes, Church fees, or abusive corregidores) tended to be perceived as expressions of general trends. As John Coatsworth has noted, whereas village uprisings in Mexico mostly arose from purely local grievances, in the Andes rural unrest responded to general economic conditions and public policy.[42] Rural protests could also ignite a process of peasant politicization because in redressing specific grievances, Andean communities often needed to question state policies and institutions and, sometimes, the working of the political order as a whole. Virtually any social conflict in the eighteenth-century Andes pushed indigenous peoples to deal with different instances of the colonial administration, to experience the gap between norms and power, to test the balances of power between peasants and rural elites. The dynamic of these processes is critical to an understanding of the roots of Indian insurgency, not only in negative terms, that is, the *failure* of specific village revolts to create the climate for large-scale upheavals, but also in positive terms: the forms whereby routine political contention at the local level shaped the nature of mass rebellion.[43]

In the La Paz area, for example, a series of defined radical ideological motifs can be found in circumscribed local protests. In exploring several social conflicts in the altiplano provinces since the 1740s, Sinclair Thomson has identified various strands of "anti-colonial consciousness" in rural riots prior to 1781. These "anti-colonial political options," unrelated to notions of Inca restoration, are defined by Thomson as "radical elimination of the colonial enemy; regional Indian autonomy that did not necessarily challenge the legitimacy of the Spanish Crown; and racial/ethnic integration under Indian hegemony."[44] Clearly the trigger of the Túpac Katari upheaval was the expansion of neo-Inca projects. But we cannot understand the specific way Aymara peasants engaged and experienced the pan-Andean insurrection without assessing the previous historical development of those discrete forms of political thought. When viewed in the light of this distinct historical experience, the La Paz movement appears much less as an outcome of the spread of new utopias—"revolutionary" as opposed to previous "reformist" ideas. Rather it evidences the unfolding of already existing radical, egalitarian ideas in a deeply transformed political context—a context of massive mobilization and generalized crisis of colonial legitimacy.

Mass rebellion in Northern Potosí was preceded by two fairly long conjunctures (1747–51 and 1775–80) of widespread public, albeit largely nonviolent, confrontation with local power groups (priests, caciques, and corregidores) over taxes, assignment of mita obligations, land distribution, and ethnic political autonomy, among other issues. These struggles bear remarkably little resemblance to the "spasmodic, localized, often extremely violent, and short-lived" nature of contemporary village riots in Mexico.[45] Instead, as peasant notions of political legitimacy were matched with the realities of colonial rule, a collective experience of contention was evolving. In this way the indigenous communities expanded their ideological horizons beyond the community level and their repertories of struggle beyond mere passive resistance or spasmodic violence. I mentioned earlier that Tomás Katari's activities were encouraged by the success of previous protest movements. I would now add that some of the distinctive political tenets and modes of collective action surfacing during the course of the great rebellion in this region directly derived from the dynamic of those local struggles. This holds true for the call to fully enforce Indian communities' corporative rights, as well as for the overlap between mass protest and judicial litigation.

The nature of Spanish colonialism in the Andes helped to turn the ideological potential of village protests into political practices. Homogenizing concepts of Indianness, reified notions of Inca imperial history, as well as universal juridical definitions of the Indian community (which endowed native groups with the same kind of corporative obligations and rights toward the state) facilitated the evolution of local grievances into sweeping claims. Equally important, Andean peoples enjoyed a relatively free, unsupervised communication with one another. If the Spanish imperial imagination encouraged ideas of common Indian identity, history, and corporative rights, the network of markets and state institutions, and the very political economy of the Andean community, fostered the formation of broad horizontal links. Multiethnic co-residence, annual migratory movements between valleys and highlands, collective gatherings in rural towns for ritual or fiscal purposes, participation in urban markets and trade routes, shared mita services in Potosí, journeys to administrative centers in order to litigate provincial magistrates and parish priests (some of whom were shared by several communities): all these interactions contributed to expanding the world of the Andean peasants well beyond the boundaries of their local villages, or what Hobsbawm defined as the "parish pump."[46] Furthermore, the dispersed pattern of settlement, which the Toledan program of *reducciones* had been unable to curb in most Andean regions, and the lack of means of social control in the rural areas, endowed Andean communities with a large measure of autonomy in their everyday life. The colonial system in the Andes provided little material conditions for the creation of a village-centered worldview that Eric Van Young, referring to the peasantry in colonial Mexico, has defined as *campanilismo:* "the tendency of villagers to see the social (and political) horizon as extending only as far as the view from the church tower."[47]

In sum, the patterns of political action during revolutionary times are tightly connected to local experiences of struggle. There are defined continuities between local political histories and the pattern of engagement of the Indians in large-scale uprisings. Certainly rural riots and protests could merely pursue discrete changes in village life. Yet reformism and village unrest might also contain, overtly or latently, quite radical undertones. Local initiatives often carried radical agendas of change and always had the potential to assume menacing effects of demonstration. Therefore, in writing a political history from below of the late-colonial era in the Andes, these strictly local trajectories must be reconstructed.[48] They provide the link between the "parish pump" and the "universe" as loci of indigenous political action. They give us a sense of why and how Andean peoples moved from local protests to millennial hopes of social and cosmological cataclysms. Mental structures—neo-Inca ideologies, millennial prophesies, messianic expectations, ideal visions of community-state relationship—and economic trends—increasing fiscal pressures and commercial monopolies, demographic growth, and the like—provide the context of social agency, not agency itself. Andean peasants became political actors through concrete experiences of contention, and these struggles generally did not take place in the context of village isolation, nor in the realm of radical expectations of change. Indian communities confronted colonial overlords by engaging state institutions, by relating their particular hardships to the rules that were supposed to govern social relations, by expressing their own visions of justice, by promoting community mobilization and solidarity over internal divisions, and by testing authorities' ability to counter popular violence. To change their small world, Andean people needed to engage the world at large. By 1780, they thought the time had come to try to change the world at large, too.

NOTES

1. Rowe, "El movimiento nacional Inca"; Flores Galindo, *Buscando un Inca;* on the colegio de caciques, see Brading, *The First America,* 342; and O'Phelan Godoy, *La gran rebelión,* 31–32; on Indian leaders' appeal to precolonial noble lineage, see Sala i Vila, "La rebelión," 281; and Rostworowski, *Curacas y sucesiones,* 54–57.

2. Flores Galindo, *Buscando un Inca,* 137–42; O'Phelan Godoy, "Aduanas," 53–72.

3. O'Phelan Godoy, *La gran rebelión,* 47–68.

4. Stavig, *The World of Túpac Amaru,* 229–33.

5. Hidalgo Lehuede, "Amarus y cataris," 117–38; Szeminski, *La utopía tupamarista;* Campbell, "Ideology and Factionalism," 110–39; Flores Galindo, *Buscando un Inca,* 127–57.

6. On Bourbon violation of Spanish contract notions, see Guerra, *Modernidad e independencias,* 56; on Habsburg model of rule and Indian rebels, see Sala i Vila, "La rebelión," 300; O'Phelan, *La gran rebelión,* 44; Thurner, *From Two Republics,* 9.

7. On Túpac Amaru's overall aim as "a cross-racial Peruvian nationalist project," see Thomson, "Colonial Crisis," 245; Walker, *Smoldering Ashes,* 40.

8. In his study of the conflicts that took place in the town of Andagua, Arequipa, in the mid-eighteenth century, Frank Salomon provides an excellent example of the dichotomous worldview prevailing among other Andean peoples; see Salomon, "Ancestor Cults," 163.

9. O'Phelan Godoy, *Un siglo de rebeliones,* 175–294; Fisher, Kuethe, and McFarlane, eds., *Reform and Insurrection.*

10. Campbell, "Social Structure," 3–49; O'Phelan Godoy, *Un siglo de rebeliones,* 268; on parish priests in the Cuzco rebellion, see Stavig, *The World,* 242; O'Phelan Godoy, *La gran rebelión,* 122–23; for an interesting study questioning the extent of the involvement of the priests in the insurrection, see Garzón Heredia, "1780: Clero," 245–71.

11. Platt, *Estado boliviano,* 20–21.

12. For recent studies on this rebellion, see Adrian, "Sociedad civil," 29–54; Adrian,

"Reformas borbónicas," 11–35; Andrade Padilla, *La rebelión;* Penry, "Transformations"; Serulnikov, "Peasant Politics," 245–74. On *cabildos indígenas* and ritual sponsors before and during the rebellion, see Abercrombie, *Pathways,* 291–304.

13. Campbell, "Ideology and Factionalism," 120–24; Szeminski, "Why Kill the Spaniards?," 171–74; Stavig, *The World,* 208.

14. Flores Galindo, *Buscando un Inca,* 146.

15. "Confesión de Nicolás Catari," in de Angelis, ed., *Colección,* 725.

16. "Confesión de Dámaso Catari," in de Angelis, ed., *Colección,* 700.

17. Thomson, "Colonial Crisis"; Valle de Siles, *La rebelión.*

18. Rowe, "El movimiento nacional Inca"; Flores Galindo, *Buscando un Inca;* Guibovich Pérez, "Lectura y difusión," 103–20; Mazzotti, "Garcilaso," 13–35.

19. Campbell, "Ideology and Factionalism," 116–17.

20. Flores Galindo, *Buscando un Inca,* 69.

21. Ibid., 136.

22. Cf. Méndez, *Incas sí, indios no*; Thurner, *From Two Republics,* 110–12; Walker, *Smoldering Ashes,* 145–50 and 193–201; and Poole, *Vision,* 146–51; on Creole uses of pre-Columbian history, see Pagden, *Spanish Imperialism,* 91–132; Brading, *The First America,* 447–64.

23. Flores Galindo, *Buscando un Inca,* 136–37.

24. On ambivalent colonial artistic evocations of the Inca past, see Espinoza, "Colonial Visions," 84–106.

25. Chartier, *Cultural Origins,* 2.

26. Stavig, *The World,* 235.

27. Ibid., 215.

28. Cf. note 12.

29. Serulnikov, "Customs and Rules," 245–74; Adrián, "Los curatos," 97–117.

30. de Certeau, *Heterologies*, 120–21.

31. O'Phelan Godoy, "Tradición y modernidad," 91; Fisher, "La rebelión," 118.

32. Brading, *The First America,* 491; Rowe "El movimiento nacional inca," 35–36; Campbell, "Ideology and Factionalism," 118; the disparate regional characteristics of the pan-Andean upheaval are underscored by the fact that while in Cuzco the continuing existence of an Indian nobility was considered a political menace. In Northern Potosí Spanish officials advocated the maintenance of hereditary or at least consensual kurakas, arguing that they reminded native communities of their subordination to the king; see Valle de Siles, *La rebelión,* 601.

33. Skocpol, *States,* 15–17; Scott, *Weapons of the Weak,* 341–44.

34. Campbell, "Ideology and Factionalism," 125; Walker, *Smoldering Ashes,* 39.

35. Tilly, *European Revolutions,* 17.

36. Serulnikov, "Disputed Images," 11–34.

37. Phelan, *The People,* 39–186.

38. For shifting historiographical approaches to the Túpac Amaru movement, see Piel, "Cómo interpretar," 71–80; and Walker, *Smoldering Ashes,* 16–22.

39. Thomson, "Colonial Crisis," 246–54; see also Cornblit, *Power and Violence,* 137–72.
40. Rowe, "El movimiento nacional inca," 51.
41. Taylor, *Drinking, Homicide, and Rebellion,* 113–51.
42. Coatsworth, "Patterns of Rural Rebellion," 49.
43. Cf. Stern, "New Approaches," 3–25.
44. Thomson, " 'We Alone Will Rule,' " 294.
45. Van Young, "The Raw and the Cooked," 91.
46. We again owe this insight to Flores Galindo's work; see his *Buscando un Inca,* 144.
47. Van Young, "The Raw and the Cooked," 88.
48. Local histories have also provided rich information on the lack of indigenous involvement in the 1780 uprising; for cases of avoiding participation in large-scale rebellion, see, Stavig, *The World,* 222–23 and 252–54; and Glave, "Sociedad campesina," 27–68.

PUBLIC OPINIONS AND PUBLIC SPHERES IN LATE-NINETEENTH-CENTURY PERU

A MULTICOLORED WEB IN A TATTERED CLOTH

Nils Jacobsen

In one of his sparkling essays on the history of the Peruvian press, Raúl Porras Barrenechea suggested how, in the absence of newspapers, church bells during the colonial period served to transmit news.[1] Lima's citizens informed themselves about the death of a celebrated *vecino,* the arrival of the new viceroy, or some alarming riot in the popular barrio Abajo el Puente, all by the manner in which "la Mónica" of San Agustín was ringing. Church bells, suggested Barrenechea, could even function as the opposition press of later epochs: for example, "that wayward bell which commenced to ring wildly when his Excellency the Viceroy scampered through the city's dark streets at night in amorous affairs."[2]

By the late nineteenth century, church bells had far from lost their communicative powers in Peru. Yet the dissemination of news and the formation of public opinions now was effected through a much broadened array of media: these ranged from the telegraph and newspapers, schoolbooks, pamphlets and fliers, assemblies of artisan societies and fire brigades, to raucous discussions in *chicherias* and solemn communal meetings. All too frequently, public opinion was still formed through *bolas,* the rumors spreading like wildfire through a barrio of a town or a rural district. Liberal-democratic political theory declares both a free press and voluntary associations of citizens as essential for modern public opinion based on rational debate, individual autonomy, and democratic political processes. In that light, Peru's nineteenth-century public opinion and the media on which it was based have been condemned by most writers as exclusivist, authoritarian, and not conducive to modern democratic governance.[3]

This chapter will present some ideas on how we might approach the formation of public opinions in republican Peru before the emergence of mass media. I focus on the last two decades of the nineteenth century, the aftermath of the traumatizing defeat in the War of the Pacific (1879–83). After briefly summarizing the notions about public opinion of Alexis de Tocqueville, Jürgen Habermas, and Ferdinand Tönnies, I will suggest a spatial map of the axes and networks through which opinions spread and became public in late-nineteenth-century Peru. For analytical purposes, I will maintain the conventional distinction between "modern" and "traditional" types of public opinion. As I develop the argument and the evidence, it will become clear that this distinction is of limited use for late-nineteenth-century Peru. What characterized the Peruvian public sphere was the interpenetration of such putatively polar means of communicating and forming public opinions. Yet this did not create one socially and spatially integrated network of civil society; instead it forged paths to modernity distinct from those outlined by liberal-democratic theory.

Tocqueville emphasized that freedom of the press and freedom of association formed indispensable defenses of freedom against the dangers of centralized power and despotism growing in egalitarian, democratic orders. Yet the citizen's freedom, so prone to dangerous individualistic exaggeration especially in the case of the press, for Tocqueville must be tempered by ethical-religious values that ought to be internalized by the citizen rather than imposed by the state.[4] Jürgen Habermas's *Strukturwandel der Öffentlichkeit* (1962), largely based on critical Marxist theory, seeks to overcome the limitations of liberal political theory. Yet, in his depiction of the ideal-typical bourgeois public sphere during the early nineteenth century, he comes close to the vision of Tocqueville. For Habermas the rise of a bourgeois public sphere was linked to underlying socioeconomic transformations of society. The bourgeoisie used the tools of publication and of assembling in coffeehouses and political clubs to assure rational debate without interference from the absolutist state. While ultimately driven by particularistic interests derived from their status as property owners, Habermas imagined that, for a brief historical moment, this bourgeois public sphere, based on the autonomy of the individual, engaged in rational debate about the republic's common good. Since the second half of the nineteenth century, however, the public sphere in Western societies lost autonomy, besieged by the increasing monopoly power of the media, the rise of consumerism, and the interpenetration of functions between state and civil society. Hence, while vigorous public opinion based on rational debate remains as vital as ever for a democratic republic, for Habermas that goal has become more difficult to achieve under conditions of late capitalism.[5]

In his 1922 study *Kritik der Öffentlichen Meinung*, Ferdinand Tönnies (1855–1936), the German sociologist best known for his differentiation of *Gemeinschaft* and *Gesellschaft*, offers a more skeptical account of public opinion in modern democracies. For Tönnies, "opining" and "willing" the matter opined are closely related. Public opinion always has to do with the struggle to carry out publicized ideas, and thus with power. Moreover, in the formation of opinions shared in public by a few or many, there are always "leaders" who have a preponderant influence on them.

Tönnies differentiates between public opinion and *the* Public Opinion. The former means any public clash over ideas and projects, some of which may only be influential locally. *The* Public Opinion describes the condition of debate in the entire body politic in which there is overwhelming agreement among the great majority of active citizens on a policy matter, a collective judgment by the nation's rational individuals that the government ignores only at its own peril. This Public Opinion appears in different states of solidity (*Aggregatzustände*). The more fluid and "airy" Public Opinion is, the more partisan and passionate it is. Tönnies also employed his *Gemeinschaft/Gesellschaft* dichotomy for differentiating between different forms of public opinion. In a *Gemeinschaft*, the upper classes (noblemen, priests, and village elders) function as teachers of the people, passing along customs and values. Public opinion takes the form of relatively unchanging dogma, articles of faith, and traditions and connects not just the living members of the community but past and future generations. In the modern *Gesellschaft*, communication tends to be horizontal. Public opinion must persuade rather than base itself on the social standing of teachers; tradition has lost much of its power. Tönnies envisioned modern Western societies as moving toward this condition. But they still contain social, gender, regional, and educational groups little affected as yet by this horizontal, rational formation of public opinion.[6] In short, while Tönnies follows some of the tenets of liberal-democratic theory, he builds in caveats that suggest the ambiguous outcome of public opinion even when society has become preponderantly modern.

THE SO-CALLED MODERN FORMS OF PUBLIC OPINION

If one mapped the diffusion of print media and modern associations onto the space of the Peruvian republic around 1895, one would find that they largely replicated the volume and spread of "modern," monetarized economic activity and industrial-era means of transportation and communication (steamships, railroads, and, of course, telegraphs). Concentrated in the capital Lima, from there they radiated along the coast to departmental and provincial capitals and a few bustling district capitals. Print media penetrated Andean Peru primarily along railroad lines and a few heavily traveled mule roads. Away from these major arteries, print media were published only in some of the major regional Andean towns, such as Cuzco (connected to the railroad only in 1908) and Ayacucho in the south and Cajamarca in the north. Many Andean provincial capitals away from the modern arteries of trade still had no printing press. Further east, in the *ceja de la selva* and Peru's vast Amazonian territories, print media were spread extremely thin, limited to no more than a half dozen towns. One can characterize the spatial distribution of print media in late-nineteenth-century Peru as follows: a primary diffusion zone radiating from Lima along the entire coast and into the central and northern sierra; a secondary, semidetached diffusion zone focused on Arequipa in the south, spreading along the railroad corridor from Mollendo to Lake Titikaka and north as far as Sicuani in the high provinces of Cuzco; and last a series of unconnected Andean archipelagos (more isolated cities and towns and their hinterlands), thinning out toward the east. Lima newspapers were available in the primary diffusion zone, much less so in the secondary diffusion zone, and rarely, with delays of two to four weeks, in the archipelagos. On the other hand, a few copies of most newspapers published anywhere in the republic ultimately—often after several weeks—found their way to Lima. The editors of major papers eagerly scanned them for important news "de provincias" to be inserted into their own paper, while provincial residents in Lima were anxious to find out about the latest scandal or festivity in their home province. Provincial papers were also disseminated in narrower regional circuits. The Arequipa dailies, for example, inserted items from papers in Mollendo, Puno, Sicuani, Cuzco, and Moquegua. In coastal cities close to the northern and southern borders, newspapers from nearby foreign towns—Guayaquil and Panamá in the north and Tacna, Arica, Iquique, and Valparaiso in the south—found some readers as well.[7] Between the 1910s and 1930s, once the rail link from Buenos Aires through Bolivia to Lake Titikaka was completed, newspapers from the Argentine capital were distributed more broadly in Puno and Cuzco than those from Lima.

Until the 1890s, the growth of circulation remained modest, due to low literacy rates, the cost of papers, and newspaper technology. The great technological innovations (linotype and rotation press) which made it feasible to cheaply print tens of thousands of copies per hour were introduced in Lima just after the turn of the century at two or three papers. Until then, even the most advanced Peruvian papers did not achieve the mass circulation common in large cities of the United States, Great Britain, and France since the 1830s (e.g., the "penny press" in the United States). By the 1890s, even the most important Peruvian papers were hardly great capitalist enterprises serving a mass market and optimizing profits. In smaller papers the owner and editor also served as the only writer/journalist. Dominant Lima dailies as *La Opinión Nacional*, *El Comercio*, and *El Nacional* had a staff of at most two dozen employees, including five or six writers/journalists.[8] Many editors and owners still personified the nonprofessional journalism practiced in Peru since independence. Trained in law, theology, or medicine, they edited a paper to promote a political, ideological, or social agenda, ingratiate themselves with their elite friends, and perhaps satisfy their own penchant for public writing and debate. Depending on political fortunes, many leading figures of Lima's press moved back and forth between editing a paper, elected offices as congressional senator or deputy, or a high position in government. In the provinces, where the income and prestige derived from a newspaper remained meager, many editors and writers maintained another occupation in order to survive. Some editors ran their printing press also for other contract publications, others worked as shopkeepers, pharmacists, lawyers, or teachers. By the 1890s, the transition toward a professional journalism, practiced as a primary occupation throughout one's career, was just beginning.

During the last decade of the nineteenth century, between 100 and 150 newspapers and periodicals appeared during any given year in the entire republic. Numbers fluctuated from year to year due to political and economic circumstances but tended toward the estimate's upper bound after 1895. This may represent only a modest increase from previous cycles of growth, such as that of the 1820s–30s and especially that of the early 1860s through 1879. For example, Charles Walker has tallied a total of thirty-four newspapers and periodicals launched in Cuzco between 1825 and 1837. During a similar thirteen-year period, from 1885 to 1897, a minimum of forty-four newspapers and periodicals were launched in Cuzco.[9] By the 1890s some eight to ten different daily and weekly papers and periodicals appeared in Cuzco during any given year, including those surviving for only a few numbers.

It is virtually impossible to find reliable statistics on Peruvian newspaper and periodical circulations for the late nineteenth century. But considering literacy rates, urban population size, and a few scattered circulation figures, we can arrive at reasonable estimates. Lima's population during the late 1890s was about 110,000. With an urban literacy rate of perhaps 25 percent, active readers of papers could not have exceeded 30,000. This pool of potential readers was shared by four or five daily newspapers appearing at any given time between 1883 and 1900. Juan Gargurevich, the most knowledgeable historian of the Peruvian press, has estimated the circulation of *El Comercio* at no more than 10,000 copies during this period.[10] Other well-established daily papers must have sold between 2,000 and 8,000 copies. In the largest provincial cities, such as Arequipa, Cuzco, Trujillo, and Piura, with populations between 15,000 and 30,000 inhabitants, circulations of individual daily papers could not have surpassed 2,000 copies, especially if the market had to sustain more than one daily (as in Arequipa after 1890). In Cuzco, with a lower literacy rate than the more commercial coastal cities, papers may have struggled to sell 1,000 copies. In smaller towns circulations below 1,000 must have been the norm. This was also the case for the great majority of the virulently partisan political and satirical weekly or monthly papers. By the 1890s, there existed at least half a dozen of these *periodiquillos* in Lima, with colorful names such as *El Microbio, Luz Eléctrica, Fray Leguito San José, La Tunda, Ño Bracamonte,* and *El Halcón. El Microbio* suggested in October 1892 that the paper sold 525 copies of its previous number.[11] Sales for these papers fluctuated enormously from one week to the next, perhaps by as much as 100 percent, depending on political circumstances and the sensationalism of lead articles.[12]

Who were the readers of newspapers and periodicals? A first indication comes from the fact that most copies of daily papers were sold through subscriptions. In Lima few copies were sold in shops around town and in the adjacent rural or resort districts and the port of Callao.[13] We may assume the densest distribution occurred through the streets and quarters close to the plaza de armas where most of the well-to-do and professionals still lived. The primary target audience of the established dailies were merchants (including the foreign business community), large landholders, industrialists, directors of railroad lines and utility companies, financiers, high government officials and military officers, leading members of the church hierarchy, and the roughly 200 members of congress. But these economic and power elites, at most 3,000 men, only accounted for a fraction of the 30,000 potential readers of newspapers in Lima. The readership extended through high-level professionals, such as lawyers, doctors, engineers, and university professors, into broader middle- and lower-middle-class groups, such as shopkeepers, white-collar commercial and government employees, artisan masters, junior military and police officers, teachers, and university students. Probably even among blue-collar workers, as well as police and army petty officers, a minority regularly read papers.[14] When Enrique López Albújar was arrested in 1893 for publishing an anti-Cáceres poem in *La Tunda,* the police sergeant delivering him to jail considered the young troublemaker a celebrity: he had read that poem, and so had all the officers in his *comisaría.* The driver of the coach delivering the poet to jail now felt free to confess that he too was a regular reader of the virulent opposition paper.[15] Similarly, some of the journeymen, skilled factory workers, and mechanics who were members of mutual aid societies in Lima most likely read newspapers. In fact, all those groups who were treated in its columns as subjects and not as objects formed part of a paper's readership. That is, they were treated with respect by the newspapers, recognized as social, political, and moral agents with at least some autonomy who contributed to the "material and moral well-being of the republic." This was true for all civil-society associations, from the elite social clubs to fire brigades, and artisan and worker mutual-aid societies. Their activities were reported on as praiseworthy, and they themselves had communications about meetings and projects inserted in the papers. The same can be said about the readership of provincial papers, except that here literacy was more restricted: many provincial shopkeepers and artisans, especially in the highlands, were poor and illiterate.

Newspapers and other print products left an impact considerably beyond the social space of the literate and the geographic space of the towns where they were published. The driver of the coach taking López Albújar to jail in 1893 reported how in his *callejón* (tenement) neighbors crowded around him "like flies" when he sat down to read *La Tunda.*[16] Reading aloud to illiterate friends and family must have been frequent.[17] It could happen on public plazas, in semipublic spaces such as the patios of the *callejones* and *chicherias,* or in artisans' workshops or private homes.

The print material disseminated in this fashion was not limited to regular newspapers and periodicals. Political parties issued papers and fliers in the departmental capitals for months before elections, and these were distributed down to the district level in the rural hinterlands. There they could only be effective if the few literate party stalwarts read the nasty invectives about opponents to illiterate potential followers. In the civil war of 1894–95, both the government and the irregular montonera forces issued bulletins, fliers, and manifestoes in the towns they occupied. It was vital for the residents to inform themselves of their contents (usually concerning forced loans, arms, and penalties for infractions of any decree). Illiterate families needed literate neighbors, relatives or compadres to read or tell them what these imprints said. Beginning in the late 1880s, Protestant mission societies sold bibles and tracts for proselytizing. They drew crowds of hundreds first in Callao and Lima, then in towns in the central coast and sierra, and after 1895 in Arequipa and Cuzco. They read aloud to their audiences from their unorthodox Christian texts. During his first year of missionary work in Peru, 1888–89, the Methodist Francisco Penzotti sold some 7,000 bibles in 110 coastal and highland towns.[18] Those who purchased them in many cases must have read passages aloud or reported on their novel interpretations at home and at work. Perhaps the broadest dissemination of print materials was achieved through schoolchildren. In 1906, 150,506 children were enrolled in primary schools, some 20 to 30 percent of their age cohort.[19] Many of these children represented the first generation in their family to learn how to read and write. When they brought their primers and elementary Peruvian histories home, much was read aloud and marveled at by their illiterate parents and other household members. Clearly print media were disseminated much more broadly in Peru by the late nineteenth century than the meager figures for newspaper circulation would suggest.

But how did these variegated exposures to print media actually shape public opinions? What messages did newspapers and other print media convey to their readers and what messages did these readers take away? How did it involve the readers in public debates? Here we are on speculative ground and there are no general answers applicable to the entire reading (and listening) public. Much depended on the fluency of reading, familiarity with concepts espoused in the media, and, of course, on the socioethnic and ideological position of the reader. For a university student a pamphlet was easily recognizable as presenting a particular ideological or political position. But for a barely literate artisan or farmer who through some happenstance had acquired such a pamphlet and counted it among his prized possessions, it opened up unheard-of combinations of ideas. It would be pulled out from under the straw mattress again and again and queried as to how the claims and combinations proposed might be integrated into the vision of the world on which such a reader had relied to date. What resulted was an idiosyncratic integration of odd facts and claims from the text into the reader's representation of the world in a manner very distinct from the intentions of the text's writer and publisher.[20]

On the broadest level, newspapers and other print material produced two contradictory effects on Peru's late-nineteenth-century public opinions. Simultaneously, they reinforced notions of hierarchical order and honor—and undermined these very notions.[21] This could not help but give Public Opinion on many issues an "airy" aggregate state, easily switching from one position to another, and often extremely vehemently. The "bedrock," long-standing positions held by vast majorities of Public Opinion, and rarely challenged even by the progressive-liberal or Protestant "fringe," concerned relatively few deep convictions: the centrality of honor and work, a hierarchical gender order assigning special roles to men and women needed to safeguard the saintly and regenerative but vulnerable qualities of women/mothers, and the need to make the nation strong and effective. The notion that the "common good" was more important than private interests also remained a core conviction. But this common good was no longer automatically assumed to coincide with positions of the Catholic Church, as public opinion was more divided than ever over the Church's role in the body politic.

Nearly all writers and editors espoused notions of hierarchical order in late-nineteenth-century Peru and differentiated between a literate, rational public and the unwashed, irrational masses (often thought of as "Indians" and other dark-skinned groups). Newspapers consistently drew a sharp line between people of good social standing and education who should actively form public opinion and hold power, and the masses, identified as uneducated, emotional, unreliable, or, as in many descriptions of native Andeans, essentially brain-dead. A political program for the city of Arequipa, published in May 1895, shortly after Nicolás de Piérola's civil war victory over Andrés Avelino Cáceres, did not mince words:

> The people . . . should be firmly persuaded that only its upper social classes can effect its happiness and well-being by spending the public funds in a correct manner and undertaking public works projects useful by any rational standard, carried out with the discipline, timeliness and discretion of which only they [the upper classes] are capable. No improvisations, please! Let us open a wide path to knowledge, to the distinguished social position and to the industrialist of proven honor.[22]

During the same period an editorial of Arequipa's *La Bolsa* castigated the "popular demonstrations" in Callao of people complaining that collaborators of the old regime were getting jobs, leaving partisans of the revolution empty-handed. The editorial warned that any excitement could make popular sentiment "vibrate," as a consequence of an excess of emotion. In such circumstances, it was easy but very dangerous to seduce the masses. The masses cannot use reason, and, due to their passions, blindly obey their caudillos. If Peru wanted to overcome the tyrannical and corrupt regimes of its past, this emotional, passionate, and irrational behavior of the masses needed to be discouraged.[23] Widely disseminated in the press, distrust of the masses was a mainstay of liberal thought. José Maria Quimper, leading ideologue of liberalism in Peru wrote in 1886 that "public opinion that directs all issues in free countries, is not, in practice, the opinion of all, but rather the opinion of those capable of having one."[24] And those incapable of having their own opinion, were, besides criminals and imbeciles, the illiterate majority of Peruvians.

Conservative and pro-clerical newspapers frequently published articles on hierarchical family structures as the healthy base of society in which the father needed to rule wisely, just like the president in the nation.[25] Everybody should take their rightful place in society, as in the family. For the majority, including women and the emotional masses, this meant obeying rather than opining about public affairs that they could not understand. Some writers defined the bounds of modern public opinion not through this authoritarian hierarchical principle, nor by race or social class, but by literacy itself. In this interpretation, public opinion became exclusivist on its own terms: the deemed incapacity to participate in modern public opinion itself excluded one from active citizenship.

The boundary, however, between those whom the newspapers included in Public Opinion and those whom they wished excluded remained vague. In the most ebullient statements about the effects of Public Opinion on the affairs of state the net seemed to be cast wide. For example, in early February 1895, after the revolutionaries defeated the government's forces in the city of Arequipa with the overwhelming support of middle- and lower-class civilians, an editorial in Mollendo's *El Puerto* pronounced that Cáceres's continued rule had become impossible because "public opinion is against him." Cáceres lost the south in spite of his "brilliant army," not because it was grabbed from him by a few "brave and audacious armed citizens," but because "the *pueblo en masse* desires it."[26] The meaning of "pueblo"—here explicitly including lower classes—was unstable during the late nineteenth century: at times still used in the plural ("los pueblos peruanos"), identifying Peru as an agglomeration of corporate towns, more frequently it was used as a synonym for the entire nation. Other writers implied a social meaning, setting off "el pueblo" from "vecinos notables," or "the better classes." Ironically, many newspaper articles excluded certain social strata from reasonable Public Opinion who clearly belonged to their readership (e.g., the artisans and workers attending demonstrations).

And yet the press simultaneously contributed to undermining that sense of hierarchical order most writers strove to defend. This was achieved both through the contents of writing and, more subtly, through the demonstration effect of information. It would be difficult to remain unaffected by the vilification, abuse, and searing satire partisan political papers heaped on their enemies in prose, verse, and cartoons. Witness the following aggressive and mocking verses against Cáceres, published in *El Microbio* after a government-sponsored attack on the fellow opposition paper *La Tunda* in June 1893:

Against this wicked
one-eyed, cunda [?] bandit
Hit him and hit him again

With cudgel blows,
Keep hitting him
Until his last bone is smashed.
. . .
Blow after blow,
Without compassion
For the squinting,
Thieving tyrant
Let's not fear him
Don't let him get away
The entire people
Wants to hang him,
Wants to beat him up,
leave him stiff
Wants to spit
On his corpse
. . .
[Contra ese Tuerto
malvado y cunda
Facineroso
Tunda y mas tunda
y "garrotazos
y tente tieso
y no dejarle
Ni un solo hueso."
. . .
Golpe y más golpe
sin compasión
Con el tirano
Tuerto ladrón
No hay que temerle
No hay que dejarlo,
Que el pueblo entero
Quiere colgarlo.
Quiere palearlo,
Dejarlo yerto,
Quiere escupirlo,
Después de muerto . . .][27]

Such sophomoric expression of violence against one's political enemies was commonplace in the political press. As Robert Darnton, Roger Chartier, and others have suggested for publications in prerevolutionary France, it gradually whittled away, like the steady drip of water on stone, the respect for figures of political authority and the entire edifice of hierarchical order.[28] The lamentations and hand-wringing about ineptitude, *empleomania,* and spineless opportunism characteristic of *política criolla* published in the more mild-mannered daily press could hardly help but contribute to growing skepticism about the republic's authorities.

Perhaps even more important were the demonstration effects of seeing in print petitions, complaints, proposals by individual citizens and associations, the whole gamut of citizens' participation in civil society laid out before the paper's readers every day. Reading newspapers undoubtedly did have the emancipatory impact claimed by liberal public-opinion theory: an instrumental connection between what one read about what others of one's own condition were doing and how one might proceed oneself. In the cities, newspapers publicized abuses by the government, the police, or the army: the arrest of a citizen without cause, the maltreatment of "political prisoners" (a term used even by the government), or fraudulent electoral practices. This bright light, focused on the activities of those with power, dimmed considerably as one moved out to the smaller towns with no press, and especially to the Andean countryside. Here events (from massacres to the more regular daily abuses of power) could still pass without a broad reading public finding out about them.

Readers, then, received conflictive messages from their engagement with print media: on the one hand they were called to order, the rigid, hierarchical order envisioned by the narrow upper- and middle-class groups controlling newspapers and periodicals. But on the other hand they learned to doubt much of what the government was claiming, although the credibility of the printed word itself was severely strained given the shrillness of partisan papers.[29] Reactions to these conflicting messages obviously varied from person to person and between various social groups, depending on what they could hope to gain by adhering to the call to order. Yet such conflictive messages reinforced a longstanding, "traditional" approach to politics: that of personalism. If it was the wisdom of publicized opinion that, on the one hand, you could not trust most politicians and authorities, but, on the other hand, you should strictly adhere to the established order, then it was convenient and ethically correct to put your trust in specific leaders and politicians to whom you felt close and who you considered to be of high moral standing.[30] Personalism played a strong role in the press itself: in the way it covered political stories as much as in hiring practices of writers/journalists.[31] The continued vitality of *folleteria* (pamphleteering) until after 1900 owed a great deal to the strength of personalism in the public sphere: many pamphlets were written, published, financed, and distributed by individuals to dispute claims by personal enemies or to satisfy their own vanity.

This personalistic aspect of Peru's late-nineteenth-century press closely relates to a preoccupation with honor. Elites discussed with alarm how freedom of the press so often was abused for slanderous attacks on the honor of individuals, as in the anti-Caceres doggerel above. In 1889, Piérola dedicated fully three-and-one half pages of the thirty-odd-page program of his *Partido Demócrata* to "honor," calling for strict slander laws to make publishers responsible for "character assassination" in their papers.[32] Yet the impact of public opinions on honor was ambiguous. Clearly the press also served to establish the honor of individuals and social groups who had not been publicly recognized to have honor before.

The other side of "modern" public-opinion formation concerns associations and public gatherings, such as demonstrations and public ceremonies. For reasons of space, I shall limit myself to a few cursory remarks on their role in late-nineteenth-century Peru.[33] Just like print media, associations were an expression of the republican spirit of the age. Belonging to one of them brought advantages related to the purpose of the association and established networks of protection and aid. In theory, associations did this with a more egalitarian ethos than the Catholic Church had traditionally done.[34] But membership of most associations in Peru remained small even during the 1890s. It was more costly to become a member in an association than to read a newspaper. Moreover, the great majority of associations were consciously exclusive, smugly confirming the members' own advanced civilization in contrast to that of the vast majority of Peruvians.[35]

Public ritual was accessible to far greater numbers of people.[36] And here the divide between civil society and the political arena was crossed quite easily.[37] To be sure, religious processions, which still drew the greatest street crowds by the 1890s, belonged to Habermas's representative public of an older, prebourgeois era.[38] But civic ritual—such as independence day celebrations—was now imbued with the same intense emotions once reserved for the religious sphere. Besides reenacting the notions of hierarchical honor copied from religious processions, civic ritual included the paternalistic recognition of republican virtue, as well as popular entertainments.[39] The "electoral demonstrations" of the various parties prominent since Manuel Pardo's campaign of 1871–72 were becoming routine by the 1890s and involved large numbers of citizens.[40] The concluding rally of Piérola and his Partido Demócrata for the 1890 presidential election purportedly brought out 10,000 party members in Lima. They were all in their Sunday finest, lined up by electoral clubs—each with its own banner—in perfect marching order, ready to follow their leader Don Nicolás. Decked out in fanciful uniform and plumed hat, he rode in front of his loyal partisans on a white horse.[41]

Electoral demonstrations were held for three competing parties in virtually every provincial capital, and even in smaller pueblos. In provincial towns participation rates reached 10 percent of the population, which means 20–30 percent of adult men coming out to support just *one* party (women remained rare at public demonstrations)![42] Electoral campaigns were tightly controlled by a small urban social and political elite. Party bosses enticed mass supporters to attend demonstrations with free meals and promises, and many participating artisans, workers, and other common folk came as clients of bosses or powerful businessmen. In that sense, civic demonstrations had little in common with the grassroots organizing, debating, and politicking extolled in Tocqueville's notion of public opinion. Nevertheless, they provided symbolic affirmation of being part of the patria. Moreover, campaigns could easily get out of control, especially in rural districts and popular urban quarters where elite control thinned considerably. The popular supporters ("gente de acción") whom parties readied for violent confrontations with adversaries sometimes pursued their own agendas, battling it out with local police, with hostile clientele groups, even with hacendados and traders.[43] Such "slippage" usually remained local, easily squashed after the election. But with eroding power and divisions among elites (as in the aftermath of the War of the Pacific), mobilization for electoral campaigns could radicalize into autonomous popular movements.

THE SO-CALLED TRADITIONAL FORMS OF PUBLIC OPINION

Following political theory of the day, the Peruvian elite during the late nineteenth century proclaimed that the people who could not read and who did not participate in "modern" civic life could not form part of Public Opinion. They thus meant to exclude the majority of Peru's population from active participation in the affairs of the republic. But public opinions were being formed constantly throughout the vast and diverse realm of rural communities, estates, smallholder hamlets, popular districts, and *callejones* of cities. Two issues were at stake: how did these spheres of public opinion differ from the idea and practice of the "modern" public opinion, and were there any connections or overlaps between the two spheres?

Let us begin with a brief depiction of the spatial spread of "traditional" public opinions in late-nineteenth-century Peru. In contrast to "modern" public opinion, it did not radiate out from focal points, such as the largest cities. Since it relied for its transmission primarily on the spoken word and public rituals, its spread was coterminous with the spread of population on the Peruvian map. "Traditional" public opinion was not excluded from the cities, diffusion zones, and archipelagos in which "modern" public opinion had established a foothold. Here they existed side by side, overlapping considerably. Take the literate artisan reader of a newspaper who engaged in heated debates of public affairs in a chicheria or at his cousin's saint's day celebration; or the literate muleteer moving back and forth between city and countryside where he spread information from the city's papers among his rural customers. By its very nature "traditional" public opinion was more localized, disseminated among smaller groups of people. But if we count patron-saint festivities as one of its forms, it included gatherings of large crowds.

It would be wrong to characterize "traditional" public opinion in Peru as atomized, myriad opinion-forming spheres isolated from each other. Even without considering the frequent overlaps with the "modern" sphere, there were plenty of mechanisms to propel public opinions along linear axes and through radial spaces. Throughout Andean Peru there still existed numerous networks of exchange among rural producers entirely outside the control of urban merchants or state authorities. Scholars have long recognized how these networks served to disseminate information and projects since the colonial era (for example, during the Great Rebellion of 1780–81). Patron-saint festivals in a community or small town, pilgrimages to shrines of revered miraculous images, and the trade fairs connected to them brought together hundreds, thousands, or even tens of thousands of rural and urban people from various districts, provinces, or departments. Exchanges of news and gossip—e.g., who was betrothed to whom, who was found drunk in whose cottage, how Moroorcco community intended to react to the tax collector and the subprefect's latest decree for corvée laborers—were vital activities of such festivities. Thus the sphere of "traditional" public opinion should not be depicted as countless isolated atoms but rather as a tattered piece of cloth, consisting of numerous swaths of interwoven material, each quite strong in itself, but held together with other swaths by only a few threads. The rhythm in which "traditional" public opinion was propagated also differed from that of "modern" public opinion. Rather than following a linear calendar of daily or periodical publications, "traditional" public opinion was propagated through the cycles of the religious and agricultural calendars and the corresponding ebb and flow of exchange activities.[44]

I wish to focus briefly on one especially important site of non-"modern" public opinion making: rural communities. By the late nineteenth century, many communities faced an ascending local or provincial elite of large landholders, merchants, and government officials basing their power on the exploitation of Andean peasants. In this oppressive environment, communicating, forming opinions, and deciding courses of action for the entire communal group unwittingly turned into acting out communal identity.[45] Deciding on when to sow the chacras in the open fields, how many *cargas* of potatoes to bring to the governor, who would become *varayok* (mayor) during the coming year—these were more than technical decisions. By reenacting the community's rituals, customs, and beliefs, its identity was reaffirmed. In the formation of the community's Public Opinion, appeal to how it was always done, and how the heroic ancestors would have wanted it to be done, played a strong role.

Such appeals, however, usually were not based on unchanging tradition. They normally involved recreating or inventing traditions and foundational myths in order to gain legitimacy and help the community adjust to new challenges from the outside. No doubt, these types of decision-making processes were "rational" in the pursuit of community goals. Yet they differed from the ideal-typical "modern" sphere of public opinion in two ways: (a) they aimed at securing collective goods, and thus neither relied on nor fostered the autonomous rationality of individuals;[46]and (b) history—in the sense of relating causes and effects of specific events—and myth were not clearly separated in communal Public Opinion. For an outsider, this would make it difficult to evaluate the truth value of its claims. In a sense, then, the ideal-typical community fostered a type of Public Opinion just as exclusive as that which the national elite sought to construct. It arrived at pronouncements and collective expressions of will based on its own norms and customs, seen as distinct from those of Hispanized national society. This exclusivity would have been the consequence of the oppressive neocolonial regime threatening the very survival of the community.

But most peasant communities in late-nineteenth-century Peru differed to some extent from this ideal type. Rural settlements of farmers and herders appeared in many guises in Peru's diverse ecological, social, and ethnic landscapes.[47] They varied as to landholding regimes, modes and intensity of commercial exchange, governance and internal cohesion, and the peasants' own notion of their sociocultural identity. Thus we cannot expect the meaning and functioning of opinion formation within communal publics to follow one rigid pattern. It depended on local power constellations, and the degree to which local elites accepted the claims of peasant communities as legitimate. It also depended on a community's engagement with the republic and its debates, on civic rituals, literacy, and associative organizations. For example, the fact that there were quite a few rural schools in the vicinity of Huancayo (Mantaro Valley) even by 1900, while there were virtually none in the altiplano, must have made a difference in both regions' rural public spheres.[48]

Mark Thurner and others have argued that indigenous communities fully embraced the republic, sought alliances, and wished to participate in the public and political spheres on their own terms but were tragically rebuffed and repressed by the elite-controlled state.[49] This is indeed the logical consequence of the exclusivity and hierarchical nature claimed for the nation's "modern" Public Opinion by political and social elites. Yet, as suggested above, this was only one side of "modern" public opinion in late-nineteenth-century Peru. There were instances where a well-entrenched indigenous community forged peacetime alliances with elite factions (Catacaos), founded associations (Laraos), and conducted competitive communal election campaigns (sierra de Piura).[50] While in many parts of the republic communities were under increasing assault since the mid-1880s, in some regions new communities were founded, as for example in the sierra de Piura, in northern Peru. This new coming together was based partly on a "modern" public sphere, with interest representation, and competitive elections of leaders reflecting communal public opinion.

Moreover, at least since the 1860s, there were a few progressive elite liberals, such as Gregorio Paz Soldan, who understood native peasant protests—usually denounced as revolts or even "race wars" by hysteric hacendados—as the normal exercise of civic rights.[51] Even though the overwhelming majority of elite politicians were unwilling to respect public opinions of native peasants, this did not mean that most communities stopped incorporating elements of the "modern" public sphere into their institutional framework and their very identity. Native communities, just as other social spheres, could be "modern" and exclusive at the same time. And among the native peasantry, just as among Peru's Hispanized elites, literacy and/or participation in public debate did not automatically translate into Western-style "democratic" notions about the polity, such as separation of powers and due process of law.

But to what extent and how did public opinions formed in peasant communities, among colonos of estates, workers of a bread factory, or muleteers and itinerant traders meeting at an annual fair matter for the Public Opinion at the national level? Did they have any impact on the processes of decision making over the distribution of material and symbolic resources in public and private spheres of power? Widespread evidence for repression of subaltern opinions and interests in late-nineteenth-century Peru make it easy to answer this quintessential question pessimistically. Many of these decentralized public opinions were not voiced in a form easily understood by the national power elite, nor were they necessarily intended to be heard by that elite. On a certain level, many subaltern Peruvians still accepted a hierarchically ordered society and polity. One could be both a humble farmer, pastoralist, muleteer, or cobbler putting much stock in the protection of a benevolent *padrino* or *patrón, and* a proud citizen of the republic. Moreover, people in chicherias, in communities, and at trade fairs lacked information on many issues they discussed and formed opinions about. Many "matters of state" were dealt with secretively and through informal ties in the exclusive elite social clubs, rather than through public media. This resulted in *bolas* and *chismes,* the variegated forms of rumor. These can be read as the "national sentiment" about which thoughtful contemporary observers were so concerned, as it found scant expression in elite-controlled Public Opinion.[52] Rumor reinforced a politics of arbitrariness, seducing popular groups and authorities to militant action or repression with at times devastating consequences.

Under these conditions, public opinions in the diverse spaces of Peru's social life communicated with elite-dominated Public Opinion at the national level in two distinct ways: clientelistic ties between individuals and families of different social and ethnic backgrounds, and the instable utilization of liberal and republican discourses and practices by large segments of Peru's citizens. The very broadening of interclass, interethnic communications in the context of an exclusivist political regime led to the reinforcement of vertical, clientelistic ties, all the way from the callejon to the president's palace.[53] Just as important, however, were the frequent occasions in Peru's late-nineteenth-century political life when critical impasses of national politics forced those in power to listen to the rumors and rumbles of discontent bubbling up from rural districts in various regions, and from the marketplaces, chicherias, and callejones in towns. While repression was an option deemed legitimate in the dominant elitist, hierarchical vision of the polity, it could only be applied against localized challenges. The state did not have the capacity to enforce decrees rejected by public opinions throughout the republic's territory. When Andean farmers, miners, or artisans and day laborers in the towns justified such ubiquitous grumbling with liberal or republican notions, it could occasionally shape the Public Opinion.[54]

• • • • •

I have tried in this chapter to demonstrate that a rigid differentiation of "modern" and "traditional" spheres or sectors of public opinion in late-nineteenth-century Peru is not very helpful. There were too many overlaps between them. More importantly, the Tocquevillian liberal theory of a rational, democratic public sphere as the more or less automatic outcome of newspaper circulation and lively associational activity does not hold up for Peru during the late nineteenth century. While the circulation of Peru's press before 1900 looks paltry by international standards, its diffusion in the cities and towns may have been surprisingly wide. Even illiterate artisans and blue-color workers seem to have been greatly interested in the opposition's latest sensational blast against the president and his regime. In many quarters of the towns there was a genuine excitement for public affairs. This fits well with Tönnies' notion of an "airy" or wavering aggregate state of Public Opinion that appears especially passionate.

Also Tönnies' idea of differentiating between *the* Public Opinion and the back-and-forth banter of public opinions has turned out to be useful for understanding Peru during the late nineteenth century. In contrast to the Tocquevillian ideal type, elite controlled, "modern" Public Opinion in Peru sought to be exclusive and hierarchical, the very opposite of an open, associative, grassroots model. But the meaning and effects of the press and civil society could not be so tightly controlled by elite designs, and so they also had the opposite effect. Similarly one can argue that the "traditional" public sphere, as I have discussed it here especially in the context of indigenous communities, had its own contradictory patterns of exclusivity and increasingly open debate. Given the multiple overlaps between both supposedly separate spheres, in fact one can envision a tattered web of opinion formation and diffusion through communities, chicherias, religious festivities, and trade fairs interwoven with strands of the cloth formed by opinion diffusion through newspapers and associations: a multicolored cloth accommodating many different public opinions side by side with each other throughout Peru's vast geographic, social, and ethnic space.[55] But this diverse network was always prone to being smothered by the gray sheet of elite exclusivity seeking to establish its Public Opinion.

NOTES

1. I thank Teresa Jacobsen, Michel Gobat, and participants of the Latin American History Workshop at the University of Chicago for their thoughtful comments.
2. Porras Barrenechea, *El periodismo,* 7–8.
3. Gargurevich Regal, *Historia de la prensa,* 87.
4. Tocqueville, *Democracy in America,* esp. vol. 2, bk. 2; cf. Aron, *Main Currents,* 1:252–54.
5. Habermas, *The Structural Transformation;* Habermas, "The Public Sphere," 49–55; for a critique, see Eley, "Nations," 289–339.
6. Tönnies, *Kritik.*
7. Tacna, Arica, and Iquique continued to have a vigorous pro-Peruvian press for decades after their occupation by Chile in 1879–80.
8. López Martínez, *Los 150 años,* 308.
9. Walker, "A Journalistic Orgy"; figures for 1885–97 derived from Hazen, *Bibliography.*
10. Gargurevich, *Historia de la prensa,* 113; on newspaper readership in Mexico City during the Porfiriato, see Piccato, "The Court."

11. *El Microbio,* 1:2 (Oct. 29, 1892).
12. For exaggerated circulation claims for *La Tunda* (up to 15,000 copies!), see López Albújar, *Memorias,* 47, and *Fray Leguito San José,* 1:11 (April 20, 1893).
13. *Periodiquillos,* stridently partisan papers, depended on corner stores for distribution; del Aguila, *Callejones y mansiones,* 114.
14. On newspaper readers in Buenos Aires, see Prieto, *El discurso criollista,* chap. 1.
15. López Albújar, *Memorias,* 51.
16. Ibid.
17. Cf. del Aguila, *Callejones y mansiones,* 114; on "readers" in Cuban cigar factories, see Ortiz, *Cuban Counterpoint,* 89–90; so far, no comparable evidence has come to light for Peruvian factories.
18. Armas Asin, *Liberales,* 141–42.
19. Deustua and Rénique, *Intelectuales,* 21, table 6.
20. Personal observation (1975–76) of a migrant farmer and carpenter in Puno.
21. Cf. del Aguila, *Callejones y mansiones,* esp. chaps. 4, 5.
22. S. Ortiz de la Puente, "Breve estudio político-social . . .," *La Bolsa* (Arequipa), May 3 and 4, 1895.
23. "Interior: Callao," *La Bolsa,* April 17, 1895.
24. Quimper, *El Liberalismo,* 13–16.
25. "Crónica: Decálogo del padre," *El Deber* (Arequipa), Nov. 28, 1894.
26. *El Puerto* (Mollendo), Febr. 9, 1895, reprinted in *La Bolsa,* Febr. 11, 1895.
27. "Sinapismos: La Tunda! [A mi compatriota el Dr. D. Belisario Barriga]," *El Microbio,* 1:34, June 22, 1893; italics in original.
28. Chartier, *Cultural Origins,* 91 and chap. 6; Darnton, *The Forbidden Bestsellers,* esp. chaps. 5 and 9.
29. On press credibility, see *El Comercio* (Lima), April 3, 1894, afternoon edition.
30. Cf. del Aguila, *Callejones y mansiones,* esp. chap. 4.
31. On routine patronage for newspapers positions, see *Rasgos biográficos del Sr. José Fermin Herrera candidato a la diputación en propiedad por la provincia de Canta* (Lima, July 1895).
32. *Declaración de principios,* 22–27; on honor in Mexico City's Porfirian press, see Piccato, "The Court."
33. On nineteenth-century Peruvian civil society, see Forment, "La sociedad civil y la invención de la democracia" and also "La sociedad civil en el Perú"; Chambers, *From Subjects to Citizens,* esp. chap. 7.
34. Sabato, *La política,* 286–87.
35. For broadening of civic society in Cuzco since the late 1890s, see Krüggeler, "Indians," esp. 166, 171–75.
36. Cf. del Aguila, *Callejones y mansiones,* chap. 5; on Mexico, see Vaughn, "The Construction," 213–46; Lomnitz, "Ritual," 20–47.
37. On Buenos Aires ca. 1860–1880, see Sabato, *La política,* chap.10; on nineteenth-century U.S. cities, see Ryan, *Civic Wars.*

38. In 1886, the 300th anniversary celebrations of Santa Rosa's birth drew the largest crowds to date in Lima; see Middendorf, *Beobachtungen,* 1:339–40.

39. See the detailed account of *fiestas patrias* in Callao in *El Amigo del Pueblo* (Callao), July 27, 1895; on transformations of civic ritual in a Mexican town, see Vaughan, "The Patriotic Festival."

40. On 1871–72 campaign, see Mücke, *Der Partido Civil,* chap. 3.1; McEvoy, *La utopía republicana,* chap. 2.

41. Dulanto Pinillos, *Nicolás de Piérola,* 363–66.

42. Subprefect of Provincia del Cercado to Prefect of Dpto. de Huanuco, March 31, 1890, Archivo General de la Nación (AGN), Min. del Interior, Prefecturas, 1890, Paq. 14.

43. Jacobsen and Diez Hurtado, "Montoneras."

44. In reality, Peru's "modern" media also ebbed and flowed according to electoral calendars, government press policies, and business cycles.

45. Cf. Abercrombie, *Pathways,* 21, and part 3.

46. On public spheres in Alto Peru peasant communities, 1750–80, see Penry, "Transformations," esp. 134–36.

47. Jacobsen, "Liberalism," 123–70.

48. Deustua and Rénique, *Intelectuales,* 18–19.

49. Thurner, *From Two Republics,* chap. 2 and 146–52.

50. Jacobsen, "Liberalism," 149–51; Mayer, "Tenencia y control comunal," 65; Diez Hurtado, *Comunes y haciendas,* 179–84.

51. See Vasquez, *La rebelión,* 320.

52. Capelo, *Sociologia,* 3:15–21; on rumor in Mexico, see Lomnitz, "Ritual."

53. del Aguilar, *Callejones y mansiones,* chaps. 4 and 7.

54. Cf. Contreras's chapter on the fate of *contribución personal.*

55. On public opinion as a flexible net of strings and nodes, see Capelo, *Sociologia,* 3:32–41.

THE LOCAL LIMITATIONS TO A NATIONAL POLITICAL MOVEMENT

GAITÁN AND GAITANISMO IN ANTIOQUIA

Mary Roldán

Liberal populist Jorge Eliécer Gaitán is perhaps the most famous of Colombia's twentieth-century politicians. An outspoken critic of oligarchic rule and an assiduous advocate of the Colombian pueblo, Gaitán left an indelible mark on the ideology and symbolism of the Liberal Party and on the character and practice of Colombian politics as a whole. His assassination by a mentally unstable gunman on April 9, 1948, in downtown Bogotá set off widespread riots that destroyed nearly half of the Colombian capital and wreaked considerable damage and death elsewhere in Colombia as well. The *Bogotázo* became a catalyst for the seminal event of twentieth-century Colombian history, la Violencia—a fratricidal struggle initially waged by Liberal and Conservative partisans that left more than 200,000 dead between 1948 and 1963.[1] Despite the significance of Gaitán and the movement he founded (*gaitanismo*) to an understanding of Colombian political and social history over the last half-century, Gaitán and gaitanismo have remained surprisingly understudied subjects.[2]

This chapter explores Gaitán's impact on regional and local politics in one Colombian province—Antioquia—between 1944 and 1954, the years immediately before and after the onset of la Violencia. On the face of it, the northwestern department of Antioquia seems an unlikely context in which to examine either Gaitán or gaitanismo. In marked contrast to other Colombian provinces with major urban centers such as Bogotá, Cali, or Barranquilla, where Gaitán won 50 percent or more of the total vote cast in the 1946 presidential election, Gaitán garnered less than 5 percent of the vote in Medellín (Antioquia's capital) and did little better in the province as a whole.[3] Gaitán's electoral failure in Antioquia—Colombia's premier industrial and commercial center, and the second most populous midcentury Colombian province—has been blamed on the fact that "Medellín was a traditional Conservative Party stronghold" where paternalistic employers and regional anti-Gaitán union leaders "exerted considerable control" over worker votes.[4] To the extent that such an explanation suggests that *Conservatives* posed the greatest obstacle to Gaitán's success in Antioquia, it is unpersuasive. While it is true that Antioquia had historically been a bastion of Conservative Party strength, Medellín had more Liberal than Conservative voters by the decade of the forties, and even during the worst years of Conservative repression between 1949 and 1953, a Liberal majority dominated the city's municipal council. Indeed, a good percentage of Medellín's *Concejo* was made up of self-defined "gaitanistas" who continued to hold political office after Gaitán's assassination. The city's "anti-Gaitán" union leadership and many of the city's "paternalist" employers, moreover, belonged to the Liberal rather than the Conservative Party.

Gaitán's significance in the Colombian political arena and his impact on Antioquia's political culture in any case cannot be measured in simple electoral terms. Indeed, Gaitán's inability during his lifetime to cohere significant electoral support in Antioquia belies the extraordinary popularity of his ideas and the impact of his movement on politics in Antioquia after his assassination. An exclusively electoral gauge of Gaitán's impact also obscures the extent to which gaitanismo—reinterpreted in local terms—fundamentally influenced the scope and shape of popular resistance during the period of la Violencia. Ultimately, Gaitán's importance lay not so much in what he did, but in what and whom he represented, and the ways in which his approach and language—specifically geared to appeal to the interests and aspirations of the pueblo—inspired and shaped political practice among sectors of society who felt politically, socially, and culturally marginalized by the elite-driven leadership style and agenda of Colombia's two traditional parties. Gaitán's willingness to defy the unspoken rules of the "gentleman's politics" that typified Colombian political practice before 1945 cohered the real but diffuse ambitions and beliefs of a generation of Colombians and opened up avenues of political possibility notwithstanding his untimely demise.

Unlike other Latin American nations in the mid-twentieth century, populist politics and discourse did not attract an enduring, significant following in Colombia. But the mobilization of workers and urban middle class professionals in midcentury Colombia did reflect demographic, economic, and educational changes typical of other countries in Latin America in the 1930s and 1940s.[5] These transformations—the shift from predominantly rural to urban residence, exposure to labor organizing and socialist and communist political mobilization, access to university education, and limited economic and social mobility—brought into stark relief the disjunction between formal (electoral) and participatory democracy. Like movements generated by other notable Latin American populists such as Getulio Vargas in Brazil and Juan Domingo Perón in Argentina, or, closer to Colombia, Ecuador's General Velasco or Peru's Haya de la Torre, gaitanismo capitalized on rising expectations of economic, political, and social change that crystallized in the aftermath of the Second World War. Rising expectations, increased social mobility, and greater access to education combined to foster new representations of the body politic, and new symbolic political practices, that marked a profound shift in Colombia's political culture. But Gaitán differed to some extent from populist leaders who emerged elsewhere in Latin America. Gaitán was a sometime dissident from the Liberal Party (one of Colombia's two traditional parties) and although he founded a separate movement, the populist leader made his way back to the Liberal fold by 1947 and assumed the party's leadership.[6] Gaitanismo, moreover, never became institutionalized nor achieved the distinctly autonomous political character of either peronism or aprismo. Gaitán's demise, however, enabled his admirers to pursue their own selective interpretation of his ideas and to adopt political strategies unhampered by the populist leader's potential opposition or disapproval, much the way peronists and apristas were able to improvise in the aftermath of their respective leaders' exile or eventual demise.

This essay is divided into three parts. In the first I briefly examine Gaitán's discourse and self-representations as these emerge in selected speeches, interviews, and writings. I next analyze the impact of Gaitán's movement, the reasons why different sectors identified with and supported him, and the problems that arose in coordinating divergent constituencies in the specific case of Antioquia. A final section explores the transformations of Antioqueño gaitanismo in the aftermath of Gaitán's assassination, and the ways in which different groups adapted his ideas and image to suit their own circumstances. My objective is to explore the ways national political movements and leaders operate in regional and local contexts and to expose the sometimes surprising internal workings of "political culture" even in apparently "traditional," two-party, elite-dominated political systems such as Colombia's.

GAITÁN: PUBLIC MAN, IMAGE, AND DISCOURSE

Jorge Eliécer Gaitán was the material and symbolic embodiment of midcentury change in Colombia. A dark-skinned, physically striking individual who early gave promise of intellectual brilliance and oratorical skill—abilities highly prized within the Colombian political arena—Gaitán grew up in a respectable but poor urban neighborhood of Bogotá, the only son of a public school teacher and unsuccessful bookseller. As a young lawyer (educated on party-sponsored and merit-based scholarships) Gaitán first attracted national political attention when he denounced the Conservative government's complicity in the massacre of United Fruit workers during the 1928 strike in Santa Marta. In the 1930s, his dissatisfaction with the leadership and direction of Colombia's traditional parties and the tendency of that leadership to collaborate in closed-door, bipartisan deal making coalesced into a dissident political movement: UNIR (Unión Nacional de Izquierda Revolucionaria). The manifesto that accompanied the creation of UNIR in 1933 later became a blueprint for the platform adopted by the Liberal Party when Gaitán became its leader in 1947. Aside from his law school thesis, "Las ideas socialistas en Colombia" (1924), the manifesto constitutes Gaitán's most detailed explanation of his political ideology and program.[7]

In UNIR's manifesto, Gaitán identified himself as a socialist who understood Colombian reality in essentially economic terms. "There are two forces in conflict: on the one side those in possession of the means of production, and on the other those who possess nothing but their labor power." Gaitán refused to call this confrontation "class struggle." Neither class struggle nor government by the people could exist in Colombia, Gaitán believed, because the pueblo was devoid of consciousness.[8] Gaitán resolved the problem of the pueblo's inability to govern itself by suggesting that able men could rule *for* the pueblo.[9] He repudiated change by revolutionary means and defined UNIR's struggle as "not merely . . . for the workers; it incorporates all productive forces. We must concern ourselves as much for the worker as for the peasant, for the middle class, for professionals, small industrialists, tradespeople. In other words, for all those who work."[10] "We are not opposed to wealth," Gaitán insisted, "but to poverty." Gaitán and his movement embodied a conscious rejection of corrupt political bossism and restricted elite bipartisan collaboration, practices that had historically compromised the transparency of Colombian politics and the democratic participation of the pueblo majority. Yet at first gaitanismo relied on charismatic and exclusive leadership as much as the traditional political parties, if not more so. At the same time, Gaitán's political discourse left considerable leeway for diverse sectors to interpret his meaning and intentions as they saw fit. Labor, on the one hand, could understand his emphasis on an interventionist state that mediated between Colombia's different social groups as a sign that Gaitán intended to fundamentally restructure national power. Workers could thus link him and his political project with the early days of Alfonso López Pumarejo's "Revolution on the March" when such an approach on the part of the state resulted in the creation of the Colombian Workers Confederation (hereafter CTC) and the favorable resolution of labor disputes.[11]

Middle-sector professionals, on the other hand, downplayed the radical implications of Gaitán's message. They found solace in gradualism and in the notion of a mediating group of brokers whose existence ultimately guaranteed that political initiative and power would remain in the hands of leaders rather than followers. The retention of a privileged place for middle-class adherents where "men of learning counted more than workers," was characteristic of the group of Gaitán's closest associates who, in 1945, organized his presidential campaign in Antioquia.[12] The tension between popular and middle sector conceptions of Gaitán's political message had a determinant effect on the nature of his constituency in the region.

Geography, class, and ethnic/racial identity played important roles in shaping the nature of gaitanismo's support in Antioquia. These factors explain to some degree why sectors that supported Gaitán elsewhere in Colombia did not do so in a significant way in the province. They also account for why the two extreme poles of gaitanista loyalty in Antioquia—Medellín-based middle sector professionals and militant organized workers residing in the province's geographical periphery or border regions—proved so difficult to coordinate into a cohesive movement during Gaitán's lifetime. Gaitán's earliest enthusiasts in Antioquia were men who shared his petit bourgeois origins, university education, or social aspirations. Some of these middle class supporters were professionals—doctors, engineers, lawyers, and journalists.[13] Through kinship and common interests these educated professionals had links to literate, politically active, and mobile artisans (tailors, printers, shoemakers), skilled tradesmen (barbers, butchers, bus drivers/owners) and small shopkeepers (*graneros* [grain dealers], bar/tavern/gas station owners).

Like Gaitán, many middle-sector professionals came to political maturity in the 1920s and 1930s, after a long period of Conservative rule. Like him, too, they found that educational opportunities, professional status, and affiliation to the party in power were no guarantee of admission into the restricted circle of political leadership.[14] Antioquia's Liberal Party, however, did not have the kind of militant, sometimes radical tradition of "left-liberalism" which could be found to operate among Liberals on the Atlantic Coast, within parts of Cundinamarca, and in the eastern provinces of the Santanderes. A left-liberal tradition on which Gaitán could build support for a reformist and dissident political movement did exist in the province, but it was centered in geographically peripheral areas. Here many of the settlers were migrants from coastal departments, the Chocó, Bolivar, and the Santanderes, and landless squatters or organized workers employed in extractive and foreign-owned enterprises such as mining and oil production.

Gaitán's popularity with rural workers and tenants in some parts of Colombia—especially those areas characterized by land disputes in the 1930s—also had little echo in Antioquia, where the area of densest rural settlement was the southwestern coffee zone. Large haciendas and landlessness did not predominate in the Antioqueño southwest, nor had the area experienced land conflicts in the 1930s. By contrast, support for Gaitán was strong in the geographically peripheral Antioqueño areas characterized by cattle ranching, commercial agriculture, and extractive industries (western Antioquia, Urabá, the Bajo Cauca, and parts of the northeast and Magdalena Medio) where land disputes *had* occurred in the 1930s. Though peripheral areas were strategically and economically valuable, they were also among the least populated and least politically integrated Antioqueño regions, which diminished their political clout.

Gaitán's followers in Antioquia therefore understood his message to mean different things depending on their geographical location, class, and ethnic/cultural background. Some viewed Gaitán and his movement as an alternative way to attain political office, while others considered gaitanismo an alternative way of envisioning how politics should operate. These distinctions were reflected, for instance, in two different categories of middle-sector gaitanistas in Antioquia. Known as "parlor gaitanistas," one middle-sector group eschewed the real empowerment of the pueblo.[15] Parlor gaitanistas were often intellectuals seduced by a romantic notion of political radicalism, but they had little direct contact with the popular classes. Their support for Gaitán was abruptly cut short when they witnessed the force of popular wrath in the aftermath of Gaitán's assassination in 1948.[16] A second group of middle-sector gaitanistas understood Gaitán's project in more progressive terms and envisioned gradually including the pueblo in real positions of power.[17] This latter sector continued to be loyal gaitanistas even after the outbreak of popular violence in the wake of Gaitán's death.

The effects of internal gaitanista dissension became sadly apparent in the May 1946 presidential election. A mere 1,740 voters in Medellín chose dissident Liberal Gaitán compared to the 15,883 votes cast for Conservative Mariano Ospina Pérez and the 17,054 votes cast for the official Liberal Gabriel Turbay. In the industrial towns around Medellín such as Envigado, Bello, Caldas, and Itaguí, an average of only 5 percent of the electorate supported Gaitán.[18] Reeling from their movement's catastrophic performance at the polls, middle-sector politicians blamed the movement's poor showing on the official Liberal Party's power of intimidation. The election, gaitanista regional leader Froilán Montoya Mazo insisted, served to reveal the bankruptcy of elite led politics: "they believe that they still enjoy the support of the masses, but in reality a drastic reaction has set in which rejects them completely."[19]

For middle-sector gaitanistas associated with the least populist faction of Gaitán's movement, however, it had not been "the brutal fashion in which the official apparatus had been employed during the previous election" which had guaranteed Gaitán's defeat in Antioquia, but the absence of a clearly designated regional leadership.[20] Ex-Turbay supporters, Lopistas, the nonaligned, a group of workers and drivers (*choferes*) known as "los Negros," and a "leftist" Liberal youth group led by Hernando Jaramillo Arbeláez all clamored unsuccessfully to be recognized as Gaitán's official representatives in Antioquia.[21] Multiple petty rivalries led one gaitanista to conclude that "the lack of respect for hierarchy logically led to an uneasy expectation of total equality, lack of discipline and in the end anarchy."[22]

In addition to the absence of a well-defined corps of regional representatives, political recruitment for Gaitán's cause was also inhibited by mainstream (*oficialista*) Liberal fears that support for Gaitán might erode their hard-won control of certain areas of public sector patronage hiring in Antioquia. Liberal workers were discouraged from supporting Gaitán with threats of job dismissal in positions where Liberal brokers exerted considerable influence such as the regionally owned railroad, public works, customs collection, and so forth. In addition, Gaitán had to struggle against a tendency for Antioqueño politicians in both parties to put regional above partisan interests.[23] Regional 'ethnocentrism' led gaitanistas to bitterly blame Gaitán's loss on Antioqueños as a "race."[24] "You know how Antioquia which is so utilitarian," Delio Jaramillo Arbelaez reminded Gaitán, "has proved incapable of embracing our movement built on patriotism."[25] "As the focal point of the turbayista campaign [Antioquia] is a hostile environment for the enterprise which we, the gaitanistas, are promoting,"[26] middle-sector leaders insisted. They begged Gaitán to be patient with Antioquia, because "the struggle here is very fierce as it is here that much of oligarchic power is concentrated."[27]

Gaitanistas correctly attributed the difficulties in recruitment faced by middle-sector supporters to the weight of elite power, regional pragmatism, and a narrow sense of politics among Antioquia's inhabitants (regardless of partisan affiliation). In Antioquia Gaitán ran up against the nation's most cohesive elite and a regional hegemonic project that aspired to privilege regional interests and identification above partisan differences or appeals.[28] Members of the regional elite who embraced a bipartisan approach to politics had struggled since the nineteenth century to craft and disseminate an image of Antioquia as a place where individual merit rather than birth formed the basis for political and economic influence. Regional politics was consciously represented as being conducted for the public good by disinterested, technically inclined statesmen, and material progress and social welfare were preferred to partisanship or *politiquería.*[29] While by no means as civic-minded or altruistic as they liked to represent themselves, on the whole Antioquia's regional leaders could point to the vibrancy of the regional economy, the possibility of social mobility, and the absence of overt social conflict as evidence that Antioquia was a more efficiently governed region than many other Colombian provinces of the time. Regional identity, constructed around a circumscribed sense of geographic space, moral values, religious practice, and race, moreover, was inextricably bound up in bourgeois political discourse. This led Antioqueños to understand "the nation primarily as their own region" and had given rise over time to a regional political culture in which politics was envisioned as an exercise in pragmatic negotiation rather than as a set of rigid partisan-inspired principles to be defended to the death.[30]

Thus, while Gaitán's attack against oligarchic politics resonated with the region's inhabitants, Antioqueños in core areas tended to associate political bossism and corruption with Bogotá rather than with their regional party leadership or the regional government. Indeed, in some respects Gaitán's ideas regarding the need to moralize politics sounded a lot like regional leaders' discourse of "good government" already rooted in local consciousness. This discourse, to some extent, had found expression in the relative material and social progress of the core towns surrounding Medellín and the southwestern coffee zone, rendering these areas largely indifferent to gaitanismo's appeal.

Voting patterns during the 1947 and 1949 national, regional, and local elections reveal the peculiarities of regional political perception and practice. Candidates running on a dissident Liberal list as gaitanistas won 23.6 percent of Medellín's Liberal vote in the municipal council elections of October 1947. This was almost three times the number of votes cast for Gaitán during his bid for the presidency in 1946, and nearly double the number of votes cast for Gaitán and his followers in the elections to the provincial assembly and the national congress of March 1947.[31] These results suggest that while Medellín's residents were reluctant to vote for non-Antioqueño gaitanista candidates in national elections, they *were* willing to experiment with support for native sons running in local elections as gaitanistas. Medellín's gaitanista candidates—who emphasized the reformist rather than revolutionary aspects of Gaitán's message—may also have capitalized on a shared regional identity to assuage voters who might otherwise have been skittish about voting for a potentially subversive movement. Citizens' different strategies in local and national elections reveal another important characteristic of politics in pre-Violencia Colombia. Despite an accelerated trend toward the centralization of power in Colombia that would result in the eclipse of municipal and regional autonomy by the 1950s, the 1940s were still a period of some fluidity and struggle over local and national spheres of authority and patronage.[32]

Notwithstanding the peculiarities of regional political practice and the obstacles faced by political candidates who challenged a rigid and entrenched hostility to political "outsiders," Gaitán managed to raise his share of regional Liberal votes from 8.7 percent in 1946 to an impressive 39 percent in March 1947. Yet it was just as gaitanismo appeared to be achieving a meaningful presence in regional politics that Gaitán lost interest in pursuing his project of political mobilization in Antioquia.[33] This may have been due to the fact that Gaitán's newly won electoral support in Antioquia did not come from Liberals in Medellín, its surrounding industrial towns, or the densely settled coffee zone, but from militant workers on Antioquia's periphery linked to Communist union leaders.

I use the terms "periphery" and "peripheral" to denote towns and peoples whose cultural traditions and physical location placed them on the margins of traditional Antioqueño settlement and custom. Many of the inhabitants of these towns were migrants from outside Antioquia. In mining towns such as Segovia, Puerto Berrío, Zaragoza, and Remedios, such migrants were also often militant, organized workers. In contrast to middle-sector Antioqueños and industrial workers residing in the geographic and cultural core, they were not reluctant to jeopardize participation in the traditional parties by supporting a maverick. The regional ethos of "good," "disinterested" political leadership that supposedly underwrote a regional hegemonic political project in core areas of Antioquia had never been extended to the residents of Antioquia's periphery, nor had they witnessed any evidence that the region's bourgeoisie actively considered them a legitimate part of Antioquia's political constituency.

Gaitanistas in peripheral areas were largely employed in public works projects or by foreign-owned mining companies such as the Pato Consolidated Mining Company, the Frontino Gold Dredging Company, and Shell Oil. Maritime workers and those employed in the mining sector were often affiliated with a Communist labor leadership. But regardless of their actual political sympathies or union affiliation, workers in peripheral areas tended to be viewed with suspicion by Antioquia's authorities as dangerous, promiscuous, largely black, and godless individuals ("*sin Dios ni ley*") and were indiscriminately accused of threatening Antioquia's social stability and sense of identity (*raza*).[34] Accustomed to having their grievances and labor disputes squashed by coercion and the deployment of national and regional troops (the army and police), workers employed by foreign-owned companies or in what were perceived as strategic areas such as river transport were often denied their political rights.[35]

Unlike Gaitán's supporters in core Antioqueño areas, organized workers on the periphery reveled in Gaitán's more revolutionary postures. For them Gaitán's movement seemed to represent an escape from provincial marginality and from the limitations imposed by the traditional parties and their embedded power in the region. Yet while militant periphery workers and inhabitants delivered a large percentage of their votes for Gaitán, he was ambivalent and cautious about the degree to which he should either court or encourage this sector's enthusiastic endorsement. The fact that Gaitán's richly suggestive but ambiguous discourse found its greatest support among the very Antioqueño sectors to have experienced most palpably the effects of regional cultural, political, and social marginalization led to an especially malleable and unstable trajectory of left-liberal "populist" politics in the province.

WORKERS AND GAITÁN

A series of events precipitated the shift of political support to Gaitán among miners, oil workers, and road construction crews in Antioquia. First, the majority of these workers were affiliated with the CTC, the labor confederation whose legal recognition had been won during Liberal Alfonso López Pumarejo's first presidential administration. López Pumarejo's government, like other Latin American Popular Front governments in the 1930s, formed alliances with sympathetic parties on the left for the purpose of passing into law labor and social legislation that might otherwise have been effectively blocked by conservative political sectors. The bulk of CTC affiliates and union leaders—including those not affiliated with the Liberal party—came to rely on the Liberal government's willingness to intercede on labor's behalf in disputes with management. The era of relative cooperation between Liberals and Communists came to an end, however, as both the balance of power shifted between conservative and left-sympathizing factions within the Liberal party and as Cold War anticommunism emerged in the aftermath of the Second World War. Global and domestic changes sparked dissension between rank and file members, some union leaders, and the Communist Party. This dissension prompted workers on the periphery who had not identified themselves as gaitanistas before the presidential election of 1946 to shift their support to Gaitán after that time.

In the towns of the northeast, Bajo Cauca, Magdalena Medio, and western Antioquia, where Jorge Eliécer Gaitán found his most loyal adherents, elite political leadership and traditional party discipline had historically been weakest. Compared to the regional average of 58.4 percent, an average of only 34 percent of the eligible voters in Caucasia, Segovia, Cáceres, Puerto Berrío, San Roque, Turbo, Zaragoza, and Remedios cast ballots in the 1946 election.[36] In the Antioqueño heartland (Medellín and its surrounding industrial towns, Oriente, Suroeste, and the immediate northern and southern municipalities), 77 percent of eligible voters cast votes in the 1946 election. The towns where Gaitán garnered the most votes, moreover, were typically ones where inhabitants had voted in previous years for alternative parties (not just the Liberal or Conservative parties), and where a precedent of support for alternative political movements existed within local culture.

The correspondence exchanged between Gaitán and union members employed in oil, mining, and transport sectors as well as periphery voting patterns in various elections between 1947 and 1949 underscores peripheral residents' exasperation with traditional party leadership and structures. The letters demonstrate why militant workers and inhabitants residing in Antioquia's periphery supported Gaitán after 1946 even when Gaitán himself sometimes proved a lukewarm ally. Throughout 1946, workers in the mines, oil camps, and on the Magdalena River wrote Gaitán to complain not only of their daily work conditions but also of the abuse heaped on them by both the official Liberal and Conservative authorities. Ship crews in Puerto Berrío complained that union members were arbitrarily accused of missing a day's work in order to justify firing them, while miners who worked for the Pato Consolidated Gold Dredging Company in El Bagre (Bajo Cauca) accused the government of favoring foreign management and ignoring worker grievances.[37]

Gaitán, however, refused to be roped in as a broker on labor's behalf. He answered workers' letters politely but referred them to Liberal headquarters or instructed them to submit their grievances directly to the minister of labor.[38] Accustomed to his remorseless criticism of the highly bureaucratic and corrupt machine politics of the traditional parties, some workers expected Gaitán to circumvent protocol and intercede on their behalf. Workers in peripheral areas appealed to Gaitán as a potentially powerful intermediary who could help build direct political links between their own marginal localities, a national political movement, and the central government. To elude the engrained regional political structures based in Medellín that had historically eschewed alliances with inhabitants and workers on the periphery, workers there insisted on dealing directly with Gaitán and refused to communicate with him through his regional middle-sector leaders in Medellín.[39]

The gulf between periphery and core residents and their relationship to Gaitán may be observed in the marked differences in voting patterns that emerged among Gaitán's supporters in Antioquia. When Gaitán ran as a dissident for a seat in Antioquia's assembly in 1947, for example, he drew an overwhelming amount of support from peripheral towns as well as a respectable and significant number of votes from core area towns with a Liberal majority. Yet while core Liberal inhabitants were willing to vote for Gaitán for regional office, they did not vote for him in the presidential election of 1946 and proved unwilling for the most part to vote for gaitanista candidates in local municipal elections held in 1947 and 1949. Few voters in periphery towns lent their support to Gaitán when he ran for president in 1946, though like core area voters, they proved willing to vote for him in the regional assembly election of 1947. Unlike core area voters, however, voters in Antioquia's periphery continued to vote in significant numbers for gaitanista candidates in local municipal council elections in 1947 and even after Gaitán's death, in 1949. This trend in gaitanista support in local elections was most marked in periphery towns settled by non-Antioqueños where public road personnel and miners constituted an important presence (Cáceres, Dabeiba, Frontino, Puerto Berrío, Segovia, and Turbo).[40]

Differences in voting patterns among Gaitán's followers reflect the distinct understandings and objectives present within Antioqueño gaitanismo. Core area politicians used their association with Gaitán to maneuver themselves into positions of power from which to leverage greater inclusion and recognition by the traditional parties, but showed little interest in radically redefining the practice of Colombian politics. Voters in core areas, moreover, were reluctant to brook the loss of patronage and modest partisan inclusion that voting for dissident party lists (when these were not a majority) might represent at the local level. The municipal council after all was a powerful source of patronage and employment—appointing teachers, public works personnel, policemen, etc.—and core towns such as those in the coffee-producing southwest were well inscribed in the traditional parties' regional and national networks. In peripheral towns, in contrast, the parties were weak and traditional patronage networks were less in evidence, making the balance of risk and gain a fundamentally different one. Electing a predominantly gaitanista municipal council might not appear to represent a grand political achievement in Medellín or Bogotá. But in economically and geographically strategic towns such as Puerto Berrío, Segovia, and Turbo it meant that the elected representatives could act as allies of militant workers and advance a radical agenda locally in the appointment of sympathetic policemen, work inspectors, and public works personnel.

In March 1947, a wave of sympathetic strikes broke out in Antioquia to protest the dismissal of workers and their repression by the police. In those selected periphery towns where gaitanista strength by that time had become consolidated at the local level, workers did not abandon gaitanismo even when Gaitán repudiated the strikers and left them to face the retribution of regional Conservative authorities alone.[41] Instead, they redefined it for their own ends. Miners and road construction workers suffered an escalating campaign of intimidation and violence at the hands of the Conservative regional government and unsympathetic right-leaning factions of the regional Liberal party. As these sectors' increasingly deployed the terms "gaitanista," and later "*nueve abrileño*" to justify the use of coercion against workers deemed to be militant and Communist sympathizers, the identification in the periphery with gaitanismo was reinforced.[42] The term "gaitanista" was used selectively by conservative Liberal politicians and regional Conservatives, not against Liberal industrial workers but against public road crews, miners, and oil workers employed on the periphery.[43] A collective identity as "gaitanistas" among periphery inhabitants was thus consolidated at the very moment when gaitanismo's strength might have been expected to wane as a result first of Gaitán's own repudiation of militant support and later as a result of his demise. Among people in the periphery who felt marginalized socially, racially, and in terms of regional origin, gaitanismo as political practice emerged as a marker of oppositional identity in the face of rising discrimination or neglect by elite politicians in Medellín.

RESURRECTION: GAITANISMO AFTER GAITÁN'S DEATH

All non-Conservative workers in Antioquia employed in sectors where political influence played a direct or indirect role in hiring after 1949 suffered some degree of official intimidation. But those workers able to forge a collective identity around a particular symbol or political project such as gaitanismo were able to construct strategies of resistance and self-defense. Within hours of Gaitán's assassination, oil workers created a revolutionary junta that assumed control of the Shell Oil camp for several days.[44] A year later, gaitanistas in mining towns such as Caucasia drove local Conservative authorities to distraction by playing the record "Mataron a Gaitán" (They Killed Gaitán) over and over again in the jukeboxes of all the local cantinas.[45] Despite having prohibited any form of political propaganda, the regional governor personally forbade the town's mayor (a Conservative regional appointee who was not native to the town) from taking any punitive action against the townspeople lest he provoke a "revolutionary" response among Gaitán's followers. Demonized as gaitanista "savages" and "agitators," workers successfully capitalized on their reputed militancy and violence to intimidate the authorities and defy attempts to limit popular political expression.

Road construction workers labeled by the authorities as gaitanistas were among those most successful in resisting Conservative harassment.[46] With the support of engineers such as gaitanista Humberto White (who had run in the congressional election of 1947), the road workers employed in the construction of the Santa Fé de Antioquia-Anzá-Bolombolo trunk road in northwestern Antioquia exploited both the governor's reluctance to jeopardize public works projects and regional preconceptions of gaitanista unruliness and violence to defend their jobs and lives. Workers insisted on reading excerpts from the banned gaitanista newspaper *Jornada* over the town radio and effectively wielded the threat of work stoppages to block government attempts to replace White and dismiss workers.[47] Two years later, in 1951, road workers in Dabeiba—a town that had voted overwhelmingly for Gaitán from 1946 until 1949 (in local as well as national elections)—went a step further than their coreligionists in Anzá. They threatened to kill Conservative engineers and scab workers sent to usurp their jobs.[48] In the Casabe oil camp, moreover, Shell workers explicitly identified as *nueve abrileños* impeded the efforts of Conservative engineers to dismiss work inspectors appointed locally (by a majority gaitanista town council) who doubled as labor brokers for the company as late as 1953.[49]

Regional authorities were unable to fundamentally alter the partisan composition of Antioquia's most militant labor sectors (oil workers, miners, and road construction crews) during la Violencia. These groups' demonization as gaitanistas, their willingness to exploit government fears and stereotypes, and their coalescence around a shared sense of themselves as the heirs to a "revolutionary" political movement enabled them to mount a successful challenge against Conservative harassment and intimidation. In the course of elaborating a strategy of resistance, however, workers on the periphery also ranged well beyond Gaitán's own ideology and notions of appropriate behavior to embrace a form of gaitanismo that fit their specific and immediate needs.

MIDDLE-SECTOR GAITANISTAS AND POPULAR EMPOWERMENT

While workers on the periphery used their identity as gaitanistas to withstand and retaliate against Conservative violence, the chaotic condition of the Liberal Party in Medellín in the aftermath of Gaitán's death paradoxically made possible what had never been achieved while Gaitán was alive. This city without a 'left-liberal' tradition for the first time saw the incorporation and day-to-day participation in party organization of the urban pueblo. For a brief period (1949–54) Medellín's popular neighborhoods and such members of the pueblo as truck drivers, artisans, small shopkeepers, and some industrial workers helped construct what has remained to this day one of the few experiments in twentieth-century Medellín of political organization from the bottom up. How was it possible to achieve after Gaitán's death what was never realized during his lifetime?

The regional Liberal Party (which had not supported Gaitán) was particularly hard hit by the intensification of Conservative and police harassment in the year following Gaitán's assassination. Meetings at the party's headquarters in downtown Medellín were made the target of assaults by Conservative Party members acting alone or with the tacit approval or help of some of the party leadership, the police, and regional detectives. Unauthorized searches, surveillance, phone and wiretaps, and vandalism increasingly discouraged Liberals from meeting publicly.[50] Disagreements about how to deal with an escalating climate of violence, moreover, further fractured Liberals. Some (known as *lentejos*) preferred to cooperate with selected regional Conservatives and continued to enjoy the patronage jobs within the government to which they had been appointed. Others were riven by ideological or personal differences that weighed as much or more than did hostility toward local Conservatives. Finally, elite party members, like their regional Conservative counterparts, dismayed by the populist and increasingly vituperative tenor of partisan politics, simply withdrew from active participation in the daily affairs of the party.[51] Those left to run the party were forced to search for alternative forms of financing and new ways of maintaining party loyalty among the rank and file.

In 1949, national Liberal leader Carlos Lleras Restrepo traveled to Medellín hoping to persuade the regional membership to reconcile their differences and form a unified front to oppose Conservative intimidation. But he found that the only sector of the party willing to shoulder such a burden was the progressive wing of the old gaitanista leadership—men such as Froilán Montoya Mazo—and a few non-gaitanista middle-sector politicians such as Alberto Jaramillo Sánchez and Francisco Cardona Santos. The rise to positions of authority by gaitanistas such as Montoya Mazo was made possible only because the traditional sectors of party leadership withdrew from an active role in politics during la Violencia. The need to find alternative meeting places and financial support for the regional Liberal party, moreover, combined to shift the party's focus to the pueblo. By late 1949, party meetings were held in working-class neighborhoods such as Aranjuéz, Berlín, and Manrique Oriental, not in elite-dominated downtown Medellín.[52] These neighborhoods, while Liberal, did not necessarily identify themselves as gaitanista, but they welcomed their party's new interest in them and embraced leaders such as Montoya Mazo who made the shift in party focus possible. A Coordinadora Revolucionaria (Revolutionary Coordinating Committee) was organized to communicate with emergent Liberal guerrilla groups in Antioquia's countryside and to aid rural refugees of violence.[53] Artisan and worker cooperatives were organized to collect dues deducted from weekly wages to provide the funds necessary to keep the party running and to defray the expenses of transportation and aid to Liberal refugees. The pueblo, moreover, agreed to take in such refugees and provide them with shelter and job training (carpentry, cabinet-making skills, etc.). In cases where party members continued to be employed as foremen (*jefés de fáb-*

rica) in Medellín's textile mills and light industries, they used their authority to hire Liberal refugees.

Liberal Party organization underwent a radical transformation. Eighty *directorios de barrio* were set up in the poor neighborhoods encircling Medellín. These elected their own representatives (drawn from among the inhabitants of each neighborhood) and established networks for the distribution of information and party instructions. Montoya Mazo, the architect of these barrio headquarters, considered them "thermometers for the party leaders," a daily gauge of pueblo opinions and attitudes.[54] Each *junta* or directorio de barrio appointed a jefé de debate who acted as an intermediary between the neighborhood membership and the central leadership of the party located in the *directorio munícipal* (which incorporated all of Medellín). The neighborhood party associations met on a weekly basis with the municipal headquarters to discuss party issues, news, and maintain morale. Via the clandestine use of radio the barrios kept up the "Liberal Fridays," a weekly radio program that during Gaitán's lifetime had been a crucial vehicle of political mobilization and information.[55] When the national leadership of the party ordered regional and local party headquarters to close down because violence made it impossible to protect the lives of Liberals, moreover, Antioquia's Liberals refused. The directorios de barrio continued to function throughout the period of la Violencia.

What are we to make of this experiment in popular participation? One might argue that party organization continued to be hierarchically structured in ways that did not differ much from the highly centralized organization of the Liberal Party before la Violencia. In fact, however, the party organization developed by gaitanistas such as Froilán Montoya Mazo did represent a departure from tradition and an example of real popular participation. First, although neighborhoods had been mobilized before la Violencia, such mobilization tended to occur only during periods of electoral campaigning. Once speeches were made and votes committed, neighborhood organizations disbanded or were left unused until the next electoral season. During la Violencia, in contrast, directorios de barrio functioned continuously.

Second, the directorios de barrio represented entities through which the pueblo could air its grievances and where the contours of its party obligations could be negotiated. For instance, the inhabitants of the barrios extracted a commitment that once violence in rural areas had diminished, the party leadership would ensure that refugees were shipped back to the countryside. Barrio dwellers made their reasoning for this demand explicit. They feared that the unlimited migration of rural inhabitants would ultimately undermine their ability to bargain in the workplace and threaten their livelihoods. In hindsight, the impossibility of enforcing this commitment seems pathetically apparent, but what is important is that neighborhood Liberals made their donations and participation in the effort to support refugees and keep the party functioning contingent on the adequate consideration of demands of their own.

Third, in contrast with earlier periods of party organization, it was the pueblo, and not the wealthy membership of the Liberal party, that kept the party afloat during the period of la Violencia. This gave ordinary people a sense that they were indeed critical to the party's existence and enabled them to regard their participation in the party as a reciprocal one, marked by mutual responsibilities and obligations. Their day-to-day integration, moreover, enabled them to be far more critical of their traditional jefes. Several individuals interviewed remarked that "there were plenty of activists from the pueblo; it was the jefes who were missing."[56] The elite leadership in particular was disdained and rejected by popular members who viewed their tendency to go into exile in Miami and Mexico, or to retreat to their economic activities and abandon the daily work of the party, as evidence of the bankruptcy of traditional party leadership.[57] Only those leaders who, like Montoya Mazo, remained by the pueblo's side during the entire period of la Violencia despite frequent jailings and police harassment enjoyed the pueblo's respect and loyalty.

Perhaps the clearest indication that the popular organization given the party during this period represented something fundamentally distinct and, indeed, dangerous in the eyes of traditional party leaders is provided by what happened in the aftermath of la Violencia. Liberal politicians who had remained aloof from party activities during la Violencia deliberately dismantled and in some cases violently destroyed the contents and offices of the directorios de barrio. The posters of Gaitán that had decorated the humble neighborhood sites used as the seats of party organization, the painstakingly collected "archives" of biographical information on rural Liberal guerrillas, the paper vestiges of cooperative networks to aid refugees and finance the party were burnt or otherwise destroyed by individuals who today enjoy positions of leadership within the regional Liberal Party.[58]

The product in part of historical accident, Medellín's Liberal Party organization during la Violencia made reality what had only been a vague promise during Gaitán's lifetime: the democratization of party organization and the empowerment of popular sectors. Gaitán's assassination paradoxically made possible popular participation in Antioquia by creating a vacuum of authority within the party leadership. None but the most popularly disposed gaitanista leaders were willing to undertake the rescue and maintenance of party structure during la Violencia. Granted little hands-on political participation in Antioquia while Gaitán was alive even though they were the rhetorical focus of his political discourse, the pueblo now was able to capitalize on the party's need of it. During la Violencia they achieved a receptive audience for their grievances and could experiment with the exercise of local power.

• • • • •

The malleability and ambiguity of Gaitán's self-representations and language—which could be interpreted as both revolutionary and reformist—offered unparalleled opportunities for individuals with varying interests to see in Gaitán what they chose to. Gaitán's Antioqueño supporters accordingly contested, shaped, and embraced his image and political discourse in distinct, contradictory ways that reflected their geographic, political, cultural, and sector-specific beliefs and needs. As Gaitán moved closer to attaining real political power and the presidential office, however, the differences of strategy and expectations among his adherents brought his movement in Antioquia to the edge of collapse. Ironically, Gaitán's real impact on Antioqueño politics emerged only after his assassination in 1948.

Freed by Gaitán's untimely death from having to reconcile their conflicting agendas and understandings of gaitanismo, militant workers and inhabitants in Antioquia's periphery were able to build a sense of collective identity around a radical image of Gaitán. This enabled them to retain local autonomy and defend themselves against the worst effects of Conservative repression between 1949 and 1953. Meanwhile, the withdrawal of Medellín's traditional Liberal Party leadership from political activism in the wake of Gaitán's assassination enabled both progressive gaitanista leaders and non-gaitanista sectors of the pueblo to achieve something approximating the popular political participation for which Gaitán had fought during his lifetime. Thus, although ultimately Gaitán and his political movement were unsuccessful in their attempt to build a lasting or coherent basis of electoral support in Antioquia, his rhetoric and ideas had a tremendous impact on regional political strategy and the empowerment of the pueblo during la Violencia. The emergence of a grassroots radical political practice around gaitanismo, however briefly, brought to the political forefront previously marginalized members of Antioquia's popular sectors (especially those residing in the periphery), thus permanently disrupting any illusion of smoothly functioning, unchallenged regional elite political control.

NOTES

1. The literature on la Violencia is too extensive to cover in its entirety here, but see Guzmán, Fals Borda, and Umaña, *La Violencia;* Sánchez and Meertens, *Bandoleros;* Alape, *El Bogotázo;* Oquist, *Violence;* Pécaut, *Orden y violencia;* and Bergquist, Peñaranda, and Sánchez, eds., *Violence in Colombia.* For a detailed examination of la Violencia in Antioquia, see Roldán, *Blood and Fire.*

2. Among the few works on Gaitán or gaitanismo are Braun, *The Assassination;* Sharpless, *Gaitán of Colombia;* López Giraldo, *El apostol desnudo;* Sánchez, *Los dias de la revolución;* and Díaz Callejas, *El 9 de abril 1948.* For a rare study of Gaitán in a regional context, see Green, "Vibrations," 283–311. Green, *Gaitanismo,* provides an unprecedented and careful analysis of the phenomenon of gaitanismo in Colombia as a whole.

3. Colombia, Departamento de Antioquia, Contraloría Departamental, *Anuario Estadístico de Antioquia, años 1944–1945–1946,* app. 2, 219–22.

4. Green, "Sibling Rivalry," 99.

5. See, for instance, various essays in Conniff, ed., *Latin American Populism,* and Rock, ed., *Latin America in the 1940s.*

6. Conservative Antioqueño critics explicitly compared gaitanismo to peronism and described Gaitán's followers as *descamisados* (shirtless ones); see *El Colombiano,* May 3, 1951.

7. Gaitán, "Las ideas socialistas"; for the 1933 manifesto and 1947 platform, see Eastman, ed., *Gaitán, Obras selectas,* 1:129–55, 203–13.

8. Ibid., 1:130, 133.

9. Ibid., 1:132.

10. Ibid., 1:138.
11. Urrutia, *The Development,* 119.
12. Braun, *The Assassination of Gaitán,* 88; Green, however, disagrees with Braun's characterization of gaitanismo's leadership as mainly middle class in origin.
13. Author's interviews with Froilán Montoya Mazo and Bernardo Ospina Román, Medellín, October 1986 and April 1987; *El Colombiano* (1946–50), *La Defensa* (1946–50), *El 9 de Abril* (1948) and *El Correo* (1946–49); Gaitán's correspondence in the Centro Gaitán, Bogotá (1946–1947); and biographical information in Mejía Robledo, *Vidas y empresas.*
14. Braun, *The Assassination of Gaitán,* 13–38; for Antioquia, see Roldán, *Blood and Fire,* 44–45.
15. *9 de Abril,* June 4, 1948.
16. *9 de Abril,* May 21, 1948.
17. Montoya Mazo, interview with author, Medellín, October 1986.
18. Dto. de Antioquia, *Anuario Estadístico . . . 1944–1945–1946,* 219–20.
19. Montoya Mazo to Gaitán, Medellín, June 19, 1946, *Correspondencia.*
20. Ibid.
21. Hernando Jaramillo Arbeláez to Gaitán, Medellín, June 24, 1946; Oscar Rincón Noreña to Gaitán, n.d., 1946, *Correspondencia.*
22. Jorge Ospina Londoño to Gaitán, Medellín, June 14, 1946, *Correspondencia.*
23. Oscar Rincón Noreña to Gaitán, n.d. (1946), *Correspondencia.*
24. Jairo de Bedout to Gaitán, Medellín, July 29, 1946, *Correspondencia.*
25. Delio Jaramillo Arbeláez to Gaitán, Medellín, July 8, 1946, *Correspondencia.*
26. Delio Jaramillo Arbeláez, Julio Hincapie Santa María, and Jairo Arango Gaviria to Gaitán, Medellín, Aug. 8, 1946, *Correspondencia.*
27. Montoya Mazo to Gaitán, Medellín, Sept. 17, 1946, *Correspondencia.*
28. Fontana, *Hegemony and Power,* 33–34.
29. See the biographical entries for Francisco Moreno Ramirez and Ricardo Olano in Mejía Robledo, *Vidas y empresas,* 117–19, 126–29, and the critique of regional bipartisan "pragmatism" in Restrepo Jaramillo, *El Pensamiento conservador,* 15–16, 20, 25–32.
30. Uribe de Hincapie and Alvarez, *Las raíces,* 87.
31. Contraloría Departamental, *Estadística electoral . . . el dia 5 de Mayo 1946,* App. 2, 4.
32. For a general discussion of this phenomenon, see Tirado Mejía, *Descentralización;* for the case of Antioquia, see Roldán, "La política antioqueña," 161–75.
33. Montoya Mazo to Gaitán, Medellín, Sept. 17, 1946, *Correspondencia.*
34. Secretaría de Gobierno de Antioquia (hereinafter SGA), 1949, v.3, letter, Nechí (Caucasia), March 31, 1949; Archivo Privado del Sr. Gobernador de Antioquia (hereinafter AGA), 1949, no volume number (hereafter no vol. no.), letter, Puerto Berrío, Sept. 8, 1949.

35. SGA, 1948, vol. 1, "Proposición #1, Asamblea General del Sindicato de Trabajadores de Pato Consolidated Gold Dredging Ltd.," Jan. 1948.
36. "Resultado . . . 1946," in *Anuario estadístico,* 219–22.
37. Fabio Acuña Parra to Gaitán, Puerto Berrío, Nov. 25, 1946; G. Pernett Miranda to Gaitán, El Bagre, Oct. 9, 1946, *Correspondencia.*
38. Benjamín Jaramillo Zuleta to Gaitán, Pato, June 27, 1946; Rionegro residents to Gaitán, n.d. (Sept. 1946), *Correspondencia.*
39. Letter to Gaitán, San Rafael, June 26, 1946, *Correspondencia.*
40. "Resultado . . . 5 de octubre de 1947;" "Resultado . . . 5 de junio de 1949," in *Anuario Estadístico,* 274–77.
41. Ibid.
42. AGA, 1952, vol. 12, "Secretaría de Obras Públicas—Informe para el Sr. Gobernador de Antioquia," Nov. 10, 1952.
43. AGA, 1947, no vol. no., "Telegramas," June 1947.
44. Díaz Callejas, *El 9 de Abril 1948,* 91–92.
45. SGA, 1949, vol. 3, Visitador Administrativo to Secretario de Gobierno, Caucasia, March 31, 1949.
46. AGA, 1949, no vol. no., "Papeles del Sr. Gobernador, 1949–1950," telegram, Anza, April 30, 1949.
47. SGA, 1949, vol. 2, telegram, Yarumal, May 28, 1949.
48. AGA, 1951, vol. 7, telegram, Dabeiba, Jan. 10, 1951.
49. AGA, 1952, vol. 12, telegram from Obras Públicas, Medellín, Nov. 10, 1952; SGA, 1953, vol. 8, telegrams from Obras Públicas engineer, Casabe, April 6, 1953 and May 11, 1953.
50. AGA, 1950, vol. 9, Detectives to Governor, Medellín, Nov. 21, 1949; AGA, 1952, vol. 6, Oficio #329, Medellín, Dec. 7, 1951; AGA, 1950, vol. 3; Rafael Mejía Toro (Policia Nacional), Oficio #2421, Medellín, July 4, 1952; AGA, 1952, vol. 6, Dir. Gral. de la Pol. Nac. to Governor, Bogotá, Feb. 5, 1952.
51. SGA, 1951, vol. 6, "Plan A," Aug. 10, 1951.
52. Montoya Mazo, interview with author, Medellín, April 1987.
53. *El Colombiano,* Dec. 8, 1951.
54. Montoya Mazo, interview with author, Medellín, Oct. 1986.
55. AGA, 1951, vol. 2, telegram (in code), Orden Público, Bogotá, May 17, 1951; AGA, 1951, vol. 6, report on clandestine radio stations, Ministerio de Guerra, Bogotá, April 7, 1951; SGA, 1951, vol. 6, report of clandestine radio station, Jefé de Rentas e Impuestos to Administrador de Hacienda Nacional, Segovia, April 4, 1951.
56. Capitán Corneta (Francisco Montoya), Liberal guerrilla leader, interview with author, Medellín, April 1987.
57. Montoya Mazo, personal archive, letter from Fidelino Urrego, Adán Cartagena, and Hotabio [*sic*] Gónzalez, Urrao, March 8, 1954.
58. Montoya Mazo, interview with author, Medellín, April 1987.

CONCLUDING REMARKS

ANDEAN INFLECTIONS OF LATIN AMERICAN POLITICAL CULTURES

Nils Jacobsen and
Cristóbal Aljovín de Losada

Volumes of collected essays do not easily lend themselves to summations of central, shared ideas. Still, the rich studies presented here demonstrate that Andean political cultures during the formative centuries between the waning colony and the waxing nation-states shared key issues and practices with other nations of Latin America while also showing distinct inflections, making them uniquely Colombian or Bolivian, or—for a few issues—perhaps even uniquely Andean. One of the more subtle yet highly significant insights that emerges from this book is that seemingly minor shifts or variations in policies or political practices can set different polities on substantially different trajectories. This is what we mean by inflections of political cultures. It is comparable perhaps to how minor changes of chords and rhythm produced the shift from *son* to *rumba* in Cuban music.

Alan Knight has presented a cogent model of Latin American political economies during the nineteenth century, suggesting how different commodity markets, institutions, and labor regimes have lead to distinct types of political trajectories in various polities. Specific mixes of market opportunities, types of commodities, property regimes, and means of covering labor demands have strongly shaped political elite decisions and practices concerning the inclusivity or exclusivity of polities and how much coercion—in the social as well as political spheres—was deemed legitimate or even necessary. Clearly distinct socioeconomic structures (and their epochal changes) had a strong influence on Andean political regimes. Knight's brilliant comparative overview of distinct trajectories during the long nineteenth century eloquently encapsulates results of a venerable tradition of social-scientific and historical scholarship on our region in this regard.

Our notion of distinct inflections in local, national, and region-wide politics also suggests that political cultures may be less "hard-wired" than some socioeconomic structures. Trajectories of polities are set in specific historical conjunctures; political decisions arising out of values and interests and negotiations between different agents may shape trajectories for years to come. But inflections can be changed in new rounds of negotiation and decision making. Path dependency is not absolute. The approach to political cultures and their inflections espoused in this book suggests the tension between path dependency and the openness or malleability of political regimes based on the agency of diverse social, ethnic, and regional groups. In these brief concluding remarks we wish to highlight a few of the similarities and distinct inflections of modern Andean political cultures.

"RACE," STATE, AND NATION

Andean politicians, intellectuals, and societies at large have been preoccupied—often morbidly so—with how "multiracial" populations in their territories affect state building and the formation of national communities. Six chapters in this book impressively demonstrate how regional and national Andean elites at various conjunctures constructed widely differing models to categorize and deal with indigenous, mestizo, cholo, black, and mulatto populations. Most of these models served to buttress the elites' pretensions to exclusionary power. Distinct identities, cultural memories, alliance politics, and power potentials of the various subaltern groups themselves—fluctuating between periods of encirclement and loss, relative stability and regeneration—contributed to shifts in racial orders. The chapters also point to the distinct positioning of indigenous populations on the one hand, and black and mulatto populations on the other within colonial and national states. The fascinating pair of chapters by Garrido and Helg about people of African descent on Nueva Granada's Atlantic coast during the transition from colony to republic suggests how two scholars' different approaches can result in distinct but complementary "histories" of the same place and time (perhaps they also suggest different perspectives resulting from an "internal" and an "external" gaze). Helg stresses the *collective* failure of Afro-Colombians of the Atlantic coast during the wars of independence to challenge the socioracial order that subjected them, ultimately allowing elites in the highland regions to dominate the Atlantic region and define the republic of Nueva Granada as Andean, white, and mestizo. Garrido highlights *individual* challenges by *libres de todos colores.* Through publicly insisting on recognition of their personal accomplishments, they subverted socioracial hierarchies of honor. Such individual struggles derived from and helped forge plebeian popular culture, but—as Helg finds—did not question honor and power hierarchies per se. Derek Williams's chapter suggests the ambivalent outcome of García Moreno's authoritarian Catholic state-building project in Ecuador, and how notions of race and gender were central for its success. Women and indigenous groups turned the Catholic dictator's patriarchal, gender-segregated, and ethnically hierarchical vision of Ecuador around and insisted on their own terms for political and social inclusion. Most surprisingly, Williams shows that this ultramontane *and* modernizing project did more to improve access of women and native Andeans to education than many contemporary Liberal governments in neighboring republics.

For the southern Andes, Serulnikov's chapter convincingly analyzes the Great Rebellion of the late 1770s and early 1780s as regionally distinct processes of cultural and political empowerment of native Andean commoners and kurakas. In stressing the *process* of local and regional insurrections, Serulnikov perceptively demonstrates the fluidity between ameliorative movements, insisting on ancient rights, and the development of revolutionary postures among native Andeans, ready to throw out much of the colonial order. This fluidity and border crossing between ameliorative politics and more radical or even revolutionary projects was also observed in the very different settings of mid-twentieth-century crises in Colombia and Bolivia, in the chapters by Roldán and Gotkowitz.

The chapters by Larson and Gotkowitz offer exciting new analyses of the whole gamut of elite projects on race and nation in Bolivia during the first half of the twentieth century and the native Andeans' engagement with national politics during the crucial decade preceding the revolution of 1952. Larson stresses the common denominator among all Paceño elite intellectuals writing on these issues during the early twentieth century: their call for protection and uplift of racialized "Indians," to make them effective workers, taxpayers, and soldiers for the Creole nation, while limiting their citizens rights and repressing grassroots movements; and their fear of mestizos and cholos, increasingly viewed as corrupting and dangerous, as populist strategies mobilized them for support in political contests. But Larson's chapter intriguingly also outlines significant variance among these elite projects: between quasi-seigneurial visions of Creole hacendados' control over their Indian wards (Arguedas), and those foreseeing a central role for the state (Tamayo); and between writers/politicians imagining Indians as a tabula rasa for whom every aspect of their social and cultural ways needed the civilizing impact of Hispanic elite guidance (Saavedra) and those who wrote approvingly of core aspects of native Andean civilization as the ayllu (Paredes). In spite of their pervasive racism and exclusivism, visions such as those of Paredes and Tamayo foreshadow more statist and antiliberal indigenista projects of middle-class and military populists during the late 1930s and 1940s. Gotkowitz demonstrates how these could be transformed and appropriated by native Andean social and political movements into a politics of republican entitlement and indigenous identity. She suggests continuities between midcentury populists and earlier elite indigenists by her convincing argument that even the MNR—protagonist of the 1952 revolution—wavered between subsuming native Andeans within the category of social classes and special legislation inscribing native Andean cultural and social institutions in the framework of national institutions. On the level of political projects, then, there was no complete and irreversible shift "from caste to class."

THE LIMITS OF ANDEAN STATE-BUILDING PROJECTS

Charles Walker's chapter persuasively argues that the Bourbon civilizing project in the central Andes, and especially in cities like Lima, largely failed. He adduces four reasons for that failure: the incapacity or reluctance to dedicate sufficient finances for the program's realization; the unresolved contradiction between the Bourbon reform-mongers' notion of a socioracially fragmented and hierarchical society and their goal to create a uniform enlightened polity and society; the Bourbons' lukewarm commitment to their own civilizing program; and resistance to the program by diverse popular groups. If not complete failures, most republican projects to revamp their states and societies administratively, socially, and culturally also show stark limitations.

At least for the postcolonial period, Walker's list of the causes for failure or limited success of state-building projects should also include the fragility or absence of elite consensus, and the capacity of regional or sectoral elites and clientele groups excluded from the governing coalition to block state-building projects in their bailiwick. This clearly played a role in the failure of Lima governments after the War of the Pacific to establish a decentralized tax collection system autonomous from regional and provincial executive authorities, as analyzed by Contreras. Both regional power holders and the native Andeans insisted on the old collection mechanisms for direct taxes, with roots in the colonial "reciprocity compact." Moreover, at least the Andean liberal and positivist state-building projects between the 1850s and 1920s, from their very inception, often converted their universalist republican pretensions into justifications for strengthening hierarchical and exclusive social, ethnic, and gender orders. Modernizing state building in this sense often seemed little more than a formal *aggiornamiento* of those orders. This was true for the trumpeting of the centrality of public opinion by Peruvian elites as much as for García Moreno's efforts for education and moral reforms to build a "Catholic people" in Ecuador. While frequently touting European ideological models, state-building projects were usually highly eclectic endeavors, responding to perceived crises of the state or society—and elite control—much more than to ideological demands.

But the overt failure or stark limitations of many Andean state-building projects certainly did not mean that nothing changed in the course of their flawed implementation. It rather means that outcomes usually were somewhat different from the stated goals. The Bourbon reforms largely failed to reshape Andean society in the image of enlightened civilization. But they did usher in the slow decomposition of the Habsburg corporate order, contribute to novel ideological, regional, and socioethnic tensions or ruptures, and unwittingly open the colonial order to challenges from multiple fronts, both elite and subaltern. Santa Cruz's eclectic project to recompose the "Andean space" in the guise of an efficient federated, personalist, and authoritarian republic, with elements of modern constitutional and ethnic institutions of governance, also failed. But he accentuated the political role of the army and jelled the politics of regional blocs that would remain crucial in central Andean affairs for the next fifty years. García Moreno's project of an Ecuadorian Catholic people appears to have died with him, but the paternalistic recruitment of native Andeans for the nation in exchange for social and educational benefits would become more pronounced during the Liberal era after 1895. The strenuous efforts of fiscal decentralization in Peru after the War of the Pacific ultimately resulted in a reform of the taxation system that in crucial aspects did the opposite of the initial reform goals. It centralized the collection apparatus and shifted taxation once more toward indirect revenues on consumption, although it did accomplish the separation between tax collector and regional or local executive authorities. And the elitist and exclusivist notion of the public sphere entertained by Peru's late-nineteenth-century upper and professional classes was too contradictory and unreflective of reality to tidily shut out the pueblo from public deliberation. In Bolivia during the mid-1940s, the attempts by President Villarroel and urban populists to neutralize grassroots indigenous mobilizing through a politics of symbolic inclusion and modest social legislation instead contributed to radicalization in parts of the altiplano and the Cochabamba valleys. Even the unleashing of the Violencia in Antioquia by Conservative-controlled forces after 1948 unexpectedly resulted in the empowerment of the more radical and popular followers of Gaitán vis-à-vis the cautious middle-class and elite Liberal Party bosses. Thus the cunning of history—a cipher for unexpected social, economic, cultural, political, and international influences on the course of events—reliably gave Andean state-building projects a different direction and meaning than the initiating elites intended.

THE ENTANGLED RELATIONS BETWEEN AUTHORITARIAN/CLIENTELISTIC AND ENLIGHTENED/LIBERAL POLITICS

In his portrayal of the ideas and practices on which Andrés de Santa Cruz sought to build his Peru-Bolivian Confederation, Aljovín coins the felicitous phrase describing postcolonial Latin America as a "laboratory of politics." Those vying for power and in the process building republican political cultures in the decades immediately following independence relied on a "tool box" of ideas, practices, and institutions of governance that had become vastly larger over the preceding fifty years. Habsburg patrimonialism and corporatism; compacts between indigenous authorities and communities and the state; Andean notions of governance and legitimacy; distinct variants of liberal and constitutional conceptions; republicanism; vertical Caesarist notions of governance, with personalist ties between a quasi-charismatic president claiming the *suma de poder* and atomized citizens, kin, and client networks, articulated through the military as a vertebral column; and briefly even monarchy drawing on different fonts of legitimacy (European dynasties and the Incas): all formed part of the repertoire of Andean state making between the 1820s and 1840s. It was the extraordinary ethnic, social, regional, and economic disarticulation of the newly carved national spaces that made this phase of experimentation longer and more conflictual in most of Latin America than in the other republic emerging from the liberal-democratic revolutions, the United States.

In the Andean republics various unstable amalgams were forged from this repertoire, stressing the one or the other conception of governance more and downplaying or excluding others. During subsequent decades, the amalgams were frequently recomposed, and some conceptions of governance, such as those associated with native Andean authorities and Spanish corporatism and patrimonialism, were increasingly deemphasized (although not entirely forgotten by segments of the citizenry). Republicanism, with its emphasis on virtuous citizens, rule of law, and citizens' participation in public affairs through elections, militias, and public opinion, gained strength in most regions of the Andes during the century after independence. It formed ambiguous and as yet not fully understood amalgams both with liberalism and Caesarist or Catholic authoritarian conceptions of governance. In later eras of crisis—especially between the 1930s and 1970s—new conceptions of governance as state interventionism and socialism were added and older, chastised ones were remembered and reinvigorated in a new garb (Andean communalism and corporatism, most prominently). Again Andean and Latin American political experimentation seemed especially protracted and messy.

A prominent recent interpretation of Latin American politics during the nineteenth century has explained this messiness as the consequence of the confrontation between modern liberal and constitutional imaginaries quite suddenly imported from the North Atlantic during the revolutions of independence and "traditional" social structures. The drag from these social structures would have impeded the full implementation of "modern" political cultures and institutions. This interpretation has the merit of highlighting the tremendous innovation that liberalism, constitutionalism, and republicanism brought to Latin American political cultures and institutions in the years after 1810. But it is hard to see why Latin America's interaction with the rest of the world should have led to a tabula rasa in political imaginaries in favor of the new imports from the North Atlantic while social structures simply remained "traditional." Social historians of Latin America have shown how—since the very onset of European colonization—the gradual and uneven penetration of markets and capitalist complexes of production created a frequently changing and regionally diverse patchwork of social structures, conjoining—often within the same social group—elements of "traditional" and "modern" social structure. Aljovín demonstrates the same patchwork nature for the political imaginary of the Peru-Bolivian Confederation. Thus it appears more reasonable to envision instable amalgamations between elements derived from different historical and ethnic contexts for all dimensions of Andean societies and polities, mutually reinforcing or destabilizing each other, rather than imagining a conflict between modernity and tradition neatly aligned with the political and social dimensions. This is so especially since large segments of the Andean population did not think in terms of separated dimensions of politics, society, economy, and culture, a classification system only introduced by enlightened and liberal thinkers since the late eighteenth century.

In a simplified manner, we can say that many of the contributions to this volume demonstrate how enlightened/liberal and authoritarian/clientelistic elements of political ideas and practices have been entangled in the shifting political cultures of the postcolonial Andes. Depending on currents of ideas, political coalitions, and economic conjunctures, the liberal or authoritarian elements of these amalgams gained relative strength or were weakened. But at least before the mid-twentieth century, political movements, parties, or coalitions in the Andes (grassroots and elite-dominated) that entirely eschewed the one or the other of these elements in their explicit programs and in the praxis of politics remained rare and marginal.

The conclusions from the essays in this volume highlighted so far are hardly specific to Andean political cultures. The concern with race and gender for nation-state formation, the challenges to projects seeking to strengthen the state, and an eclectic amalgamation of various systems of governance and political doctrines have characterized most Latin American states in the past two centuries, although the way these issues played out obviously differed considerably, in, say, Argentina, Costa Rica, or Mexico from the way they did in Colombia or Ecuador. Anthropologists have little problem identifying what practices and norms are peculiar to native Andean cultures (at least between Quito and the Bolivian altiplano)—from reciprocity, verticality, and emphasis on dual and quadripartite systems of social and cultural classification to ancestor worship, and specific kinship, settlement, and land-use patterns. It is much harder to identify what may be specific to modern Andean political cultures. In the introduction we mentioned the important role that representations of the Incas and other native Andean civilizations have repeatedly played for providing a foundation myth for the nations of Ecuador, Peru, and Bolivia. Here we would like to propose two other facets of the region's emerging political cultures that may show unique inflections in the Andes compared with other parts of Latin America.

THE RELATION BETWEEN THE LOCAL AND THE NATIONAL OR STATEWIDE

We start with Serulnikov's perceptive observation about the difference between eighteenth-century rebellions or grassroots movements in Mexico and the southern Andes. He writes that William Taylor's characterization of village revolts in late-colonial New Spain as purely local affairs, arising out of local grievances and lacking broader ties and repercussions, does not work for Chayanta and other places in revolt during the Great Rebellion of the late 1770s and early 1780s. Serulnikov convincingly demonstrates how local grievances in Chayanta in that specific conjuncture were transformed into a more encompassing project, tying together ayllus, villages, and towns across broad regions. Could it be that this observation is applicable as well to social and political movements in other parts of the Andes and during other historical conjunctures?

Ever since the pre-Hispanic civilizations, Andean villages, ethnic polities, and, later, districts and provinces have shown an unusually strong and conflictive juxtaposition of local autonomy and engagement with regional, national, or pan-Andean cultural and political movements and patterns of exchange. This may well be grounded in the singular geographic environment of the Andes and the cultural, social, political, and economic adaptations to this environment that Andean societies have forged during the pre-Hispanic, colonial, and national eras. More than anywhere else in the Americas, ecologically highly diverse locales—ranging from tropical rain forests to temperate or frigid inter-Andean valleys and plains, and coastal deserts and riverine oases—are in close proximity to each other yet separated by forbidding mountain crags and steep gorges. Hundreds of Andean ethnic groups built cultures and polities well adapted to these diverse local environments, anchored in their own deities and foundation myths. But it was the pragmatic genius of these peoples to embrace the necessity of communications, exchange, and alliance with peoples in neighboring valleys and plains or further afield, or to colonize favorable spots in distinct ecological zones. Andeans have always been consummate travelers through this difficult terrain, whether to distant communities or towns for barter and trade, to religious shrines, or to centers of political power.

One image that has been employed to depict the relation between the local and the statewide in the Andes is that of "nested units." Just as with the Russian dolls within a doll, Andeans often have viewed their own well-defined and distinct local community as being encapsulated within the sphere of a regional authority which in turn is harbored and nourished by statewide authorities. An image coined for local communities and regional polities within the Inca empire, one still finds native Andean, mestizo, and Hispanic farmers and town folks during the nineteenth and twentieth centuries thinking about legitimate governance in such terms of nested units. In order to be viewed as legitimate on the local level, Andean governments have had to walk a tightrope: enforcing the general laws and incorporating communities, villages, and towns into the larger body politic on the one hand, and, on the other, protecting the autonomy and interests of those locales.

Movements in which the pursuit of local grievances quickly latched onto broader regional or national alliances of contestation can be found in various Andean settings throughout the nineteenth and twentieth centuries. From the Great Rebellion in the southern Andes and the Comunero Rebellion in the northern Andes around 1780, to the Bustamante Rebellion (1866–68), the anti-Chilean guerrillas of 1882–83, the Peruvian revolution of 1895, the Bolivian Federal Revolution of 1899, the cacique movement in Bolivia during the years between 1910 and 1930 and the simultaneous cycle of insurgency throughout southern Peru, the rural mobilizations throughout much of highland Bolivia in 1946–47 analyzed here by Gotkowitz, and perhaps even recent events such as the insurgency orchestrated by Sendero Luminoso in Peru and the nationalized movements for indigenous rights in Bolivia and

Ecuador: in all of them, local groups protesting local grievances—from abusive authorities to unfair tax collections, electoral fraud, theft of community lands, exploitation by outside business interests, inadequate schools and social programs—in short order proclaimed broader goals, allied with other groups in the region or nationally, and answered to supralocal leadership either forged from their own ranks or accepted from urban intellectuals-politicians. But once the crisis or insurgency was over and people returned home, the majority of citizens in communities or towns would revert to defending local autonomy within reciprocal ties to higher authorities.

THE POLITICS OF STALEMATE IN ANDEAN REPUBLICS

In his contribution to this volume, Charles Walker suggests that the failure of the Bourbon civilizing project initiated a period of political stalemates in the Andes, at least through the Liberal era, perhaps until today. He stresses two elements substantiating such a stalemate or impasse: the capacity of the various Andean subaltern groups to block ruling groups and the state from severe regulation and restriction of popular culture; and the internal divisiveness of those subaltern groups, which in turn prevented them from defeating those ruling groups.

We propose to broaden this notion of a politics of stalemate in the postcolonial Andes beyond the struggles over popular culture and the relations between subalterns and ruling groups. The notion has been applied to other parts of Latin America as well, but a case can be made that quasi-structural stalemates (recurring and/or persistent) have been especially damaging in the politics of the Andean republics. Besides the obvious and massive unresolved conflicts between variegated elite and popular groups, these have also involved regional and sectoral elites and political actors, vertical clientele groups, the military, and civil associations. The relative incapacity of the state to implement major reform projects thus not only owed to weaknesses of the state institutions themselves but also to the relation between the state and civil society and the feeble or absent consensus about the legitimacy of basic institutions and the rules of the game. This has meant that governing coalitions have often fragmented soon after coming to power so that their reforms remained truncated, or were reversed by subsequent governments. While the politics of stalemate has allowed experimentation, it has made institutionalization difficult. It seems to affect highly centralized political regimes such as that of Peru as much as those with a comparatively weak center, as in the case of Colombia. It has fostered, and in turn has itself been exacerbated by, a perception widely held among Andean politicians that the struggle over public-resource distribution is a zero-sum game, with very high stakes.

In Colombia the stalemate involved regional power blocs and the reluctance of those in power to extend state-resource distribution to peripheral areas and populations. This type of stalemate, with overlapping regional *and* socioethnic components, in large measure blocked the national accords of the entrenched elite parties from becoming a sufficiently broad basis of national consensus. The rupture of minimal elite consensus in the Violencia since the late 1940s demonstrated the explosiveness and potency of radical-populist alternative visions in the mantle of gaitanismo, as Mary Roldán shows in her chapter on Antioquia. In other words, Colombia's was a mediated stalemate in which elite consensus was too weak to inhibit or institutionally channel violent conflict between social and political groups and in regions outside its immediate control.

What has made the politics of stalemate so particularly severe in the Andean republics is this overlay of exclusivist elite norms and practices of socioethnic order *and* the fragility of consensus between elites, coalitions, and power contenders in distinct regions and sectors. The shallowness of sanctioned social and ethnic participation in national politics at least until the mid-twentieth century has meant that the deep crises of elite politics developing from insufficient basic consensus between regional and sectoral elites frequently erupted in militant and violent forms. Since native Andeans, African Americans, and other popular groups had routinely been treated as second-class citizens (or worse), their mobilization in these crises revealed a reservoir of resentments and far-reaching demands that their elite allies were unwilling or unable to support. The stalemates thus often owed their severity to the mutually reenforcing effects of the lack of broad-based elite consensus, the entrenched practices of social and political exclusion of popular groups, and their routine authoritarian subordination. Stalemate has meant that it has proved extraordinarily difficult to overcome these legacies.

• • • • •

This book has sought to advance an understanding of changing political cultures during two formative centuries of the modern Andean republics.

Much appears in these pages that could make the reader fainthearted or even dismissive of politics in the Andes: the elites' pretensions to exclusive power, and their hierarchical norms and practices regarding race, gender, and class; the limited success of state-building projects, and the concomitant routine gap between beautiful political plans and declarations and their indifferent realization; the frequent use of violence to achieve political ends; in short, the narrow space of maneuver for a decent, democratic politics in republics still adequately characterized as neo- or postcolonial. But the careful reader will also notice far less gloomy tones in the authors' depictions of Andean political cultures: the repeated and ongoing capacity of popular groups to wrest concessions from exclusivist elites; the frequent mollification or abandonment of the most draconian and repressive political projects; popular groups' appropriation and recasting of political concepts espoused by the elites; and the emergence of middle sectors—in terms of class, education, and ethnic identity—not easily categorized by the exclusivist, polarizing, black-and-white terms of elite pretensions. The authors in this volume share an appreciation of the fact that in the Andes the harsh authoritarian relations of power have been contingent and less stable than often assumed. The pragmatic approach to political culture espoused in this book suggests that scholars need to explore the dimensions of both longer-term trajectories or path dependencies and the short-term plasticity or malleability of specific historical conjunctures. There are no preordained structures that now or at any time in the past have condemned the citizens of the Andean republics to be beggars sitting on a mountain of gold, or commoners crouched under the sable of authoritarian rulers. Through painful struggles Andean political cultures have developed their own paths toward more inclusive politics.

BIBLIOGRAPHY

Abercrombie, Thomas. "To Be Indian to Be Bolivian: 'Ethnic' and 'National' Discourses of Identity." in *Nation-States and Indians in Latin America*, edited by Greg Urban and Joel Sherzer, 95–130. Austin: University of Texas Press, 1991.

——. "La fiesta del carnaval postcolonial en Oruro: Clase, etnicidad y nacionalismo en la danza folklórica." *Revista Andina* 10, 2 (1992): 279–352.

——. "Q'aqchas and *la plebe* in 'Rebellion': Carnival vs. Lent in Eighteenth Century Potosí." *Journal of Latin American Anthropology* 2, 1 (1996): 62–111.

——. *Pathways of Memory and Power. Ethnography and History Among an Andean People.* Madison: University of Wisconsin Press, 1998.

Adelman, Jeremy, ed. *Colonial Legacies: The Problem of Persistence in Latin American History.* New York: Routledge, 1999.

——. "Introduction: The Problem of Persistence in Latin American History." In *Colonial Legacies: The Problem of Persistence in Latin American History*, edited by Jeremy Adelman, 1–14. New York: Routledge, 1999.

——. *Republic of Capital. Buenos Aires and the Legal Transformation of the Atlantic World.* Stanford: Stanford University Press, 1999.

Adler Lomnitz, Larissa, and Ana Melnick. *Chile's Political Culture and Parties: An*

Anthropoligical Explanation. Notre Dame, Ind.: Notre Dame Univresity Press, 2000.

Adorno, Theodor, Else Frenkel-Brunswick, Daniel Levinson and Sanford Nevitt. *The Authoritarian Personality.* New York: Norton, 1950.

Adrian, Mónica. "Sociedad civil, clero y axiología oficial durante la rebelión de Chayanta. Una aproximación a partir de la actuación del cura doctrinero de San Pedro de Macha." *Boletín del Instituto de Historia Americana "Dr. E. Ravignani,"* 8 (1993, 2nd semester), 29–54.

——. "Reformas borbónicas y políticas locales. Las doctrinas de Chayanta durante la segunda mitad del siglo XVIII." *Revista del Instituto de Derecho* 23 (1995): 11–35.

——. "Los curatos en la provincia de Chayanta durante la segunda mitad del siglo XVIII." *Data* 6 (1996): 97–117.

Aguila, Alicia del. *Callejones y mansiones: Espacios de opinión pública y redes sociales y políticas en la Lima del 900.* Lima: PUCP, 1997.

Aguilera Peña, Mario, and Renán Vega Cantor. *Ideal democrático y revuelta popular: Bosquejo histórico de la mentalidad política popular en Colombia, 1781–1948.* Bogotá: ISMAC, 1991.

Aguirre, Carlos. *Agentes de su propia libertad: Los esclavos de Lima y la desintegración de la esclavitud, 1821–1854.* Lima: Pontifícia Universidad Católica del Perú, 1993.

Alape, Arturo. *El Bogotazo, memorias del olvido.* Bogotá: Editorial Pluma, 1983.

Alarcón, José C. *Compendio de historia del departamento del Magdalena (desde 1525 hasta 1895)* [1900]. Bogotá: Editorial El Voto Nacional, reprint 1973.

Albó, Xavier. "From MNRistas to Kataristas to Katari." In *Resistance, Rebellion and Consciousness in the Andean Peasant World, Eighteenth to Twentieth Centuries,* edited by Steve Stern, 379–419. Madison: University of Wisconsin Press, 1987.

——. "Andean People in the Twentieth Century." In *The Cambridge History of the Native Peoples of the Americas,* vol. 3, *South America,* part 2, edited by Frank Salomon and Stuart B. Schwartz, 765–861. Cambridge: Cambridge University Press, 1999.

Aljovín de Losada, Cristóbal. *Caudillos y constituciones: Perú 1821–1845.* Lima: PUCP, IRA, FCE, 2000.

Almond, Gabriel A. "Comparative Political Systems," *Journal of Politics* 18 (1956): 391–409.

——. "Foreword: The Return to Political Culture." In *Political Culture and Democracy in Developing Countries,* edited by Larry Diamond. Boulder and London: Lynne Rienner, 1993.

——. "The Study of Political Culture." In *Political Culture in Germany,* edited by Dirk Berg-Schlosser and Ralf Rytlewski. New York: St. Martin's, 1993.

——. and Sidney Verba. *The Civic Culture. Political Attitudes in Five Nations.* Princeton: Princeton University Press, 1963.

——. and Sidney Verba, eds. *The Civic Culture Revisited.* Boston: Little, Brown, 1980.

Anderson, Benedict. *Imagined Communities: Reflections on the Origins and Spread of Nationalism.* London: Verso, 1986.

Andrade Padilla, Claudio. *La rebelión de Tomás Katari.* Sucre: CIPRES, 1994.

André, Edouardo. "América equinoccial (Colombia-Ecuador)." In *América pintoresca: Descripción de viajes al nuevo continente por los más modernos exploradores, Carlos Wiener, Doctor Crevaux, D. Charnay, etc., etc.* Barcelona: Montaner y Simon, Editores, 1884.

Anna, Timothy E. "Spain and the Breakdown of the Imperial Ethos: The Problem of Equality." *Hispanic American Historical Review* 62 (1982): 242–72.

Annino, Antonio, ed. *Historia de las elecciones en Ibero-América, siglo XIX: la formación del espacio político nacional.* Bueno Aires: Fondo de Cultura Económica, 1995.

Antezana E., Luis and Hugo Romero B. *Los sindicatos campesinos. Un proceso de integración nacional en Bolivia.* La Paz: Consejo Nacional de Reforma Agraria, Departamento de Investigaciones Sociales, 1973.

Appelbaum, Nancy. "Whitening the Region: Caucano Mediation and 'Antioqueño Colonization' in Nineteenth Century Colombia." *Hispanic American Historical Review* 79, 4 (1999): 631–68.

Appleby, Joyce, Lynn Hunt and Margaret Jacob. *Telling the Truth About History.* New York: Norton, 1994.

Aranda, Ricardo. *La Constitución del Perú de 1860, con sus reformas hasta 1893.* Lima, 1893.

Ardant, Gabriel "Financial Policy and Economic Infrastructure of Modern States and Nations." In *The Formation of National States in Western Europe,* edited by Charles Tilly, 164–242. Princeton: Princeton University Press, 1975.

Arguedas, Alcides. *Pueblo Enfermo* [1909]. La Paz: Puerta del Sol, 1936.

——. *Raza de Bronce* [1919]. La Paz: Gisbert y Cía., 1976.

——. *Historia general de Bolivia* [1922]. La Paz: Gisbert y Cía., 1975.

——. *Los caudillos bárbaros* [1928]. La Paz: Gisbert y Cía., 1975.

Armas Asin, Fernando. *Liberales, protestantes y masones: modernidad y tolerancia religiosa: Perú, siglo XIX.* Cusco and Lima: CBC and Pontifícia Universidad Católica del Perú, 1998.

Aron, Raymond. *Main Currents in Sociological Thought.* 2 vols. Garden City, N.Y.: Anchor, 1968.

Arrázola, Roberto. *Los mártires responden.* Cartagena: Ediciones Hernández, 1973.

——, ed. *Documentos para la historia de Cartagena.* 2 vols. Cartagena: Edición Oficial, 1963.

Arrom, Silvia M. *Containing the Poor: The Mexico City Poor House, 1774–1871.* Durham, N.C.: Duke University Press, 2001.

Arrom, Silvia M., and Servando Ortoll, eds. *Riots in the Cities: Popular Politics and the Urban Poor in Latin America 1765–1810.* Wilmington, Del.: SR Books, 1996.

Aubert, Roger et al. *The Church in the Age of Liberalism.* Translated by Peter Becker. New York: Crossroad Pub. Co., 1981. [Series: *History of the Church,* v. 8]

Ayala Mora, Enrique. *Historia de la revolución liberal ecuatoriana.* Quito: Corporación Editora Nacional, 1994.

Baker, Keith M. "Introduction." In *The French Revolution and the Creation of Modern Political Culture*, vol. 1, *The Creation of the Old Regime,* edited by Keith M. Baker, xi–xxiv. Oxford: Pergamon Press, 1987.

——. *Inventing the French Revolution.* Cambridge: Cambridge University Press, 1994.

Baltes, Peter. "José María Pando, colaborador de Gamarra." B.A. thesis, Pontifícia Universidad Católica del Perú, 1968.

——. "José María Pando, colaborador peruano de Simón Bolívar." Ph.D. dissertation, Pontifícia Universidad Católica del Perú, 1968.

Barragan Romano, Rossana. *Indios, mujeres y ciudadanos: Legislación y ejercicio de la ciudadanía en Bolivia (siglo XIX).* La Paz: Fundación Diálogo, 1999.

Basadre, Jorge. *La multitud, la ciudad y el campo en la historia del Perú.* Lima: Ediciones Treintaitrés & Mosca Azul, 1980.

Baumeister, R. F. *Identity, Cultural Change and the Struggle for Self.* Oxford and New York: Oxford University Press, 1986.

Baylin, Bernard. *The Ideological Origins of the American Revolution.* Cambridge, Mass: Harvard University Press, 1967.

Beezley, William H., Cheryl E. Martin, and William E. French, eds. *Rituals of Rule, Rituals of Resistance: Public Celebrations and Popular Culture in Mexico.* Wilmington, Del.: SR Books, 1994.

Bell Lemus, Gustavo. "Conflictos regionales y centralismo: Una hipótesis sobre las relaciones políticas de la Costa Caribe con el gobierno central en los primeros años de la república, 1821–1840." In *El Caribe colombiano. Selección de textos históricos,* edited by Gustavo Bell Lemus, 39–48. Barranquilla: Editorial Uninorte, 1988.

——. *Cartagena de Indias: de la colonia a la república.* Bogotá: Fundación Simón y Lola Guberek, 1991.

Bendix, Reinhard. *Max Weber: An Intellectual Portrait.* Garden City, N.Y.: Anchor Books, 1962.

Benjamin, Thomas. *A Rich Land, a Poor People.* Albuquerque: University of New Mexico Press, 1989.

Bergquist, Charles, Ricardo Peñaranda and Gonzalo Sánchez, eds. *Violence in Co-*

lombia: The Contemporary Crisis in Historical Perspective. Wilmington, Del.: SR Publications, 1992.

Berg-Schlosser, Dirk. *Politische Kultur: Eine neue Dimension politikwissenschaftlicher Analyse.* München: Ernst Vögel Verlag, 1972.

Blackmore, Susan. *The Meme Machine.* Oxford: Oxford University Press, 1999.

Blanchard, Peter. "The Recruitment of Workers in the Peruvian Sierra at the Turn of the Century: The Enganche System." *Inter-American Economic Affairs* 33 (1979): 63–83.

——. *Slavery and Abolition in Early Republican Peru.* Wilmington, Del.: SR Books, 1992.

Bobbio, Norberto. *Democracy and Dictatorship.* Minneapolis: University of Minnesota Press, 1989 [1978].

Bolívar, Simón. *Obras completas.* Edited by Vicente Lecuña. 2 vols. La Habana: Editorial Lex, 1947.

——. *Discursos, proclamas y epistolario político.* Edited by M. Hernández Sánchez-Barba. Madrid: Editora Nacional, 1975.

Bonilla, Heraclio. "The War of the Pacific and the National and Colonial Problem in Peru." *Past and Present* 81 (1978): 92–118.

——. "The Indian Peasantry and 'Peru' During the War With Chile." In *Resistance, Rebellion and Consciousness in the Andean Peasant World, Eighteenth to Twentieth Centuries,* edited by Steve J. Stern, 219–31. Madison: University of Wisconsin Press, 1987.

Bossa Herazo, Donaldo. *Cartagena independiente: Tradición y desarrollo.* Bogotá: Ediciones Tercer Mundo, 1967.

Bourdieu, Pierre. *El sentido práctico,* Madrid: Taurus, 1991 [first French ed. 1982].

Brading, David A. *The Origins of Mexican Nationalism.* Cambridge: Cambridge University Press, 1975.

——. "Bourbon Spain and Its American Empire." In *Cambridge History of Latin America,* vol. 2, edited by Leslie Bethell, 112–62. Cambridge: Cambridge University Press, 1987.

——. *The First America. The Spanish Monarchy, Creole Patriotism, and the Liberal State, 1492–1867.* Cambridge: Cambridge University Press, 1991.

Braun, Herbert. *The Assassination of Gaitán: Public Life and Urban Violence in Colombia.* Madison: University of Wisconsin Press, 1985.

Burga, Manuel. *Nacimiento de una utopía: Muerte y resurrección de los incas.* Lima: Instituto de Apoyo Agrario, 1988.

Burns, Kathryn. *Colonial Habits: Convents and the Spiritual Economy of Cuzco.* Durham, N.C.: Duke University Press, 1999.

Bushnell, David. *The Making of Modern Colombia: A Nation in Spite of Itself.* Berkeley: University of California Press, 1993.

Cahill, David. "Popular Religion and Appropriation: The Example of Corpus Christi in Eighteenth-Century Peru." *Latin America Research Review* 31, 2 (1996): 67–110.

Caicedo, Amanda and Ivan Espinosa, "'Públicos ladrones' en la Gobernación de Popayán." *Historia y Espacio* (Cali), no. 16 (2000): 91–108.

Calisto, Marcela. "Peasant Resistance in the Aymara Districts of the Highlands of Perú, 1900–1930: An Attempt at Self-Governance." Ph.D. dissertation, University of California at San Diego, 1993.

Campbell, Leon. *The Military and Society in Colonial Peru, 1750–1810.* Philadelphia: American Philosophical Society, 1978.

——. "Social Structure of the Túpac Amaru Army in Cuzco, 1780–81." *Hispanic American Historical Review* 61 (1981): 3–49.

——. "Ideology and Factionalism during the Great Rebellion, 1780–1782." In *Resistance, Rebellion, and Consciousness in the Andean Peasant World, Eighteenth to Twentieth Centuries,* edited by Steve Stern, 110–42. Madison: University of Wisconsin Press, 1987.

Campbell, Peter R. *Power and Politics in Old Regime France, 1720–1745.* New York: Routledge, 1966.

Campos Harriet, Fernando. *Desarrollo educacional, 1810–1960.* Santiago: Editorial Andrés Bello, 1960.

Cañaberal y Ponce, J. de. "El deber de vivir ordenadamente para obedecer al rey." In *Anuario Colombiano de Historia Social y de la Cultura,* no. 20 (1992): 109–131.

Capelo, Joaquin. *Sociologia de Lima.* 3 vols. Lima, 1895–1900.

Casalino Sen, Carlota. "Higiene pública y piedad ilustrada: La cultura de la muerte bajo los Borbones." In *El Perú en el siglo XVIII,* edited by Scarlett O'Phelan Godoy, 325–44. Lima: Pontifícia Universidad Católica del Perú, 1999.

Castro Trespalacios, Pedro. *Culturas aborígenes cesarenses e independencia de Valle de Upar.* Bogotá: Biblioteca de Autores Cesarenses, 1979.

Catholic Church. Ecuador. *Decretos del Primer Concilio Provincial Quitense celebrado en el año de 1863.* Quito, 1869.

——. *Segundo Sinodo Diocesano Quitense Celebrado en la Iglesia Metropolitana de Quito por el Ilmo. y Rmo. Señor Doctor Don José Ignacio Checa y Barba, Arzobispo de Quito, en los dias 6, 20 y 22 de junio del año de 1869.* Quito: Imprenta de J. Campuzano, por J. Villavicencio, 1869.

Cevallos, Pedro Fermín. *Resumen de la historia del Ecuador.* Vol. 6. Guayaquil: Imprenta de la Nación, 1889.

Chambers, Sarah. *From Subjects to Citizens, Honor, Gender and Politics in Arequipa, Peru, 1780–1854.* University Park: Pennsylvania State University Press, 1999.

——. "Republican Friendship: Manuela Sáenz Writes Women into the Nation, 1835–1856." *Hispanic American Historical Review* 81, 2 (2001): 225–58.

Chartier, Roger. *Cultural Origins of the French Revolution.* Durham, N.C.: Duke University Press, 1991.

Chatterjee, Partha. *The Nation and its Fragments: Colonial and Postcolonial Histories.* Princeton: Princeton University Press, 1993.

Chiaramonti, Gabriella. "Andes o nación: la reforma electoral de 1896 en Perú." In *Historia de las elecciones en Iberoamérica, siglo XIX,* edited by Antonio Annino, 315–47. Mexico: FCE, 1995.

Choque, Roberto. *La sublevación de Jesús de Machaqa.* La Paz: Chitakolla, 1986.

——. "Las rebeliones indígenas de la post-guerra del Chaco. Reivindicaciones indígenas durante la prerevolución." *Data* 3 (1992): 37–53.

Choque, Roberto, et al., eds. *Educación indígena: ¿Ciudadanía o colonización?* La Paz: Aruwiyiri, 1992.

Choque, Roberto, and Esteban Ticona. *Jesús de Machaca, la marka rebelde: Sublevación y masacre de 1921.* La Paz: CIPCA/CEDOIN, 1996.

Clark, Kim. *The Redemptive Work: Railway and Nation in Ecuador, 1895–1930.* Wilmington, Del.: SR Books, 1998.

Clement, Jean-Pierre. "El nacimiento de la higiene urbana en la América española del siglo XVIII." *Revista de Indias* 171 (1983): 77–95.

Coatsworth, John H. "The Limits of Colonial Absolutism: The State in Eighteenth-Century Mexico." *Essays in the Political, Economic and Social History of Colonial Latin America,* edited by Karen Spalding, 25–51. Newark: University of Delaware Press, 1982.

——. "Patterns of Rural Rebellion in Latin America: Mexico in Comparative Perspective." In *Riot, Rebellion, and Revolution: Rural Social Conflict in Mexico,* edited by Friedrich Katz, 21–64. Princeton: Princeton University Press, 1988.

Colmenares, Germán. "La nación y la historia regional en los paises andinos, 1870–1930." *Revista Andina* 3, 2 (1985): 311–42.

——. "Región-nación: problemas de poblamiento en la época colonial." *Revista de Extensión Cultural de la Universidad Nacional de Colombia* (Medellín), nos. 27–28 (June 1991): 6–15.

Colombia, República de. Sala de Negocios Generales del Consejo de Estado. *Codificación nacional de todas las leyes de Colombia desde el año de 1821, hecha conforme a la ley 13 de 1912.* 24 vols. Bogotá: Imprenta Nacional, 1924–33.

Comaroff, Jean and John Comaroff. *Of Revelation and Revolution: Civilization, Colonialism, and Consciousness in South Africa.* Vol. 1. Chicago: University of Chicago Press, 1991.

Comaroff, John L. "Foreword." In *Contested States: Law, Hegemony and Resistance,* edited by Mindie Lazarus-Black and Susan F. Hirsch, ix–xiii. New York: Routledge, 1994.

——. "Legality, Modernity, and Ethnicity in Colonial South Africa: An Excursion in the Historical Anthropology of Law." In *Law, Society, and Economy: Centenary Essays for the London School of Economics and Political Science, 1895–1995*, edited by Richard Rawlings, 247–69. Oxford: Oxford University Press, 1997.

Condarco Morales, Ramiro. *Zarate, el temible Willka: Historia de la rebelión indígena de 1899.* La Paz: n.p., 1965.

Conde Calderón, J. "Castas y conflictos en la provincia de Cartagena del Nuevo Reino de Granada a finales del siglo XVIII." *Historia y Sociedad* (Medellín), no. 3 (1996): 83–101.

Condori Chura, Leandro and Estaban Ticona Alejo. *El escribano de los caciques apoderados; kasikinakan purirarunakan qillqiripa.* La Paz: HISBOL/THOA, 1992.

Conniff, Michael, ed. *Latin American Populism.* Albuquerque: University of New Mexico Press, 1982.

Consejo Regional de Planificación de la Costa Atlántica. *Mapa cultural del Caribe colombiano.* Santa Marta: Consejo Regional de Planificación de la Costa Atlántica, 1993.

Constant, Benjamin. "The Liberty of the Ancients Compared with That of the Moderns [1819]." In *Benjamin Constant: Political Writings,* edited by Biancamaria Fontana. Cambridge: Cambridge University Press, 1989.

Contreras, Carlos. "Estado republicano y tributo indígena en la sierra central en la postindependencia." *Histórica* 13, 1 (1989): 9–44.

——. "La descentralización fiscal en el Perú después de la guerra con Chile, 1886–1895." *Relaciones. Estudios de Historia y Sociedad,* nos. 67–68 (1996): 203–31.

Cope, R. Douglas. *The Limits of Racial Domination: Plebeian Society in Colonial Mexico City, 1660–1720.* Madison: University of Wisconsin Press, 1994.

Cornblit, Oscar. *Power and Violence in the Colonial City: Oruro from the Mining Renaissance to the Rebellion of Túpac Amaru (1740–1782).* New York: Cambridge University Press, 1995.

Corrales, Manuel Ezequiel, ed. *Documentos para la historia de la provincia de Cartagena de Indias, hoy estado soberano de Bolívar en la unión colombiana.* 2 vols. Bogotá: Imprenta de Medardo Rivas, 1883.

——, ed. *Efemérides y anales del estado de Bolívar.* 4 vols. Bogotá: Casa Editorial de J. J. Pérez, 1889.

Corrigan, Philip and Derek Sayer. *The Great Arch: English State Formation as Culture Revolution.* Oxford: Oxford University Press, 1985.

Cosamalón Aguilar, Jesús. *Indios detrás de la muralla.* Lima: Pontifícia Universidad Católica del Perú, 1999.

Crespo, Alfonso. *Santa Cruz, el cóndor indio.* México: FCE, 1944.

Dancuart, Pedro E. and José M. Rodríguez. *Anales de la hacienda pública del Perú.* 24 vols. Lima: Lit. y Tip. Scheuch, 1902–1921.

Dandler, Jorge and Juan Torrico. "From the National Indigenous Congress to the Ayopaya Rebellion: Bolivia, 1945–1947." In *Resistance, Rebellion, and Consciousness in the Andean Peasant World, Eighteeenth to Twentieth Centuries*, edited by Steve J. Stern, 334–78. Madison: University of Wisconsin Press, 1987.

Darnton, Robert. "An Enlightened Revolution?" *The New York Review of Books*, Oct. 24, 1991.

——. *The Forbidden Bestsellers of Pre-Revolutionary France.* New York: Norton, 1995.

De Angelis, Pedro. *Colección de obras y documentos relativos a la historia antigua y moderna de las provincias del Río de la Plata* [1836]. Buenos Aires: Plus Ultra, 1971.

de Certeau, Michel. *The Practice of Everyday Life.* Berkeley: University of California Press, 1984.

——. *Heterologies: Discourse on the Other.* Translated by Brian Massumi. Minneapolis: University of Minnesota Press, 1986.

de la Cadena, Marisol. *Indigenous Mestizos: The Politics of Race and Culture in Cuzco Peru, 1919–1991.* Durham, N.C.: Duke University Press, 2000.

de la Fuente, Ariel. *Children of Facundo: Caudillo and Gaucho Insurgency During the Argentine State-Formation Process (La Rioja, 1853–1870).* Durham, N.C.: Duke University Press, 2000.

Dealy, Glen. "Prolegomena on the Spanish American Political Tradition." *Hispanic American Historical Review* 48 (1968): 37–58.

Deans-Smith, Susan. "The Working Poor and the Eighteenth-Century Colonial State: Gender, Public Order, and Work Discipline." In *Rituals of Rule, Rituals of Resistance: Public Celebrations and Popular Culture in Mexico*, edited by William Beezley et al., 47–75. Wilmington: SR Books, 1994.

Deas, Malcolm. *Del poder y la gramática; y otros ensayos sobre historia, política y literatura colombiana.* Bogotá: Tercer Mundo, 1993.

Declaración de principios del Partido Demócrata, Perú. Lima: Tip. La Voce d'Italia, 1912 [1889].

Demélas, Marie Danielle. "Darwinismo a la criolla: El darwinismo social en Bolivia, 1880–1910." *Historia Boliviana* 1–2 (1981): 55–82.

Demélas-Bohy, Marie Danielle. *L'invention politique: Bolivie, Equateur, Pérou au XIX siècle.* Paris: Editions Recherches sur les Civilisations, 1992.

——, "Modalidades y significación de eleccciones generales en los pueblos andinos." In *Historia de las elecciones en Iberoamérica, siglo XIX*, edited by Antonio Annino, 291–314. México: FCE, 1995.

Demélas-Bohy, Marie Danielle, and Yves Saint-Geours. *Jerusalén y Babilonia: religión y política en el Ecuador.* Quito: Corporación Editora Nacional, 1988.

Denegri, Francesca. *El abanico y la cigarrera: La primera generación de mujeres ilustradas en el Perú.* Lima: Ed. Flora Tristan and IEP, 1996.

Dennett, Daniel C. *Darwin's Dangerous Idea.* London: Penguin, 1996.

Dennis, Philip A. *Conflictos por tierras en el Valle de Oaxaca.* Mexico: INI, 1976.

Denoon, Donald. *Settler Capitalism: The Dynamics of Dependent Development in the Southern Hemisphere.* Oxford: Clarendon Press, 1983.

Deustua, José, and José Luis Rénique. *Intelectuales, indigenismo y descentralismo en el Perú, 1897–1931.* Cuzco: CBC, 1984.

Diamond, Larry. "Introduction: Political Culture and Democracy." In *Political Culture and Democracy in Developing Countries,* edited by Larry Diamond, 1–33. Boulder: Lynne Rienner, 1993.

Díaz Callejas, Apolinar. *El 9 de abril 1948 en Barrancabermeja: Diez días de poder popular.* Bogotá: El Labrador, 1988.

Diez Hurtado, Alejandro. *Comunes y haciendas: Procesos de comunalización en la Sierra de Piura, siglos XVIII a XX.* Piura and Cuzco: CIPCA and CBC, 1998.

Doering, Juan Gunther, and Guillermo Lohmann Villena. *Lima.* Colección Ciudades de Iberoamérica, 4. Madrid: Editorial MAPFRE, 1992.

Dore, Elizabeth. "One Step Forward, Two Steps Back: Gender and the State in the Long Nineteenth Century." In *Hidden Histories of Gender and the State in Latin America,* edited by Elizabeth Dore and Maxine Molyneux, 3–32. Durham and London: Duke University Press, 2000.

Dulanto Pinillos, Jorge. *Nicolás de Piérola.* Lima: Comp. de Impresiones y Publicidad, 1947.

Dunkerley, James. *Rebellion in the Veins: Political Struggle in Bolivia, 1952–82.* London: Verso, 1984.

Earle, Rebecca. "Popular Participation in the Wars of Independence in New Granada." In *Independence and Revolution in Spanish America: Perspectives and Problems,* edited by Anthony McFarlane and Eduardo Posada-Carbó, 87–101. London: Institute of Latin American Studies, University of London, 1999.

——. *Spain and the Independence of Colombia, 1810–1825.* Exeter: University of Exeter Press, 2000.

Eastman, Jorge Mario, ed. *Jorge Eliécer Gaitán, Obras selectas.* Vol. 1, *Colección pensadores políticos colombianos.* Bogotá: n.p., 1979.

Eckstein, Harry. *Division and Cohesion in Democracy: A Study of Norway.* Princeton: Princeton University Press, 1966.

——. *Regarding Politics. Essays on Political Theory, Stability, and Change.* Berkeley: University of California Press, 1992.

Ecuador. Minister of Interior. *Informe del Ministro de lo Interior . . . del Ecuador . . . 1872 y 1873.* Quito: Imprenta del Gobierno, 1873.

——. *Leyes, decretos legislativos y ejecutivos y circulares espedidos en 1869, 1870, 71, 72, 73 y 74.* Quito: Imprenta Nacional, 1874.

Eley, Geoff. "Nations, Publics, and Political Cultures: Placing Habermas in the Nineteenth Century." In *Habermas and the Public Sphere,* edited by Craig Calhoun, 289–339. Cambridge, Mass.: MIT Press, 1992.

Elkins, Stanley M. *Slavery: A Problem in American Institutional and Intellectual Life.* Chicago: University of Chicago Press, 1959.

Escritores políticos. Puebla: J.M. Cajico Jr., 1960. [Series: Biblioteca ecuatoriana minima. La colonia y la república]

Espinosa Descalzo, Victoria. *Cartografía de Lima (1654–1893).* Lima: Seminario de Historia Rural Andina-UNMSM, 1999.

Espinoza, Carlos. "Colonial Visions: Drama, Art, and Legitimation in Peru and Ecuador." In *Native Artists and Patrons in Colonial Latin America,* edited by Emily Umberger and Tom Cummins, 84–106. Tempe: Arizona State University, 1995.

Estenssoro Fuchs, Juan Carlos. *Música y sociedades coloniales: Lima 1680–1830.* Lima: Colmillo Blanco, 1989.

——. "Modernismo, estética, música, y fiesta: Elites y cambio de actitud frente a la cultura popular, Perú 1750–1850." In *Tradición y modernidad en los Andes,* edited by Henrique Urbano, 181–96. Cusco: CBC, 1992.

——. "La plebe ilustrada: El pueblo en las fronteras de la razón." In *Entre la retórica y la insurgencia: Las ideas y los movimientos sociales en los Andes, siglo XVIII,* edited by Charles Walker, 33–66. Cuzco: CBC, 1996.

——. "Los colores de la plebe: razón y mestizaje en el Perú colonial." In *Los cuadros de mestizaje del Virrey Amat,* edited by Natalia Majluf, 68–107. Lima: Museo de Arte de Lima, 2000.

Esteva Fabregat, C. *El mestizaje en Iberoamérica.* Madrid: Alhambra, 1988.

Ezyaguirre, Ignacio Victor. *Los intereses católicos en América.* Vol. 2. Paris: Garnier Hermanos, 1859.

Fals Borda, Orlando. *Historia doble de la costa.* Vol. 2, *El presidente Nieto.* Bogotá: Carlos Valencia Editores, 1981.

Farnsworth Alvear, Ann. *Dulcinea in the Factory: Myths, Morals, Men and Women in Colombia's Industrial Experiment, 1905–1960.* Durham, N.C.: Duke University Press, 2000.

Federación Rural de Cochabamba. *Memoria de la tercera conferencia nacional de agricultura, ganadería e industrias derivadas realizada en Cochabamba.* Cochabamba: Editorial Atlantic, 1946.

Fidalgo, Joaquín Francisco. "Expedición Fidalgo: Derrotero de las costas de la América septentrional desde Maracaibo hasta el río de Chagres. . . ." [1790s]. In *Colección de documentos inéditos sobre la geografía y la historia de Colombia,* edited by Antonio B. Cuervo, 1: 1–305. 4 vols. Bogotá: Imprenta de Vapor de Zalamea Hermanos, 1891.

Fisher, John R. *Government and Society in Colonial Peru: The Intendant System, 1784–1814.* London: Athlone Press, 1970.

——. "La rebelión de Túpac Amaru y el programa imperial de Carlos III." In *Túpac Amaru II-1780,* edited by Alberto Flores Galindo, 107–28. Lima: Retablo de Papel Ediciones, 1976.

——. "Royalism, Regionalism, and Rebellion in Colonial Peru, 1808–1815." *Hispanic American Historical Review* 59, 2 (1979): 232–57.

——, Allan Kuethe, and Anthony McFarlane, eds. *Reform and Insurrection in Bourbon New Granada and Peru.* Baton Rouge: Louisiana State University Press, 1990.

Fitzgibbon, Russell, and Julio A. Fernandez, eds. *Latin America: Political Culture and Development.* Englewood Cliffs, N.J.: Prentice Hall, 1981.

Flores Galindo, Alberto. *Aristocracia y plebe: Lima, 1760–1830.* Lima: Mosca Azul, 1984.

——. *Buscando un Inca: identidad y utopía en los Andes.* Lima: Instituto de Apoyo Agrario, 1987.

Fontana, Benedetto. *Hegemony and Power: On the Relation Between Gramsci and Machiavelli.* Minneapolis: University of Minnesota Press, 1993.

Fontana, Josef. *La crisis del antiguo régimen.* Barcelona: Crítica, 1979.

Forment, Carlos. "La sociedad civil en el Perú del siglo XIX: democrática o disciplinaria?" In *Ciudadanía política y formación de los naciones: perspectivas históricas de América Latina,* edited by Hilda Sabato, 202–52. Mexico, D.F.: Colegio de México and Fondo de Cultura Económica, 1999.

——. "La sociedad civil y la invención de la democracia en el Perú del tardío siglo diezinueve: una perspectiva Tocquevilliana." In *Culturas políticas en los Andes, 1750–1950,* edited by Cristóbal Aljovín de Losada and Nils Jacobsen. Lima: Universidad Nacional Mayor de San Marcos, forthcoming.

——. *Democracy in Latin America, 1760–1900.* Vol. 1, *Civic Selfhood and Public Life in Mexico and Peru.* Chicago: University of Chicago Press, 2003.

Formisano, Ronald. "The Concept of Political Culture." *Journal of Interdisciplinary History* 31, 3 (2001): 393–426.

Foucault, Michel. *Discipline and Punish: The Birth of the Prison.* New York: Vintage Books, 1995.

Furet, François. *Interpreting the French Revolution.* Cambridge: Cambridge University Press, 1981.

Gaitán, Jorge Eliécer. *Las Ideas Socialistas en Colombia.* Bogotá: n.p., 1984.

Galvez, Manuel. *Vida de Don Gabriel García Moreno.* Buenos Aires: Editorial Difusión, 1942.

Gargurevich Regal, Juan. *Historia de la prensa peruana, 1594–1990.* Lima: La Voz Ediciones, 1991.

Garrido, Margarita. *Reclamos y representaciones. Variaciones sobre la política en el Nuevo Reino de Granada 1770–1815.* Bogotá: Banco de la República, 1993.

Garzón Heredia, Emilio. "1780: Clero, elite local y rebelión." In *Entre la retórica y la insurgencia,* edited by Charles Walker, 245–72. Cusco: CBC, 1995.

Geertz, Clifford. *The Interpretation of Cultures: Selected Essays.* New York: Basic Books, 1973.

Gendzel, Glen. "Political Culture: Genealogy of a Concept." *Journal of Interdisciplinary History* 28, 2 (1997): 225–51.

Giménez Fernández, Manuel. "Las doctrinas populistas en la independencia de Hispanoamérica." *Anuario de Estudios Americanos* 3 (1946): 517–666.

Glave, Luis Miguel. "Sociedad campesina y violencia rural en el escenario de la gran rebelión indígena de 1780." *Histórica* 14, 1 (1990): 27–68.

Gomez, Adolfo. "¡García Moreno!" In *García Moreno!,* edited by Eloy Proaño y Vega. Quito: Fundación de Tipos de Manuel Rivadeneira, 1875.

González, Luis. *San José de Gracia: Mexican Village in Transition.* Austin: University of Texas Press, 1974.

González Prada, Manuel. *Pájinas libres.* Lima: Ediciones Nuevo Mundo, 1964.

Gootenberg, Paul. "Carneros y Chuñu: Price Levels in Nineteenth-Century Peru." *Hispanic American Historical Review* 70, 1 (1990): 1–56.

——. *Imagining Development: Economic Ideas in Peru's "Fictitious Prosperity" of Guano, 1840–1880.* Berkeley: University of California Press, 1994.

Gordillo, José M. *Campesinos revolucionarios en Bolivia: Identidad, territorio y sexualidad en el Valle Alto de Cochabamba, 1952–1964.* La Paz: Plural, 2000.

Gotkowitz, Laura. "Race and Education in Early Twentieth Century Bolivia." Unpublished Paper, 1991.

——. "Within the Boundaries of Equality: Race, Gender, and Citizenship in Bolivia (Cochabamba, 1880–1953)." Ph.D dissertation, University of Chicago, 1998.

Gould, Jeffrey. *To Die This Way: Nicaraguan Indians and the Myth of Mestizaje, 1880–1965.* Durham, N.C.: Duke University Press, 1998.

Graham, Richard. *Patronage and Politics in Nineteenth-Century Brazil.* Stanford: Stanford University Press, 1990.

——, ed. *The Idea of Race in Latin America, 1870–1940.* Austin: University of Texas Press, 1990.

Grandin, Greg. *The Blood of Guatemala: A History of Race and Nation.* Durham, N.C.: Duke University Press, 2000.

Green, W. John. " 'Vibrations of the Collective:' The Popular Ideology of Gaitanismo on Colombia's Atlantic Coast, 1944–1948." *Hispanic American Historical Review* 76, 2 (1996): 283–311.

——. "Sibling Rivalry on the Left and Labor Struggles in Colombia During the 1940s." *Latin American Research Review* 35, 1 (2000): 85–118.

——. *Gaitanismo, Left Liberalism, and Popular Mobilization in Colombia.* Gainesville: University Press of Florida, 2003.

Gruening, Ernest. *Mexico and its Heritage.* London: Stanley Paul, 1928.

Guardino, Peter. *Peasants, Politics, and the Formation of Mexico's National State: Guerrero, 1800–1857.* Stanford: Stanford University Press, 1996.

Guerra, François Xavier. *México: del antiguo régimen a la revolución.* México: FCE, 1988.

——. *Modernidad e independencias. Ensayos sobre las revoluciones hispánicas.* Mexico: Fondo de Cultura Económica, 1993.

——. "The Spanish American Tradition of Representation and Its European Roots." *Journal of Latin American Studies* 26, 1 (1994): 1–35.

——, and Annick Lempérière. "Introducción." In *Los espacios públicos en Iberoamérica: Ambiguedades y problemas, siglos XVIII–XX,* edited by F. X. Guerra and A. Lempérière, 5–24. Sierra Leona, Mexico: Centro Francés de Estudios Mexicanos y Centroamericanos, 1998.

Guerrero, Andrés. "Curagas y tenientes políticos: La ley de la costumbre y la ley del estado (Otavalo 1830–1875)." *Revista Andina,* no. 14 (1989): 321–66.

——. *La semántica de la dominación: El concertaje de indios.* Quito: Libri Mundi, 1991.

——. "La loi de la coutume et la loi de l'Etat." *Annales, Economies, Sociétés, Civilisations* 2 (1992): 331–54.

——. "The Construction of a Ventriloquist's Image: Liberal Discourse and the 'Miserable Indian Race' in Late 19th-Century Ecuador." *Journal Latin American Studies* 29 (1997): 555–90.

Guerrero, J. Augustin. *La música ecuatoriana desde su origen hasta 1875.* Quito: Imprenta Nacional, 1876.

Guibovich Pérez, Pedro. "Lectura y difusión de la obra del Inca Garcilaso en el virreinato peruano (siglos XVII–XVIII): El caso de los *Comentarios Reales.*" *Revista Histórica* 37 (1990–92): 103–20.

Guillermoprieto, Alma. *The Heart that Bleeds: Latin America Now.* New York: Vintage Books, 1994.

Gutiérrez Gutiérrez, José Antonio. *Los altos de Jalisco.* Mexico: Consejo Nacional Para la Cultura y las Artes, 1991.

Gúzman, Germán, Orlando Fals Borda and Eduardo Umaña. *La Violencia en Colombia.* 2 vols. Bogotá: Carlos Valencia Editores, 1980.

Haber, Stephen. "Anything Goes: Mexico's 'New' Cultural History." *Hispanic American Historical Review* 79, 2 (1999): 309–30.

Habermas, Jürgen. *Strukturwandel der Öffentlichkeit: Untersuchungen zu einer Kategorie der bürgerlichen Gesellschaft.* Neuwied: Luchterhand, 1962. [Published in English as *The Structural Transformation of the Public Sphere: An Inquiry into a Category of Bourgeois Society.* Cambridge, Mass.: MIT Press, 1989].

——. "The Public Sphere: An Encyclopedia Article. [1964]" in *New German Critique* 3 (1974): 49–55.

Hale, Charles A. *The Transformation of Liberalism in Late Nineteenth-Century Mexico.* Princeton: Princeton University Press, 1989.

Halperín Donghi, Tulio. *The Aftermath of Revolution in Latin America.* New York: Harper Torchbooks, 1973.

——. *Politics, Economics, and Society in Argentina in the Revolutionary Period.* Cambridge: Cambridge University Press, 1975.

——. "The Cities of Spanish America, 1825–1914: Economic and Social Aspects." In "Urbanization in the Americas: The Background in Comparative Perspective." Special issue of *Urban History Review* (1980): 63–75.

——. "Argentina: Liberalism in a Nation Born Liberal." In *Guiding the Invisible Hand: Economic Liberalism in Latin American History,* edited by Joseph L. Love and Nils Jacobsen, 99–116. New York: Praeger, 1988.

——. *The Contemporary History of Latin America.* Edited and translated by John Charles Chasteen. Durham, N.C.: Duke University Press, 1993.

Hamnett, Brian. "Process and Pattern: A Re-Examination of the Ibero-American Independence Movements, 1808–1826." *Journal of Latin American Studies* 29 (May 1997): 279–328.

Harris, Olivia. "Ethnic Identity and Market Relations: Indians and Mestizos in the Andes." In *Ethnicity, Markets and Migration in the Andes: At the Crossroads of History and Anthropology,* edited by Brooke Larson, Olivia Harris, and Enrique Tandeter, 351–390. Durham, N.C.: Duke University Press, 1995.

Hartup, Cheryl. "Artists and the New Nation: Academic Painting in Quito during the Presidency of Gabriel Garcia Moreno (1861–1875)." M.A. thesis, University of Texas at Austin, 1997.

Haskett, Robert S. *Indigenous Rulers: The Ethnohistory of Town Government in Cuernavaca.* Albuquerque: University of New Mexico Press, 1991.

Hassaurek, Friedrich. *Four Years Among the Ecuadorians.* Edited by C. Harvey Gardiner. Carbondale and Edwardsville: Southern Illinois University Press, 1967.

Hazareesingh, Sudhir. *Political Traditions in Modern France.* Oxford: Oxford University Press, 1994.

Hazen, Dan. *Bibliography and Peruvian Union List of Serial Publications From Southern Peru, 1880–1950: Departments of Arequipa, Cuzco and Puno.* Berkeley-Stanford Occasional Publications in Latin American Studies, No. 1. Berkeley: Center for Latin American Studies, 1988.

Helg, Aline. "Race in Argentina and Cuba, 1880–1930: Theory, Policies and Popular Reaction." In *The Idea of Race in Latin America,* edited by Richard Graham, 37–70. Austin: University of Texas Press, 1990.

——. "The Limits of Equality: Free People of Colour and Slaves during the First Independence of Cartagena, Colombia, 1810–1815." *Slavery and Abolition* 22, 2 (1999): 1–30.

——. "A Fragmented Majority: Free 'of All Colors,' Indians, and Slaves in Caribbean

Colombia during the Haitian Revolution." In *The Impact of the Haitian Revolution in the Atlantic World,* edited by David Geggus. Charleston: University of South Carolina Press, forthcoming.

——. "Liberty and Equality: Free People of Color, Elite Whites, Slaves, and Indians in Caribbean Colombia, 1770–1851." Book manuscript, in progress.

Henderson, James D. *When Colombia Bled: A History of the Violencia in Tolima.* Tuscaloosa: University of Alabama Press, 1985.

Hidalgo Lehuede, Jorge. "Amarus y cataris: aspectos mesiánicos de la rebelión indígena de 1781 en Cusco, Chayanta, La Paz y Arica." *Revista Chungara* 10 (1983): 117–38.

Hopf, Christel and Wulf Hopf. *Familie, Persönlichkeit, Politik: Eine Einführung in die politische Sozialisation.* Weinheim: Juventa Verlag, 1997.

Hora, Roy. *The Landowners of the Argentine Pampas: A Social and Political History, 1860–1945.* Oxford: Clarendon Press, 2001.

Humboldt, Alejandro de. *Cartas Americanas.* Caracas: Biblioteca Ayacucho, 1980.

Hünefeldt, Christine. "Poder y contribuciones: Puno 1825–1845." *Revista Andina,* no. 14. (1989): 367–403.

——. *Paying the Price for Freedom: Family and Labor Among Lima's Slaves, 1800–1854.* Berkeley: University of California Press, 1994.

——. "Contribución indígena, acumulación mercantil y reconformación de los espacios políticos en el sur peruano, 1820–1890." In *Circuitos mercantiles y mercados en Latinoamérica, siglos XVIII–XIX,* edited by Juan Carlos Grosso, Jorge Silva Riquer, and Carmen Yuste, 523–561. Mexico: Instituto Mora, UNAM, 1995.

——. *Liberalism in the Bedroom: Quarreling Spouses in Nineteenth Century Lima.* University Park: Pennsylvania State University Press, 2000.

Hunt, Lynn. *Politics, Culture and Society in the French Revolution.* Berkeley: University of California Press, 1984.

Huntington, Samuel. P. *The Third Wave: Democratization in the Late Twentieth Century.* Norman: University of Oklahoma Press, 1991.

Ibarra, Hernan. *Indios y cholos: origenes de la clase trabajadora ecuatoriana.* Quito: Ed. El Conejo, 1992.

Inkeles, Alex. *National Character: A Psycho-Social Perspective.* New Brunswick: Transaction Publishers, 1997.

Irurozqui Victoriano, Marta. *La armonía de las desigualidades: Elites y conflictos de poder en Bolivia, 1880–1920.* Cusco: CBC, 1994.

——. "La amenaza chola: La participacion popular en las elecciones bolivianas, 1900–1930." *Revista Andina,* no. 13 (1995): 357–386.

——. *'A bala, piedra y palo:' La construcción de la ciudadanía política en Bolivia, 1826–1952.* Sevilla: Diputación de Sevilla, 2000.

Jacobsen, Nils. *Mirages of Transition: The Peruvian Altiplano, 1780–1930.* Berkeley: University of California Press, 1993.

——. "Liberalism and Indian Communities in Peru, 1820–1920." In *Liberals, the Church, and Indian Peasants: Corporate Lands and the Challenge of Reform in Nineteenth-Century Spanish America,* edited by Robert Jackson, 123–70. Albuquerque, N.M.: University of New Mexico Press, 1997.

——, and Alejandro Diez Hurtado. "Montoneras, la comuna de Chalaco y la revolución de Piérola: La sierra piurana entre el clientelismo y la sociedad civil, 1868–1895." In *Los ejes de la disputa: Moviminetos sociales y actores colectivos en América Latina, siglo XIX,* edited by Antonio Escobar Ohmstede and Romana Falcón, 57–131. Madrid and Frankfurt: AHILA, Vervuert, 2002.

Jaimes Peñaloza, Sonia Milena. "Balance y reflexión: Alrededor de la cultura política en la historiografía colombiana." B.A. thesis, Universidad del Valle (Cali), Department of History, 2000.

Jaramillo Uribe, Jaime. *Ensayos sobre historia social colombiana.* Bogotá, Universidad Nacional de Colombia,1968.

Jaramillo, Carlos Eduardo. *Los guerrilleros de novecientos.* Bogotá: CEREC, 1991.

Jiménez Molinares, Gabriel. *Los mártires de Cartagena de 1816 ante el consejo de guerra y ante la historia.* 2 vols. Cartagena: Imprenta Departamental, 1947.

Johnson, Lyman L., and Sonya Lipsett-Rivera. "Introduction." In *The Faces of Honor in Colonial Latinamerica,* edited by L L. Johnson and S. Lipsett-Rivera, 1–17. Alburquerque: University of New Mexico Press, 1998.

Joseph, Gilbert and Daniel Nugent, eds. *Everyday Forms of State Formation: Revolution and the Negotiation of Rule in Modern Mexico.* Durham, N.C.: Duke University Press, 1994.

Kershaw, Ian. *Hitler, 1889–1936. Hubris.* New York: Norton, 1999.

King, James F. "The Colored Castes and American Representation in the Cortes of Cádiz." *Hispanic American Historical Review* 33 (1953): 33–64.

King, William. "Ecuadorian Church and State Relations under Garcia Moreno, 1859–1863." Ph.D. dissertation, University of Texas at Austin, 1974.

Klaren, Peter F. *Modernization, Dislocation, and Aprismo. Origins of the Peruvian Aprista Party, 1870–1932.* Austin: University of Texas Press, 1975.

Klein, Herbert. *Parties and Political Change in Bolivia, 1880–1952.* Cambridge: Cambridge University Press, 1969.

——. *Bolivia: The Evolution of a Multi-Ethnic Society.* Oxford: Oxford University Press, 1982.

Klor de Alva, J. Jorge. "The Postcolonization of the (Latin) American Experience: A Reconsideration of 'Colonialism.'" In *After Colonialism: Imperial Histories and Postcolonial Displacements,* edited by Gyan Prakash, 241–278. Princeton: Princeton University Press, 1995.

Knight, Alan. "Racism, Revolution, and Indigenismo: Mexico, 1910–1940." In *The Problem of Race in Latin America,* edited by Richard Graham, 71–114. Austin: University of Texas Press, 1990.

——. "Popular Culture and the Revolutionary State in Mexico, 1910–40." *Hispanic American Historical Review* 74, 3 (1994): 393–444.

——. "México bronco, México manso: reflexiones sobre la cultura cívica mexicana." *Política y gobierno* 3, 1 (1996): 5–30.

——. "Subalterns, Signifiers, and Statistics: Perspectives on Mexican Historiography." *Latin American Research Review* 37, 2 (2002): 136–58.

Kolchin, Peter. *American Slavery, 1617–1877.* New York: Hill and Wang, 1993.

Konetzke, Richard. *Colección de documentos para la historia de la formación social de Hispanoamérica 1493–1810.* 3 vols. Madrid: CSIC, 1962.

König, Hans Joachim. *En el camino hacia la nación: nacionalismo en el proceso de la formación del estado y de la nación de la Nueva Granada, 1750–1856.* Bogotá: Banco de la República, 1994.

Krüggeler, Thomas. "Indians, Workers, and the Arrival of 'Modernity:' Cuzco, Peru (1895–1924)." *The Americas* 56, 2 (1999): 161–89.

Kuethe, Allan J. *Military Reform and Society in New Granada, 1773–1808.* Gainesville: University Presses of Florida, 1978.

——. "Flexibilidad racial en las milicias disciplinadas de Cartagena de Indias." *Historia y Cultura* (Cartagena), no. 2 (May 1994): 177–91.

Kuper, Adam. *Culture: The Anthropologists' Account.* Cambridge, Mass.: Harvard University Press, 1999.

Landes, David. *The Wealth and Poverty of Nations.* London: Little Brown, 1998.

Langer, Erick D. "El liberalismo y la abolición de la comunidad indígena en el siglo XX." *Historia y Cultura* (La Paz) 14 (October 1988): 59–95.

——. "Andean Rituals of Revolt: The Chayanta Rebellion of 1927." *Ethnohistory* 37, 3 (1990): 227–53.

Larson, Brooke. "Race, Democracy, and the Politics of Indian Education in Bolivia, 1900–1920." Unpublished paper presented at the Convention of Latin American Studies Association, Chicago, September 1998.

——. *Cochabamba 1550–1900: Colonialism and Agrarian Transformation in Bolivia.* 2nd ed. Durham, N.C.: Duke University Press, 1998.

——. "Highland Andean Peasants and the Trials of Nation Making in the Nineteenth Century." In *The Native Histories of the Americas: South America,* vol. 3, *South America,* part 2, edited by Frank Salomon and Stuart Schwartz, 558–703. Cambridge: Cambridge University Press, 1999.

——. "National Pedagogy, Andean Resurgence, and the Struggle over Public Culture." Unpublished paper presented at the Convention of the Latin American Studies Association, Miami, March 2000.

Lauria-Santiago, Aldo A. *An Agrarian Republic: Commercial Agriculture and the Politics of Peasant Communities in El Salvador, 1823–1914.* Pittsburgh: Pittsburgh University Press, 1999.

Leal Buitrago, Francisco, and Leon Zamosc, eds. *Al filo del caos: Crisis política en la Colombia de los 80.* Bogotá, 1991.

Lehm A., Zulema and Silvia Rivera C. *Los artesanos libertarios y la ética del trabajo.* La Paz: THOA, 1988.

León Mera, Juan. *Catecismo de geografía de la Republica del Ecuador.* Quito: Imprenta Nacional, 1875.

León, Francisco Javier. *Discurso del Presidente de la Cámara de Diputados al terminar las sesiones del congreso ordinario del año de 1865.* Quito: Imprenta Nacional. [Deposited in BEAEP *Miscelanea* 26.]

Lewis, Oscar. *Five Families: Mexican Case Studies In the Culture of Poverty.* [1959] London: Souvenir Press, 1975.

Lievano Aguirre, Indalecio. *Los grandes conflictos sociales y económicos de nuestra historia.* Bogotá: Ediciones Tercer Mundo, 1966.

Lockhart, James, and Stuart B. Schwartz, *Early Latin America: A History of Colonial Spanish America and Brazil.* Cambridge: Cambridge University Press, 1983.

Lomnitz, Claudio. "Ritual, Rumor and Corruption in the Constitution of Polity in Modern Mexico." *Journal of Latin American Anthropology* 1, 1 (1995): 20–47.

Londoño, Patricia. "Aspects of Religion, Culture, and Sociability in Antioquia (Colombia), 1850–1930." Ph.D. dissertation, Oxford University, 1996.

Londoño-Vega, Patricia. *Religion, Culture and Society in Colombia: Medellin and Antioquia, 1850–1930.* Oxford: Clarendon, 2002.

López Albújar, Enrique. *Memorias.* Lima: Talleres Gráficos P.L.Villanueva, 1963.

López-Alves, Fernando. *State Formation and Democracy in Latin America, 1810–1900.* Durham, N.C.: Duke University Press, 2000.

López Giraldo, Fermín. *El apóstol desnudo: o dos años al lado de un mito.* Manizales: Editorial Zapata, 1936.

López Martínez, Héctor. *Los 150 años de El Comercio.* Lima: El Comercio, 1989.

Lynch, John. *Spanish Colonial Administration, 1782–1810.* London: University of London Press, 1958.

——. *Argentine Dictator: Juan Manuel De Rosas, 1829–1852.* Oxford and New York: Oxford University Press, 1981.

——. *The Spanish American Revolution, 1808–1826.* 2nd ed. New York: W. W. Norton, 1986 [1st ed. 1973].

——. *Bourbon Spain, 1700–1808.* Oxford: Basil Blackwell, 1989.

——. *El siglo XVIII. Historia de España.* Barcelona: Editorial Crítica, 1991.

Macera, Pablo. "El indio y sus intérpretes del siglo XVIII." *Trabajos de historia.* Lima: INC, 1977, 2: 3–16.

Maiguashca, Juan. "El proceso de integración nacional en el Ecuador: el rol del poder central, 1830–1895." In *Historia y región en el Ecuador,* edited by Juan Maiguashca, 356–420. Quito: Corporación Editora Nacional, FLACSO, IFEA, 1994.

Maingot, Anthony P. "Social Structure, Social Status, and Civil-Military Conflict in

Urban Colombia, 1818–1858." In *Nineteenth-Century Cities. Essays in the New Urban History*, edited by Stephan Thernstrom and Richard Sennet, 297–355. New Haven: Yale University Press, 1969.

Mallon, Florencia. *The Defense of Community in Peru's Central Highlands.* Princeton: Princeton University Press, 1983.

——. "Nationalist and Anti-state Coalitions in the War of the Pacific: Junín and Cajamarca, 1879–1902." In *Resistance, Rebellion and Consciousness in the Andean Peasant World, Eighteenth to Twentieth Centuries*, edited by Steve J. Stern, 232–79. Madison: University of Wisconsin Press, 1987.

——. "Indian Communities, Political Cultures, and the State in Latin America, 1780–1990." *Journal of Latin American Studies* 24 (1992): 35–53.

——. "The Promise and Dilemma of Subaltern Studies: Perspectives from Latin American History" *American Historical Review* 99, 5 (1994): 1491–1515.

——. *Peasant and Nation. The Making of Postcolonial Mexico and Peru.* Berkeley: University of California Press, 1995.

——. "Constructing Mestizaje in Latin America: Authenticity, Marginality, and Gender in the Claiming of Ethnic Identities." *Journal of Latin American Anthropology* 1 (1996): 170–81.

Malloy, James. *Bolivia: The Uncompleted Revolution.* Pittsburgh: University of Pittsburgh Press, 1970.

Mamani Condori, Carlos B. *Taraqu, 1866–1935: Massacre, guerra, y "renovación" en la biografía de Eduardo L. Nina Qhispi.* La Paz: Aruwiyiri, 1991.

Manarelli, María Emma. *Limpias y modernas: Género, higiene y cultura en la Lima del novecientos.* Lima: Ed. Flora Tristán, 1999.

Manrique, Nelson. *Las guerrillas indígenas en la guerra con Chile.* Lima: CIC and Ital Perú, 1981.

——. *Yawar Mayu. Sociedades terratenientes serranas, 1879–1910.* Lima: IFEA, DESCO, 1988.

Maraval, J. A. *La literatura picaresca desde la historia social, siglos XVI–XVII.* Madrid, 1986.

Martin, Cheryl E. *Governance and Society in Colonial Mexico: Chihuahua in the Eighteenth Century.* Stanford: Stanford University Press, 1996.

——. "Public Celebrations, Popular Culture and Labor Discipline in Eighteenth-Century Chihuahua." In *Rituals of Rule, Rituals of Resistance: Public Celebrations and Popular Culture in Mexico*, edited by William Beezley et al., 95–114. Wilmington: SR Books, 1994.

Martinez Alier, Juan. *Haciendas, Plantations and Collective Farms.* Hassocks: Frank Cass, 1977.

Martinez, Josefa, et al. *La voz del deber de unas mujeres católicas.* Quito: Imprenta del Clero, 1878. [Deposited in Biblioteca Espinosa Polit (Quito), *Hojas Volantes*, vol. 1851–1880, no page.]

Martínez-Echabal, Lourdes. "Mestizaje and the Discourse of National/Cultural Identity in Latin America, 1845–1959." *Latin American Perspectives* 100, 25 (1998): 21–42.

Mayer, Enrique. "Tenencia y control de la tierra comunal: Caso de Laraos (Yauyos)." *Cuadernos del Consejo Nacional de la Universidad Peruana* 24–25 (January–June 1977): 59–72.

Mazzotti, José Antonio. "Garcilaso y los orígenes del garcilasismo: El papel de los *Comentarios Reales* en el desarrollo del imaginario peruano." *Fronteras* 3 (1998): 13–35.

McCreery, David. *Rural Guatemala, 1760–1940.* Stanford: Stanford University Press, 1994.

McEvoy, Carmen. *La utopía republicana: Ideales y realidades en la formación de la cultura política peruana (1871–1919).* Lima: Pontifícia Universidad Católica del Perú, 1997.

——. "Estampillas y votos." *Forjando la Nación.* Lima: PUCP-Sewanee, 1999.

McFarlane, Anthony. *Colombia before Independence. Economy, Society, and Politics under Bourbon Rule.* Cambridge: Cambridge University Press, 1993.

——. "Building Political Order: The 'First Republic' in New Granada, 1810–1815." In *In Search of New Order: Essays on the Politics and Society of Nineteenth-Century Latin America,* edited by Eduardo Posada-Carbó, 12–26. London: Institute of Latin American Studies, 1998.

Mejía Robledo, Alfonso. *Vidas y empresas de Antioquia.* Medellín: Imprenta Departamental, 1951.

Mendez, Cecilia. *Incas si, indios no: Apuntes para el estudio del nacionalismo criollo en el Perú.* Lima: IEP, 1993.

——. "Rebellion without Resistance: Huanta's Monarchist Peasants in the Making of the Peruvian State (Ayacucho, 1825–1850)." Ph.D. dissertation, State University of New York at Stony Brook, 1996.

Mendinueta, Pedro. "Relación del estado del Nuevo Reino de Granada, presentada por el Excmo. Sr. Virrey D. Pedro Mendinueta a su sucesor el Excmo. Sr. Don Antonio Amar y Borbón. Año de 1803." In *Relaciones e informes de los gobernantes de la Nueva Granada,* edited by Germán Colmenares, 3: 5–191. Bogotá: Talleres Gráficos Banco Popular, 1989.

Mendoza, Zoila. *Shaping Society through Dance: Mestizo Ritual Performance in the Peruvian Andes.* Chicago: University of Chicago Press, 2000.

Menten, Juan Bautista. "Discurso sobre la enseñanza." In *Programa de las materias que se enseñan en la Escuela Politécnica, establecida en Quito a 3 de octubre de 1870.* Quito: Imprenta Nacional, 1871.

Middendorf, Ernst. *Beobachtungen und Studien über das Land und seine Bewohner während eines 25jährigen Aufenthaltes.* 2 vols. Berlin: Robert Oppenheim [Gustav Schmidt], 1893.

Minchom, Martin. *The People of Quito, 1690–1810: Change and Unrest in the Underclass.* Boulder: Westview Press, 1994.

Mitchell, Timothy. "The Limits of the State: Beyond Statist Approaches and Their Critics." *American Political Science Review* 85, 1 (1991): 77–96.

Moerner, Magnus. *Region and State in Latin America's Past.* Baltimore: Johns Hopkins University Press, 1993.

Moncayo, Pedro. *Cuestión de limites entre el Ecuador y el Perú, segun el Uti Possidetis de 1810 y los tratados de 1829.* Quito: Imprenta del Gobierno, 1860.

Montesquieu, Charles de Secondat, Baron de. *The Spirit of the Laws.* Cambridge: Cambridge University Press, 1989.

Moore, Barrington. *Social Origins of Dictatorship and Democracy.* Harmondsworth: Penguin, 1969.

Moreno Cebrián, Alfredo. "Cuarteles, barrios y calles de Lima a fines del siglo XVIII." *Jahrbuch für die Geschichte von Staat, Wirtschaft und Gesellschaft Lateinamerikas* 18 (1981): 97–161.

Moscoso, Gladys. "Las imágenes de la literatura." In *Y el amor no era todo . . . : Mujeres, imágenes, y conflictos,* edited by Martha Moscoso, 85–116. Quito: Abya-Yala, 1996.

Moscoso, Martha. "Discurso religioso y discurso estatal: la mujer sumisa." In *Y el amor no era todo . . . : Mujeres, imágenes y conflictos,* edited by Martha Moscoso, 21–57. Quito: Abya-Yala, 1996.

Mücke, Ulrich. *Das Indianerbild des peruanischen Liberalismus im 19. Jahrhundert.* Hamburg: LIT Verlag, 1998.

——. *Der 'Partido Civil' in Peru, 1871–1879: Zur Geschichte politischer Parteien und Repräsentation in Lateinamerika.* Stuttgart: F. Steiner Verlag, 1998. [translated into English as *Political Culture in Nineteenth-Century Peru: The Rise of the Partido Civil.* Pittsburgh: University of Pittsburgh Press, 2004.]

Muller, Edward N., and Mitchell A. Seligson. "Civic Culture and Democracy: The Question of Causal Relationships." *American Political Science Review* 88 (1994): 635–52.

Muratorio, Blanca. *The Life and Times of Grandfather Alonso: Culture and History in the Upper Amazon.* New Brunswick: Rutgers University Press, 1991.

——. "Nación, identidad, y etnicidad: Imágenes de los indios ecuatorianos y sus imagineros a fines del siglo XIX." In *Imágenes e imagineros: Representaciones del los indígenas ecuatorianos, siglos XIX–XX,* edited by Blanca Muratorio, 109–96. Quito: FLACSO, 1994.

Nichols, Theodore E. *Tres puertos de Colombia: Estudio sobre el desarrollo de Cartagena, Santa Marta y Barranquilla.* Bogotá: Banco Popular, 1973.

Noboa, Alejandro. *Recopilación de mensajes dirigidos por los presidentes de la república, jefes supremos y gobiernos provisorios a las convenciones nacionales desde el año 1819 hasta nuestros dias.* Vols. II-III. Guayaquil: Imprenta de El Tiempo, 1906–1907.

Noboa, Tomás H. *Sermón pronunciado . . . en la festividad del aniversario de nuestra independencia el dia 10 de agosto de 1861. . . .* Quito: Imprenta de los Huerfanos de Valencia, 1861.

North, Douglass C. "New Institutional Economics and Third World Development." In *The New Institutonal Economics and Third World Development,* edited by John Harris, Janet Hunter and Colim M. Lewis, 17–26. London: Routledge, 1995.

Novick, Peter. *That Noble Dream: The 'Objectivity Question' and the American Historical Profession.* Cambridge: Cambridge University Press, 1988.

Nugent, David. *Modernity at the Edge of Empire: State, Individual and Nation in the Northern Peruvian Andes, 1885–1935.* Stanford: Stanford University Press, 1997.

Nye, Robert A. *The Origins of Crowd Psychology: Gustave LeBon and the Crisis of Mass Democracy in the Third Republic.* London: Sage, 1975.

O'Connor, Erin. "Dueling Patriarchies: Gender, Indians, and State Formation in the Ecuadorian Sierra, 1860–1925." Ph.D. dissertation, Boston College, 1997.

O'Phelan Godoy, Scarlett. "Aduanas, mercado interno y elite comercial en el Cuzco antes y después de la gran rebelión de 1780." *Apuntes* 19 (1986): 53–72.

——. "El mito de la independencia concedida: Los programas políticos del siglo XVIII y del temprano XIX en el Perú y Alto Perú (1730–1814)." In *Independencia y Revolución,* edited by Alberto Flores Galindo, 2: 145–99. 2 vols. Lima: Instituto Nacional de Cultura, 1987.

——. *Rebellions and Revolts in Eighteenth Century Peru and Upper Peru.* Köln, Wien: Böhlau, 1985. [Published in Spanish as *Un siglo de rebeliones coloniales: Perú y Bolivia 1700–1783.* Cusco: CBC, 1988].

——. "L'utopie andine: Discours parallèles à la fin de l'époque coloniale." *Annales, Histoires, Sciences Sociales* 49, 2 (1994): 471–95.

——. "Tradición y modernidad en el proyecto de Túpac Amaru." In *Tres levantamientos populares. Pugachóv, Túpac Amaru, Hidalgo,* edited by Jean Meyer. Mexico: CEMCA, 1992.

——. *La gran rebelión en los Andes: de Túpac Amaru a Túpac Catari.* Cusco: CBC, 1995.

——. "Discurso y etnicidad en las Cortes de Cadiz." In *Culturas políticas andinas, 1750–1950.* Ed. by Cristóbal Aljovín and Nils Jacobsen. Lima: Universidad Nacional Mayor de San Marcos, forthcoming.

——, ed. *El Perú en el siglo XVIII: La era Borbónica.* Lima: Pontificia Universidad Católica del Perú, 1999.

Omi, Michael and Howard Winant. *Racial Formation in the United States from the 1960s to the 1980s.* New York: Routledge, 1994.

Oquist, Paul. *Violence, Conflict and Politics in Colombia.* New York: Academic Press, 1980.

Ortiz, Fernando. *Cuban Counterpoint: Tobacco and Sugar.* Durham, N.C.: Duke University Press, 1995 [1st Span. ed. 1943].

Ortiz, Sergio Elías. *Franceses en la independencia de la Gran Colombia.* Bogotá: Editorial ABC, 1971.

Ortner, Sherry. "Theory in Anthropology since the Sixties." *Comparative Studies in Society and History* 16 (1984): 126–66.

——. "Resistance and the Problem of Ethnographic Refusal." *Comparative Studies in Society and History* 37, 1 (1995): 173–93.

Otero, Gustavo Adolfo. "Temperamento, cultura y obra de Alcides Arguedas." In *Alcides Arguedas. Juicios bolivianos sobre el autor de 'Pueblo Enfermo,'* edited by M. Baptista Gumucio, 83–107. La Paz: Los Amigos del Libro, 1979.

Oviedo, Juan. *Colección de leyes, decretos y órdenes publicadas en el Perú desde el año de 1821 hasta el 31 de diciembre de 1859.* 16 vols. Lima: Felipe Baily, 1861–1872.

Pagden, Anthony. *Spanish Imperialism and the Political Imagination.* New Haven: Yale University Press, 1990.

Palacios de la Vega, J. *Diario de viaje entre los indios y negros de la provincia de Cartagena en el Nuevo Reino de Granada (1787–1788).* Edited by Gerardo Reichel-Dolmatoff. Bogotà: Editorial ABC, 1955.

Paladines Escudero, Carlos. *Pensamiento pedagógico ecuatoriano.* Quito: Banco Central del Ecuador/Corporación Editora Nacional, 1988. [Series: Biblioteca Básica del Pensamiento Ecuatoriano, 23]

Pardo, Manuel. "Prólogo." In Felipe Pardo y Aliaga. *Poesías y escritos en prosa.* París: Imprenta de los Caminos de Hierro, 1872.

Paredes Ramirez, Willington. "Economia y sociedad en la costa: siglo XIX." In *La nueva historia del Ecuador,* vol. 7, *Época Republicana I,* edited by Enrique Ayala Mora. Quito: Corporación Editora Nacional/Grijalbo, 1990.

Paredes, Manuel Rigoberto. *Provincia de Inquisivi.* La Paz: Gamarra, 1906.

——. *Política parlamentaria de Bolivia* [1907]. La Paz: Velarde, 1911.

——. *La altiplanície: Anotaciones etnográficas, geográficas y sociales de la comunidad aymara* [1914]. La Paz: Ed. ISLA, 1965.

Parkerson, Phillip. *Andrés de Santa Cruz y la Confederación Perú-Boliviana 1835–1839.* La Paz: Librería Editorial Juventud, 1984.

Pateman, Carole. "Political Culture, Political Structure, and Political Change." *British Journal of Political Science* 1 (1971): 291–305.

Patiño Millán, B. "Indios, negros y mestizos, la sociedad colonial y los conceptos sobre las castas." In *Ciencia, cultura y mentalidades en la historia de Colombia,* edited by Amado Guerrero, 41–76. VIII Congreso de Historia de Colombia. Bucaramanga: Universidad Industrial de Santander, 1992.

——. *Criminalidad, ley penal y estructura social en la provincia de Antioquia, 1750–1820.* Medellín: IDEA, 1994.

Pattee, Richard. *Gabriel García Moreno y el Ecuador de su tiempo.* Quito: Editorial Ecuatoriana, 1941.

Paz, Octavio. *The Labyrinth of Solitude* [1950]. London: Penguin, 1967.

Pécaut, Daniel. *L'ordre et la violence: évolution socio-politique de la Colombie entre 1930 et 1953.* [Published in Spanish as *Orden y violencia: Colombia 1930–1954.* 2 vols. Bogotá: Siglo Veintiuno Editores, 1987]

Peloso, Vincent. "Liberals, Electoral Reform, and the Popular Vote in Mid-Nineteenth Century Peru." In *Liberals, Politics and Power: State Formation in Nineteenth-Century Latin America,* edited by Vincent Peloso and Barbara Tenenbaum, 186–211. Athens: University of Geogia Press, 1996.

Penry, Elizabeth. "Transformations in Indigenous Identity and Authority in Resettlement Towns of Colonial Charcas (Alto Peru)." Ph.D. dissertation, University of Miami, 1996.

Peralta Ruiz, Víctor. *En pos del tributo: Burocracia estatal, elite regional y comunidades indígenas en el Cusco rural (1826–1854).* Cuzco: Bartolomé de Las Casas, 1991.

——, and Marta Irurozqui Victoriano. *Por la concordia, la fusión y el unitarismo: estado y caudillismo en Bolivia, 1825–1880.* Madrid: Consejo Superior de Investigaciones Científicas, 2000.

Pérez Cantó, María Pilar. *Lima en el siglo XVIII.* Madrid: Universidad Autónoma de Madrid, ICI, 1985.

Pérez Velasco, Daniel. *La mentalidad chola en Bolivia.* La Paz: Ed. López, 1928.

Phelan, John Leddy. *The Kingdom of Quito in the Seventeenth Century.* Madison: University of Wisconsin Press, 1967.

——. *The People and the King: The Comunero Revolution in Colombia, 1781.* Madison: University of Wisconsin Press, 1978.

Piccato, Pablo. "The Court of Public Opinion: The Honor of Journalists in Porfirian Mexico." Paper presented at the Conference on "Republic in Print: Mexican Journalism in Sociological and Historical Perspective," University of Chicago, Nov. 12–13, 1999.

Piel, Jean. "Cómo interpretar la rebelión panandina de 1780–1783?" In *Tres levantamientos populares: Pugachev, Túpac Amaru, Hidalgo,* edited by Jean Meyer, 71–80. Mexico: CEMCA, 1992.

Pitt-Rivers, Julian. "Honour and Social Status." In *Honour and Shame, The Values of the Mediterranean Society,* edited by J.G. Peristiany, 19–97. Chicago: University of Chicago Press, 1966.

Pius IX. "Syllabus of Modern Errors. A Condemnation of Modernist, Liberal Errors. Encyclical Letter of Pope Pius IX, December 8, 1864." *The Reformation Online,* //www.reformation.org/syllabusþofþpius.html.

Planas, Pedro. *La descentralización en el Perú republicano, 1821–1998.* Lima: Municipalidad Metropolitana de Lima, 1998.

Platt, Tristan. *Estado boliviano y ayllu andino: Tierra y tributo en el norte de Potosí.* Lima: IEP, 1982.

Pocock, J.G.A. *The Machiavellian Moment: Florentine Political Thought and the Atlantic Republican Tradition.* Princeton: Princeton University Press, 1975.

Poole, Deborah. "Antropología e historia andinas en los EE.UU.: Buscando un reencuentro." *Revista Andina* 10, 1 (1992): 209–45.

——. *Vision, Race and Modernity: A Visual Economy of the Andean Image World.* Princeton: Princeton University Press, 1997.

——, ed. *Unruly Order: Violence, Power and Cultural Identity in the High Provinces of Southern Peru.* Boulder: Westview Press, 1994.

Porras Barrenechea, Raúl. "Don Felipe Pardo y Aliaga, satírico limeño." *Revista Histórica* (Lima) 20 (1953): 237–304.

——. *El periodismo en el Perú.* Lima: Instituto Raúl Porras Barrenechea, 1970.

Posada-Carbó, Eduardo. *The Colombian Caribbean: A Regional History, 1870–1950.* Oxford: Clarendon Press, 1996.

——, ed. *Elections Before Democracy: The History of Elections in Europe and Latin America.* Houndshill and London: Macmillan and ILAS, 1996.

Posada Gutiérrez, Joaquín. *Memorias histórico-políticas.* 4 vols. Bogotá: Imprenta Nacional, 1929.

Prieto, Adolfo. *El discurso criollista en la formación de la Argentina moderna.* Buenos Aires: Editorial Sudamericana, 1988.

Przeworski, Adam. *Democracy and the Market.* Cambridge: Cambridge University Press, 1991.

Purnell, Jennie. *Popular Movements and State Formation in Revolutionary Mexico.* Durham, N.C.: Duke University Press, 1999.

Pye, Lucien W. *Politics, Personality, and Nation Building: Burma's Search for Identity.* New Haven: Yale University Press, 1962.

——, and Sydney Verba, eds. *Political Culture and Political Development.* Princeton: Princeton University Press, 1965.

Quimper, José Maria. *El liberalismo.* Ghent: De Busscher, 1886.

Rama, Angel. *The Lettered City.* Durham, N.C.: Duke University Press, 1996.

Ramón Valarezo, Galo. *Regreso de las runa: la potencialidad del proyecto indio en el Ecuador contemporáneo.* Quito: COMUNIDEC, 1993.

Ramón, Gabriel. "Urbe y orden: Evidencias del reformismo borbónico en el tejido limeño." In *El Perú en el siglo XVIII,* edited by Scarlett O'Phelan Godoy, 295–324. Lima: Pontifícia Universidad Católica del Perú, 1999.

Ramos, Alcida Rita. *Indigenism: Ethnic Politics in Brazil.* Madison: University of Wisconsin Press, 1998.

Rappaport, Joanne. *The Politics of Memory: Native Historical Interpretation in the Colombian Andes.* 2nd ed. Durham, N.C.: Duke University Press, 1998 [1st ed. 1990].

Rasnake, Roger. *Domination and Cultural Resistance: Authority and Power Among an Andean People.* Durham, N.C.: Duke University Press, 1988.

Regal, Alberto. *Castilla educador.* Lima: Imp. "Gráf. Industrial," 1968.

Reis, João José. " 'Death to the Cemetery:' Funerary Reform and Rebellion in Salvador, Brazil, 1836." In *Riots in the Cities: Popular Politics and the Urban Poor in Latin America 1765–1810,* edited by Silvia M. Arrom and Servando Ortoll, 97–113. Wilmington, Del.: SR Books, 1996.

República de Bolivia. *Redactor de la Convención Nacional de 1945.* 2 vols. La Paz, 1945.

Restrepo Jaramillo, Gonzalo. *El pensamiento conservador.* Medellín: Editorial Bedout, 1936.

Restrepo Piedrahita, Carlos. *El congreso constituyente de la villa del Rosario de Cúcuta, 1821.* Bogotá: Universidad Externado de Colombia, 1990.

Restrepo Tirado, Ernesto. *Historia de la provincia de Santa Marta* [1921]. Bogotá: Instituto Colombiano de Cultura, reprint 1975.

Restrepo, José Manuel. *Historia de la revolución de la república de Colombia.* [1827] 6 vols. Medellín: Editorial Bedout, reprint 1969–70.

Rivera Ayala, Sergio. "Lewd Songs and Dances from the Streets of Eighteenth-Century Mexico." In *Rituals of Rule, Rituals of Resistance: Public Celebrations and Popular Culture in Mexico,* edited by William Beezley et al., 27–46. Wilmington, Del.: SR Books, 1994.

Rivera, Alberto. *Los terratenientes de Cochabamba.* Cochabamba: CERES/FACES, 1992.

Rivera, Silvia. *Oprimidos pero no vencidos: Luchas del campesinado aymara y qhechwa, 1900–1980.* La Paz: UNRISD, 1986. [Published in English as *'Oppressed But Not Defeated:' Peasant Struggles Among the Aymara and Qhechwa in Bolivia, 1900–1980.* Geneva: UNRISD, 1987].

——. " 'Pedimos la revisión de límites:' Un episodio de incomunicación de castas en el movimiento de caciques-apoderados de los Andes bolivianos, 1919–1921." In *Reproducción y transformación de las sociedades andinas, siglos XVI–XX,* edited by Segundo Moreno and Frank Salomon, 1: 603–52. Quito: Abya Yala, 1991.

Rizo-Patrón Boylan, Paul. *Linaje, dote y poder: la nobleza de Lima de 1700 a 1850.* Lima: Pontifícia Universidad Católica del Perú, 2001.

Robalino Dávila, Luis. *Origenes del Ecuador de hoy: García Moreno.* Puebla: Editorial José M. Cajica Jr. S.A., 1967.

Rocha, José Antonio. *Con el ojo de adelante y con el ojo de atrás: Ideología étnica, el poder y lo político entre los quechua de los valles y serranías de Cochabamba (1935–1952).* La Paz: Plural, 1999.

Rock, David, ed. *Latin America in the 1940s.* Berkeley: University of California Press, 1994.

Rockwell, Elsie. "Schools of the Revolution: Enacting and Contesting State Forms in Tlaxcala, 1910–1930." In *Everyday Forms of State Formation: Revolution and the Negotiation of Rule in Modern Mexico,* edited by Gilbert Joseph and Daniel Nugent, 170–208. Durham, N.C.: Duke University Press, 1994.

Rodríguez O., Jaime E. *The Independence of Spanish America.* Cambridge: Cambridge University Press, 1998.

Rodríguez Ostria, Gustavo, and Humberto Solares S. *Sociedad oligárquica, chicha y cultura popular: ensayo sobre la identidad regional.* Cochabamba: Ed. Serrano, 1990.

Rodríguez, José M. *Estudios económico financieros y ojeada sobre la hacienda pública del Perú y la necesidad de su reforma.* Lima, 1895.

Rodríguez, Linda Alexander. *The Search for Public Policy: Regional Politics and Government Finances in Ecuador, 1830–1940.* Berkeley: University of California Press, 1985.

Roldán, Mary. "La política antioqueña de 1946 a 1958." In *La historia de Antioquia,* edited by Jorge Orlando Melo, 160–76. Bogotá: Editorial Presencia, 1988.

——. *Blood and Fire: La Violencia in Antioquia, Colombia, 1946–1953.* Durham, N.C.: Duke University Press, 2002.

Romero Jaramillo, Dolcey. *Esclavitud en la provincia de Santa Marta, 1791–1851.* Santa Marta: Fondo de Publicaciones de Autores Magdalenenses-Instituto de Cultura y Turismo del Magdalena, 1997.

Romero, Carlos. *Las tareas de nuestra democracia.* La Paz: ARNO, 1919.

Rosas Lauro, Claudia. "Educando al bello sexo: La mujer en el discurso ilustrado." In *El Perú en el siglo XVIII,* edited by Scarlett O'Phelan Godoy, 369–413. Lima: Pontifícia Universidad Católica del Perú, 1999.

Roseberry, William. "Hegemony and the Language of Contention." In *Everyday Forms of State Formation: Revolution and the Negotiation of Rule in Modern Mexico,* edited by Gilbert Joseph and Daniel Nugent, 355–66. Durham, N.C.: Duke University Press, 1994.

Rostworowski de Diez Canseco, María. *Curacas y sucesiones: Costa Norte.* Lima: Minerva, 1961.

Rowe, John. "El movimiento nacional inca del siglo XVIII." *Revista Universitaria* (Cusco) 107 (1954): 17–47. [Reprinted in Alberto Flores Galindo, ed. *Túpac Amaru II—Antología.* Lima, 1976]

Rubin, Jeffrey W. *Decentering the Regime: Ethnicity, Radicalism and Democracy in Juchitán. Mexico.* Durham, N.C.: Duke University Press, 1997.

Ryan, Mary. *Civic Wars: Democracy and Public Life in the American City During the Nineteenth Century.* Berkeley: University of California Press, 1998.

Saavedra, Bautista. "Proceso Mohoza: Defensa del Abogado Bautista Saavedra" [1901]. *El ayllu: Estudios sociológicos.* La Paz: Juventud, 1987.

——. *El ayllu* [1904]. La Paz: Ed. Nacimento, 1938.

——. *La democracia en nuestra historia.* La Paz: González y Medina, 1921.

Sabato, Hilda. *La política en las calles: Entre el voto y la movilizción: Buenos Aires, 1862–1880.* Buenos Aires: Ed. Sudamericana, 1998. [Published in English as *The Many and the Few: Political Particpation in Republican Buenos Aires.* Stanford: Stanford University Press, 2001].

——. "On Political Citizenship in Nineteenth Century Latin America." *American Historical Review* 106, 4 (2001): 1290–1315.

——, ed. *Ciudadanía política y formación de las naciones: Perspectivas históricas de América Latina.* México: Colegio de México, 1999.

Safford, Frank. *The Ideal of the Practical: Colombia's Struggle to Form a Technical Elite.* Austin: University of Texas Press, 1976.

——. "Race, Integration and Progress: Elite Attitudes and the Indian in Colombia." *Hispanic American Historical Review* 71, 1 (1991): 1–34.

——, and Marco Palacios. *Colombia: Fragmented Land, Divided Society.* New York and Oxford: Oxford University Press, 2001.

Saignes, Thierry. "Hacia la formación de sociedades nacionales." In *Estados y naciones en los Andes: Hacia una historia comparativa: Bolivia, Colombia, Ecudor, Perú,* edited by J.P. Deler and Y. Saint-Geours, 1: 349–52. 2 vols. Lima: IEP and IFEA, 1986.

Sala i Vila, Núria. "La rebelión de Huarochirí en 1783." In *Entre la retórica y la insurgencia,* edited by Charles Walker, 273–308. Cusco: CBC, 1995.

Salazar, Francisco Javier. *El método productivo de la enseñanza primaria aplicada a las escuelas de la República del Ecuador.* Quito: Imprenta Nacional, 1969.

Salomon, Frank. "Andean Ethnology in the 1970s: A Retrospective." *Latin American Research Review* 17, 2 (1982): 75–128.

——. "The Historical Development of Andean Ethnology." *Mountain Research and Development* 5, 1 (1985): 79–98.

——. "Ancestor Cults and Resistance to the State in Arequipa, ca. 1748–1754." In *Resistance, Rebellion, and Consciousness in the Andean Peasant World, Eighteenth to Twentieth Centuries,* edited by Steve Stern, 148–65. Madison: University of Wisconsin Press, 1987.

——. "Testimonies: The Making and Reading of Native South American Historical Sources." In *The Cambridge History of Native Peoples of the Americas,* vol. 3, *South America,* part 1, edited by Frank Salomon and Stuart Schwartz, 19–95. Cambridge: Cambridge University Press, 1999.

Salzedo del Villar, Pedro. *Apuntaciones historiales de Mompox. Edición conmemorativa de los 450 años de Mompox.* [1939] Cartagena: Gobernación del Departamento de Bolívar, reprint 1987.

Sánchez Albornoz, Nicolás. *Indios y tributos en el Alto Perú.* Lima: IEP, 1978.

Sánchez Gómez, Gonzalo. *Los dias de la revolución: Gaitanismo y 9 de abril en provincia.* Bogotá: Centro Gaitán, 1983.

——. *Guerra y política en la sociedad colombiana.* Bogotá: El Ancora, 1991.

——, et al., *Violencia y democracia: Informe al Ministerio de Gobierno.* Bogotá, 1987.

——, and Donny Meertens. *Bandoleros, gamonales y campesinos.* Bogotá, 1983.

Sarmiento, Domingo F. *Educación Popular.* Buenos Aires: Librería la Facultad, 1915 [Series: Biblioteca Argentina, 4]

Scott, James C. *Weapons of the Weak: Everyday Forms of Peasant Resistance.* New Haven: Yale University Press, 1985.

——. *Domination and the Arts of Resistance: Hidden Transcripts.* New Haven: Yale University Press, 1990.

Seed, Patricia. "Social Dimensions of Race: Mexico City, 1753." *Hispanic American Historical Review* 62 (1982): 559–606.

Seligson, Mitchell A. "Toward a Model of Democratic Stability: Political Culture in Central America." *Estudios Interdisciplinarios de América Latina y el Caribe* 11, 2 (2000): 5–30.

Serulnikov, Sergio. "Disputed Images of Colonialism. Spanish Rule and Indian Subversion in Northern Potosí, 1777–1780." *Hispanic American Historical Review* 76 (1996): 189–226.

——. "Su verdad y su justicia: Tomás Catari y la insurrección Aymara de Chayanta, 1777–1780." In *Entre la retórica y la insurgencia: Las ideas y los movimientos sociales en los Andes, siglo XVIII,* edited by Charles Walker, 205–43. Cuzco: Centro Bartolomé de las Casas, 1996.

——. "Peasant Politics and Colonial Domination: Social Conflicts and Insurgency in Northern Potosi, 1730–1781." Ph.D. dissertation, State University of New York at Stony Brook, 1998.

——-. "Customs and Rules: Bourbon Rationalizing Projects and Social Conflicts in Northern Potosí during the 1770s." *Colonial Latin American Review* 8, 2 (1999): 245–74.

——. *Subverting Colonial Authority: Challenges to Spanish Rule in Eighteenth-Century Southern Andes.* Durham, N.C.: Duke University Press, 2003.

Sharpless, Richard E. *Gaitán of Colombia: A Political Biography.* Pittsburgh: Pittsburgh University Press, 1978.

Siegfried, André. *Tableau politique de la France de l'Ouest sous le Troisième République.* Paris: Colin, 1913.

Silva, Vicente. *Legislación de las Juntas Departamentales.* Lima, 1901.

Silverblatt, Irene M. *Sun, Moon and Witches; Gender Ideologies and Class in Inca and Colonial Peru.* Princeton: Princeton University Press, 1987.

Skinner, Quentin. *The Foundations of Modern Political Thought.* Cambridge: Cambridge University Press, 1978.

Skocpol, Theda. *States and Social Revolutions: A Comparative Analysis of France, Russia and China.* Cambridge: Cambridge University Press, 1979.

Smith, Carol A. "Origins of the National Question in Guatemala: A Hypothesis." In

Guatemalan Indians and the State, 1540–1988, edited by Carol Smith, 72–95. Austin: University of Texas Press, 1990.

——. "Myths, Intellectuals, and Race/Class/Gender Distinctions in the Formation of Latin American Nations." *Journal of Latin American Anthropology* 2, 1 (1996): 148–69.

Sourdis de la Vega, Adelaida. *Cartagena de Indias durante la primera república, 1810–1815.* Bogotá: Banco de la República, 1988.

Sourdis Nájera, Adelaida. "Ruptura del estado colonial y tránsito hacia la república, 1800–1850." In *Historia económica y social del Caribe colombiano,* edited by Adolfo Meisel Roca, 155–228. Bogotá: Ediciones Uninorte-Ecoe Ediciones, 1994.

Sowell, David. *The Early Colombian Labor Movement: Artisans and Politics in Bogotá, 1832–1919.* Philadelphia: Temple University Press, 1992.

Spalding, Karen. "Kurakas and Commerce: A Chapter in the Evolution of Andean Society." *Hispanic American Historical Review* 54, 4 (1973): 581–99.

——. *Huarochirí: An Andean Society Under Inca and Spanish Rule.* Stanford: Stanford University Press, 1984.

Spierenburg, Pieter. "Violencia, castigo, el cuerpo y el honor: una revaluación." In *Figuraciones en proceso,* edited by Vera Weiller. Bogotá: Universidad Nacional de Colombia, 1998.

Stavig, Ward. *The World of Túpac Amaru: Conflict, Community, and Identity in Colonial Peru.* Lincoln: University of Nebraska Press, 1999.

Stepan, Nancy Leys. *The Hour of Eugenics: Race, Gender, and Nation in Latin America.* Ithaca: Cornell University Press, 1991.

Stephenson, Marcia. *Gender and Modernity in Andean Bolivia.* Austin: University of Texas Press, 1999.

Stern, Steve, ed. *Resistance, Rebellion and Consciousness in the Andean Peasant World, Eighteenth to Twentieth Centuries.* Madison: University of Wisconsin Press, 1987.

——. "New Approaches to the Study of Peasant Rebellion." In *Resistance, Rebellion, and Consciousness,* edited by Steve Stern, 3–28. Madison: University of Wisconsin Press, 1987.

——. *The Secret History of Gender: Women, Men, and Power in Late Colonial Mexico.* Chapel Hill: University of North Carolina Press, 1995.

Stoetzer, Carlos. *Las raíces escolásticas de la emancipación de la América española.* Madrid: Centro de Estudios Constitucionales, 1982.

Stutzman, Ronald. "El Mestizaje: an All-Inclusive Ideology of Exclusion." In *Cultural Transformations and Ethnicity in Modern Ecuador,* edited by Norman Whitten, 45–94. Urbana: University of Illinois Press, 1981.

Sullivan-González, Douglass. *Piety, Power, and Politics: Religion and Nation Formation in Guatemala, 1821–1871.* Pittsburgh: University of Pittsburgh Press, 1998.

Sutherland, Stuart. *Irrationality.* Harmondsworth: Penguin, 1992.

Szeminski, Jan. *La utopía tupamarista.* Lima: Pontifíca Universidad Católica del Perú, 1984.

——. "Why Kill the Spaniards? New Perspectives on Andean Insurrectionary Ideology in the Eighteenth Century." In *Resistance, Rebellion, and Consciousness in the Andean Peasant World, Eighteenth to Twentieth Centuries,* edited by Steve Stern, 166–92. Madison: University of Wisconsin Press, 1987.

Tamayo, Franz. *Creación de una pedagogía nacional* [1910]. La Paz: Juventud, 1988.

Taylor, C. *Las fuentes del yo: La construcción de la identidad moderna.* Barcelona: Paidós Básica, 1996.

Taylor, William. *Drinking, Homicide, and Rebellion in Colonial Mexican Villages.* Stanford: Stanford University Press, 1979.

Tejera Gaona, Hector, ed. *Antropología política: Enfoques contemporáneos.* Mexico: INAH and Plaza y Valdés, 1996.

Thompson, E. P. *Costumbres en común.* Barcelona, Crítica, 1991.

Thompson, Michael, Richard Ellis and Aaron Wildavsky. *Culture Theory.* Boulder: Westview, 1990.

Thomson, Sinclair. "La cuestión india en Bolivia a principios del siglo: el caso de Rigoberto Paredes." *Autodeterminación* 4 (1987–88): 83–116.

——. "Colonial Crisis, Community and Andean Self-Rule: Aymara Politics in the Age of Insurgency (Eighteenth Century La Paz)." Ph.D. dissertation, University of Wisconsin, Madison, 1996.

——. " 'We Alone Will Rule . . . :' Recovering the Range of Anticolonial Projects among Andean Peasants (La Paz, 1740s to 1781)." *Colonial Latin American Review* 8: 2 (1999): 275–99.

——. *We Alone Will Rule: Native Andean Politics in the Age of Insurgency.* Madison: University of Wisconsin Press, 2002.

Thurner, Mark. *From Two Republics to One Divided: Contradictions of Postcolonial Nation-making in Andean Peru.* Durham, N.C.: Duke University Press, 1997.

Ticona, Esteban and Xavier Albó. *Jesús de Machaqa: La marka rebelde.* Vol. 3, *La lucha por el poder comunal.* La Paz: CIPCA/CEDOIN, 1997.

Tilly, Charles. *European Revolutions, 1492–1992.* Cambridge, Mass.: Blackwell, 1993.

Tirado Mejía, Alvaro. *Descentralización y centralismo en Colombia.* Quito: Fundación Friedrich Naumann, and Bogotá: Editorial Oveja Negra, 1983.

Tobar Donoso, Julio. *García Moreno y la instrucción pública.* 2nd ed. Quito: Editorial Ecuatoriana, 1940.

Tocqueville, Alexis de. *Democracy in America.* 2 vols. New York: Vintage, 1945.

Tomasek, Robert B., ed. *Latin American Politics: Twenty-four Studies of the Contemporary Scene.* New York: Anchor Books, 1966.

Tönnies, Ferdinand. *Kritik der Öffentlichen Meinung.* Berlin: Julius Springer, 1922.

Tovar Pinzón, Hermes. "Guerras de opinión y represión en Colombia durante la independencia (1810–1820)." *Anuario Colombiano de Historia Social y de la Cultura* 11 (1983): 187–232.

——, et al., eds. *Convocatoria al poder del número: Censos y estadísticas de la Nueva Granada.* Bogotá: Archivo General de la Nación, 1994.

——, et al. "Introducción." In *Convocatoría al poder del número,* edited by H. Tovar Pinzón et al., 43–46. Bogotá: Archivo General de la Naciòn, 1994.

Trazegnies, Fernando de. *La idea de derecho en el Perú republicano.* Lima: PUCP, 1992.

Twinam, Ann. *Public Lives, Public Secrets: Gender, Honor, Sexuality and Illegitimacy in Colonial Spanish America.* Stanford: Stanford University Press, 1999.

Urbano, Henrique, ed. *Modernidad en los Andes.* Cusco: CBC, 1991.

Urbina María, et al. "Otra igual que las madres de familia de la misma ciudad de Guayaquil eleven a la Representación Nacional con el mismo objeto" [29 Jan. 1850]. Deposited in Biblioteca Espinosa Polit (Quito), *Miscelánea de Historia,* v. 12, p. 20.

Uribe de Hincapie, Maria Teresa and Jesús Alvarez. *Las raíces del poder regional: el caso antioqueño.* Documento Preliminar, No. 5. Medellín: Universidad de Antioquia, 1986.

Uribe-Urán, Victor M. *Honorable Lives: Lawyers, Family, and Politics in Colombia, 1780–1850.* Pittsburgh: University of Pittsburgh Press, 2000.

Urrutia, Miguel. 1969. *The Development of the Colombian Labor Movement.* New Haven: Yale University Press.

Valcárcel, Carlos Daniel. *Breve historia de la educación peruana.* Lima: Editorial Educación, 1975.

Valle de Siles, María Eugenia. *La rebelión de Túpac Catari, 1781–1782.* La Paz: Editorial Don Bosco, 1990.

Van Young, Eric. "The Raw and the Cooked: Elite and Popular Ideology in Mexico, 1800–1821." In *The Middle Period in Latin America: Values and Attitudes in the Seventeenth-Nineteenth Centuries,* edited by Mark Szuchman, 75–102. Boulder: Lynne Rienner, 1989.

——. "Agrarian Rebellion and Defense of Community: Meaning and Collective Violence in Late Colonial and Independence-Era Mexico." *Journal of Social History* 27, 2 (1993): 245–69.

——. "Conclusion: The State as Vampire—Hegemonic Projects, Public Ritual, and Popular Culture in Mexico, 1600–1990." In *Rituals of Rule, Rituals of Resistance: Public Celebrations and Popular Culture in Mexico,* edited by William Beezley et al., 343–74. Wilmington, Del.: SR Books, 1994.

——. "Doing Regional History: Methodological and Theoretical Considerations." *Conference of Latin Americanist Geographers Yearbook* 20 (1994): 21–34.

——. "To See Someone Not Seeing: Historical Studies of Peasant Politics in Mexico." *Mexican Studies/Estudios Mexicanos* 6, 1 (1990): 133–59.

——. "The New Cultural History Comes to Old Mexico." *Hispanic American Historical Review* 79, 2 (1999): 211–47.

——. "Conclusion: Was There an Age of Revolution in Spanish America?" In *State and Society in Spanish America during the Age of Revolution,* edited by Víctor Uribe-Uran, 219–46. Wilmington, Del.: SR Books, 2001.

——. *The Other Rebellion: Popular Violence, Ideology, and the Mexican Struggle for Independence, 1810–1821.* Stanford: Stanford University Press, 2001.

Vargas Ugarte, Ruben, S. J. *Historia del Perú, virreinato.* 5 vols. Lima: Librería e Imprenta Gil, 1956.

Vasquez, Emilio. *La rebelión de Juan Bustamante.* Lima: Mejía Baca, 1976.

Vaughn, Mary Kay. "The Construction of Patriotic Festival in Tecamachalco, Puebla, 1900–1946." In *Rituals of Rule, Rituals of Resistance: Public Celebrations and Popular Culture in Mexico,* edited by William Beezley, Cheryl Martin and William French, 213–46. Wilmington, Del.: Scholarly Resources, 1994.

Vedoya, Juan Carlos. *Cómo fue la enseñanza popular en la Argentina.* Buenos Aires: Editorial Plus Ultra, 1973.

Veyne, P. "El individuo herido en el corazón por el poder público." In *Sobre el individuo: Contribuciones al coloquio de Royaumon,* edited by P. Veyne et al. Barcelona: Paidós, 1990. First French ed., 1985.

Villavicencio, Manuel. *Geografía de la República del Ecuador.* New York: Imprenta de Robert Craighead, 1858.

Viotti da Costa, Emilia. *The Brazilian Empire. Myths and Histories.* Chapel Hill: University of North Carolina Press, 2000.

——. "New Publics, New Politics, New Histories: From Economic Reductionism to Cultural Reductionism" In *Reclaiming the Political in Latin American History: Essays from the North,* edited by Gilbert Joseph, 17–31. Durham, N.C.: Duke University Presss, 2001.

Viqueira Albán, Juan Pedro. *Propriety and Permissiveness in Bourbon Mexico.* Wilmington, Del.: SR Books, 1999.

Voekel, Pamela. "Peeing on the Palace: Bodily Resistance to Bourbon Reforms in Mexico City." *Journal of Historical Sociology* 5, 2 (1992): 183–208.

——. "Piety and Public Space: The Cemetery Campaign in Veracruz, 1789–1810." In *Latin American Popular Culture: An Introduction,* edited by William Beezley and Linda Curcio-Nagy, 1–27. Wilmington, Del.: SR Books, 2000.

Wade, Peter. *Blackness and Race Mixture: The Dynamics of Racial Identity in Colombia.* Baltimore: Johns Hopkins University Press, 1993.

——. *Race and Ethnicity in Latin America.* London: Pluto, 1997.

Walker, Charles F. "A Journalistic Orgy: The Press and Political Culture in Cusco, Peru, 1820–1840." Unpublished paper, 1995.

——. *Smoldering Ashes. Cuzco and the Creation of Republican Peru, 1780–1840.* Durham, N.C.: Duke University Press, 1999.

Welch, Stephen. *The Concept of Political Culture.* Basingstoke: MacMillan, 1993.

Whitecotton, Joseph W. *The Zapotecs: Princes, Priests and Peasants.* Norman: University of Oklahoma Press, 1977.

Whitehead, Christine. "Cochabamba Landlords and the Agrarian Reform." B. Phil, Oxford University, 1970.

Whitehead, Lawrence. "Bolivia." In *Latin America Between the Second World War and the Cold War, 1944–1948,* edited by Leslie Bethell and Ian Roxborough, 120–46. Cambridge: Cambridge University Press, 1992.

Wiarda, Howard. "Toward a Framework for the Study of Political Change in the Iberic-Latin Tradition: The Corporative Model." *World Politics* 25 (1973): 206–36.

Wiatr, Jerzy. "The Civic Culture from a Marxist Sociological Perspective." In *The Civic Culture Revisited,* edited by Gabriel Almond and Sidney Verba, 103–123. Boston: Little, Brown, 1980.

Williams, Derek. "Assembling the 'Empire of Morality': State Building Strategies in Catholic Ecuador, 1861–1875." *Journal of Historical Sociology* 14, 2 (2001): 149–74.

——. "Negotiating the State: National Utopias and Local Politics in Andean Ecuador, 1845–1875." Ph.D. dissertation. State University of New York at Stony Brook, 2001.

——. "Popular Liberalism and Indian Servitude: The Making and Unmaking of Ecuador's Anti-Landlord State, 1845–1868." *Hispanic American Historical Review* 83, 4 (2003): 697–734.

Williams, Robert G. *States and Social Evolution. Coffee and the Rise of National Governments in Central America.* Chapel Hill: University of North Carolina Press, 1994.

Wilson, Baronesa [Emilia Serrano de]. *La ley del progreso (paginas de instrucción pública para los pueblos sud-americanos).* Quito: Imprenta Nacional, 1880.

Wolf, Eric R. *Envisioning Power: Ideologies of Dominance and Crisis.* Berkeley: University of California Press, 1999.

——. *Pathways to Power: Building an Anthropology of the Modern World.* Berkeley: University of California Press, 2001.

Womack, John. *Zapata and the Mexican Revolution.* New York: Knopf, 1968.

Wood, Gordon S. *The Radicalism of the American Revolution.* New York: Knopf, 1992.

Woodward, Jr., Ralph Lee. *Rafael Carrera and the Emergence of the Republic of Guatemala, 1821–1871.* Athens: University of Georgia Press, 1993.

Wortman, Miles L. *Government and Society in Cental America, 1680–1840.* New York: Columbia University Press, 1982.

Wuffarden, Luis Eduardo. "Los lienzos del virrey Amat y la pintura limeña del siglo xviii." In *Los cuadros de mestizaje del Virrey Amat,* edited by Natalia Majluf, 48–65. Lima: Museo de Arte de Lima, 2000.

Yashar, Deborah J. *Demanding Democracy. Reform and Reaction in Costa Rica and Guatemala, 1870s-1950s.* Stanford: Stanford University Press, 1997.

Yuval-Davis, Nira, and Floya Anthias. "Introduction." In *Women-Nation-State,* edited by Yuval-Davis and Anthias, 1–15. London: Macmillan, 1989.

Zamalloa, Raúl. "El pensamiento político del Directorio a través de la Guardia Nacional." B.A. thesis, Pontifícia Universidad Católica del Perú, 1964.

——. " 'La Guardia Nacional:' Estudio de un periódico vivanquista por Felipe Pardo y Aliaga." Ph. D. thesis, Pontifícia Universidad Católica del Perú, 1964.

Zaz Friz, Johnny. *La descentralización fictícia: Perú, 1821–1998.* Lima: Universidad del Pacífico, 1999.

Zuluaga, F. "Conformación de las sociedades negras del Pacífico." In *Historia del Gran Cauca,* edited by Alonso Valencia Llano, 231–37. Cali: Universidad del Valle, 1996.

CONTRIBUTORS

Cristóbal Aljovín de Losada (BA, Pontifícia Universidad de Católica del Perú, 1988) received his Ph.D. at the University of Chicago and is Professor and Coordinator of the Masters Program in History at the Universidad Nacional Mayor de San Marcos in Lima. He is the author of *Caudillos y constituciones: Perú 1821–1845* (Lima, 2000) and a number of articles on Peru's political and economic history during the eighteenth and nineteenth centuries. He is currently principal investigator of a major project on the history of elections in Peru.

Carlos Contreras is Associate Professor in the Department of Economics of the Pontifícia Universidad Católica del Perú in Lima and a member of the Instituto de Estudios Peruanos. His most recent book is *El aprendizaje del capitalismo: Estudios de historia económica y social del Perú republicano* (Lima, 2004). He is currently working on a book about the fiscal aspects of the late-nineteenth-century reform of the Peruvian state in the aftermath of the crisis caused by the War of the Pacific.

Maragarita Garrido received her D. Phil. at Oxford University and is currently Professor and Head of the Masters Program in History at the Universidad de los Andes, Bogotá. She is the author of *Reclamos y representaciones, variaciones sobre la* *política en el Nuevo Reino de Granada, 1770–1815* (Bogotá, 1993) and, most recently, "Contrarrestando los sentimientos de lealtad y obediencia: Los sermones en defensa de la Indepepndencia en el Nuevo Reino de Granada," (Actas do XII Congresso Internacional AHILA, 2002). She edited the third volume of *Historia de América Andina,* entitled *El Sistema Colonial Tardío* (Quito, 2001).

Laura Gotkowitz is Assistant Professor of History at the University of Iowa. Her work on race and gender in twentieth-century Bolivia has appeared in collections published in Bolivia and the United States. She is the author of the forthcoming book *Within the Boundaries of Equality: Citizenship, Race, and Nation: Bolivia, 1880–1952.*

Aline Helg is Professor of History at the University of Geneva in Switzerland. Her works include *Liberty and Equality in Caribbean Colombia, 1770–1835* (forthcoming), the award-winning *Our Rightful Share: The Afro-Cuban Struggle for Equality, 1886–1912* (Chapel Hill, 1995), and *Civiliser le peuple et former les élites: L' éducation en Colombie, 1918–1957* (Paris, 1984) as well as articles on comparative race relations in the Americas.

Nils Jacobsen, Director of the Center for Latin American and Caribbean Studies at the University of Illinois, Urbana-Champaign, is the author of *Mirages of Transition: The Peruvian Altiplano, 1780–1930* (Berkeley, 1993) and coeditor of volumes on the Mexican and Peruvian economies during the late-colonial period and on Latin American economic liberalism. He is currently working on a book on the Peruvian revolution of 1894–95.

Alan Knight was educated at Oxford University and held posts at the Universities of Essex, and Texas, before returning to Oxford, where he is currently Professor of the History of Latin America. He is the author of *The Mexican Revolution* (2 vols., Cambridge, 1986) and of two volumes (*Mexico: From the Beginning to the Conquest* and *The Colonial Era,* Cambridge, 2002) of a proposed three-volume general history of Mexico. He has written more broadly on Mexican politics and modern Latin American history, including foreign relations. He is completing a more detailed (archive-based) study of Cardenista Mexico, provisionally entitled *The Triumph of the Revolution? Mexico in the 1930s.*

Brooke Larson, a historian at the State University of New York at Stony Brook, has published several books on the Andes, including, most recently, *Trials of Nation Making: Liberalism, Race, and Ethnicity in the Andes, 1810–1910* (Cambridge, 2004). Her article in the present volume comes out of her current book project on the cultural politics of Indian schooling in the early-twentieth-century Bolivian Andes.

Mary Roldán is Associate Professor of History at Cornell University. Her most recent work includes *Blood and Fire: La Violencia in Antioquia, Colombia, 1946–1953* (Durham, 2002). The Spanish edition of her book won the 2003 Fundación Alejandro Angel Escobar Prize for Research in the Humanities and Social Sciences. She is currently at work on a book about the cultural and political impact of radio in Colombia from the 1930s to the 1980s.

Sergio Serulnikov is Assistant Professor of History at Boston College. His book *Subverting Colonial Authority: Challenges to Spanish Rule in Eighteenth-Century Southern Andes* was published by Duke University Press in 2003. He is currently working on a study of Spanish elites, the colonial state, and urban social conflicts in eighteenth-century Charcas.

Charles Walker is the author of *Smoldering Ashes: Cuzco and the Creation of Republican Peru, 1780–1840* (Durham, 1999) and the editor of two books in Spanish. He is finishing a book on a massive earthquake and tsunami that struck the Lima area in 1746. He teaches Latin American history at the University of California, Davis.

Derek Williams is Assistant Professor of History at the University of Toronto. His current research interests include religion, race, and modernity in nineteenth-century Latin America. He is completing a book manuscript entitled *A Truly Catholic Nation: Politics and Religion in Ecuador, 1845–1895.* His articles have appeared in *Hispanic American Historical Review*, *Journal of Historical Sociology*, and *Procesos*, an Ecuadorian historical journal.

INDEX

Library of Congress Cataloging-in-Publication Data
Political cultures in the Andes, 1750–1950 /
edited by Nils Jacobsen and Cristóbal Aljovín de Losada.
p. cm. — (Latin America otherwise)
Includes bibliographical references (p.) and index.
ISBN 0-8223-3503-4 (cloth : alk. paper)
ISBN 0-8223-3515-8 (pbk. : alk. paper)
1. Political culture—Andes Region—History—18th century.
2. Political culture—Andes Region—History—19th century.
3. Political culture—Andes Region—History—20th century.
4. Andes Region—Politics and government— 18th century.
5. Andes Region—Politics and government—19th century.
6. Andes Region—Politics and government—20th century.
I. Jacobsen, Nils. II. Aljovín de Losada, Cristóbal.
III. Series.
JL1866.P637 2005
306.2′098′0903—dc22 2004025959